Royal Armouries Research Series

Volume III

Gunpowder Technology in the Fifteenth Century

Royal Armouries Research Series

About the series

Royal Armouries Research Series is published in partnership with Boydell and Brewer. The series is a forum for the study of arms and armour and cognate subjects from antiquity to the present day.

We welcome proposals for future volumes – either edited collections or monographs – from the broad world of arms and armour study, unlimited by geography, discipline or time period. Volumes that focus on objects within the Royal Armouries collection, or that support the organisation's research strategy (available at www.royalarmouries.org) are particularly encouraged. Critical editions and translations of arms and armour texts (such as fencing manuals and fight books) will also be considered.

Proposals and queries should be sent in the first instance to the Publishing Manager at the address below:

Dr Martyn Lawrence
Royal Armouries Publishing
Armouries Drive
Leeds LS10 1LT
Email: martyn.lawrence@armouries.org.uk

About the Royal Armouries

The Royal Armouries is Britain's national museum of arms and armour, and one of the most important museums of its type in the world. Its origins lie in the Middle Ages, and at its core is the celebrated collection originating in the nation's working arsenal, assembled over many centuries at the Tower of London. In the reign of Elizabeth I, selected items began to be arranged for display to visitors, making the Royal Armouries heir to one of the oldest deliberately-created visitor attractions in the country. The collection is now housed and displayed at three sites: the White Tower at the Tower of London, a purpose-built museum in Leeds, and Fort Nelson near Portsmouth.

Previously published volumes are listed at the back of this book.

Gunpowder Technology in the Fifteenth Century

A Study, Edition and Translation of the *Firework Book*

Axel E. W. Müller

THE BOYDELL PRESS

© Axel E. W. Müller 2024

All Rights Reserved. Except as permitted under current legislation
no part of this work may be photocopied, stored in a retrieval system,
published, performed in public, adapted, broadcast,
transmitted, recorded or reproduced in any form or by any means,
without the prior permission of the copyright owner

The right of Axel E. W. Müller to be identified as
the author of this work has been asserted in accordance with
sections 77 and 78 of the Copyright, Designs and Patents Act 1988

First published 2024
The Boydell Press, Woodbridge

ISBN 978-1-78327-731-5

The Boydell Press is an imprint of Boydell & Brewer Ltd
PO Box 9, Woodbridge, Suffolk IP12 3DF, UK
and of Boydell & Brewer Inc.
668 Mt Hope Avenue, Rochester, NY 14620–2731, USA
website: www.boydellandbrewer.com

The publisher has no responsibility for the continued existence or accuracy of
URLs for external or third-party internet websites referred to in this book, and
does not guarantee that any content on such websites is, or will remain, accurate
or appropriate

A catalogue record of this publication is available
from the British Library

This publication is printed on acid-free paper

Contents

	List of Figures	vi
	Acknowledgements	vii
	Introduction	1
1.	The *Firework Book* Tradition	10
2.	The Use and Reception of the *Firework Book*	35
3.	The Leeds *Firework Book*	56
4.	The Text of Royal Armouries I.34	80
	Editorial Principles	80
	Edition and Translation	83
5.	Analysis of the Text	304
	Conclusion	345
	Bibliography	349
	Index	374

Figures

All images © Royal Armouries

Fig. 1 Royal Armouries, I.34, fol. 83 in gathering 7 (picture provided by Royal Armouries). 58

Fig. 2 Royal Armouries, I.34, fol. 117 in gathering 11 – a watermark (picture provided by Royal Armouries). 58

Fig. 3 Royal Armouries, I.34, fol. 1r – preamble in Part 1 (picture provided by Royal Armouries). 61

Fig. 4 Royal Armouries, I.34, fol. 52r, first folio of Part 2 (picture provided by Royal Armouries). 62

Fig. 5 Royal Armouries, I.34, fols 90v and 90r – in the field (pictures provided by Royal Armouries). 70–71

Fig. 6 Royal Armouries, I.34, fols 89v and 86v – in the workshop (pictures provided by Royal Armouries). 72–73

Fig. 7 Royal Armouries, I.34, fols 85v and 87r – in the workshop (pictures provided by Royal Armouries). 74–75

Fig. 8 Royal Armouries, I.34, fols 94v and 95v – incendiary devices (pictures provided by Royal Armouries). 76–77

Fig. 9 Royal Armouries, I.34, fols 6r, 14r, 42v and 57r – initials in Parts 1 and 2 (pictures provided by Royal Armouries). 81

Fig. 10 Royal Armouries, I.34, fols 87v and 88r (pictures provided by Royal Armouries). 330–31

Fig. 11 Royal Armouries, I.34, fol. 89r – possible depiction of mass manufacturing of wheel hub incendiaries – top right, and fol. 88v – possible mass production of fire arrows (picture provided by Royal Armouries). 336–37

Fig. 12 Royal Armouries, I.34, fols 52v and 57r (pictures provided by Royal Armouries). 338

Acknowledgements

It is always a challenge to mention everyone who has been involved in a project conceived and developed over so many years, and I am certain (though it is not for want of trying) that I may well have overlooked one or more of those many people who have provided support and advice throughout the process of this project. This study has relied on many friends, family, colleagues, and fellow researchers along the way – far too many to mention individually –, and I am extremely grateful for all their help, support, and encouragement.

Particular thanks and gratitude go to Kay Smith and Ruth Rhynas Brown for the ongoing, highly valued support and encouragement, and all the other members of the *HO Group: Medieval Gunpowder Research* and everybody at the Middelaldercentret in Nykøbing Falster (Denmark). In particular, I would like to thank for their very helpful comments and suggestions Kelly DeVries, Bert Hall, Peter Vemming Hansen, Dan Spencer, Clifford J. Rogers, and Steven A. Walton.

The late and sorely missed John Tailby for introducing me to the pleasures of Early New High German and for providing such a wide range of insights into the world of fifteenth-century vernacular literacy.

Everybody at the *Frühneuhochdeutsches Wörterbuch* (*FWB*), especially its editors Oskar Reichmann and Anja Lobenstein-Reichmann, for allowing me wide-ranging access to the *FWB* as well as much unpublished material, while simultaneously allowing me to see into their own linguists' brains.

The Royal Armouries and all their staff – past and present – for enabling this research on one of their many treasures; in particular, Stuart Ivinsen, Philip Lankester, Thom Richardson, Graeme Rimer, Peter Smithurst, Karen Watts, and Bob Woosnam-Savage.

Everybody in the Institute for Medieval Studies and the School of History at the University of Leeds, both staff and students, past and present, for facilitating this research, for providing me with a platform on which to engage with so many medievalists, and for highlighting the joy and fascination that research into the Middle Ages can bring. In particular, thanks to my colleagues Iona McCleery and Emilia Jamroziak for guidance and advice on academic directions and context.

Many thanks to Sarah Bastow, Glenn Foard, Katherine J. Lewis, Richard Morris, and Tim Thornton, and everybody else at the Arms & Armour Research Institute at the University of Huddersfield, who played their part at various stages throughout the study.

Acknowledgements

All the librarians and archivists across the globe who act as custodians of the treasures of the past, all of whom when consulted have been immensely helpful to the solitary researcher who enquires about their holdings in – what to them must have appeared to be, at best – a niche subject. In particular, Arnold Otto and Karin Zimmermann.

Many thanks to Herwig Weigl and Jacqueline Schindler from the University of Vienna for help and assistance with the Early New High German.

Everybody working for and with Boydell & Brewer and the Royal Armouries Research Series, expecially Nick Bingham, Martyn Lawrence, Laura Napran, and Caroline Palmer, for highly professional service and support throughout.

My friends Brenda Bolton and Christine Meek for commenting on drafts of the text, and for preventing me from committing the worst crimes against the English language. Needless to say, some have managed to sneak through – and the fault for that is entirely my own.

My family, having been without both parents over the process of this dissertation, for being there throughout.

Last but by no means least, my eternal thanks go to Iona, my long-suffering partner, who has helped me through this long and gruelling process with positive support and encouragement, and without whom none of this would ever have gone beyond the initial 'sort of a good idea'. I dedicate this book to her.

Introduction

Gunpowder technology has often been identified as one of the key catalysts for the transition from the Middle Ages to the Early Modern Period. By 1620, the natural philosopher Francis Bacon had placed gunpowder as one of the tripartite symbols of technological advancement: 'Printing, gunpowder, and the compass. For these three have changed the appearance and state of the whole world.'[1] As Kay Smith put it in 2010, regarding

> [...] the crucial role that gunpowder played in the development of the exploitation of energy resources from ancient times to the present. It marks the beginning of the change from animal, mechanical, or natural sources of energy [...] to the apparently unlimited power and mobility of chemical energy.[2]

However, when and how gunpowder technology emerged and spread to all corners of Europe in the fourteenth and fifteenth centuries is far less clear.

Gunpowder's early origins in China are well-known, but we know surprisingly little about how this technology was transferred across Eurasia, and even less about the way that early gunpowder weapons performed in practice.[3] This lack of understanding has had a significant effect on research into warfare in the late medieval and early modern period. Kelly DeVries and Kay Smith list a number of guns and gunners from 1326 onwards, and by the fifteenth century gunpowder artillery 'had led to significant changes on battlefields and at sieges' and 'affected every kingdom and principality'.[4] Surviving records of

---

[1] Francis Bacon and Joseph Devey (eds), *Novum Organum* (New York: P. F. Collier, 1902). https://oll.libertyfund.org/title/bacon-novum-organum#Bacon_0415_198 (accessed 10 August 2023), Book 1, Aphorism CXXIX.

[2] Kay Smith (publ. under former name of Robert Douglas Smith), *Rewriting the History of Gunpowder* (Nykøbing Falster: Middelaldercentret, 2010), 12.

[3] For these early origins, see Joseph Needham, *Military Technology: The Gunpowder Epic*, Part 7 of *Science and Civilisation in China*, Vol. 5, *Chemistry and Chemical Technology* (Cambridge: Cambridge University Press, 1986), and more recently, Tonio Andrade, *The Gunpowder Age: China, Military Innovation, and the Rise of the West in World History* (Princeton and Oxford: Princeton University Press, 2016).

[4] Kelly DeVries and Robert D. Smith, *Medieval Military Technology* (Toronto: University of Toronto Press, 2012), 138–40, and Kay Smith (publ. under former name of Robert Douglas Smith) and Kelly DeVries, *The Artillery of the Duke of Burgundy, 1363–1477* (Woodbridge: Boydell, 2005), 10–12.

master gunners are sparse from the late fourteenth century, becoming increasingly more substantial by the mid-fifteenth century, but still only amount to a patchwork of individual mentions of gunners in widely dispersed employment across Europe.[5] While the Tower of London recorded gunpowder production from 1346, increasing considerably between 1400 and 1410, the records say very little about purchase, storage, maintenance, and use.[6] In recent decades, scholars have become aware of both the gap in knowledge and the social history potential of gunpowder technology. For example, in 1996 Brenda Buchanan pointed out:

> The history of gunpowder making is a comparatively neglected subject, yet this was a technology of international significance in terms of the intellectual transfer of ideas and techniques, and the practical transfer of raw materials and finished goods across continents and oceans. Unlike many industries its product supplied a diversity of markets which mirrored the cultural, social, and economic conditions in which it flourished.[7]

Since then, a wide range of scholars from different disciplines (military history, medieval studies, manuscript studies, sinology, economic history, history of science and technology) have contributed to the field and further demonstrated the significance of gunpowder technology to warfare, trade, intellectual exchange, culture, and society. However, they have naturally interpreted the evidence from the standpoint of their particular disciplines, often retrospectively applying modern science to medieval contexts and materials.[8] And,

---

[5] Most recently, Dan Spencer, *Royal and Urban Gunpowder Weapons in Late Medieval England* (Woodbridge: Boydell Press, 2019), or Knut Schulz, 'Büchsenmeister des Spätmittelalters: Migration und Ausbreitung des neuen Wissens', in *Craftsmen and Guilds in the Medieval and Early Modern Periods*, eds Eva Jullien and Michel Pauly (Stuttgart: Franz Steiner, 2016), 221–42, 230–42, or earlier, Rainer Leng, '"*getruwelich dienen mit Buchsenwerk*". Ein neuer Beruf im späten Mittelalter: Die Büchsenmeister', in *Strukturen der Gesellschaft im Mittelalter. Interdisziplinäre Mediävistik in Würzburg*, eds Dieter Rödel and Joachim Schneider (Wiesbaden: Reichert, 1996), 303–21.

[6] Thom Richardson, *The Tower Armoury in the Fourteenth Century* (Leeds: Royal Armouries, 2016), 174–90

[7] Brenda J. Buchanan (ed.), *Gunpowder: The History of an International Technology* (Bath: Bath University Press, 1996), xvii.

[8] Notable exceptions in recent years are: Jonathan Davies, *The Medieval Cannon 1326–1494* (Oxford: Osprey Publishing, 2019), Geoff Smith, 'Saltpetre: The Soul of Gunpowder', *Journal of the Ordnance Society* 27 (2020), 5–24, and Geoff Smith, 'Sulphur: The Trigger of Gunpowder', *Journal of the Ordnance Society* 28 (2021), 115–19, Trevor Russell Smith, 'The Earliest Middle English Recipes for

Introduction

until recently, there has been little about gunpowder technology in the early fifteenth century available in English. To try to understand gunpowder technology – including its introduction, use, trade, and significance – it is crucial to study a wide range of texts and records, as well as artefacts and experimental archaeology.[9]

While there is some information to be gleaned from fragments in local chronicles and other written evidence, as well as from isolated surviving artefacts, it is arguably through the study of military manuscripts that we can obtain the most comprehensive insight into military techniques in the fifteenth century and the emergence of this technology. Particularly valuable is the genre of technical manuscripts known as the *Firework Book* (one of the first surviving group of manuals written for gunpowder technology).[10] However, no sustained, comparative analysis of the *Firework Book* genre has yet been undertaken. Accordingly, this book aims to answer some of the basic questions about gunpowder and early artillery in order to create a solid foundation of good hard evidence and research for others to build on. Future research would benefit from a multidisciplinary approach integrating the results of documentary and archival research, experimental work, and test firing of actual weapons.

Gunpowder', *Journal of Medieval Military History* 18 (2020), 183–92, Clifford J. Rogers, 'Gunpowder Artillery in Europe, 1326–1500: Innovation and Impact', in *Technology, Violence, and War: Essays in Honor of Dr. John F. Guilmartin, Jr.*, eds Robert S. Ehlers Jr., Sarah K. Douglas, and Daniel P. M. Curzon, History of Warfare 125 (Leiden: Brill, 2019), 39–71, Clifford J. Rogers, 'Four Misunderstood Gunpowder Recipes of the Fourteenth Century', *Journal of Medieval Military History* 18 (2020), 173–82, and Spencer, *Royal and Urban Gunpowder Weapons*.

[9] Experimental archaeology is a crucial method in investigating material culture and testing research hypotheses and techniques. See issues of the online journal EXARC; Peter G. Stone and Philippe G. Planel, *The Constructed Past* (London: Routledge, 2003); the research by the HO Group: Medieval Gunpowder Research with the stated aim of investigating the composition and properties of medieval gunpowder; and recent research carried out at the United States Military Academy as published in Tessy S. Ritchie, Kathleen E. Riegner, et al., 'Evolution of Medieval Gunpowder: Thermodynamics and Combustion Analysis', *ACS Omega* 6:35 (2021). 22848–22856. https://pubs.acs.org/doi/10.1021/acsomega.1c03380 (accessed 10 August 2023).

[10] The *Firework Book* is a genre with different versions, rather than a single book, as the 65 extant copies demonstrate considerable variation. This will be discussed in more detail in the 'Manuscripts and Editions' section of this Introduction, and in Chapter 1 under '*Urtext*, Production, and Transmission'.

It is clear that this technology was changing society, but little is known about the speed and format of the change. Gunpowder technology was transformative for every aspect of how wars were fought, because it had a substantial impact on resources, training, and construction. Some scholars have identified a 'Military Revolution' of the sixteenth century, in which gunpowder technology was one of the key components, but the evidence discussed in this book shows that whatever was happening was already well underway in the fourteenth and fifteenth centuries.[11] Whether the *Firework Book* can be viewed as a contribution to an earlier 'Military Revolution', or was part of a gradual change in society, will be a topic of discussion. Technological changes certainly contributed in major ways to how military interaction was conducted, and by the later fifteenth century gunpowder technology was omnipresent in Western Europe and no self-respecting local ruler could afford not to have access to gunpowder technology. There certainly was a demand for and supply of new technology such as the use of gunpowder artillery, with the consequent and overwhelming need to preserve and disseminate this knowledge, resulting in a wide range of manuals on military matters. The *Firework Book* is part of a genre emerging in the late fourteenth and early fifteenth centuries, which contains other texts related to technical military instructions such as the *Bellifortis* and the *Büchsenmeister Books*.[12]

All of these texts emerged at what was clearly a crucial point of development in this technology. It is less clear, however, what was the actual purpose of producing these texts.[13] Realistically, there are three possible explanations: a) the *Firework Book* marks the recording of a fully-fledged technology which had already been in use for decades by the early fifteenth century, well before

---

[11] For an overview on the debate on the Military Revolution, its chronology, and its conceptual debates see Geoffrey Parker, *The Military Revolution: Military Innovation and the Rise of the West, 1500–1800* (Cambridge: Cambridge University Press, 1988; rev. edn 2002), Clifford J. Rogers (ed.), *The Military Revolution Debate: Readings on the Military Transformation of Early Modern Europe* (Oxford: Westview Press, 1995), Kelly DeVries, 'Catapults are not Atomic Bombs: Towards a Redefinition of "Effectiveness" in Premodern Military Technology', *War in History* 4 (1997), 454–70, and more recently Anne Curry, 'Guns and Goddams: Was There a Military Revolution in Lancastrian Normandy 1415–50?', *Journal of Medieval Military History* 8 (2011), 171–88, and Helmut Flachenecker, 'Kanonen, Räderuhr und Brille: zur technischen Revolution des Spätmittelalters', in *Überall ist Mittelalter: zur Aktualität einer vergangenen Epoche*, ed. Dorothea Klein (Würzburg: Königshausen & Neumann, 2015), 303–29.

[12] For more on the *Firework Book* as a genre, as well as on the *Bellifortis* and the *Büchsenmeister Books*, see Chapter 1 under '*Firework Books* as a Coherent Genre'.

[13] See also Chapter 2 under 'Manuscript Evidence of Use'.

Introduction

it has been assumed by modern historians to have occurred; b) it was the result of a substantial change in gunpowder manufacture and technology, which required a tool to disseminate knowledge of the change; or c) it is a textual anomaly which does not reflect actual practice at the time.

This study will show that the third explanation can be ruled out because the text does relate to operating tasks within gunpowder technology and contains well-documented ingredients, as well as recipes and instructions which work and can be recreated.[14] It is more likely a combination of a) and b), in that it was written at a turning point of a change in technology or technological knowledge transfer, at a time when gunpowder technology had been in use for some decades. The *Firework Book* demonstrates both a demand for this type of knowledge about gunpowder technology, and that this specialist knowledge was already well established. The texts appeared during the period when vernacular writing, including the written recording (as opposed to oral transmission) of technical knowledge, was starting to appear across Europe. This was also the time when the profession of master gunner became widespread.

Manuscripts and Editions

In the Royal Armouries manuscript collection in Leeds there is a complex fifteenth-century vernacular text in German, catalogued as MS I.34, called the *Firework Book* (in German: 'Feuerwerkbuch'). It has not previously been edited and thus far has only been cursorily studied.

This study sets out to create a diplomatic edition and translation of I.34, the sole exemplar of a *Firework Book* in the United Kingdom and a unique example of the corpus as a whole. This work is crucial for a more complete understanding of *Firework Books*, in view of the paucity of editions of this genre. Only three modern editions in New High German of the Freiburg manuscript Ms. 362 of the *Firework Book* have been produced, together with one translation into English, based on one of these modern editions. The first modern edition, printed in 1941, was the work of a civil servant, Wilhelm Hassenstein, with limited historical and scientific knowledge but working in a military context.[15]

---

[14] Kay Smith (partially publ. under former name of Robert Douglas Smith), *Reports of the HO Group: Medieval Gunpowder Research*, 2002–2022, https://ahc.leeds.ac.uk/downloads/download/35/fields_of_conflict or https://www.middelalderakademiet.dk/krudt-og-kanoner (accessed 10 August 2023).

[15] The author of the earliest edition and translation of a *Firework Book* in the twentieth century, Wilhelm Hassenstein, gave his profession as being in the high-ranking civil service (*Oberregierungsrat*), and stated in the dedication that his book was

The second and third editions were produced by the physicist Ferdinand Nibler (also translated into New High German) and the chemist Gerhard Kramer (who also added a partial translation into English). Both possessed scientific knowledge but lacked sufficient historical background to understand the need for accuracy in translation.[16] In contrast, the choice here has been to offer a translation close to the original, dealing with inconsistencies when they occur, as well as rendering the sometimes monotonous and repetitive style as closely as possible to the original. This method provides scholars with greater insight into what the text actually states, rather than what modern scholars have interpreted it to be.

All 65 surviving versions of the *Firework Book* were produced in the fifteenth and sixteenth centuries in various dialects of Early New High German (defined as the version of German used between 1350 and 1650). On the basis of the predominant vernacular adopted, they may be traced to the south-western region of present-day Bavaria. Using the didactic format of a dialogue between a master gunner and an apprentice, the *Firework Book* has deservedly been described as 'the most frequently copied, changed, and extended book about the art of gunnery and chemistry of the period'.[17] However, it was frequently restructured and repackaged, with the result that no two surviving texts are identical in content.[18]

---

    presented at the 50th birthday of Reichsminister Fritz Todt (German Minister for Armaments and Ammunition, 1940–42) to honour the work carried out by German engineers and builders (Hassenstein, *Feuerwerkbuch*, inside front cover).

[16] Ferdinand Nibler, *Feuerwerkbuch: Anonym, 15. Jahrhundert; Synoptische Darstellung zweier Texte mit Neuhochdeutscher Übertragung* (online publication, 2005), https://www.ruhr-uni-bochum.de/technikhist/tittmann/5%20Feuerwerkbuch.pdf (accessed 10 August 2023). He taught electrical engineering at the German Military University in Munich, and created and maintained the website http://www.feuerwerkbuch.de/ (defunct as of 16 February 2023, although a copy of the homepage can be found on WaybackMachine at https://web.archive.org/web/20220618191626/http://www.feuerwerkbuch.de/ – accessed 10 August 2023). Kramer published one edition of Freiburg Ms. 362 in 1995: Gerhard W. Kramer, *Berthold Schwarz: Chemie und Waffentechnik im 15. Jahrhundert*, Abhandlungen und Berichte der Deutschen Museum N.F., 10 (München: Oldenbourg, 1995), as well as the only 'translation' into English in 2001: Gerhard W. Kramer and Klaus Leibnitz, *Das Feuerwerkbuch: German, circa 1400: Translation of MS 362 dated 1432 in the Library of the University of Freiburg,* Journal of the Arms & Armour Society 17.1 (London: The Arms & Armour Society, 2001).

[17] Kramer and Leibnitz, *Das Feuerwerkbuch*, 13. Kramer and Leibnitz's understanding and interpretation of the *Firework Book* will be discussed in Chapter 2.

[18] For further discussion, see Chapter 1 under '*Urtext*, Production, and Transmission'.

Introduction

An important element of the present study is the critical examination of the content of I.34, relating it to a significant subset of the other 64 surviving manuscripts of the *Firework Book* genre, thereby providing a comparative analysis of this genre and related subject areas, as well as giving a better understanding of its technical content. This study presents substantial evidence that *Firework Books* were widely popular and often reproduced, although their role and function have gradually been forgotten over time.

While Royal Armouries manuscript I.34 shares the same core content with most *Firework Books*, it also has several distinctive and unique features which make it an ideal case study. In addition to transcribing, translating, and interpreting I.34, this study aims to move beyond textuality to explain the technical content of these manuscripts and offer an interpretation of the development of early gunpowder weaponry. In contrast to most other *Firework Books*, I.34 is compiled with associated elements of text which offer a deeper insight into the knowledge of gunpowder technology and, more particularly, into the production and possible use of the *Firework Book* in the fifteenth century. I.34 contains several distinct parts of text (the second part of I.34 has long been viewed as unique) and a substantial number of images which are referred to in the manuscript text – such features are unusual for most *Firework Books*. The images vividly show the various production techniques of gunpowder explosives and their use in battle, combined with technical illustrations of mounting the equipment.[19] It is hoped that a detailed analysis will lead to a better understanding, not only of how the emergence of literacy contributed to the production of the *Firework Books*, but also of plausible theories as to their production, authorship, readership, reception, and other uses.

The approach does not follow the conventional type of textual study which compares multiple manuscripts in detail. A few previous attempts have been made to compare a number of manuscripts, both by the heading to each chapter and by the texts of each subheading.[20] In fact, Ferdinand Nibler embarked

---

[19] These illustrations allow us to appreciate better the nature and knowledge of gunpowder technicians in the period. However, while some images are included in this book, a detailed analysis of the images goes beyond the scope of this project. While they have occasionally been referred to by military historians, they have yet to be analysed by art historians and image specialists as representations of gunpowder warfare and technical manuals, or even as representations of buildings, clothing, materials, or for their use of perspective. The images have been consulted in relation to the text (at several points where the text refers to them), but it was decided that the main focus here should be limited to the presentation and interpretation of the text.

[20] See Ferdinand Nibler, 'Das Feuerwerkbuch: Eine verspätete Buchbesprechung etwa 600 Jahre nach dem Erscheinen des Feuerwerkbuches', *Zeitschrift für*

on this work but only partially completed it – demonstrating the complexity of the extant corpus and providing information which is partial at best, as each *Firework Book* manuscript differs from the next.[21] Furthermore, the considerable number of subtle differences (which increase the further one gets into the text) make this kind of study unfeasible, while the benefits would certainly be limited. Previous scholars have merely listed these variations, without comment, in the order of the key components, highlighting elements listed in one and not the other, thus providing only partial information on a text corpus.[22] Understanding the extent to which the manuscripts differ is only possible if all of them are compared, side by side – a daunting task given the number of extant manuscripts.

What emerges from my examination of the corpus of *Firework Book* manuscripts is a high proportion of similarities, albeit with sometimes subtle, sometimes more substantial differences. A comprehensive comparative analysis is beyond the scope of this study, and would likely be of limited value in any case. Instead, this focused analysis of one manuscript provides a thorough basis on which to explain the origins, use, circulation, and subsequent

---

Heereskunde 67:2 (2003), 147–54, and Nibler, *Feuerwerkbuch*. Ferdinand Nibler's work is the most comprehensive attempt in that he compared both the headings in the Freiburg manuscript Ms. 362 with the Augsburg 1529 printed book (only surviving in the reprint of Hassenstein, *Feuerwerkbuch*) in detail, while also providing a comparison of chapter headings between the two texts mentioned together with Munich Clm. 30150, Dillingen Ms. XV 50, Weimar Q 342, and a further printed book by Egenolph, Strassburg, 1529, and has made a comparative study of two versions of the texts in a 'synoptic way'. However, the benefits are difficult to ascertain, with some similarities and some differences between the versions. These differences are revealed in choice of words, phrases, different placing of chapters, or more substantial changes and omissions. As he only included some selected manuscripts, his study is of limited use. Previous attempts were substantially less comprehensive, including the investigations by Max Jähns, *Geschichte der Kriegswissenschaften vornehmlich in Deutschland*, 3 vols (München and Leipzig: R. Oldenbourg, 1889–91), http://archive.org/details/geschichtederkr00jhgoog (accessed 10 August 2023), 382–424, and Wilhelm Hassenstein, *Das Feuerwerkbuch von 1420: 600 Jahre Deutsche Pulverwaffen und Büchsenmeisterei*, Bücher der Deutschen Technik (München: Verlag der Deutschen Technik, 1941), 14–78, 84–88, Christa Hagenmeyer, 'Kriegswissenschaftliche Texte des ausgehenden 15. Jahrhunderts', *Leuvensche Bijdragen* 57 (1967), 182–95, or Franz Maria Feldhaus, *Die Technik der Antike und des Mittelalters* (Wildpark-Potsdam: Athenaion, 1931 [1971]), 362, but all of these were carried out with limited source access or discernible methodology applied.

[21] Nibler in his introductory comments to the synoptic, comparative analysis of four manuscripts and two early prints of the *Firework Book* (Nibler, *Feuerwerkbuch*, 3).

[22] See, in particular, Nibler, *Feuerwerkbuch*, or Kramer, *Das Feuerwerkbuch*.

Introduction

life-story of the *Firework Book*. Taking I.34 as an exemplar for all *Firework Book* manuscripts, this study provides a textual analysis of the single manuscript and, through comparative works of secondary material, evaluates its content, role, and function within the context of technological and military development. I.34 is ideal for the purpose, as it provides the traditional *Firework Book* components, along with an additional explanatory text. Almost all manuscripts include a series of questions, often referred to as the Master Gunner's Questions. These vary in length and content, and in the number of key elements that are omitted or added. The core, however, remains the same, giving a description of the ingredients of gunpowder, and its various uses. Whether these practices were actually used, or were imagined enhancement or wishful thinking, will be discussed in Chapters 2 and 5. MS I.34 – like all other manuscripts of the *Firework Book* – has its own order of paragraphs and thematic groupings of paragraphs, as well as distinctive additions and omissions within paragraph content, accompanied by an unusual second part and provides valuable insight into the possible uses of the text.

***

Chapter 1 discusses the complex tradition of the *Firework Book* with reference to the 65 extant manuscripts, of which I have examined 63. Also considered are how the *Firework Book* fits into the wider genre of fifteenth-century military manuals and technical writings, and how it has been studied by modern scholars. Chapter 2 provides a summary of evidence of the audience for whom the *Firework Books* were produced and what happened to individual manuscripts of the *Firework Books*. Chapter 3 gives a physical description of Royal Armouries' manuscript I.34, outlining its contents and its provenance. Chapter 4 provides editorial and translation notes, followed by a line-by-line transcription and translation of I.34. The text has to be viewed in its entirety to provide a thorough understanding of the *Firework Book* format and content, and it is essential to read it before the technology – both its terminology and its usage – can be discussed. Chapter 5 examines the key elements in the text to analyse the information that they provide and what they tell us about fifteenth-century gunpowder technology.

In summary, as the history of gunpowder technology to date has been a sort of jigsaw puzzle composed of pieces from various disciplines, the present publication aims to further our understanding of it by using I.34 as an exemplar of a *Firework Book* (albeit a unique one). Combining literary and linguistic source criticism, along with historical analysis and fieldwork, it demonstrates the role of the *Firework Book* as an essential link in the consolidation of gunpowder technology.

1 The *Firework Book* Tradition

This chapter provides an overview of the wider *Firework Book* tradition. It addresses whether a single genre existed or whether this term is more correctly applied to a collective group of more disparate texts. It considers the historiography of research on *Firework Books* and whether a distinction should be made between the different types of *Firework Books*. Ultimately, it explores how and where the *Firework Book* fits into the wider genre of fifteenth-century technical writings (with and without illustrations), and analyses the similarities and differences of existing manuscripts and how these have been interpreted by scholars.

Firework Books as a Coherent Genre

The case needs to be made for this being a coherent tradition which requires (or is entitled to include) a clearly definable group of texts. For the purpose of this chapter, I understand a *Firework Book* to be a text written in Early New High German, consisting of a number of core elements in relation to early gunpowder artillery, including: the so-called 'Master Gunner's Questions'; the handling of saltpetre, sulphur, and charcoal; instructions on how to make, improve, preserve, and revitalize gunpowder; as well as other instructions related to attacks with gunpowder technology or how to defend against these. The core of the text was reproduced many times over more than a century. From 1529 onwards, it continued to be produced as printed text.[1] The earliest

---

[1] According to Hassenstein, the first printed edition was found as an appendix to *Flavii Gegetii Renati vier Bücher von der Ritterschaft* (Augsburg, 1529). Hall refers to 'two unrelated first editions': Heinrich Stainer, Augsburg, 1529, and Christian Engenolphen, Strassburg, 1529, the latter published under the title *Büchsenmeisterei: von Geschoss, Büchsen, Pulver, Salpeter, und Feuerwerk*. The two printers, Heinrich Stainer (also known as Steyner or Steiner) in Augsburg, and Christian Egenolff or Engenolph, initially based in Strasbourg and later in Frankfurt, were both prolific printers with over 1450 different books recorded to have been printed on a wide range of subjects from theology, history, philosophy, natural sciences, and other medical texts, including texts by Hans Sachs, Melanchton, Paracelsus,

The *Firework Book* Tradition

version probably appeared during the first years of the fifteenth century and the last well into the sixteenth. The *Firework Book* was thus so frequently restructured and repackaged that no two surviving texts are identical in content.

All surviving manuscripts of the *Firework Book* were produced in the fifteenth and sixteenth centuries in the local dialects of the south-western region of present-day Bavaria. The texts of all surviving *Firework Books*, which all show variations, were written in fifteenth-century vernacular script, almost exclusively in red and dark brown ink.

As a group such books retain a coherence and similarities to an extent much greater than, for example, cookery books or fencing manuals from the same period and region. It is striking that, in fifteenth-century Germany, the south-western region of Bavaria was at the forefront of producing vernacular manuscripts of a technical nature.[2] For example, Melitta Weiss Adamson and Trude Ehlert have examined the production of vernacular cookery books and their adjacent genres in fifteenth-century Germany. Both authors highlight the simplicity and low quality of the language of their original text, and the almost accidental nature of the collation of their texts, although they have omitted the important point that these 'technical' sources appear predominantly in Bavaria.[3]

Erasmus of Rotterdam, Cicero, Petrarch, Plato, Ovid, and many others (Norbert H. Ott, 'Steiner, Heinrich', *Neue Deutsche Biographie* 25 (2013), 183, https://www.deutsche-biographie.de/pnd119838451.html#ndbcontent, and Josef Benzing, 'Egenolff, Christian', *Neue Deutsche Biographie* 4 (1959), 325–26, https://www.deutsche-biographie.de/pnd122968468.html#ndbcontent (both accessed 10 August 2023)). The most comprehensive study of the printed editions of the *Firework Book* was carried out by Klára Andresová, who identified a total of 13 printed versions of the *Firework Book* from 1529 until 1619 (Klára Andresová, 'A Bestseller among Artillery Handbooks of the 16th Century: Printed Editions of the Late Medieval *Feuerwerkbuch*', *International Journal of Military History and Historiography* (2022), 1–27, 1).

[2] The connection between the format of the *Firework Book* and fencing manuals has been highlighted by Daniel Jaquet in a so far unpublished paper, 'Fighting Experts: Fencers, Gunners, and Arbalesters as Masters in Swiss Towns', presented at the International Medieval Congress in Leeds in 2021.

[3] See, for example, Melitta Weiss Adamson, 'Vom Arzneibuch zum Kochbuch, vom Kochbuch zum Arzneibuch: Eine diätetische Reise von der arabischen Welt und Byzanz über Italien ins spätmittelalterliche Bayern', in *Der Koch ist der bessere Arzt: Zum Verhältnis von Diätetik und Kulinarik im Mittelalter und der Frühen Neuzeit*, eds Andrea Hofmeister-Winter et al. (Frankfurt am Main: Peter Lang, 2014), 39–62, and Melitta Weiss Adamson, '"mich dunkcht ez sein knöllell": Von den Mühen eines bayrischen Übersetzers mittelalterlicher Fachliteratur', in *Fachtexte des Spätmittelalters und der Frühen Neuzeit: Tradition und Perspektiven der Fachprosa- und*

The title *Firework Book* (in German: 'Feuerwerkbuch') derives from the textual reference which seems to appear in all of the identified manuscripts, usually early in the text.[4] It has, however, not been used as a title at the head of the text – this was only done by librarians and archivists from the eighteenth century onwards. In 1941, the suffix 'of 1420' was added by Wilhelm Hassenstein in the publication of the *Feuerwerkbuch von 1420*, which provided both an edition of two copies of the *Firework Book* and an additional commentary, but he offers no discernible explanation for this choice of date.[5] Hassenstein's title has been used to name this category of technical writing ever since, even though many have subsequently challenged the dating of 1420 on account of the otherwise questionable historical context in the commentary of the publication.[6] Other scholars have assigned it a different date of production. For example, Joseph Needham, historian of Chinese technology and science, refers to the 'Feuerwerkbuch von 1437'.[7] The only thing that can be agreed is that the afterlife of the *Firework Book* had started by the 1430s, as Bert Hall notes when commenting on the dating issue:

> The *Firework Book* continued to be copied, but its text seems to have stabilized after the 1430s or 1440s, and the later versions contain little that is new. When the work finally was printed in 1529, it was thoroughly obsolete.[8]

Fachsprachenforschung, ed. Lenka Vanková (Berlin: de Gruyter, 2014), 143–54, and Trude Ehlert (ed.), *Küchenmeisterei: Edition, Übersetzung und Kommentar zweier Kochbuch-Handschriften des 15. Jahrhunderts* (Frankfurt am Main: Peter Lang, 2010), and Trude Ehlert and Rainer Leng, 'Frühe Koch- und Pulverrezepte aus der Nürnberger Handschrift GNM 3227a (um 1389)', in *Medizin in Geschichte, Philologie und Ethnologie. Festschrift für Gundolf Keil*, eds Dominik Groß and Monika Reininger (Würzburg: Königshausen & Neumann, 2003), 289–313.

[4] In the Royal Armouries manuscript I.34 it is on fol. 2r, line 1, where it is referred to as '*fewrwerkpůch*'.

[5] *Das Feuerwerkbuch von 1420*, Hassenstein, *Feuerwerkbuch*, title page.

[6] Bert S. Hall, *Weapons and Warfare in Renaissance Europe: Gunpowder, Technology, and Tactics* (Baltimore: Johns Hopkins University Press, 1997), 71: '… can safely be said to stem from the period before 1420 …'; see also Kramer, *Berthold Schwarz*, 98–99.

[7] Needham, *Military Technology: Gunpowder Epic*, 33, with a reference to James R. Partington, *A History of Greek Fire and Gunpowder* (Baltimore: Johns Hopkins University Press, 1960; repr. 1999), 152, who himself lists only five *Firework Books* in existence, two of which seem to be dated 1437 while one other is dated 1420.

[8] Hall, *Warfare in Renaissance*, 88.

The *Firework Book* Tradition

Hassenstein's *Feuerwerkbuch von 1420* also provides a listing of 38 *Firework Book* manuscripts.[9] In recent decades there has been general consensus that Hassenstein's list was incomplete and was, moreover, based on rather dubious scholarship – as is the rest of the publication. Hassenstein even argues that the Milimete Gun illustration (Oxford, Christ Church MS 92 fol. 70v), which is said to be the first to display the characteristics of gunpowder weaponry in action, must have been a later addition to the 1326 manuscript, as the English, who were not sufficiently advanced in weapon technology (in comparison to the Germans), could not have invented gunpowder technology ('*[…] sind phantastische Malereien, die nachträglich in die […] Handschrift […] aus den Jahren 1326 und 1327 hineingemalt worden sind, […] und die unmögliche Vorstellung erweckt haben, daß nicht die Deutschen, sondern die schon damals im Waffenwesen rückständigen Engländer die Erfinder der Pulvergeschütze sind*').[10] It was exactly this depiction which led to the academic case being made in the 1960s that England must have been in the forefront of technological development.[11]

Hassenstein was by no means the first to emphasize the 'origin myth' of the inventors of gunpowder. Early debate was strongly influenced by national interests with the aim of establishing which nation in particular had 'invented' guns and/or gunpowder and led the field in military technology. Max Jähns among others was eager to point out that the powder gun was invented in Germany. While he does acknowledge the earlier presence of gunpowder technology in China and the Arabian peninsula, he is certain that gunpowder as the driver for projectiles was a German invention by the legendary Berthold Schwarz (Niger Bertholdus) who is mentioned in almost all *Firework Books*.[12] Kelly DeVries describes Hassenstein's publication as 'virtually useless except for the text itself'.[13] Hassenstein's publication nevertheless has been regularly used in the twentieth century as a point of reference for the presence of *Firework Books* and their circulation.

Research by Rainer Leng, a medieval historian with a special interest in technical manuscripts, has been instrumental in expanding the corpus of

---

[9] Hassenstein, *Feuerwerkbuch*, 85–88.

[10] Hassenstein, *Feuerwerkbuch*, 83.

[11] Partington, *Greek Fire and Gunpowder*, 78, and Dudley Pope, *Guns* (Feltham: Spring Books, 1969), 21–23.

[12] Jähns, *Kriegswissenschaften*, 224–26.

[13] Kelly DeVries, 'Review of Gerhard W. Kramer, ed., and Klaus Leibnitz, trans. *The Firework Book: Gunpowder in Medieval Germany (Das Feuerwerkbuch, c. 1440)*', *Ambix* 50:2 (2003), 237–38, at 237. See also Simon Werrett, who uncritically follows both Kramer and Hassenstein (Simon Werrett, *Fireworks: Pyrotechnic Arts and Sciences in European History* (Cambridge: Cambridge University Press, 2010), 27).

Gunpowder Technology in the Fifteenth Century

material available in order to show which *Firework Books (of 1420)* are extant.[14] Leng reuses Hassenstein's label of *Firework Book of 1420*, which was also used as an entry in the second edition of *Die deutsche Literatur des Mittelalters: Verfasserlexikon* ('German Literature of the Middle Ages: Dictionary of Authors'):

> This group of manuscripts known as the *Firework Book of 1420* from the first half of the fifteenth century was first printed in 1529. [...] They transmitted personal experiences, often gained through experimentation. This resulted in a considerable number of often substantial firework books, which can be grouped together because they are almost identical, as they consisted of chapters copied almost word-for-word. [...] In total, 48 manuscripts with related content exist in German-speaking regions.[15]

---

[14] Particularly in Rainer Leng, *Ars belli: deutsche taktische und kriegstechnische Bilderhandschriften und Traktate im 15. und 16. Jahrhundert*, Imagines medii aevi, 2 vols (Wiesbaden: Reichert, 2002), and Rainer Leng, 'Feuerwerks- und Kriegsbücher', in *Katalog der deutschsprachigen illustrierten Handschriften des Mittelalters*, vol. 4/2, eds Norbert H. Ott et al. (München: C. H. Beck, 2009), 145–512, http://www.manuscripta-mediaevalia.de/?xdbdtdn:%22hsk%200622a%22&dmode=doc#|3 (accessed 10 August 2023).

[15] Burghart Wachinger et al., *Die deutsche Literatur des Mittelalters: Verfasserlexikon*, 2nd edn (Berlin: de Gruyter, 1977–2008), vol. 2 (1980), cols 728–31, under the heading of '*Feuerwerkbuch von 1420*':

> Das heute unter dieser Bezeichnung geführte Kompendium einschlägiger Hss. aus der ersten Hälfte des 15. Jh.s wurde erstmals i. J. 1529, ein Jahrhundert nach seiner Entstehung [...] gedruckt [...] tradierte aufgrund seiner eigenen, häufig auch experimentell gewonnenen Erfahrungen. Auf diese Weise kam es schon in der ersten Hälfte des 15. Jh.s zu einer erheblichen Zahl mitunter sehr umfangreicher Feuerwerkbücher, deren Verwandtschaft miteinander noch heute anhand der in jeder erhaltenen Hs. auftauchenden fast identischen, weil nahezu immer wieder wörtlich abgeschriebenen Kapitel nachzuweisen ist. [...]

> Insgesamt sind bis heute 48 dieser in zumindest einem Abschnitt inhaltlich miteinander verwandten Hss. im deutschsprachigen Raum.

The first edition was published 1933–55, but as the first volume A–F included the *Firework Book* reference, it did not include the Hassenstein reference, and the new terminology was only added in the second edition published between 1977 and 2008. Even then, the article on the '*Feuerwerkbuch von 1420*' (in vol. 2, published in 1980) varies in its definition of the entries 'Instructions on the making of gunpowder, loading of guns and firing them' ('*Anleitungen, Schießpulver zu bereiten, Büchsen zu laden und zu beschießen*' [in vol. 1, published in 1978]) and of 'Guns, armour for warfare, sieges and fireworks' ('*Pixen, Kriegsrüstung, Sturmzeug und Feuerwerk*' [in vol. 7, published in 1989]). All three entries are written by the same author, Volker Schmidtchen.

The *Firework Book* Tradition

Still, no clear definition is provided of what a *Firework Book* is, or is not. Leng criticizes manuscripts he considers to be 'loose transmissions' (*Streuüberlieferungen*) as well as, in his opinion, 'wrongful attributions' (*Fehlzuschreibungen*) to the *Firework Book of 1420* tradition. Nevertheless, he produces his own attribution list of manuscripts which contain 'substantial or larger continuous parts' of the *Firework Book*, including a total of 58 manuscripts, with partial or full content associated with the genre of the *Firework Book*. He restricts his list to manuscripts but includes copies in sixteenth-century chancery hand, as well as other references to manuscripts believed to be missing ('*verschollen*') but which had been recorded at some point earlier, including one which was last recorded in private ownership.[16] Leng does not, however, provide a clear definition which could clarify how to include or exclude any texts related to this corpus.

The earliest version of the *Firework Book* was likely to have been written in the first few years of the fifteenth century, broadly agreeing with Hassenstein's dating but not his fixed date, for which no evidence could be found. The *Firework Book* is distinctively different from other technical-military texts in that it deals solely with specific questions on gunpowder artillery instead of focusing on the wider aspects of gun making and on defensive or offensive tactics. Based on this group of criteria a total of 65 manuscripts can be attributed to the genre, all but one of which are in known locations and accessible to view, including fifteenth- and sixteenth-century copies, ranging from seemingly complete texts down to smaller fragments. A list of all manuscripts identified as belonging to the genre is given in the Bibliography.

Very few copies of the *Firework Book* provide dates of production or identifiable authors, and where dates or authors are provided it is hard to verify whether these are later additions. Freiburg Ms. 362 is dated in the text as having been produced in 1432.[17] Only one copy of the *Firework Book*, that in Dillingen, has a possible attributed author: at the end of the text, the name and date, '*1466 Jodocus Foelki presbyter*',[18] have been inserted – identified as Jodocus Völki from the Vorarlberg region of Austria. A certain Jodocus Völki was documented in the 1480s as a priest in Sulz on the river Neckar.[19] This

---

[16] Leng, *Ars belli*, vol. 2, 441–62.

[17] Freiburg Ms. 362, fol. 89v, '*Anno trecesimo 2*'. This seems to be in the same hand but the ink is slightly darker in colour – although even this one is described in the Freiburg University Library catalogue entry as a copy of an earlier manuscript from around or before 1420.

[18] Dillingen Ms. XV 50, fol. 33r.

[19] See catalogue entry for Dillingen manuscript Ms. XV 50: Elisabeth Wunderle, *Die mittelalterlichen Handschriften der Studienbibliothek Dillingen* (Wiesbaden:

location seems to correlate to the manuscript's linguistic features as they have been identified as 'Alemannic with traces of Swabian dialect'.[20] However, the line containing the date and name appears to be written in a different coloured ink and by a different hand, and it is possible that it was added later, thus throwing doubt on the assumption that the reference could be used to date the manuscript. It is possible that Völki was an owner of the manuscript, rather than the author or copyist. The authors of most manuscripts are anonymous, sometimes described as 'very shadowy figures about whom little is known'.[21] Ever since the nineteenth century, there has been some speculation about the possible author of the *Firework Book*, and one long-discussed theory argues for a certain Abraham von Memmingen. Abraham was said to have been a master gunner in the early fifteenth century who was claimed to have produced a *Firework Book* for his employer, Frederick of Austria. This is based on research by Josef Würdinger, who provides no credible evidence to support this claim.[22] Hence, this theory has been widely dismissed in recent years.[23]

Most copies in existence have been rebound since production, and have often been placed together with other texts on military regimen or other technical content.[24] This makes any speculation about their state at the point of production difficult. They were all produced on good quality paper but with scarcely any illustrations, relegating them to somewhat low-status publications for more personal use.[25] This leads Kay Smith to suggest that the *Firework*

Harrassowitz, 2006), 74–77.

[20] Werner Meyer, 'Eine Abschrift des Feuerwerkbuchs. Die Hs. XV 50 der Studienbibliothek Dillingen an der Donau', *Liber Castellorum* (1981), 288–301, at 299.

[21] Bert S. Hall, *The Technological Illustrations of the So-Called "Anonymous of the Hussite Wars"*: Codex Latinus Monacensis 197, Part 1 (Wiesbaden: Reichert, 1979), 5.

[22] Josef Würdinger, *Kriegsgeschichte von Bayern, Franken, Pfalz und Schwaben: Band II von 1347 bis 1506* (München: Literarisch-Artistische Anstalt der Cotta'schen Buchhandlung, 1868), 397–402. See Jähns, *Kriegswissenschaften*, 392–93, S. J. von Romocki, *Geschichte der Explosivstoffe* (Hannover: Gebrüder Gänecke, 1895; repr. Hildesheim: Gerstenberg, 1976), 179, or Hassenstein, *Feuerwerkbuch*, 79–80.

[23] *Verfasserlexikon*, vol. 1 (1980), cols 11–12.

[24] For examples, the copies located in Dillingen, Memmingen, Darmstadt, and Strasbourg. In all of these, gaps are provided at the beginning of sections which must have been intended for a later completion (mostly made in a different colour of ink).

[25] Most primary and secondary sources related to *Firework Books* are catalogued in German academic libraries under German Literature and not under History. As there is less linguistic and literary appeal compared to other texts in German at the time, they tend to be more marginalized.

The *Firework Book* Tradition

Books could possibly be 'private notebooks of the apprentice gunner, copied during their apprenticeship from the master's copy with their own additions and later extensions'.[26] Ferdinand Nibler went one step further by suggesting that the *Firework Book* was 'a study and reference book for a master gunner'.[27]

To date, there has only been one very loose 'translation' into English of a *Firework Book*, Freiburg Ms. 362, produced in 2001 by Gerhard Kramer and his translator, Klaus Leibnitz (appearing after Kramer's death). Kramer and Leibnitz make some intriguing claims in the introductory paragraphs to the effect that the Freiburg *Firework Book* was 'written by chemists (or alchemists) for the use of master gunners'. They continue:

> It was written in German Gothic script, which is notably difficult to read. Its content is technical and arcane, its vocabulary archaic and recondite, its language – Middle High German – familiar only to scholars. The advice it contains, at least in part, is obscure and enigmatic, it's [sic!] pre-scientific concepts unfamiliar and abstruse. It could be deciphered only by a scholar who was a linguist, an historian and a chemist. Taken as a whole, however, this manuscript is an eminently sound and practical manual.[28]

This statement includes a range of suppositions, contradictions, and factual errors. The claim that the *Firework Book* was written by a chemist or alchemist is unsubstantiated in that they fail to provide a definition of what they (or a fifteenth-century expert audience) understand a chemist or alchemist to be.[29] They seem to contradict themselves by describing the text as 'technical and arcane, its vocabulary archaic and recondite', but also 'sound and practical'.[30] In fact, the vocabulary, while technical, is relatively straightforward. The language of the Freiburg *Firework Book* – as for all other *Firework Books* in existence

---

[26] Smith, *Rewriting Gunpowder History*, 95.

[27] 'Lehr- und Handbuch für den Büchsenmeister' (Nibler, *Feuerwerkbuch*, 3).

[28] Kramer and Leibnitz, *Das Feuerwerkbuch*, 20.

[29] Many scholars have tried to address the roles of alchemist and chemist in late medieval society. See Leah DeVun, *Prophecy, Alchemy, and the End of Time: John of Rupecissa in the Late Middle Ages* (New York: Columbia University Press, 2009), P. G. Maxwell-Stuart, *The Chemical Choir: A History of Alchemy* (London: Continuum, 2008), or Michela Pereira, 'Alchemy and the Use of Vernacular Languages in the Late Middle Ages', *Speculum* 74:2 (1999), 336–56. However, the scholars' main concern seems to be the role of alchemy as pseudo-science and its relation to religion. In the end, the title 'alchemist' or 'chemist' becomes a loose collective term for anyone who is more or less engaged in activities related to alchemy and associated issues.

[30] Kramer and Leibnitz, *Das Feuerwerkbuch*, 20.

– is not 'archaic' Middle High German (as Kramer and Leibnitz suggest) but Early New High German, written in the regional dialect of the respective author. Most fifteenth-century copies of the *Firework Books* – including the Freiburg *Firework Book* – are written in cursive, clear bastarda.[31] Therefore, we can see that Kramer and Leibnitz's evaluation, as evidenced in the above quote, betrays a lack of understanding of late medieval and early modern language, science, concepts, and terminology. Moreover, they undervalue the *Firework Book*'s use of the core content and invaluable rhetorical technique of question and answer, providing the reader with a familiar didactic format, similar to that found in early medical texts or later in manuals on mining, but also in scholastic texts.[32] Kramer and Leibnitz are correct, however, when they observe that a full understanding of the text requires the multidisciplinary skills of a chemist, historian, and linguist.

Up to now there have been only occasional references in scholarly publications in English to the *Firework Book* and its position within the wider genre of technical treatises on aspects of master gunners' instructions and manuals.[33] German academic scholarship, on the other hand, has attempted to identify several, different categories of firework and war books, of which the *Firework Book* tradition is only one.[34] An early reference to the *Firework Book* genre was provided by the nineteenth-century historian Max Jähns in 1889–91,[35]

---

[31] See Joachim Kirchner, *Germanistische Handschriftenpraxis* (München: Beck, 1950), 22–23. Kramer and Leibnitz refer to it as 'German Gothic Script' (Kramer and Leibnitz, *Das Feuerwerkbuch*, 20). It is difficult to get to the bottom of what Kramer and Leibnitz may have interpreted as Gothic Script. It is most likely that they confused the bastarda script (sometimes called Gothic) with the language presented.

[32] Ferdinand Nibler describes the *Firework Book of 1420* as one of the oldest, if not the oldest, German-language text with technical content (*deutschsprachige[s] Buch mit technischem Inhalt* – Nibler, *Feuerwerkbuch Buchbesprechung*, 147). It is a very bold claim, but difficult to substantiate – not only because a definition would be required for what constitutes a book, what he means by 'technical content' or even what he regards as 'German-language'.

[33] Notable exceptions include DeVries and Smith, *Military Technology*, 152, Smith, *Rewriting Gunpowder History*, 95–100, Hall, *Warfare in Renaissance*, 71, or even earlier, Partington, *Greek Fire and Gunpowder*, 144 and 155, and Needham, *Military Technology: Gunpowder Epic*, 267.

[34] Leng, *Ars belli*, vol. 1, 4–23, and Leng, 'Feuerwerks- und Kriegsbücher', 145–53.

[35] Jähns was one of the most prominent military historians in nineteenth-century Germany. After a long military career he became Professor of the History of Military Art ('*Kriegskunst*') at the Military Academy ('*Kriegsakademie*') in Berlin from 1872 to 1886. His 865-page, 3-volume *Geschichte der Kriegswissenschaften* (1889–91) provides an overview of military history from Antiquity to the end of

The *Firework Book* Tradition

who includes it in his section on technical works (*Fachwissenschaftliche Werke*) and produces an unsubstantiated explanation on the incoherent order of the instructions – describing them as 'untidy'. He suggests that the individual instructions were on separate pieces of paper, only collated with greater or less attention by the redacting editors.[36] Jähns even comments in detail about the one copy known to be in existence in French. Following the prevalent stance of German nationalism at the time, he argues that this must be a later copy, and represents an acknowledgment of the dominance of German gunpowder artillery in the fifteenth and sixteenth centuries across Europe.[37] However, Jähns fails to provide evidence for his arguments, falling back on general statements.[38]

Research into these technical texts in the nineteenth century was often driven by the antiquarian curiosity of military practitioners who wished to understand better the origins of their own discipline. Their motives and methodologies were multifaceted and produced mixed results. Max Jähns, Bernard Rathgen, and many other military historians of the period were retired officers who engaged in research into the history of artillery. Their research, in the course of collating a large number of sources and establishing early categorizations, has been described as containing substantial misinterpretations resulting from insufficient critical distance to sources.[39] Between the 1890s

---

the sixteenth century, predominantly in Germany. This text, still referred to today, has been viewed as one of the cornerstones of German military historical studies.

[36] '*Diese Unordnung, welche sämtliche Codices anhaftet, findet sich nicht überall in der selben Reihenfolge, und so darf man vermuten, daß ursprünglish einzeln auf Zettel geschrieben waren, die von Redaktoren mit größerer oder geringerer Einsicht in das Original oder in eine auch schon anderweitig verdorbene Kopie eingeschaltet worden sind*' (Jähns, *Kriegswissenschaften*, 394).

[37] His work contains statements such as 'how no other peoples in the then Europe can demonstrate' ('*wie sonst kein Volk des damaligen Europas auszuweisen hat*', Jähns, *Kriegswissenschaften*, 382), the 'esteem which German gunpowder artillery possessed even in the fifteenth century' ('*die Achtung, in welcher die deutsche Büchsenmeisterei schon im 15. Jahrhundert stand*', Jähns, *Kriegswissenschaften*, 408), or, referring to the translation into French, as a 'simple translation of the old German *Firework Book*' ('*einfache Übersetzung des alten deutschen Feuerwerkbuches*', Jähns, *Kriegswissenschaften*, 408).

[38] Jähns, *Kriegswissenschaften*, 408.

[39] Volker Schmidtchen, *Kriegswesen in späten Mittelalter: Technik, Taktik, Theorie* (Weinheim: VCH, 1990), 5, and Rainer Leng, *Anleitung Schiesspulver zu bereiten, Büchsen zu laden und zu beschiessen: eine kriegstechnische Bilderhandschrift im cgm 600 der Bayerischen Staatsbibliothek München*, Imagines Medii Aevi 5 (Wiesbaden: Reichert, 2000), 10.

and 1960s, Marcelin Berthelot, Theodor Beck, and Bertrand Gille highlighted the master gunner and gun maker traditions as one of the contributory elements in the development of the discipline of engineering. Friedrich Klemm, too, recognized the role of fifteenth-century gunnery manuals which mark the early beginnings of technical writings.[40] Franz Maria Feldhaus proposed the first typology in 1931 (revised in 1954)[41] while ignoring illustrations and the technical aspects of the content of the texts. In North America, the earliest main contribution to the subject was made by Lynn White, as part of the wider quest to revive research into medieval technology as a fundamental part of social history.[42] Since the 1960s this has changed, with scholars across Europe and North America publishing on aspects of military technology, their description and depiction in the fifteenth and sixteenth centuries. However, the main effort would appear to be focused on the illustrations with far less emphasis on the text available.[43]

Over a period of more than 30 years, the military historian Volker Schmidtchen developed a system of sub-categorization of medieval publications on military technology. It was he who first clearly subdivided the genre into five distinct categories: 1) literary sources (chronicles, annals, and other reports of events); 2) manuscripts which exclusively or partially depict and describe military technology; 3) manuals, regulations, statutes, and instructional writings; 4) account books, rolls, inventories, books of feuds (*'Fehdebücher'*), and other registers of events (*'actae')*; and 5) technical sources (arms and equipment). Even Schmidtchen admits, however, that this categorization

---

[40] See Marcelin Berthelot, 'Pour l'histoire des arts méchaniques et de l'artillerie vers la fin du moyen âge', *Annales de chimie et de physique*, ser. 6, 24 (1891), 433–521, Theodor Beck, *Beiträge zur Geschichte des Maschinenbaus* (Berlin: Julius Springer, 1899), 270–92, Bertrand Gille, 'Études sur les manuscrits d'ingénieurs du XVe siècle', *Techniques et civilisations* 5 (1956), 77–86, at 79–81, or Friedrich Klemm, *Die Geschichte des technischen Schrifttums. Form und Funktion des gedruckten technischen Buchs vom ausgehenden 15. bis zum beginnenden 19. Jahrhundert* (München: Diss. Masch, 1948).

[41] See *Feldhaus, Technik der Antike und des Mittelalters*, 324–27, as well as Franz Maria Feldhaus, *Die Machine im Leben der Völker. Ein Überblick von der Urzeit bis zur Renaissance* (Basel and Stuttgart: Birkhäuser, 1954), 229–53.

[42] See Lynn White Jr, *Medieval Technology and Social Change* (London: Oxford University Press, 1962), 96–101. See also Robert Fox (ed.), *Technological Change: Methods and Themes in the History of Technology*, Studies in the History of Science, Technology & Medicine 1 (Amsterdam: Harwood Academic, 1996), 11–15.

[43] One laudable exception was Bert Hall, who singled out the *Bellifortis* and the *Firework Book* as by far the most prominent genres produced in Germany in the fifteenth century (Hall, *Illustrations … Hussite Wars*, ch. 2).

The *Firework Book* Tradition

has its limitations and cannot be applied across all records. Each of his categories is a loose collection of different sources and formats. Nor is it helpful that many texts are untitled or are anonymous, which, in turn, leads to subjective, often artificial labelling at their respective libraries or archives.[44] Schmidtchen locates the *Firework Book* genre within his category 2, as manuscripts which depict and describe military technology.

The *Firework Book* genre is thus seen as one of the subgroups within the group of firework and war book manuscripts related to warfare technology in the German vernacular – with its main focus on the development and technologies of explosives and improved smithing and woodcraft technologies which supported those developments – emerging in the fifteenth century in vernacular cultures, and especially in German manuscripts.[45] The tradition appears not to have spread in the fifteenth century into Italian, French (with possibly one exception), or Spanish, although there is one indication of a version in Hebrew.[46] Illustrated military manuscripts were produced only in small numbers in Italy in the fifteenth and sixteenth centuries. The high level of decoration, and the use of expensive ink and materials, as well as the absence of wear and tear, suggest that they were probably used as gifts and collector's items for display rather than being intended for use as manuals in a workshop.[47]

---

[44] Schmidtchen, *Kriegswesen*, 22–23.

[45] As defined by the *Katalog der deutschsprachigen illustrierten Handschriften des Mittelalters*, see Leng, 'Feuerwerks- und Kriegsbücher', 145–512.

[46] What has survived is a sixteenth-century copy of the *Livre du secret de l'art de artillerie et cannonerie* in French. It is not possible to establish whether this text had an older original in French or is a sixteenth-century French translation of a text from a different language (Paris, Bibliothèque nationale de France, Ms. Latin 4653, https://archivesetmanuscrits.bnf.fr/ark:/12148/cc63506g (accessed 10 August 2023)). The reference on the manuscript in Hebrew comes from Partington, *Greek Fire and Gunpowder*, 179 n. 45, where the author refers to M. Ginsburger, 'Les Juifs et l'art militaire au Moyen-Âge', *Revue des Études Juives* 88 (1929), 156–66. However, when consulting the article referred to, all Ginsburger mentions is that there is meant to be a Hebrew manuscript in Munich which Ginsburger argues to be based on content from the *Firework Book*. Rather than thinking it was a translation of a German text, he believes that it is an original by a Jewish author. No reference nor justification for this assumption has been provided (Ginsburger, 'Les Juifs et l'art militaire', 157–58). The suggested manuscript could not be traced.

[47] Marcus Popplow, 'Militärtechnische Bildkataloge des Spätmittelalters', in *Krieg im Mittelalter*, ed. Hans-Henning Kortüm (Berlin: Akademie, 2001), 251–68, at 262. One of the most outstanding authors was Mariano Taccola (1381–1453/58), some of whose works survive from 1430–50. See *Mariano Taccola, Liber Tertius de Ingeneis ac edifitiis non usitatis*, ed. J. H. Beck (Milano: Edizioni il Polifilo, 1969),

The later Middle Ages saw what Lynn White called 'the emergence of a conscious and generalized lust for natural energy and its application to human purposes'.[48] This concept was further developed by Bert Hall into the emergence of literature dealing with technology and machinery in response to this new 'consciousness of a power technology'.[49] Starting with Villard de Honnecourt (whose notebook dates from c. 1235), a growing number of similarly intended writings, including Guido da Vigevano's *Texaurus regis Francie acquisitionis terre sancte* (c. 1335), depicted military technological devices for the crusades. Gradually these types of writing increased in quantity but remained largely limited to the geographical area that today includes southern Germany, Austria, and northern Italy. There are no known manuscripts of this kind in the Low Countries, Scandinavia, Iberia, or the British Isles.[50]

The *Bellifortis* and the *Büchsenmeister Book*

Most of the manuscripts of this genre in German were produced in the first few decades of the fifteenth century at a time when other genres of vernacular writing, such as treatises on technical aspects of field medicine, wound healing, and apothecary practice, were beginning to emerge.[51] Other elements in this group are texts on military technology for use at court, called the *Bellifortis*, which survives in a number of manuscripts with the first version believed to have been written between 1402 and 1405, and manuscripts related to the *Büchsenmeister Book* (literally meaning 'Master Gunner Book'), with the earliest surviving manuscript dated to 1411.[52] This means that chronologically the

---

    Mariano Taccola, De ingeneis, eds Frank D. Prager and Ulrich Montag (Cambridge, MA: MIT Press, 1971), and *Mariano Taccola, De rebus militaribus (De machinis, 1449)*, ed. Eberhard Knobloch (Baden-Baden: Koener, 1984). For an analysis of the manuscripts in historical context see Paolo Galluzzi, *Prima di Leonardo. Cultura delle machine a Siena nel Rinascimento* (Milano: Mondadori Electa, 1991).

[48] White, *Medieval Technology*, 129.

[49] Hall, *Illustrations … Hussite Wars*, 8.

[50] Hall, *Illustrations … Hussite Wars*, 9. There is one already-mentioned possible French translation.

[51] Melanie Panse, *Hans von Gersdorff: 'Feldbuch der Wundarznei'. Produktion, Präsentation und Rezeption von Wissen*, Trierer Beiträge zu den historischen Kulturwissenschaften 7 (Wiesbaden: Reichert, 2012), 204–7.

[52] For a comprehensive study of the *Bellifortis* see Leng, *Ars belli*, vol. 1, 109–49, Udo Friedrich, 'Herrscherpflichten und Kriegskunst. Zum intendierten Gebrauch früher 'Bellifortis'-Handschriften', in *Der Codex im Gebrauch. Akten des Internationalen Kolloquiums 11.–13. Juni 1992*, eds Christel Meier et al. (München: Wilhelm

The *Firework Book* Tradition

Firework Book can be placed after the production of the *Bellifortis*, and possibly around the same time or just before the earliest version of the *Büchsenmeister Book*. This leads me to speculate that the earliest *Firework Book* would have existed in the early years of the fifteenth century, and may have influenced the *Büchenmeister Book* which contains elements of the *Firework Book*. Apart from some specific mentions of the *Bellifortis* by Partington and Singer, and works on the Chinese origins by Needham, little research has been done on the relationship of these treatises and their shared roles in the history of the development of gunpowder technology.[53] As Leng observes, the main focus has been on the debate about corning – the change from individual loose powder of a floury consistency to more potent corned powder.[54]

The *Bellifortis* has generally been described as the first of the genre of illustrated manuscripts with technical military content in the later Middle Ages.[55] However, most extant *Bellifortis* manuscripts contain considerable

---

Fink, 1996), 197–210, and Lynn White Jr, 'Kyeser's *Bellifortis*: The First Technological Treatise of the Fifteenth Century', *Technology and Culture* 10 (1969), 436–41. The earliest *Büchsenmeister Books* are Vienna, Österreichische Nationalbibliothek, Cod. 3069, and Munich, Bayrische Staatsbibliothek, Cgm. 356. See Leng, *Ars belli*, vol. 2, 334–36, and 198–201, and Leng, *Anleitung Schiesspulver*, 12–22.

[53] Partington, *Greek Fire and Gunpowder*, 149–50, *A History of Technology*, ed. Charles Singer (Oxford: Clarendon Press, 1954–84), 653–56, and Needham, *Military Technology: Gunpowder Epic*, 342–65.

[54] Leng, *Ars belli*, vol. 1, 37. Corned powder or corning is a development in the production of gunpowder which involves adding water or alcohol to the ground powder and drying it so that the powder turns lumpy, which in turn improves combustion and consistency. When and how corned powder developed is a subject discussed by experts in the 1990s and beyond. There is scientific evidence that at some point in the fifteenth century gunners started using corned gunpowder, which was more powerful in its kinetic properties. This corned powder is much more advanced technologically from the earlier version of *Knollenpulver* mentioned in the Firework Book and discussed in Chapter 5. For the discussion on corned powder and corning see Kelly DeVries, 'Gunpowder and Early Gunpowder Weapons', in Buchanan, *Gunpowder: History of Technology*, 121–36, Bert S. Hall, 'The Didactic and the Elegant: Some Thoughts on Scientific and Technological Illustrations in the Middle Ages and Renaissance', in *Picturing Knowledge: Historical and Philosophical Problems concerning the Use of Art in Science*, ed. Brian Baigrie (Toronto: University of Toronto Press, 1996), 3–39, Hall, *Warfare in Renaissance*, here especially 68–87, and Gerhard W. Kramer, '*Das Feuerwerkbuch*: Its Importance in the Early History of Black Powder', in Buchanan, *Gunpowder: History of Technology*, 45–56, but also much earlier Romocki, *Geschichte der Explosivstoffe*.

[55] Leng, *Ars belli*, vol. 1, 7. This is, however, not correct, as the fourteenth-century Guido da Vigevano's *Texaurus regis Francie acquisitionis terre sancte* (c. 1335) already contains military illustrations.

Gunpowder Technology in the Fifteenth Century

material from the *Firework Book* and vice versa.[56] While changes occurred during the fifteenth century,[57] the core body of both manuscript groups can be relatively clearly defined.[58] According to Leng, 47 manuscripts of the *Bellifortis* are in existence, while a further 58 manuscripts are assumed to belong to the *Firework Book of 1420* genre.[59] It was clear that the *Bellifortis* cost much more to produce than a *Firework Book*: on high-quality paper, but written predominantly in Latin, and – most importantly – dominated by colourful (and expensive) illustrations. Conceptually, the *Bellifortis* seems much more interested in praising the military equipment depicted, usually in Latin verse, instead of explaining its actual use.[60] Thus, as argued by Theresia Berg and Udo Friedrich, the *Bellifortis*'s assumed readership is much more the untrained

---

[56] Leng, *Ars belli*, vol. 1, 199, 205–6.

[57] Leng, *Anleitung Schiesspulver*, 17–18.

[58] Leng, *Ars belli*, vol. 1, 19.

[59] Leng, *Ars belli*, vol. 1, 21, and vol. 2, 442–62. In total, Leng identifies some 100 texts produced in fifteenth-century Germany in relation to military technology and tactics, even with the exclusion of fencing and crossbow manuals, with a further 170 in the sixteenth century. However, he freely admits that this is a flawed attempt. In Leng, 'Feuerwerks- und Kriegsbücher', he provides a structure of 'manuals for fireworks and war (*Feuerwerks- und Kriegsbücher*)' as part of the 'Catalogue of German language illustrated manuscripts of the Middle Ages (*Katalog der deutschsprachigen illustrierten Handschriften des Mittelalters*)'. He provides as subcategories 1) anonymous master gunner books, 1400–1450 (*Büchsenmeisterbücher der ersten Hälfte des 15. Jahrhundert*); 2) The *Firework Book of 1420* (*Feuerwerkbuch von 1420*); 3) illustrated manuscripts of military technology for a courtly audience (*Bilderhandschriften zur Kriegstechnik für höfische Adressaten*); 4) anonymous and other master gunner books, 1450–1500 (*Anonyme und sonstige Büchsenmeisterbücher aus der zweiten Hälfte des 15. Jahrhunderts*); 5) other and anonymous war books, sixteenth century (*Sonstige und anonyme Kriegsbücher des 16. Jahrhunderts*); and 6) Arsenal inventories (*Illustrierte Zeughausinventare*); and a further 14 categories with named authors including Johannes Bengedans, Johannes Formschneider, Franz Helm, Konrad Kyeser, Martin Merz, and Philipp Mönch – with a grand total of 206 manuscripts considered. It is not entirely clear how he made editorial decisions to include or exclude certain manuscripts, which may not include illustrations.

[60] Similar to the *Firework Book of 1420*, the *Bellifortis* exists in a number of known copies. According to Graf zu Waldburg Wolfegg, 35 manuscripts are in existence, with their provenance known only from the early nineteenth century onwards. All of these manuscripts were high-quality productions, using multi-coloured illustrations on high-end paper. Christoph Graf zu Waldburg Wolfegg, 'Der Münchner "Bellifortis" und sein Autor', *Patrimonia* 137 (2000), 26–27. Bertrand Gille defines a German School of technological thought, and a movement which can be subdivided into 'The primitives', Konrad Keyser, and the manuscripts of the Hussite War – in order of sophistication. He provides a comprehensive list of *Bellifortis*

The *Firework Book* Tradition

non-expert instead of the artisan and practitioner readership of the *Firework Books* or the *Büchsenmeister Books*.[61]

As with the *Firework Book*, little is known about the *Bellifortis*: the name of its author, Konrad Kyeser, emerges in only two manuscript references.[62] Direct indications for the use of a *Bellifortis* cannot be established and the interest of a potential user can only be glimpsed from the list of dedications.[63] However, both the *Firework Book* and the *Bellifortis* have frequently been copied and their copies reveal alterations and amendments, together with additions.

The differences between the *Firework Book* and the *Bellifortis* are neatly summed up by Hall: 'The practical, prosaic, unillustrated Feuerwerkbuch and the fanciful, wide-ranging, lavishly illustrated *Bellifortis* together constitute the two main poles of the fifteenth-century Germanic tradition'.[64] Arguably, the most noticeable difference between the *Bellifortis* and the *Firework Book* is the predominant language used. The *Bellifortis* was mainly written in Latin interspersed with occasional German terms, while the *Firework Book* was composed in vernacular German, thus making the *Firework Book* the earliest textbook for specialists on military matters in any vernacular language.[65] This could possibly indicate the difference between the *Bellifortis* and the *Firework Book* with regard to their intended audience, reception, and use. It seems to be the common perception that there was a more scholarly, alchemical, and clerical tradition of texts of a technical nature which were produced in Latin – something which continued through the sixteenth and seventeenth centuries

---

copies which has been amended and enhanced by Leng, *Ars belli* (Bertrand Gille, *The Renaissance Engineer* (London: Lund Humphries, 1966), 55–77).

[61] Theresia Berg and Udo Friedrich, 'Wissenstradierung in spätmittelalterlichen Schriften zur Kriegskunst: Der "Bellifortis" des Konrad Kyeser und das anonyme "Feuerwerkbuch"', in *Wissen für den Hof. Der spätmittelalterliche Verschriftlichungsprozess am Beispiel Heidelberg im 15. Jahrhundert*, ed. Jan-Dirk Müller (München: Wilhelm Fink, 1994), 170.

[62] Friedrich, 'Herrscherpflichten und Kriegskunst', 198.

[63] Friedrich mentions one manuscript containing a list of Kyeser's dedications to previous employers, Sigismund of Hungary, Wenzel of Bohemia, and Franz of Carrara, while another contains a number of coats-of-arms, and a third specifies an *ex libris* from the Margrave Ernst Friedrich von Baden-Durlach. This, the author concludes, is an indication of presence among the political ruling classes (Friedrich, 'Herrscherpflichten und Kriegskunst', 200–1).

[64] Hall, *Illustrations ... Hussite Wars*, 20.

[65] Berg and Friedrich, 'Wissenstradierung', 215, and *Verfasserlexikon*, vol. 2 (1980), cols 730–32, where the author goes a step further and describes the *Firework Book of 1420* as the first book of technical content in German vernacular.

– while texts in vernacular languages were more practically oriented and created for a more immediate use.[66] The stated reason in the *Firework Book* as to why it was necessary to write down complex details was because there were 'so many things of which each good master gunner [and/or gun master] ought to be capable and which could not all be remembered well by a master and kept in his mind'.[67] This indicates that it was intended as an *aide memoire*, to be used frequently, as and when needed.[68] This, however, is an oversimplification about what the *Firework Book* is, as will be evidenced in subsequent chapters.

Compared to the *Bellifortis*, the *Firework Book* and the *Büchsenmeister Book* are much more clearly aimed at the practitioners themselves. They are functional and instructive texts, lacking jokes or innuendos. Instead, they focus, in a very matter-of-fact way, on disseminating information on the construction and use of guns and the production and use of gunpowder. These books have moved away from courtly entertainment to a practice-oriented role for the subject expert.[69] However, similarly to earlier comparison with the *Bellifortis*, the earliest versions of the *Büchsenmeister Book* place the main emphasis on the illustrations, with the textual references providing additional explanations, making the text of secondary importance to the illustrations. Earlier versions of the *Büchsenmeister Book* contain neither detailed recipes nor the detailed follow-through of the *Firework Book*, something that later changed, according to Leng.[70]

A key distinguishing feature of the core *Firework Book* – at first glance – is that it is unlike other associated texts such as the *Bellifortis* and the *Büchsenmeister Books* in that it hardly ever contains illustrations.[71] It is mainly restricted to the transmission of technical knowledge related to gunpowder and its components which does not require visual explanation. Leng moves one step further in his introduction to the *Firework Book* content by explaining that 'the reason was that the *Firework Book*'s limitation to transmitting chemical

---

[66] See Berg and Friedrich, 'Wissenstradierung', 174–76, or Panse, *Feldbuch der Wundarznei*, 11–16.

[67] See Chapter 3, fol. 33r.

[68] For evidence of actual use see Chapter 2.

[69] Leng, *Ars belli*, vol. 1, 109–49.

[70] Leng, *Ars belli*, vol. 1, 150–97.

[71] There are a few exceptions, such as the front page of Heidelberg Universitätsbibliothek, Cod. Pal. germ. 502, which contains an illustrated first page capital with a gun; or basic illustrations as marginalia in Vienna Cod. 3064 (not always classified as a *Firework Book of 1420*, but with some elements of it – see Leng, *Anleitung Schiesspulver*, 17–18) or Munich Cgm. 399 (see Leng, *Ars belli*, vol. 2, 454).

The *Firework Book* Tradition

knowledge on the production of gunpowder and its key components meant that the *Firework Book* did not require a visual transmission'.[72]

The fifteenth century sees the emergence of a range of technical texts. As Hall indicates, two schools of military-related writings rapidly emerge, with the Italian texts taking an all-encompassing approach, combining all aspects of military matters in one single text, while the German texts focus almost exclusively on technical matters. In the mid-fifteenth century, a treatise, *Ingenieurkunst- und Wunderbuch* ('*Book of the Art of Engineering and Miracles*') appears which contains a compilation of various instructive texts largely based on the *Bellifortis*.[73] Around the same time there emerged a group of manuscripts attributed to one Johann Formschneider, a master gunner or gun maker (*Büchsenmeister*) from Nuremberg. While only fragments of Formschneider's treatise survive, they indicate a wide ranging and detailed interest in military machines with the intention of improving some of Kyeser's writings as well as the *Firework Book*.[74] Modern scholarship has shown that these manuscripts were collected by local princes and rulers, in order to accumulate knowledge in their courtly libraries – with less of a sense as to whether they were actually used.[75] Thus, they provided access to a new technology with hitherto unknown effects.[76] Both of these statements lack supporting evidence and can only be seen as one possible interpretation of their reasons for production and usage.

One outstanding example is the *War Book* (*Kriegsbuch*) by Johannes Bengedans, surviving in three copies, which contains in parts a *Büchsenmeister Book* (literally translated as the 'master gunner' or 'gun master' book). We know from surviving letters, which have been dated to c. 1450–67, that the author Bengedans applied to the then High Master of the Teutonic Order for the

---

[72] '*Die Beschränkung auf die Vermittlung chemischen Wissens um die Herstellung von Pulverbestandteilen und Büchsenpulver erforderte keine visuelle Umsetzung*' (Leng, *Ars belli*, vol. 1, 198).

[73] Also called the 'Skanderbeg manuscript' after the Albanian nobleman George Kastrioti Skanderbeg (d. 1468), who was said to have owned it. See the anonymous *Ingenieurkunst- und Wunderbuch*, Weimar, Stiftung Weimarer Klassik / Anna-Amalia-Bibliothek, fol. 328 (unpublished).

[74] Hall, *Illustrations … Hussite Wars*, 23.

[75] Ralf G. Päsler, 'Sachliteratur (Artillerie-, Fecht-, und Ringbücher)', in *Handbuch Höfe und Residenzen im spätmittelalterlichen Reich, vol. 15.III: Hof und Schrift*, eds Werner Paravicini et al. (Ostfildern: Thorbecke, 2005), 573–84, at 579.

[76] Päsler, 'Sachliteratur', 574.

position of master gunner.[77] While no records show whether Bengedans was actually employed by the Order, he is listed as a participant on a diplomatic mission on their behalf.[78] He lists his wide-ranging skills, such as purifying saltpetre, the production of fire arrows of different types, the casting of cannons, and manufacture of other military technical devices.[79] In contrast to the *Firework Book* tradition, Bengedans emphasizes his own skills in the improving and ennoblement of precious metals.[80] The 'War Book' clearly shows that Bengedans felt the need to portray himself as multi-skilled in technical and scientific endeavours, even if most of his writing is far from original but derived from multiple other sources. Bengedans's writings, an example of the new category of reference books for military technology which emerged in the second half of the fifteenth century, are viewed as an ideal introduction to the art of artillery, a practical manual for apprentices and specialists alike.[81] The *Büchsenmeister Books* describe the establishment of the role and title of 'master gunner', and his official key functions. Most of the *Büchsenmeister Books* are attributed to a named author, and include a wide range of illustrations, usually with only small amounts of text written predominantly in German vernacular. It is clear that the *Büchsenmeister Books* relied heavily on elements of the *Firework Book* but, with the introduction of illustrations, it was produced for a different audience and a different use.[82]

Thus, the *Büchsenmeister Book* texts served a range of different purposes: as *aides memoire* for new techniques of hitherto abstract knowledge and processes which were perceived to be too complex for an individual to remember;[83] and

[77] *Kriegskunst und Kanonen: Das Büchsenmeister- und Kriegsbuch des Johannes Bengedans*, eds Hans Blosen and Rikke Agnete Olsen (Aarhus: Aarhus Universitetsforlag, 2006), vol. 2, 62.

[78] Blosen and Olsen, *Bengedans*, vol. 1, 15.

[79] Blosen and Olsen, *Bengedans*, vol. 2, 81.

[80] Blosen and Olsen, *Bengedans*, vol. 2, 66.

[81] Blosen and Olsen, *Bengedans*, vol. 1, 17.

[82] Leng puts the *Firework Book* together with earlier and later *Büchsenmeister Books* into one single category, stating that the manuscript Munich Cgm. 600 likely preceded the production of the *Firework Book*, while later named versions are described as a continuum (Leng, *Ars belli*, 150–266).

[83] The reasons for this have been explained differently by scholars, from the argument that 'new technology required accurate knowledge of abstract processes' (Päsler) to the fact that they 'have nothing to do with mechanics or ballistics as a science, but instead seem to have served as a sort of cookbook for the gunner' (Hall). See Bert S. Hall, "*Der Meister sol auch kennen schreiben und lesen*": Writings about Technology ca. 1400–ca. 1600 A.D. and their Cultural Implications', in *Early Technologies*, ed.

Sixteenth-Century Market for Science and Technology Books

In the sixteenth century, printers in Germany were the leading producers of a wide range of ground-breaking publications in the fields of both science and technology: Copernicus in astronomy, Leonard Fuchs in botany, Hieronymus Brunschwig in pharmacology, Vesalius in anatomy, as well as Agricola's *De Re Metallica*, first printed in Basel in 1556.[84] There clearly appears to have been a market for publications of this kind. It is important to point out that these publications were driven by humanists, and were exclusively written in Latin. Alongside these Latin texts, vernacular publications in Early New High German began to become more frequent, their origins being traced to early sixteenth-century text versions such as *Eyn wohlgeordnet und nützlich büchlein, wie man bergwerk suchen und finden soll* ('A well-structured and useful book on how to seek and find mines'), commonly called *Bergbüchlein*, by Ulrich Rülein von Calw, a humanist, medical researcher, and mathematician.[85]

Chronologically, the *Buch von den probierten Künsten* by Franz Helm, printed in 1535, is often seen as the culmination of the *Büchsenmeister Book* tradition.[86] This book sums up all core aspects of gunpowder technology, from powder production to firing, and includes many elements of the *Firework Book*, such as the 12 Master Gunner's Questions, which have been updated to sixteenth-century requirements and understanding of the technology. By then, the profession of master gunner had become more specialized, while the

---

Denise Schmandt-Besserat (Los Angeles: Undena Publications, 1979), 47–58, at 52–54, or Päsler, 'Sachliteratur', 578–79.

[84] David E. Connolly, 'Ulrich Rülein von Kalbe's Bergbüchlein in the Context of Sixteenth-Century German Mining/Metallurgical Literature', in *De Re Metallica: The Uses of Metal in the Middle Ages*, eds Robert O. Bork et al. (Farnham: Ashgate, 2005), 347 – in an article on sixteenth-century mining literature and Ulrich Rülein von Kalbe's *Bergbüchlein* (first printed around 1500 in Saxony).

[85] Available electronically at the Staats- und Landesbibliothek Dresden, https://digital.slub-dresden.de/werkansicht/dlf/12328/1/ (accessed 10 August 2023).

[86] Edited by Leng with critical introduction (Leng, *Franz Helm*, 3–135). Andresová's assertion that 'the late medieval *Feuerwerkbuch* […] was commonly issued under the name of the *Büchsenmeisterei* during the 16th century' is an oversimplification as no comprehensive standardization occurred (Andresová, 'Artillery Handbooks of the 16th Century', 23).

manufacture of cannons and the ingredients required for firing them (gunpowder, wadding, plugs, projectile, wedges, etc.) was delegated to others.[87]

The emergence of these texts went hand-in-hand with the development of other reference books, and could be seen as a move away from the specialist user to a more domestic audience, with texts such as the *Medieval Housebook* which include collections of drawings and texts. *Das mittelalterliche Hausbuch* (c. 1480) is attributed to the so-called 'Master of the Amsterdam Cabinet' and is often assumed to be one of the inspirations for the works of Dürer.[88] This *Hausbuch* includes a range of pyrotechnical recipes which, it has been argued, are drawn from the *Firework Book*, as well as incorporating astrological constellations and gardens of delights, together with military and domestic machines.[89] One of the many derivatives of this *Hausbuch* is the 'War Book' (*Kriegsbuch*), written in 1496 by Master Gunner Philipp Mönch (born in 1457) and illustrated as '*büch der stryt vnd buchßen*' (which can be translated as 'book of conflict and guns'), possibly made for Philip the Upright, Elector Palatine of the Rhine. A copy of this text is found in Heidelberg as Cod. Pal. germ. 126.[90]

Urtext, Production, and Transmission

Hassenstein had already noted in 1941 that the main focus of the *Firework Book of 1420* is on people, including the attribution of what qualities do (and do not) make a good master gunner, thus arguing that the *Firework Book* differs from modern technical treatises, in that the technology comes second

---

[87] '*Wie bei einem schnell immer komplexer werdenden Handwerk zu erwarten, tritt ab der zweiten Hälfte des 15. Jahrhunders eine immer deutlicher werdende Spezialisierung ein. [...] ab 1460 folgen ganze Dynastien von berühmten Büchsengießern, während die Büchsenmeister die Feuerwaffen nur noch transportieren, warten und bedienen*' (Leng, '*getruwelich dienen*', 320–21). It was only in the sixteenth century that the use of fireworks for pleasure and entertainment was recorded (see Rainer Leng, 'Feuerwerk zu Ernst und Schimpf. Die spielerische Anwendung der Pyrotechnik im Lustfeuerwerk', in *Homo faber ludens. Geschichten zu Wechselbeziehungen von Technik und Spiel*, eds Stefan Poser and Karin Zachmann (Frankfurt am Main: Peter Lang, 2003), 85–111).

[88] Christoph Graf zu Waldburg Wolfegg, *Venus and Mars: World of the Medieval Housebook* (London: Prestel, 1998), 8–9.

[89] Hall, *Illustrations ... Hussite Wars*, 15.

[90] Available online at https://digi.ub.uni-heidelberg.de/diglit/cpg126 (accessed 10 August 2023).

The *Firework Book* Tradition

– after the human factor.[91] This observation, while underlined with colourful language, arguably best describes the focus of the *Firework Book* and gives an insight into its intended use. While the uses of the book will be examined in greater detail in Chapters 2 and 5, here we can note that the differing nature of each text suggests that any possible use included a degree of oral transmission. There are three stages which could explain the production of the *Firework Book*:

(1) The author of the *urtext*: the person who first conceived the idea of producing a book of this kind, and then went on to produce or to commission it. We can surmise that the author had an in-depth knowledge of the practical aspects of gunpowder production and use. It is possible that the text was dictated to a scribe and that large parts of the content of the *Firework Book* and its components were retained in oral memory.[92]

There has been some speculation about whether an *urtext*, which is earlier than any others, might be identified. All *Firework Books* in existence appear either to be copies of an *urtext* (which in this case has not survived) or to be based on a teaching tradition derived from it. The strong similarities, yet almost predictable differences in words and configuration of the text, seem to indicate a detailed knowledge of the texts' components, and the ability of the author to distinguish between 'core texts or phrases that must not be changed' and 'interchangeable elements' which could be treated with more flexibility. Hence the preamble 'Any prince, earl, lord, knight, squire, or town who frequently fear that they may be besieged by their enemies ...' remains as it is in all copies of the text, barring a few vowel shifts resulting from regional variations and occasional additions of consonants based on the specific author's spelling preferences.[93]

One common view among modern scholars is that the Freiburg Ms. 362 may be a copy of the earliest *Firework Book*.[94] Kramer stated this with some vehemence but without necessarily providing any evidence for the claim. This has led other scholars, such as Schmidtchen, Tittmann, and

---

[91] Hassenstein, *Feuerwerkbuch*, 95.

[92] See also Chapter 2.

[93] *'Welch furst grauff her[r] ritter knecht oder stet besorgent vor iren feinden beligert vnd benot werden ...'* (Leeds, Royal Armouries, I.34, fol. 1r).

[94] Kramer, *Berthold Schwarz*, 95, and Nibler, *Feuerwerkbuch*, 3, who both argue that it is the oldest in existence, while Leng, 'Feuerwerks- und Kriegsbücher', 179, argues that Munich Cgm. 4902, dating from 1429, and Heidelberg, Cod. Pal. Germ 787, dating from 1430 (although the manuscript itself is only a sixteenth-century copy) are older.

Leng, to suspect that Kramer's preference for Freiburg resulted from the fact that he and the Freiburg manuscript shared that city as their place of origin.[95] Leng, in fact, argues that the surviving Freiburg manuscript was produced later than copies of the *Firework Books* located in Heidelberg or Munich.[96] At any rate, it seems most likely that the earliest manuscripts in Heidelberg, Munich, and Freiburg are part of the first generation of disseminated *Firework Books* descending from a no longer extant *urtext*. However, this connects closely to the question of whether the origin of the *Firework Book* can be connected to its intended use. This will be discussed in more detail in subsequent chapters.

(2) The copyist(s) and printers, medieval and post-medieval: it is clear that not all the copies were necessarily produced by those who knew or understood what they were copying. All the manuscripts I have viewed contain some scribal errors, transmission mistakes, and other forms of miscommunication or misleading information – the question is why this was so. Was the scribe not sufficiently interested in transcribing the text correctly, or did he perhaps not understand the need for accuracy of transmission, or was he a non-expert whose task was to copy but not necessarily to comprehend the content? All viewed manuscripts reveal a number of incidences where there are clear contradictions in header and text, others where the text is incomplete (e.g. lines missing).

Vienna, *Österreichische Nationalbibliothek*, Cod. 2952 is a particularly noteworthy example with a larger than usual number of scribal copying errors – many of them were corrected at (or shortly after) the time of production. There is the repeated presence of the term 'rat' which has been interpreted as a misspelling of 'rot' (meaning 'red' – which in turn would change the meaning from the colour red to something entirely different, but not obvious), but remains present in the majority of surviving manuscripts.[97]

None the less, the fact that many *Firework Books* retain a regular pattern, while yet varying in the order of the recipes and instructions, suggests that – at some level – there was both an understanding of the

---

[95] Schmidtchen, *Kriegswesen*, 29, Leng, *Ars belli*, vol. 1, 38–39 and 205–10, and Wilfried Tittmann, 2002. 'Das unaufhaltsame Ende von Berthold Schwarz. Anmerkungen zu Gerhard W. Kramer: "Das Pyr Autómaton – die selbstentzündlichen Feuer des Mittelalters"', (online publication, 2002), http://www.ruhr-uni-bochum.de/technikhist/tittmann/2%20Ende.pdf (accessed 10 August 2023), 1.

[96] Leng, *Ars belli*, vol. 1, 206 (mainly n. 880).

[97] See also Royal Armouries, I.34, fol. 6r, line 14.

subject matter, and a desire to improve it. This indicates the likelihood of an oral transmission of this knowledge to be presented or dictated to a scribe, which would explain the change of order of the elements, yet the inclusion of almost all of the key elements. These texts may have been made by new master gunners who were keen to showcase their knowledge, and to adapt it to the circumstances of their day. Therefore, the *Firework Book* marks a crucial stage in the development of gunpowder weaponry in European history, marking the transition from orally transmitted knowledge to written instructions and knowledge retention.

(3) The possible users: one stage further removed from the production of the text was the user – a master gunner, almost certainly a man, his less well-trained apprentices, or even some local authorities or rulers. Where the *Firework Books* differ from both the *Bellifortis* and the *Büchsenmeister Book* texts is that most *Firework Books* lack illustrations – even when an illustration would explain some action in a much more direct way than any text ever could. This indicates a distinctly different usage of the *Firework Books* to the *Bellifortis* and the *Büchsenmeister Books*. Apart from anything else, text without illustrations would be of little use to anyone with a low level of literacy. Nevertheless, the formulaic nature of most sections in the *Firework Books*, and the use of rubrication and headers, make it substantially easier for a less fluent reader to move relatively quickly into the relevant sections of the text.

Schmidtchen speculates that the *Firework Book* was unusually late in being printed, which in his understanding resulted from its semi-secret nature.[98] The survival of over 60 manuscripts or fragments does suggest, however, that there were substantial numbers of *Firework Books* in existence which were copied and kept (and possibly read). Many include

---

[98] *Verfasserlexikon*, vol. 2 (1980), col. 730, '*Firework Book of 1420*':

Each Master Gunner/Gun maker aimed to keep the special knowledge of the art of firework a secret – if at all possible. This is why the manuscripts were only exchanged among friendly 'colleagues', or were only passed on to successors who were closely related to the master.

(*Jeder Büchsenmeister [...] war bemüht, die [...] besonderen Kenntnisse der Feuerwerkkunst nach Möglichkeit geheim zu halten. So wurden die hsl. Aufzeichnungen allenfalls unter befreundeten 'Kollegen' ausgetauscht oder an den meist in engem verwandtschaftlichen Verhältnis zum Meister stehenden Nachfolger weitergegeben.*).

Unfortunately, the author provides no reference or support for this statement on usage. On secrecy, see also Chapter 5 under 'Features Common to Both Parts'.

'manuscripts with completely or partially depicted and described art of war' and 'war manuals, statutes, and instructive texts'.[99]

The *Firework Book* fits into a tradition of technical writings and reference books which started to emerge in the fifteenth century. Its peculiar style raises questions about usage, ownership, and purpose of production. Any attempt to define the *Firework Book* is imperfect and open to interpretation, and we need to keep an open mind for the inclusion of additional fragmentary texts into the tradition. As what is left is often broken up and rebound, it will always be a working definition as to the original intention. The extant manuscripts attributed as part of the *Firework Book* tradition, with all their variations, still share distinctive features and core elements which are surprisingly unchanged over a substantial period of more than a hundred years.

---

[99] *'Handschriften mit ausschließlich oder teilweise abgebildeter und beschriebener Kriegstechnik'* and *'Kriegsordnungen, Statuten und Lehrschriften'* (Schmidtchen, *Kriegswesen*, 22).

2 The Use and Reception of the *Firework Book*

One of the most intriguing questions that has challenged scholars over centuries is related to the use and reception of the *Firework Book*. It was relatively popular both as a manuscript and, later, in print, but there is little evidence of use in the surviving copies and no direct reference to one being consulted. While Chapter 1 discussed the *Firework Book* tradition and debates the identity and possible intentions of the author or originator of the *Firework Book*, this chapter will analyse how and in what format the *Firework Book* could have been used, and how that usage changed over time. In doing so we need to look at the status and identity of gunners, and also explore who else might have owned the *Firework Book* in subsequent decades and centuries.

Arguably the most helpful explanation of the *Firework Book* comes from Bert Hall who described its format and content in various publications. In 1979, he referred to it as 'a practical, didactic manual for artillerymen and [one that] consists principally of recipes for pyrotechnic compounds'.[1] Later in the same article he went into more detail:

> The *Feuerwerkbuch* [...] is obviously by a gunner for the use of other gunners. Most of its contents have nothing to do with mechanics or ballistics as a science, but instead seem to have served as a sort of cookbook for the gunner.[2]

For reasons already explored. Hall's interpretation of the *Firework Book* makes a lot of sense. The nature of the text, the quality of the production, the functionality and lack of flamboyant illustrations and illuminations in almost all copies – all of these seem to suggest that the *Firework Book* was intended to be used by other professionals and not by a wider, more general audience. However, Hall believed that its practical role and function – if indeed it ever was used as such – was short-lived, and that when the *Firework Book* came

---

[1] Hall, 'Der Meister sol auch kennen', 49.

[2] Hall, 'Der Meister sol auch kennen', 54.

to 'be printed, it functioned more as a collectors' item for antiquarians'.[3] Yet Hall did not explain why he believed that the *Firework Book* had become obsolete. Clearly, if the printer felt it was worth printing it in 1529, there must have been a market for this kind of publication, and the book was surely less obsolete than he implies. It was certainly the case that, by then, gunpowder technology was more widespread, as was general public knowledge of its use, but there was also an apparent and continuous need to refer to these texts, perhaps for reassurance. Or, did the use of the *Firework Book* change between first production and first printing, a period of more than a hundred years?

Gunners and their Status

To come closer to an understanding of those who produced a *Firework Book*, the starting point should be to consider who gunners were in the fifteenth century. What was their status in society, and how did they emerge?[4] For Simon Werrett, they were 'lowly, anonymous craftsmen, notorious for drunkenness, and mistrusted as outsiders', and furthermore, 'the gunner's status was lower even than that of the common soldier, for the nobility deeply resented the cannon's power, to put them at the mercy of the vulgar, and commoners feared the terrible destruction by new-fangled ordnance'. However, Werrett bases his view on only two examples, one from a nineteenth-century secondary source written by a retired artillery officer, the other from a single 1588 account from a Flemish camp after the Armada.[5] The fact is that little is known about a gunner's background, his education, or his standing among fellow soldiers, especially in the fifteenth century. Rainer Leng describes gunners thus:

> Most of the master [gunners] [...] had been working as blacksmiths or metal-workers in medieval urban settlements. They left their traditional workplaces in order to specialize and thus to climb the social ladder. They often changed employers, they were very well paid and relatively rare. Lords and cities depended on their detailed knowledge of chemistry and weapon technology.[6]

[3] Hall, *Warfare in Renaissance*, 88.

[4] See Werrett, *Fireworks*, 13–45, developing an idea raised by Steven A. Walton, 'The Art of Gunnery in Tudor England' (unpublished PhD dissertation, University of Toronto, 1999), 280.

[5] Werrett, *Fireworks*, 13.

[6] Rainer Leng, 'Social Character, Pictorial Style, and the grammar of Technical Illustration in Craftsmen's Manuscripts in the Late Middle Ages', in *Picturing Machines 1400–1700*, ed. Wolfgang Lefèvre (Cambridge, MA: MIT Press, 2004), 88. In this

The Use and Reception of the *Firework Book*

Unfortunately, Leng provides no reference for this description and even goes as far as to attribute the 'solitary travelling' lifestyle as the reason for setting down the 'technical know-how' in writing, as it 'was always in danger of being lost in perilous military engagement'.[7] Although plausible, this theory seems somewhat simplistic, if not circular, as very few biographical details survive for master gunners for the period.

Several attempts have been made to piece together the little evidence there is about master gunners. Surviving records of master gunners are sparse from the late fourteenth century, becoming increasingly more substantial by the mid-fifteenth century, but all remain a patchwork of individual mentions of gunners in widely dispersed employment across Europe.[8] Even the terminology used, for example 'a gunner', 'a master gunner', 'a gunner's troop', or a 'cannoneer', cannot be fully ascertained until later centuries. There is thus a risk of imposing back-projected modern definitions on the terms, and thereby giving rise to misinterpretation.

The former Deputy Master of the Royal Armouries, Thom Richardson, dates the first recorded gunpowder production in the Tower of London to 1333, with the purchase of raw materials as well as already mixed gunpowder.[9] However, the quantities mentioned would have allowed for only a very small number of shots to be fired. Quantities increased rapidly between 1400 and 1410.[10] The first mention of a recipe in English has recently been traced to a

---

article published in English, the translation does not distinguish sufficiently clearly between the different types of ordnance personnel, using interchangeably 'master gunner', 'gun master', 'gun maker', and 'gunner'. It is likely that there was a substantial overlap between these roles, with at the same time some distinct differences.

[7] Leng, 'Social Character', 88–89.

[8] Most recently, Schulz, 'Büchsenmeister des Spätmittelalters', 221–42, Leng, '*getruwelich dienen*', 303–21, Schmidtchen, *Bombarden, Befestigungen, Büchsenmeister*, 176–96, or even earlier with Bernard Rathgen, *Pulver und Salpeter: Schießpulver Kunstsalpeter Pulvermühlen im frühen Mittelalter* (München: Barbara-Verlag, 1926). Schulz and Schmidtchen highlight the internationality of the recorded master gunners, and the predominance of gunners recorded with an apparently German language background (Schulz, 'Büchsenmeister des Spätmittelalters', 236).

[9] Richardson, *The Tower Armoury*, 176.

[10] Richardson mentions Ranulph Hatton's account E 101/400/22–3, which records purchases of '584 lb of saltpetre, 96 lb of gunpowder, and a barrel of willow charcoal. Of this, after issues, 256 lb of saltpetre, 56 lb of sulphur, and the barrel of charcoal remained at the end of his account, E 101/403/20.' 'In 1396–9 Lowick passed on 108 lb of saltpetre, and John Norbury bought in 1,000 lb of sulphur in addition, as well as 8,000 lb of ready-made gunpowder. 1,300 lb of gunpowder

Gunpowder Technology in the Fifteenth Century

manuscript which is likely to have been produced before 1450.[11] Most recently, and based on a substantially more comprehensive body of sources, the Southampton 'Soldier in Late Medieval England' project – which unfortunately ends in 1453 – has listed a substantial increase of gunnery units and individual master gunners in the decades up to 1453 (with the evidence remaining patchy).[12] This is not helped by a 'surprisingly high turnover of personnel', while other soldiers, such as archers, served as gunners at times which made Andy King wonder about the 'surprising lack of specialization'.[13]

What we can say is that a master gunner was likely to have been an intelligent individual with the ability to read and write, and to be at ease in social interaction with local lords (as their potential employees).[14] Being a gunner was a dangerous business, and it is likely that anyone who chose this profession would have come from a lower-class background with aspirations to rise in the ranks and grow rich.[15] Those who were successful required a unique

---

was then manufactured within the Tower, from 1,370 lb of saltpetre and 400 lb of sulphur, E 101/404/25.' (Richardson, *The Tower Armoury*, 182–83.).

[11] Smith, 'The Earliest Middle English Recipes for Gunpowder', 183–92. This is only a fragmentary text of two folios listing the production of 'good gunpowder' and 'colourful powder' in London, Society of Antiquaries, Ms. 101, fols 76r and 76v.

[12] There have been countless, sometimes contradictory, attempts to establish the number of gunners in the fifteenth century. For a comprehensive overview on gunpowder artillery troops considered by the Southampton 'Soldier' project, see *The Soldier in Later Medieval England*, eds Adrian R. Bell et al. (Oxford: Oxford University Press, 2013), 194–202. The ordnance lists of the gunners' guild of Ghent from 1480 to 1560 provide detailed listings of activities and numbers of master gunners in Ghent alone (unpublished document, then at the Bijloke Abbey and now in the STAM (Stad Museum), Ghent, Sint Antonius, 155/2).

[13] Andy King, 'Gunners, Aides and Archers: The Personnel of the English Ordnance Companies in Normandy in the Fifteenth Century', *Journal of Medieval Military History* 9 (2011), 65–75.

[14] This is closely mirrored by other professions at the time, such as the master mason. See, for example, John Harvey, *The Mediaeval Architect* (New York: St. Martin Press, 1972), 69–86, or Walton, 'Statics in Theory and Practice', 356–65. There are some parallels to the *Firework Book* text such as comprehensive knowledge of all aspects of the work ('jack-of-all-trades'), sense of how to operate equipment properly and safely, and some understanding of scholastic basics but merely applying it pragmatically.

[15] Andy King challenges Werrett's assertion on rates of pay for ordnance companies. While King admits to pay being higher, he attributes this to longer working hours and overtime on religious festival days. He asserts that, in an ordnance company, little opportunity existed to make a fortune quickly (King, 'Gunners, Aides and Archers', 74). Neither Werrett nor King, however, consider the broader issue raised

The Use and Reception of the *Firework Book*

skill set to enable them to engage with an unfamiliar community and ascend rapidly through the social order – thus increasing the likelihood of resentment from their fellow soldiers.[16]

Hall's definition of a *Firework Book* as something written by a gunner for a gunner raises the question: what was it that the other gunner needed to know? Was it that the books contained knowledge which needed to be passed on, or did they serve a rite-of-passage function, by demonstrating their knowledge? Possessing a *Firework Book* would certainly have provided access to the basic skills required of a master gunner. The similar linguistic backgrounds and slight variations in copies of the *Firework Book* would seem to suggest that the habit of copying (and 'improving' – either deliberately or accidentally) an earlier version was customary within a certain regional and linguistic group, but did not go beyond it.

What assumptions can, therefore, be made about those who kept copies of the *Firework Book* or similar texts? Were they actual practitioners of gunnery – whether master or apprentice gunners – or other interested parties? Leng argued that the emergence of the *Firework Book*, and other technical treatises in the fifteenth century, was the result of fast-moving technological innovation. This, he claimed, created a tension between individually acquired knowledge and diverse prior knowledge which brought about a pressing need for information from practitioners to be readily accessible to potential newcomers to the trade. He further identified an increasing desire on the part of the employer that a potential master gunner should come with references, proving his skills and expertise as a future employee.[17] Meanwhile, Schmidtchen contributed his own theory to this discussion by stating that the manuscript not only served as an *aide memoire* for the master gunner or any family member or apprentice (who might be following the master gunner's trade), but also as an 'advertising method to inform potential employers about

---

by Rainer Elkar of travelling tradesmen in the period, when migration of younger apprentices contributed substantially to the dissemination of technology and development: *'eine gleichmäßige Diffusion von Technologie und Fortschritt'*, Rainer S. Elkar, 'Lernen durch Wandern? Einige kritische Anmerkungen zum Thema Wissenstransfer durch Migration', in *Handwerk in Europa. Vom Spätmittelalter bis zur Frühen Neuzeit*, ed. Knut Schulz, Schriften des historischen Kollegs, Kolloquien 41 (München: Oldenbourg, 1999), 224.

[16] Werrett, *Fireworks*, 43: 'Gunners [...] engaged directly with the nobility as employees and clients. Many sought patronages by dedicating their works to noble artillery officers [...]', although the examples provided are from the first decade of the seventeenth century.

[17] Leng, *Ars belli*, vol. 1, 105–6.

their range of skills and expertise'.[18] The more boastful elements in the text, as well as the repetition of the language, certainly suggest a strong marketing element. This is coupled with a sense of passive-aggressive threat that, if gunners are not paid, then they can 'cause rotten harm' (fol. 26r) by turning against their previous employers. However, whether this threat was ever carried out cannot be ascertained by documentary evidence from the fifteenth century. What purposes were served by a *Firework Book* after it was produced, and whether it was passed on from the master gunner to an apprentice or anyone else, are matters about which we can only speculate.

Manuscript Evidence of Use

Turning to the manuscript evidence, this furnishes a set of clues which provides further insight into the discussion of who used *Firework Books*, and why. They were produced on good quality paper, and since each copy appears to be in a different hand the implication is that they were produced in a number of different locations. As mentioned in Chapter 2, the watermarks suggest that the geographic origin of the paper is Austro-Bavarian, from regions between the Rhine and the Danube. The regional dialects of the language differ from book to book, and at times even within a given manuscript. For example, the language of Part 1 of the Leeds *Firework Book* I.34 indicates that the scribe might have come from southern Bohemia, an area northeast from Bavaria, and north of Passau. The language of Part 2 is in a distinctly different dialect to that of Part 1. This is more likely to come from a Bavarian region with some elements from Swabia, pointing towards a region to the west of Augsburg.[19]

Speculation has focused on whether the manuscripts were written by professional scribes or by professional gunners. In relation to I.34, Sarah Barter Bailey states that 'the compiler was adding to the collection or improving it as he compiled it, without taking the trouble to go back and eliminate duplication. The hand, however, is a regular copyist's hand rather than that of a man making a series of scribbled personal notes'.[20] This seems to imply that professional scribes were employed to produce the manuscripts.

---

[18] '... *in Sinne eines Werbeeffekts, zur Information potentieller Auftraggeber bezüglich ihrer Fähigkeiten ...*' (Schmidtchen, *Kriegswesen*, 30).

[19] Personal correspondence with Karin Zimmermann, Deputy Head of Special Collections, Heidelberg University Library, and specialist on late medieval German manuscripts, email, 21 March 2013.

[20] Sarah Barter Bailey, 'The Royal Armouries "Firework Book"', in *Gunpowder: The History of an International Technology*, ed. Brenda Buchanan (Bath: Bath University

The Use and Reception of the *Firework Book*

The surviving *Firework Books* provide very little evidence of being much used. Hall comments that 'some of the copies I [Hall] have examined show stains and charring to indicate that they were used […] in the workshop or arsenal'.[21] However, it has not been possible to substantiate this theory. His comment refers to only two manuscripts,[22] and it should be recognized that these are the exception rather than the rule. There is also no evidence that the spill (Munich manuscript) and the burn mark (Leipzig manuscript) occurred in the fifteenth century; the damage could have been caused centuries after production. Apart from these exceptions, none of the 61 other surviving manuscripts of the *Firework Books* viewed show signs of use, wear and tear, nota signs, spillage, discolouration, marginalia, marks, insertions, additions, or changes to the original text. At least some of these signs would be expected for books in common use, especially for those intended for practical purposes similar to cookery or surgery.[23] There are, however, many cookery and surgical texts without damage caused by use, but many of those often contain annotation and other marks made by an avid reader. The *Firework Books* do not have any of these marks. Does this suggest that the surviving copies are those which ended up not being used, perhaps being kept as archive copies or spares, or is it rather an indicator of why they were produced? The former certainly is the view of Klára Andresová for printed versions in the sixteenth century without providing much further evidence.[24] Whether the printed version of the later sixteenth and early seventeenth centuries would actually be used by gunners, or 'artillerymen' – as she calls them – remains debatable.

It is impossible to establish how many *Firework Books* were produced overall, and hence to ascertain what proportion of the genre is represented by the surviving manuscripts and prints. Is what survives perhaps the majority of all

---

Press, 1996), 57–86, at 58, and Leng, 'Feuerwerks- und Kriegsbücher', 147–48.

[21] Hall, 'Der Meister sol auch kennen', 54.

[22] Hall specifies that the manuscripts in question were Leipzig Ms. 1597, 1r–88r, which shows a burn mark possibly from a rod or poker, and Munich Cgm. 399, 1r–48v, which had one spillage on one folio. However, he admits that he may have overstated the usage signs. His revised theory about the *Firework Books'* usage is that the copies 'seem strangely pristine, especially […] copies that are parts of a larger *Sammelcodex* [a collection of miscellaneous manuscripts], as if they were made as archival records that were not to be used in the field.' Personal correspondence with Bert Hall, email, 23 February 2014.

[23] Joseph Burnley Trapp, 'Literacy, Books and Readers', in *The Cambridge History of the Book in Britain, Vol. III, 1400–1557*, eds Lotte Hellinga and Joseph Burnley Trapp (Cambridge: Cambridge University Press, 1999), 31–43, at 40–41.

[24] Andresová, 'Artillery Handbooks of the 16th Century', 24.

that were ever produced? Or do they instead represent the very small number of those that became forgotten in libraries and collections? If the surviving *Firework Books* are a major proportion of all *Firework Books* ever produced, a number of likely conclusions follow: it can be assumed that practical use was not their main purpose, that their audience was a very small and select group of professional gunners, their patrons and their associates, and accordingly that they were to be treated with great care. If, on the other hand, the surviving *Firework Books* represent only a small proportion of once-existing *Firework Books*, the opposite conjecture can be applied: that they were widely distributed and used in the workshop but also fragile, and that a large proportion would probably have been discarded and destroyed after use or even because of use. Such an explanation could be compared to the maps of modern shipping companies where a copy of the map is kept on the wall of the headquarters, while other maps go out with the ships (experiencing substantially different levels of wear and tear). In late medieval cartography, the surviving maps are mainly high-status elite gifts presented to rulers which remained safely preserved in libraries – such as the Catalan atlas (c. 1380) presented to Charles VI of France, now in the Bibliothèque nationale de France in Paris.[25]

A *Firework Book* text is relatively short, and, in most of the surviving cases, is bound together with one or more technical texts in vernacular German.[26] Almost all copies viewed appear to have post-medieval bindings, and it is impossible to be certain about the original content. Whether these were originally grouped together at or shortly after production remains in question, and the Royal Armouries manuscript I.34 copy may well be an example of how *Firework Books* were initially intended to be used, starting with the 'core' text, followed by a second part for the 'recipient' of the book to list their own experiments, experiences, and recipes, and a final part on illustrations.[27]

---

[25] See *The Hereford World Map: Medieval World Maps and Their Context*, ed. Paul Dean Adshea Harvey (London: British Library, 2006), 408–9, and Evelyn Edson, *The World Map, 1300–1492: The Persistence of Tradition and Transformation* (Baltimore: Johns Hopkins University Press, 2007), 1.

[26] Heidelberg Cod. Pal. Germ. 502 is bound together with 123 unsorted recipes on horse medication, all written in different hands, while Heidelberg Cod. Pal. Germ. 562 is combined with a text on defensive building structures and materials and a treatise on how to defend oneself while on the move, as well as 159 unsorted recipes on medicine, charms, and potions. It seems to have been common practice to combine *Firework Book* texts with other medical and technical military texts of the period. However, it is not clear whether this is a medieval practice or only applied to the post-medieval period as the result of later rebinding.

[27] In this, I.34 shows some similarities to Strasbourg Ms. 2259 and New York Spencer Collection Ms. 104.

The Use and Reception of the *Firework Book*

All *Firework Books* in existence are written in vernacular German with slight regional variations. What then does the choice of language indicate? A German vernacular is used throughout with an almost complete absence of Latin (even for the chemical elements), suggesting a usage and readership on an applied level.[28] Might this have been part of the 'graduation process' for a master gunner to demonstrate that he possessed the core skills and knowledge to write this text? In that case, the owner would not go out to buy a copy, but instead would be expected to commission or write his own copy. This would explain the differences in regional dialects expressed in the manuscripts, as well as the absence of illustrations and elaborate colorations (other than red rubrics and occasional initials) or any further attempts to make the *Firework Book* more decorative. If it was a private copy, the question arises as to whether it was intended to be read by anyone else, thus making the *Firework Book* a private and personal item. The printed version in 1529 suggests that, by that date, any once 'secret' knowledge of gunpowder technology had become 'public', but also suggests an interesting possibility that the text may well have included some deliberate obfuscations. This would mean that the *Firework Book* could be read by the general public while the recipes could not be recreated in full.[29]

The *Firework Book* stresses that master gunners needed to be literate as otherwise they would be unable to memorize all the details of gunpowder technology. Hall explains the importance of the master gunner's ability to read and write, '*der Meister sol auch kennen schreiben und lesen* [...]' because without literacy he could not possibly 'keep in mind all the elements that belong to this art' (fol. 33r). He concludes not only that this was the result of 'technological complexities' but that it also contributed to 'create a class of literate technicians who could and did speak for themselves, taking over the roles once held by physician-astrologers, alchemists or other interested amateurs of technology'.[30] This could explain the persistent presence in most of the manuscripts of the mythical figure of Berthold Schwarz or Niger Bertholdus, which provides a foundation story for an emerging profession of almost patron-saint status. This level of literacy might not necessarily have applied to all users of the *Firework Book*. The repetitive nature of the introductory phrases '*Welch furst grauff her[r] ritter knecht oder stet*' would have been familiar even to someone barely literate, and it thus provides a visually recognizable phrase comparable to widely used prayers, such as the *Pater Noster* or *Ave Maria*.

---

[28] See Mechthild Habermann, *Deutsche Fachtexte der frühen Neuzeit. Naturkundlich-medizinische Wissensvermittlung im Spannungsfeld von Latein und Volkssprache*, Studia linguistica Germanica 61 (Berlin: de Gruyter, 2002), 1–54.

[29] See Chapter 5, under 'Features Common to Both Parts', for discussion on secrecy.

[30] Hall, 'Der Meister sol auch kennen', 52.

Book Trade, Ownership, and Libraries

To better understand how the *Firework Book* was used, it is worth considering the book trade and book ownership in the fifteenth and early sixteenth centuries. If the *Firework Book* was something that was intended to be owned by key professionals (current or aspiring gunners and their families), there must have been some network for acquiring a copy, either by personal contact or by a wider distribution network. The fact that at least two printed versions were produced further suggests that there was an increasing demand for this type of publication. However, there is no evidence for the existence of any of these networks; hence much depends on the already-discussed issue of the quantity in which the manuscripts were produced.

In the early sixteenth century, from which time substantially more comprehensive records survive, printing and copying were carried out side-by-side in the same workshop, and by the same group of practitioners.[31] Melanie Panse argues that when a book became popular it was printed, while one-off copies were produced by hand, which implies both an existing demand and a buoyant market.[32] For early printed books, little or no evidence survives for print runs, reasons for printing, sale prices, or related information.[33] Evelyn Welch goes even further, stating that bookshops worked more on a commission basis, producing publications on demand, and suggests that 'printed books were often sold unbound, and customers could choose how they wanted their edition collated'.[34] As put by Leah Tether, in relation to production of Grail literature, 'texts were manipulated and modified so as to please different target

---

[31] David McKitterick, *Print, Manuscript and the Search for Order, 1450–1830* (Cambridge: Cambridge University Press, 2003), 30–32 and 47–48.

[32] Panse, *Feldbuch der Wundarznei*, 10–15.

[33] Benito Rial Costas, *Print Culture and Peripheries in Early Modern Europe*, Library of the Written World 24, The Handpress World 18 (Leiden: Brill, 2013), xix–xxiii.

[34] Evelyn Welch, *Shopping in the Renaissance: Consumer Cultures in Italy 1400–1600* (New Haven: Yale University Press, 2005), 151. Welch lists the library of one Zanobi di Mariano whose library inventory included 80 manuscripts and 141 printed books including 30 unbound copies of Josephus, *De bello iudaico* (Welch, *Shopping in the Renaissance*, 331). Zanobi was an important Florentine *cartolaio*, whose life (1415–1495) coincided with the shift from handwritten to printed book. He first rented a shop in Florence in 1448 and produced manuscripts, as well as selling secondhand manuscript books (see Christian Bec, 'Une librarie florentine de la fin du xve siècle', *Bibliothèque d'humanisme et renaissance* 31 (1969), 321–32, at 323).

markets'.[35] They became personal copies of books which were produced on a pick-and-mix principle, thus making each book virtually unique.

One example of this is the *Household Book*, and a comparison with the genre may provide a possible insight into for what the *Firework Book* was intended. A *Household Book* was a private text compiled with the personal preferences of the author in mind. For example, John Paston commissioned his *Great Book* – a compilation of military treatises and texts of a historical and instructional nature – in the 1470s.[36] This genre was to become hugely popular in the latter part of the fifteenth century with instructional publications such as house-books, commonplace books and household books, compendia of related tasks and chores, with often personally adjusted content, focusing on how to run all aspects of a household properly, or miscellaneous parts thereof.[37] The *Firework Book* shows signs of similar compartmentalization and of the compiler's mix-and-match approach.

Turning now to what little is known about *Firework Books*, their owners at or after the time of production, and the survival of copies into the post-medieval period, the following survey will explore the various levels of provenance of copies. One way is to attempt to trace ownership backwards from the

---

[35] Leah Tether, *Publishing the Grail in Medieval and Renaissance France* (Cambridge: D. S. Brewer, 2017), 9.

[36] Still preserved in the British Library as Lansdowne Ms. 285.

[37] The genres of the medieval housebook and its post-medieval developments are discussed in detail by Graf zu Waldburg Wolfegg, *World of the Medieval Housebook*. There are different cultural traditions for miscellanies of different kinds and scholars have argued that the housebook tradition developed in different directions through the later Middle Ages and early modern period across Europe. The Italian tradition is referred to as *Libri di Ricordanze* or *Libri di Famiglia* and dates back to the fourteenth century at least – e.g. Datini, a prominent and well-studied merchant of Prato, was known to have one. In Germany, the housebook developed more of an official exemplary character. For the English household and commonplace book see David Parker, 'The Importance of the Commonplace Book: London, 1450–1550', *Manuscripta* 40 (1996), 29–48, Julia Boffey, 'Bodleian Library, manuscript Arch. Selden. B.24 and Definitions of the "Household Book"', in *The English Medieval Book: Studies in Memory of Jeremy Griffiths*, eds Anthony Edwards et al. (London: British Library, 2000), 125–34, Julia Boffey and John Jay Thompson, 'Anthologies and Miscellanies: Production and the Choice of Texts', in *Book Production and Publishing in Britain, 1375–1475*, eds Jeremy Griffiths and Derek Pearsall (Cambridge: Cambridge University Press, 1989), 279–315; for the French tradition, see Gina Greco and Christine Rose, trans., *The Good Wife's Guide:* Le Ménagier de Paris, *A Medieval Household Book* (Ithaca and London: Cornell University Press, 2009); and for the early-modern tradition, see Ann Moss, *Printed Commonplace Books and the Structuring of Renaissance Thought* (Oxford: Clarendon Press, 1996).

present-day. Another is to trace ownership forwards in time (from or near the author to later owners). If neither of these approaches enables the establishment of a continuous line of ownership, can glimpses of ownership be detected at any stage? And is it possible to make any assumptions as to what the earliest known ownership may indicate?

Working backwards gives a multi-faceted picture of ownership of the existing known copies, with most of them entering public ownership in the mid-twentieth century. Tracing ownership further back is both arduous and challenging, as such records tend not to go back much before the early nineteenth century. Their ownership is linked to the rise of antiquarianism and the enthusiasm to catalogue and compile lists, which was not common practice before the nineteenth century. However, even then records such as the *Firework Book* could easily be overlooked or miscatalogued because of its content or a misunderstanding of it. The provenance of the *Firework Book* can usually only be traced back to provincial libraries in the eighteenth and nineteenth centuries. Occasionally, there are glimpses of possible ownerships before this period, but they are always accompanied by common phrases used by librarians such as 'likely to have been in the possession of the duke since the establishment of the library'. Only three copies have references to the fifteenth century: Freiburg Ms. 362, with a textual addition at the end of the text of '*Anno trecesimo 2*', seemingly by the same hand, but in different coloured ink; the Dillingen manuscript at the end of the text providing a signature, '*1466 Jodocus Foelki presbyter*', written in a different hand; and one of the Heidelberg manuscripts, Col. Pal. germ. 502, with a signature at the beginning showing it to have been the property of Johann von Mosbach.[38]

---

[38] Also identified by Leng, 'Feuerwerks- und Kriegsbücher', 183. Leng gives further information on the Heidelberg manuscript, Cod. Pal. germ. 502, saying that it was from the property of the Provost of Augsburg who was a nephew of Pfalzgraf Friedrich I (1451–76) whose inheritance became part of the Bibliotheca Palatina ('*Besitzeintrag (?) des 16. (?) Jahrhunderts [...] aus dem Besitz des Domprobst zu Augsburg Johann von Mosbach, Neffe des Pfalzgrafen und Kurfürsten Friedrich I (1451–1476), aus dessen Nachlaß in die Palatina gelangt*'). Leng also provides details on two other manuscript origins:

p. 161: Heidelberg Cod. Pal. germ. 787: presumably at an early stage, property of a master gun-maker ('*Zuerst vermutlich im Besitz eines Büchsenmeisters*') but no record of when it entered the *Bibliotheca Palatina* (now Heidelberg University Library). Possibly mentioned in 1610 catalogue but not identifiable with certainty ('*nicht eindeutig identifizierbar*').

p. 190: Nuremberg Ms. 1481a: origins unknown; first recorded in private library of founder of Germanic National Museum, Hans von und zu Aufseß. Donated to the museum by the owner in 1852.

The Use and Reception of the *Firework Book*

While the earliest records of the English Old Royal Library do not contain any *Firework Books* or similar technical treatises,[39] we know that gunpowder was being used, both from the Tower of London records edited by Richardson, and from the earliest mention of a gunpowder recipe mentioned above. We might have expected *Firework Books* to have existed later on, yet, even in the sixteenth century, customs rolls record imported books but only as 'containing books of diverse histories'.[40] They rarely identified particular texts or editions, unless they were of more specific value – whether the result of their content or their physical attributes.[41]

Books were viewed as precious commodities and, therefore, were regularly mentioned in inventories and wills. However, those listings give only partial information as single volumes cannot usually be matched up with book lists of wills and inventories. Customs rolls give details on quantities of traded commodities without providing the details of individual items. All that can be ascertained is that books on hawking and hunting, veterinary medicine, and the art of war were widely circulated.[42] For example, King Richard III is known to have owned copies of *De Regimine Principum* ('On the Government of Rulers') – a series of compilations of an instructional nature intent on making him a better prince – which, while not stating the individual components, could well have included technical military treatises such as the *Firework Book*. It is highly likely that these compilations included texts of a more intellectual, strategic, and chivalric nature.[43] Anything that was not part of devotional, romantic, or historical literature was perceived to be of lesser interest and was generally not specified in detail.[44] Manuscripts of a technical and secular nature, especially when written in the vernacular, were not usually

---

[39]   The collection was donated to the British Museum in 1757 by King George II. It was known as the 'Royal Library' until the arrival in the building of the library of King George III in 1828 (manuscript material associated with this collection is in the Department of Manuscripts).

[40]   *The Cambridge History of the Book in Britain, Vol. III, 1400–1557*, eds Lotte Hellinga and Joseph Burnley Trapp (Cambridge: Cambridge University Press, 1999), 151: '*libris diversarum istoriarum*'.

[41]   See Hellinga and Trapp (eds), *Cambridge History of the Book*, xxii–xxiv.

[42]   Margaret Lane Ford, 'Importation of Printed Books into England and Scotland', in Hellinga and Trapp (eds), *Cambridge History of the Book*, 179–201, at 180.

[43]   Anne F. Sutton, *Richard III's Books* (Stroud: Sutton, 1997), 283.

[44]   Diane E. Booton, *Manuscripts, Market and the Transition to Print in Late Medieval Brittany* (Farnham: Ashgate, 2010), 168, and Trapp, 'Literacy, Books and Readers', 33: '[B]ooks are seldom mentioned, let alone particularized, unless they were especially prized or had some special association'.

Gunpowder Technology in the Fifteenth Century

individually described in catalogues, wills, book lists, or inventories. Even further afield, at the Portuguese Royal Court, King Duarte (1391–1438) was known to have been aware of firepower technology, and possessed an extensive library in the 1430s, and had the unusual habit at the time of listing vernacular texts by title – yet no *Firework Book* or related text is mentioned.[45] Books were precious and listed in wills, but only those which were perceived to be of value (because of the content or the production cost/style) were specifically named. It has not been possible to find any *Firework Book* in any record of a fifteenth- or sixteenth-century book ownership list.[46]

One may ask whether exploring the book trade and any available records could shed further light on the presence of books such as the *Firework Book*. Lotte Hellinga describes the 'book trade's importance as mediator between owner and reader', and any book of interest would have been commercially available across Europe – yet, once again, available lists do not specify in sufficient detail the precise content of any vernacular secular texts before the eighteenth century.[47]

Certain assumptions can be made as to who owned and kept books in the fifteenth century. A range of books existed in libraries and in private possession,[48] with varied levels of readership and use,[49] from personal and

[45] Duarte 'contrasted deceitful alchemy and sorcery to marvels that he had himself witnessed such as water divining, miraculous cures and gunpowder' (Iona McCleery, 'Both "illness and temptation of the enemy": Melancholy, the Medieval Patient and the Writings of King Duarte of Portugal (r. 1433–38)', *Journal of Medieval Iberian Studies* 1:2 (2009), 163–78, at 172).

[46] The first mention of a book inventory by an English monarch is recorded in 1535 as 143 manuscripts and printed works seen by an anonymous French visitor to Richmond Palace (Jenny Stratford, 'The Early Royal Collection and the Royal Library to 1461', in Hellinga and Trapp (eds), *Cambridge History of the Book*, 255–66, at 256).

[47] Hellinga and Trapp (eds), *Cambridge History of the Book*, xxi, and Ford, 'Importation of Printed Books into England and Scotland', 179.

[48] Neil Ker's list is a laudable but deeply flawed attempt to list books which were available in scriptoria and libraries in the Middle Ages. As he admits, the listings available are patchy, 'for the majority [...] no medieval catalogues of book-lists survive' (p. vii), and thus the main reliance is on referencing of medieval books in modern catalogues. Furthermore, he particularly excludes 'cartularies, rentals, inventories, surveys, statutes of cathedrals and colleges, mortuary rolls, letter-books and all books concerned with business and administration' (Neil R. Ker, *Medieval Libraries of Great Britain* (London: Royal Historical Society, 1987), viii). Whether a *Firework Book* would fall under any of these categories could not be established.

[49] Trapp, 'Literacy, Books and Readers', 34. He distinguishes between 'reading' and 'comprehending', and lists the type of books as well as of users on subsequent pages.

The Use and Reception of the *Firework Book*

lay to professional and scholarly use.[50] Reasons for ownership are unlikely to have differed from that of present-day ownership, including monetary value, retention or acquisition of knowledge, entertainment, vanity, and pastimes. Books were viewed as assets and were used as dowry, gifts, and bequests, but only if the book in question was perceived to be of value, either monetary or usefulness, or both.[51] Diane Booton's classification of book acquisition in the fifteenth century by literary category places a *Firework Book* into her final category, namely, 'Medicine and Science'. This includes 'books best described as miscellaneous or unclassifiable, because the titles are unspecific, ambiguous, too general to categorize, or are part of collections not fully described in documents'.[52] This makes one wonder how these items managed to survive at all until they emerged in the early nineteenth-century catalogues. Or, did only those copies survive which were fortunate enough to have librarians who kept books for books' sake – even if they did not understand their content?

Some records of book ownership survive from a number of personal libraries, ranging from royal households to personal local libraries belonging to those of lesser nobility or to merchants or businessmen. Even for King Edward IV, founder of the Old Royal Library, no inventory exists for his books, nor is it possible to establish how much of his library survived. Insights of what might have been owned by Kings Edward IV and Henry VII can be gained by inclusions of their arms, badges, or other personal comments.[53] Similarly, one of King Henry VII's leading supporters, John de Vere, the 13th Earl of Oxford (1442–1513), had the following listing of books recorded in his will (dated 10 April 1509): 'a book called a Cowcher', a 'mass-book', 'a masse boke wt clapsys of silver; iiij masse bokes written in velom; [...] ij half Legendes; ij printid masse bokis; vij Pricke song bokis bounde in leder; and xij Prick son bokis', and a 'gospel boke wt thone sde covered wt silver and a picktur of or Lorde' – yet when the list reaches non-devotional items it suddenly becomes substantially more generic: 'and a chest full of frenshe and englisshe bokes' – without specifying any further details.[54]

---

[50] Hellinga and Trapp (eds), *Cambridge History of the Book*, viii–ix.

[51] Booton, *Manuscripts, Market in Late Medieval Brittany*, 146–49, and 204: 'Many early books and manuscripts circulated in passive ownership, that is, they were presented as gifts or descended by inheritance within a family'.

[52] Booton, *Manuscripts, Market in Late Medieval Brittany*, 209.

[53] See Janet Backhouse, 'The Royal Library from Edward IV to Henry VII', in Hellinga and Trapp (eds), *Cambridge History of the Book*, 267–81.

[54] William St John Hope, 'The Last Testament and Inventory of John de Vere, 13th Earl of Oxford', *Archaeologia* 66 (1914–15), 310–48, at 300.

One of the leading late fifteenth- and early sixteenth-century merchant families, the Fuggers from Augsburg, based in the area where most *Firework Books* can be located linguistically, were prolific book buyers and collectors. Their libraries moved in various directions, the library of Ulrich Fugger (1441–1510) eventually passed, in 1567, to Heidelberg where it became the foundation of the *Bibliotheca Palatina*; the library of Johann Jakob Fugger (1459–1525 – Ulrich's youngest brother) went to the *Hofbibliothek* of Albrecht V in Munich; and the library of Georg Fugger (1453–1506 – the middle brother) to the *k.k. Hofbibliothek* in Vienna in 1654.[55] Significantly, the three libraries of Vienna, Munich, and Heidelberg have a combined holding of seventeen copies of the *Firework Books* in their collections today – just over a quarter of all existing manuscripts.

The Fugger libraries are known to have included a range of technical and medical texts, but usually only items of exceptional value were singled out for particular mention in earlier catalogues.[56] The catalogues available are based on records from existing book seller receipts and bills, bills from bookbinders, and from the early library inventories such as that of the library of Ulrich before it was transferred from Augsburg to Heidelberg in 1567. Paul Lehmann's two-volume publication on the Fugger library has brought together the surviving records on library holdings of the key members of the Fugger family, and the records repeat the common collective term 'various treatises in German' ('*allerlei teutsche tractatlin*') without being able to specify them further.[57] His lists, however, specify by title other technology-related pub-

---

[55] The provenances of these libraries and their contents are described by Paul Lehmann (1956 and 1960).

[56] Such as the 'Erotianus: Dictionarium medicum, vel, expositiones vocum medicinalium', CERL Thesaurus, cnp00986997 (accessed 10 August 2023). See also letter exchange between Anton Fugger and the Benedictine Monk Veit Bild about scientific books and their shared interest in acquisition (Paul Lehmann, *Eine Geschichte der alten Fuggerbibliotheken* (Tübingen: Kommission für Bayerische Landesgeschichte/Schwäbische Forschungsgemeinschaft, 1956), 45).

[57] These include various scientific texts, but they are invariably grouped together as 'various unbound treatises in German' ('*Item ettlich deutsche ongebunden allerhand tractatlin*', Lehmann, *Eine Geschichte der alten Fuggerbibliotheken*, 405), 'various treatises and songs in German […] a German book of additions with other treatises in German' ('*Ettlich deutsche tractetlin und lieder […] deutsch rechenbuch mit andern deutschen tractatlin*', Lehmann, *Eine Geschichte der alten Fuggerbibliotheken*, 412), '42 pieces of various treatises in German' ('*zwei unnd vierzig stuck allerlei teutscher tractetlin*', Lehmann, *Eine Geschichte der alten Fuggerbibliotheken*, 435), 'Book on wounds and Surgery in the field. A further thirteen medical books and a cooking book' ('*Feldbuch der Wundartznei. Mehr dreizehn artznei büchlin unnd ein*

lications such as combat and tournament manual manuscripts, all of which include illustrations.[58] No evidence could be traced for the provenance of the *Firework Books* in Heidelberg in relation to the Fugger library, while the only reference in the Heidelberg manuscript Col. Pal. germ. 502 states on fol. 1r that it was in the possession of a certain Johann von Mosbach, who describes himself as provost at Augsburg cathedral and who died in 1486.[59] Whether the manuscript was produced for Johann, or bought by him at a later stage, is unclear.

Similar records are available from the former *k.k. Hofbibliothek*, now the Austrian National Library (*Österreichische Nationalbibliothek*) in Vienna, which had been established at some point before the first catalogue was compiled in 1576 by Hugo Blotius.[60] The holdings of the library are based on a combination of individual libraries and collections, most notably those of Duke Albrecht III (1365–95), his son and successor Albrecht IV (1395–1404), the Habsburg Emperor Frederick III (1440–93), and his successor Maximilian I (1493–1519). Ernst Trenkler attributes to Frederick III 69 texts,[61] and Maximilian I would have added to the collection through his marriages to Mary of Burgundy (1473) and Bianca Mary Sforza (1493), both of whom brought a large number of notable manuscripts into the collection. Listings on the content of the collection mention a range of religious and instructional texts, histories, legal and instructional treatises, and other

---

kochbuch', Lehmann, *Eine Geschichte der alten Fuggerbibliotheken*, 447), or 'Furthermore, thirty-three pieces in quarto printed in German related to medicine and cooking books' (*'Ferners auch ein unnd dreissig stuck in quarto. Allerlei deutsche truckt artznei, kochbuchlien'*, Lehmann, *Eine Geschichte der alten Fuggerbibliotheken*, 450).

[58] Lehmann, *Eine Geschichte der alten Fuggerbibliotheken*, 596–97, mentioning a number of tournament and fencing books (*'Turnierbücher und Fechtbücher'*).

[59] Berg and Friedrich, 'Wissenstradierung', 216.

[60] Josef Stummvoll, 'Die Druckschriftenbestände der Österreichischen Nationalbibliothek und die Abschreibung des alphabetischen Kataloges 1501 bis 1929', in *Buch und Welt: Festschrift für Gustav Hofmann zum 65. Geburtstag*, eds Hans Striedl and Johannes Wieder (Wiesbaden: Harrassowitz, 1965), 108. Hugo Blotius (1534–1608) was made imperial court librarian in 1575. By then, the library was said to have contained c. 9,000 printed books and manuscripts. However, the exact date of the foundation of the library is unclear (see Ernst Trenkler, 'Die Frühzeit der Hofbibliothek (1368–1519)', in *Geschichte der Österreichischen Nationalbibliothek. Erster Teil. Die Hofbibliothek (1368–1922)*, ed. Josef Stummvoll (Wien: Georg Prachner, 1968), 1–58, at 3–7 and 27–28).

[61] 35 theological, 10 historical, 8 mathematical, astronomical and medical, 16 on other sciences, and only 2 literary texts (Trenkler, 'Frühzeit der Hofbibliothek', 11).

Gunpowder Technology in the Fifteenth Century

texts,[62] but even Maximilian's will in 1518 produced only a generic list of the books he owned, referring to 'Boxes of individual leaves, bound books, chronicles, etc. to be kept safely and looked after'.[63] Blotius's catalogue of 1576 has only survived in a fragmentary state. In total, it lists over 1,500 manuscripts, of which 1,039 were medieval and 599 from the sixteenth century. Among the medieval manuscripts, 104 of them were written in German vernacular.[64] Blotius did not apply a categorization system but listed his manuscripts in alphabetical order. His precision suggests that had there been a *Firework Book* in the collection at that time, it would have been mentioned. The closest text to a *Firework Book* in the catalogue is a '*Feuerbuch in folio manuscriptum 1556*' which is given a supplementary comment to classify it as a philosophical treatise – not a reference usually attributed to a *Firework Book*.[65] It is noteworthy that this *Feuerbuch* was recorded under a German title, while its content was in Latin.[66] There are also a number of sixteenth-century Arsenal Books (*Zeughausbücher* (C923, W5296, A265 – books incorporating inventories and regulations within an arsenal)), the first two of which are copies of Franz Helm's *Buch von den probierten Künsten* (c. 1527–35), while the third is an *Innsbrucker Zeughausbuch* (c. 1540–60).[67] All include information about ammunition and fireworks, as well as supplies such as saltpetre, sulphur, and charcoal, revealing some similarities to the *Firework Book*, but seemingly more for administrative than applied purposes.

At the *Österreichische Nationalbibliothek* in Vienna, one copy of particular interest indicates that it may have come from a monastic library. Ms. Cod. 2952 is recorded in the catalogue as becoming part of the Vienna library, via Linz, from the Benedictine monastery of Mondsee in Upper Austria when the

---

[62] Trenkler, 'Frühzeit der Hofbibliothek', 20–24.

[63] '… *all under khöcher, puecher, chronikhen und dergleichen trewlich zu verwaaren und zu fursehen bis auf unser lieben sun willen und weiter fursehung.*' Haus-, Hof-, und Staatsarchiv, Urkunde No. 1117, dated 30 December 1518, quoted in Trenkler, 'Frühzeit der Hofbibliothek', 39.

[64] Hermann Menhardt, *Das älteste Handschriftenverzeichnis der Wiener Hofbibliothek von Hugo Blotius 1576* (Wien: Rudolf M. Rohrer, 1957), 31. See also Paula Molino, *L'impero di carta: Hugo Blotius, Hofbibliothekar nella Vienna di fine Cinquecento* (unpublished PhD thesis, European University Institute, Fiesole, 2011).

[65] Menhardt, *Handschriftenverzeichnis der Wiener Hofbibliothek*, 19.

[66] Today, it is catalogued as Cod. 10945 '*Instructiones germanicae de pyrotechnica praecipue de sic dictis bombardis et mortariis rite praeparandis*'.

[67] Menhardt, *Handschriftenverzeichnis der Wiener Hofbibliothek*, 72, 99. The modern references to these are Vienna, Österreichische National Bibliothek, Cod. 10898, Cod. 10952, and Cod. 10815.

The Use and Reception of the *Firework Book*

monastery was suppressed by Emperor Leopold II in 1791. Leng assumes that the manuscript only entered the monastery in the sixteenth century, as it lacks the typical binding given to all codices by Abbot Benedict Eck (1463–99).[68] It is interesting to note, however, that this copy of the *Firework Book* starts and finishes half-way down the page, and that there is a substantially larger number of errors than in other *Firework Books*.[69] The scribe or an overseer must have noticed them after writing, since there are numerous deletions and additions – few of which are of content-altering character.[70] This is the only copy with this kind of annotations in existence, which contributes to the argument that some surviving manuscripts were archived copies rather than copies for practical use. It equally could suggest that some copies were produced on demand, but never actually used, and any scribal corrections remained unnoticed. Was the demand for Firework Book copies such that it was a must-have item – but not necessarily one that needed to be studied, read, or practised?

The foundation of the *herzögliche Hofbibliothek* (Ducal Court Library) of the Wittelsbach family in Munich has been attributed to Duke Albrecht V of Bavaria (1550–79), who combined a number of libraries, including that of Johann Jakob Fugger, Johann Albrecht Widmanstetter (1506–57), and Hartmut Schedel (1440–1514). The Ducal Court Library became the backbone of the Bavarian State Library (*Bayerische Staatsbibliothek*) and the latter was first catalogued in 1582, with no distinction made between manuscripts and early printed books, although it did distinguish between Latin and non-Latin texts and included technical and scientific texts. In total, the library is reported to hold over 300 manuscripts, and over 500 volumes containing 900 printed books.[71] Once again, the catalogue mentions no *Firework Books* by name, but

---

[68] Leng, 'Feuerwerks- und Kriegsbücher', 241.

[69] It starts at fol. 32r, after 14 lines of previous text, and finishes on fol. 80r with a further 10 lines spare, followed by a treatise on weights and powder recipes.

[70] For example: many deletions are simple repetitions of mostly single words, such as '*schirmen*' (fol. 36r, line 8) or '*sechs*' (fol. 48r, line 4); additions include single words or phrases such as '*als vor geschriben stat*' (fol. 39v, line 17) or '*in dissem*' (fol. 54v, line 17). The scribe clearly did not consider the subject matter, but purely copied everything that was there whether it was required for content or not. I noted more than 50 of these errors, while other *Firework Books* have none or one.

[71] See Hans Striedl, *Der Humanist Johann Albrecht Widmanstetter 1506–57 als klassischer Philologe* (Wiesbaden: Harrassowitz, 1953), 4, and Otto Hartig, *Die Gründung der Münchner Hofbibliothek durch Albrecht V. und Jakob Fugger* (München: Königlich Bayerische Akademie der Wissenschaften, 1917), and Lehmann, *Eine Geschichte der alten Fuggerbibliotheken*.

refs to a copy of Robertus Valterius's *De Re Militari* and to various fencing books ('*Fechtbücher*'), but only lists those which include illustrations.[72]

All library listings differentiated between religious and secular books; those in Latin and various vernaculars, those with or without illustrations, but they itemized in particular only those with spiritual or monetary value. Technical manuals and instructive texts of little perceived value – especially when lacking illustrations – containing lists, complete books or only parts thereof, were usually grouped into a generic category. It is unfortunate that the *Firework Book* falls into quite a few of these categories. It is relatively short, with hardly any illustrations, written in vernacular German, and with no discernible value to a lay reader or librarian. It can be argued, however, that the reason for the survival of the Leeds *Firework Book* I.34 with its subsections may be the fact that it included illustrations. This is also the case with most other surviving copies of the *Firework Book*, which can be found nowadays bound together with other texts that include illustrations, including personifications of the planets and virtues in armour. This fact would have elevated the book's status substantially for a lay reader or librarian, and ensured that it was not broken up or discarded. Some modern scholars continue this collective catch-all terminology by failing to identify individual texts and instead only referring to them as 'impressive secular manuscripts'.[73]

***

This chapter has explored by whom the *Firework Book* was written, and its potential ownership, the position of gunners in fifteenth-century society, and their use of the *Firework Book*. The evidence for all of these points is sparse and yet cumulatively and circumstantially compelling: we cannot ascertain the names of the authors of the *Firework Book*, but it is clear that each one must have been a trained individual within the world of gunpowder artillery in the earlier years of the fifteenth century, writing a manual for colleagues and apprentices to share and disseminate information. The authors may also have intended to do more than this: to elevate the status of gunpowder artillery into a literary-scientific genre, by writing down knowledge which could be preserved for future generations. Similarly, as shown above, the *Firework Book* became a desirable object to have, clearly one which was worth copying and presumably in expectation of payment – whether it was commissioned to be copied or not. At the same time, owning and displaying a *Firework Book*

---

[72] Hartig, *Die Gründung der Münchner Hofbibliothek*, 341–45.

[73] Backhouse, 'The Royal Library', 267.

could serve as a powerful advertising tool for a master gunner to present to future employers.

The question remains as to whether the surviving *Firework Books* are a relatively small or a large proportion of all *Firework Books* ever produced. A clear distinction needs to be made between the user and the owner of the manuscript. The fact that in the post-medieval period the surviving copies are linked to libraries of the nobility indicates a potential clientele. That said, was a copy of the *Firework Book* presented to them by the gunners, was was it part of the employment condition, or was it part of a later interest by the nobility to retain an archive copy for their library collection? The scribal errors identified in some manuscripts point towards them being copies, not made by a gunner but carried out as a commission by a future owner. The evidence as laid out above points strongly in the direction of substantially more copies having been produced, as technical vernacular manuscripts of this kind were particularly vulnerable to decay and destruction, and as a result to being discarded – assuming here that the gunners had their own copies. Thus, it is most likely that those surviving were the archived copies, never actually used in practice, instead forgotten and left behind, or 'dropped behind the sofa'. This would account for the very good condition in which they remain; despite being relatively low-status manuscripts, they have surprisingly few marks and blemishes.

As we shall see, Royal Armouries manuscript I.34 followed this tradition, but further adds to it. It was not broken up to be used for different purposes; nor was it bound together with other materials. Instead, it was allowed to remain intact and to live on as a single book. It was both an archive copy as well as a copy that was added to post-production, almost certainly by someone who had practical gunpowder experience. The second part of I.34 made a link to the images which were still of a practical nature, and not wholly decorative. At the same time, the addition of the images will have aided the survival of I.34 in its entirety. The next chapter provides a detailed analysis of the Royal Armouries manuscript I.34.

3 The Leeds *Firework Book*

Having discussed the ownership of this and other *Firework Books*, and their possible use, we will now focus on the physical characteristics, structure, and content of Royal Armouries manuscript I.34, in order to place it among other manuscripts of this genre. It is clear that I.34 is a highly distinct manuscript but serves as an ideal platform to explore some of the issues shared by many of the others.

Codicology and Palaeography

I.34 is described in the Armouries' catalogue as a '"*Firework Book*", an illuminated manuscript showing the manufacture and use of gunpowder'.[1]

Reference Code:	RAR.00345; I.34
Title:	*Firework Book* (South German, mid-15th century)
Title:	Illuminated manuscript showing the manufacture and use of gunpowder
Dates:	mid-15th century
Extend/Media:	Manuscript
Archival History:	In the Library of Feldzeugmeister von Hauslab in Vienna when Demmin published drawings copied from it in 1869 (*Guide des Amateur d'Armes*) and when Essenwein published figures from it in 1877 (*Quellen zur Geschichte der Feuerwaffen*)
Acquisition:	Bought from E. Weil and presented to the Armouries by the National Art Collections Fund for £550. Acquired 1950
[…]	
Phys. Character:	11.9 inches x 8.5 inches (300mm x 220 mm)

---

[1] Royal Armouries catalogue entry, record 2465.

The Leeds *Firework Book*

[...]

Phys. Character:	4 leaves, which should have been numbered lxxxxvij, lxxxviij, cvj and cxlj were torn out after the foliation was inserted
Phys. Character:	fflxjv. – lxxxiijv. Blank. All leaves are pricked and ruled as if it had been intended to show an illustration opposite a page of text throughout
Phys. Character:	fflxxxiiijv. – cxiiij illustrated atlas of military strata-gems and devices, some showing firemaster in action, none captioned
Phys. Character:	ff.cxiijv. – cxliijv. Blank. Some water damage to last few pages
Phys. Character:	Limp parchment binding, reinforced down the back, with two decorated studs, possibly for a loop fastening, inserted
Phys. Character:	Centres of each gathering reinforced with narrow strip of re-used parchment
Phys. Character:	Pencilled notes in German, on contents and com-paranda, and bookplate, Ex Libris Liechtensteinianis, inside front cover [...]

The catalogue gives the date as 'mid-fifteenth century', and suggests that the geographic range is 'South German'. The entry is limited to four pages, in which the content of the text is scarcely mentioned. Instead, the main focus of the catalogue entry is on individual descriptions of the illustrations.

In 1996, Sarah Barter Bailey, at that time librarian of the Royal Armouries, produced the first scholarly article to address I.34 directly, but – similar to the catalogue entry which is also accredited to her – she devoted only five pages to the text, concentrating mainly on its physical characteristics, with the main focus of her article being her interpretation of the illustrations, dismissing the text as a 'version of the standard Firework Book text'.[2]

In total, the manuscript contains 140 folios, in 12 gatherings, each of six sheets folded in half, numbered straight through at the top of each page from fol. i to fol. cxliii, the front flyleaf being unnumbered. Barter Bailey states that '4 leaves, which should have been numbered lxxxxvij, lxxxviij, cvj and cxlj were torn out after the foliation was inserted', as described in the catalogue.

---

[2] Barter Bailey, 'The Royal Armouries "Firework Book"', 57.

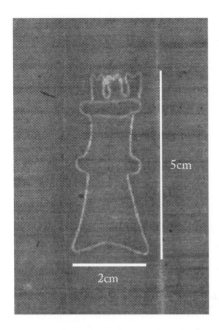
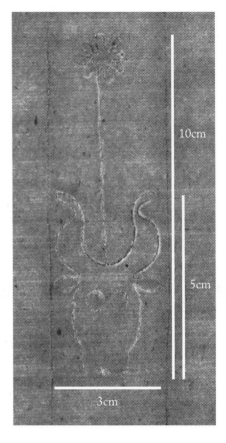

Fig. 1. (above) Royal Armouries, I.34, fol. 83 in gathering 7 (picture provided by Royal Armouries).

Fig. 2. (right) Royal Armouries, I.34, fol. 117 in gathering 11 – a watermark (picture provided by Royal Armouries).

The paper has two different watermarks.[3] The removal of single leaves and the two different watermarks could indicate that this was not a particularly high-status book. It could have been ruled and numbered close to the time of its production, using up already produced paper in a maker's workshop. This situation could also explain the removal of the leaves, cutting out single pages either because they were of poor quality, or because they were needed for other

---

[3] Royal Armouries catalogue entry, record 2465:

Phys. Character: Watermarks: Gatherings 1–7 and 12: a triple-crenellated tower. ? Piccard II 207. Gatherings 8–11: Ox head with flower between its horns. ? Piccard XII 486. 1 sheet (5/12 of gathering 7) has a mark of a Greek cross patee [sic]. ? Piccard XI 314 […]

The catalogue mentions a third mark, described as a 'Greek cross patee', but this mark could not be found, by either the current librarian or myself.

purposes. There is certainly no evidence that any of the text is missing; none of the prior folios are cut off in mid-sentence.

Gatherings 1–7 and 12 contain a triple-crenelated tower which is two centimetres wide and five centimetres high (see Figure 1). Barter Bailey compares the watermark to PICCARD II 207.[4] This is a relatively commonly used watermark with a wide range of subcategories. Based on the Watermark Classification System (*Wasserzeichen-Informationssystem*), the nearest likely match was II 311, and the *Wasserzeichen-Informationssystem* records a total of 546 paper examples in existence, with the bulk dated to be from c. 1438 to 1480. The earliest dated example is from c. 1301, and the latest is from 1573.[5]

Gatherings 8–11 contain a watermark of an ox head with eyes, with a flower on a single stem, containing eight petals, above its head (see Figure 2). Barter Bailey suggests a closeness to PICCARD XII 486.[6] This was even more commonly used in the later Middle Ages, and as a result of its wide-ranging use the subcategories are yet more varied. The most likely match in the *Wasserzeichen-Informationssystem* lists a total of 62 examples, with the bulk from c. 1444–1453. The earliest dated example is from c. 1439, and the latest is from 1472.[7]

Both watermarks have been associated with paper mills all over Germany and Austria from the fourteenth to the sixteenth centuries, and it has been impossible to find more detailed attributions. It is quite likely that the paper of I.34 was produced from c. 1430–1450 onwards, following Theodor Gerardy's suggestion that most paper produced during this period would usually have been expected to be used within three or four years after production.[8]

---

[4] Barter Bailey, 'The Royal Armouries "Firework Book"', 57.

[5] https://www.wasserzeichen-online.de/cron_distribution2.php?class=006001002001001001002001002&filter1=Realien+/+Bauwerke+/+Turm+(mit+Zinnen)+/+ein+Turm,+frei+/+ohne+Anbau+/+ohne+Fenster+/+mit+Wulst+/+ohne+Beizeichen+/+mit+Binnenzeichnung% (accessed 10 August 2023).

[6] Barter Bailey, 'The Royal Armouries "Firework Book"', 57.

[7] https://www.wasserzeichen-online.de/cron_distribution2.php?class=002007002002002001005001&filter1=Fauna+/+Ochsenkopf+/+frei,+mit+Oberzeichen+/+mit+einkonturiger+Stange+/+Blume+/+ohne+weiteres+Beizeichen+/+acht+BlÃ¼tenblÃ¤tter+/+mit+Augen% (accessed 10 August 2023).

[8] See Theodor Gerardy, *Datieren mit Hilfe von Wasserzeichen, beispielhaft dargestellt an der Gesamtproduktion der Schaumburgischen Papiermühle Arensberg von 1604–1650*, Schaumburger Studies 4 (Bückeberg: n.pub., 1964), 64–71, and Theodor Gerardy, 'Die Beschreibung des in Manuskripten und Drucken vorkommenden Papiers', *Codicologia* 5 (1980), 37–51, at 38.

I.34 is bound in leather from the skin of an unspecified animal and appears not to have been rebound in recent times, making the cover possibly of the same age as the manuscript itself. However, this is not verifiable without further scientific analysis which is beyond the scope of this study. While it is not possible to establish for certain that the I.34 copy was originally bound as one single volume, it must be assumed that it was indeed bound like this at some point in the fifteenth century. This could have been the time at which the second part of the text was written and the illustrations were added, as the continuous numbering and the page referencing would only have been possible if it already formed one single volume. This may also explain the reason for the two separate watermarks from slightly different time periods.

Returning to the manuscript itself, it consists of four distinct parts: two parts of text, one part left blank, and lastly the illustrations. As Barter Bailey notes, the first part of the text (fols 1r–51r) is 'a version of the classic German *Firework Book* text' (see Figure 3).[9] The second part of the text (fols 52r–61r) is written in a different hand (see Figure 4), and is that part which directly engages with the illustrations (fols 84v–114r). It is notable that between the second part of the text and the illustrations there is a further part of the book which is currently blank (fols 61v–84r), but is pricked and ruled, ready to be written on. The implication is that I.34 was left incomplete, although there is no indication of what the intended content may have been. The only other manuscript of the *Firework Book* tradition where this occurs is New York, Spencer Collection, Ms. 104.

The presence of these four distinct parts in one manuscript, however, provides an important indication as to why the *Firework Book* was made. One of the core questions which this study addresses is the intended readership of the *Firework Book* and its purpose. What caused it to be written and how can the existence of a considerable number of copies be explained? And indeed, who were the users (readers, owners, and re-writers) and recipients of the *Firework Book*?[10]

The manuscript cannot be attributed to any particular author, and there is no textual reference to the identity of either author or scribe. The two distinct parts of the text are written in clear bastarda,[11] in brown ink, in a single column on pricked paper. The rubrics and header texts are written in red ink, seemingly by the same hand and at the same time. The text is written in an area c. 300

---

[9] Barter Bailey, 'The Royal Armouries "Firework Book"', 57.

[10] See Chapter 2, where this question is further explored under 'Manuscript Evidence of Use' and 'Book Trade, Ownership, and Libraries'.

[11] Kirchner, *Germanistische Handschriftenpraxis*, 22–23.

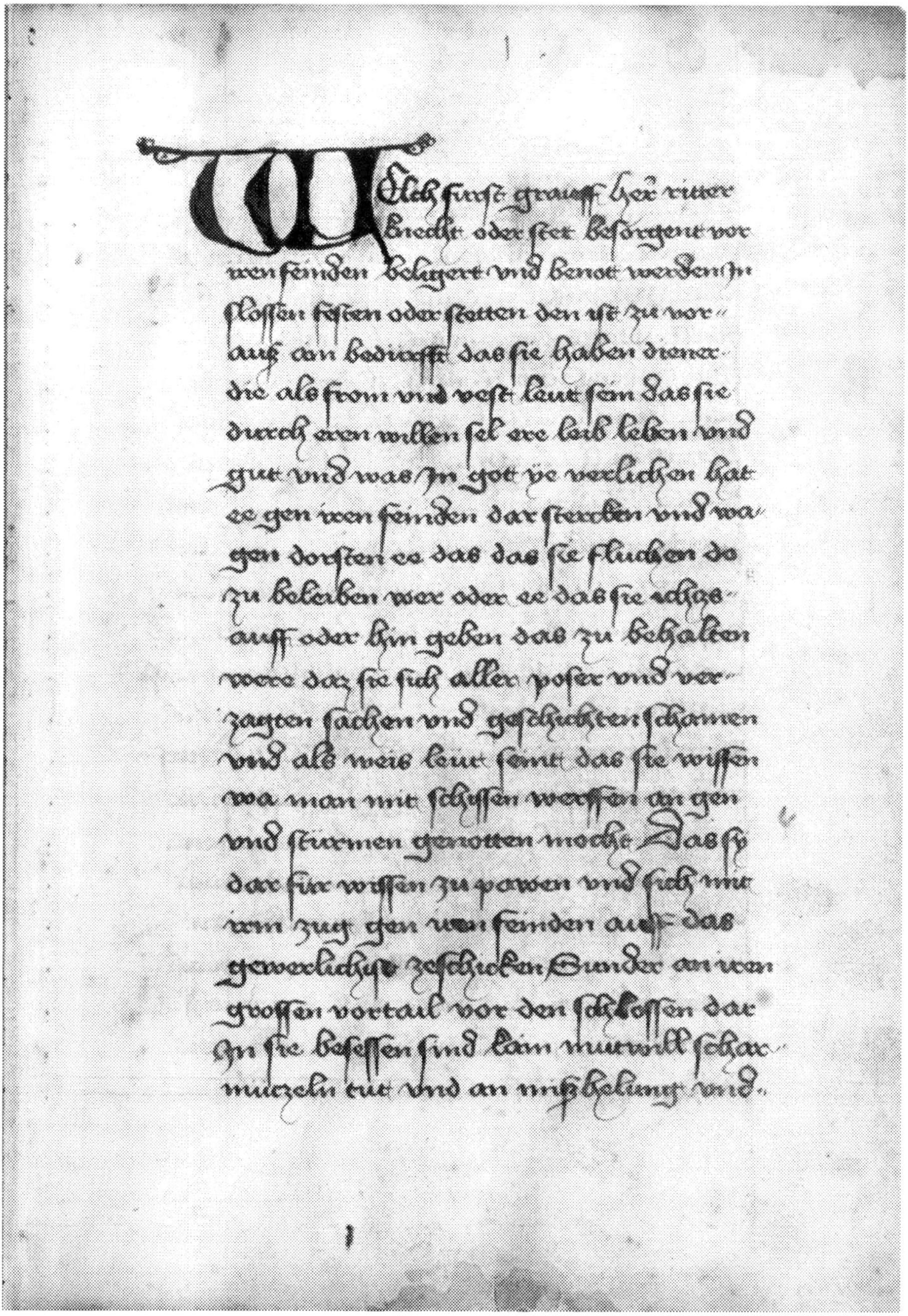

Welch fürst grauff herr ritter
knecht oder stet besorgent vor
iren feinden belägert vnd benöt werden jn
slossen festen oder stetten den ist zu vor //
auß den bedingt das sie haben diener
die als from vnd vest leut sein das sie
durch iren willen setzt ire leib leben vnd
gut vnd was jn gott ye verlichen hat
ze gen iren feinden dar strecken vnd wa
gen dorsten es das das sie fliehen da
zu beleiben wer oder es das sie ichtes
auff oder hin geben das zu behalten
were dar sie sich aller poser vnd ver //
zagten sachen vnd geschichten schamen
vnd als weis leut sent das sie wissen
wa man mit schissen werffen den gen
vnd stürmen geratten mochte Das sy
dar für wissen zu parren vnd sich mit
vom zug gen iren feinden auff das
geuerlichst zeschicken Sunder an iren
grossen vortail vor den schlossen dar
jn sie besessen sind kain muttwill schar
mützeln tut vnd an niß kelung vnd.

Fig. 3. Royal Armouries, I.34, fol. 1r – preamble in Part 1
(picture provided by Royal Armouries).

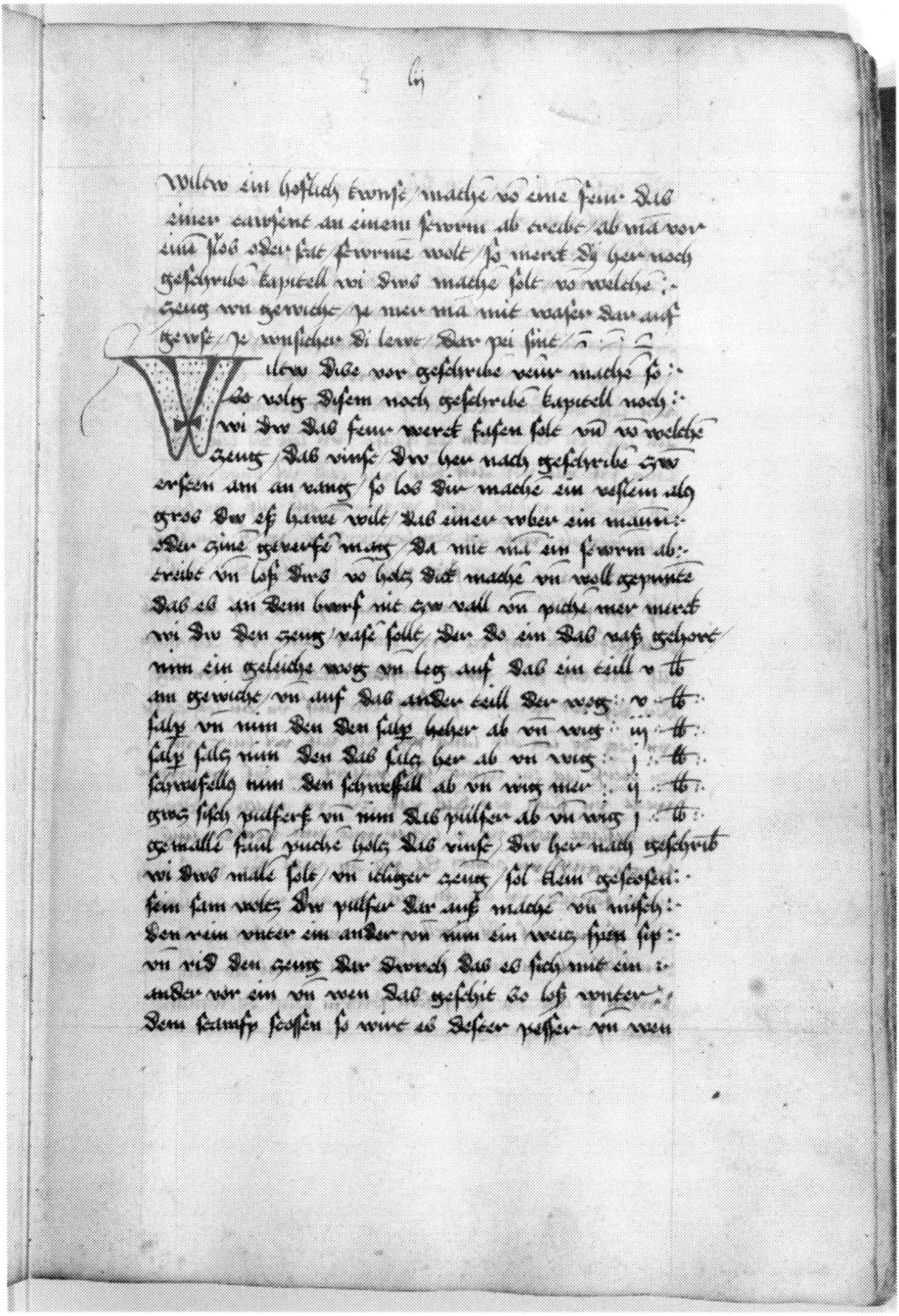

Fig. 4. Royal Armouries, I.34, fol. 52r, first folio of Part 2
(picture provided by Royal Armouries).

mm x 220 mm in both parts with an average of 22–23 rows per folio in Part 1, and 30–31 rows per folio in Part 2. Initials – mostly at the beginning of new sections of text – are listed in red, sometimes not inserted, and at others traced in brown ink to allow for later additions which were not always made. While the text parts contain no illustrations, some section headings are decorated with a mild flourish, seemingly by the same scribe who produced the text.

A clear distinction can be made between the two hands in the text, not only in the handwriting but also in the language used. With regional variations clearly distinguishable between Parts 1 and 2, both texts were written in Early New High German. The *Early New High German Dictionary* (*Frühneuhochdeutsches Wörterbuch*) defines it as 'a period in German history, which not only precedes the modern period in chronological terms, but also provides the historical, social, economic, and spiritual foundations for contemporary culture up to the present'.[12]

Content and Illustrations

Part 1 of the text in I.34 has been characterized as being part of the core *Firework Book* genre as described in Chapter 1. At fols 1v and 2r the text even provides the name for this 'book which is called the *Firework Book*' (*püch das do haist das fewr werkpüch*'). This part can be subdivided into seven different subgroups of topics – almost all of which can be found in other *Firework Book* manuscripts, but not always in the same order:

1. A preamble – containing general instructions that any ruler who is required to defend their property against enemy attack ought to employ a master gunner within his staff.

2. Twelve Master Gunner's Questions – listing the core principles of gunpowder artillery which should be known to any good master gunner.

3. Recipes and instructions related to all aspects of gunpowder, its constituent parts, and their uses. These instructions are often versions of some core recipes with slight variations.

   • Boiling saltpetre
   • Making different types of gunpowder: long-range, 'good'

---

[12] '*Eine Epoche der deutschen Geschichte, die der Neuzeit nicht nur im rein zeitlichen Sinne vorausgeht, sondern in der auch historische, soziale, ökonomische und geistige Grundlagen der neuzeitlichen bis hin zur gegenwärtigen Kultur gelegt wurden.*' *Frühneuhochdeutsches Wörterbuch Online*, Introduction, https://adw-goe.de/forschung/forschungsprojekte-akademienprogramm/fruehneuhochdeutsches-woerterbuch/woerterbuch/ (accessed 10 August 2023).

- Bringing back spoiled powder, and how to separate the core constituents from previously made gunpowder
- Making fireballs, frightening shots
- Growing saltpetre on walls
- Instructions on which ingredients make gunpowder strong
- Boiling and purifying saltpetre
- Making different types of gunpowder: 'masterful', even better
- Properly purifying saltpetre
- Recognizing adulterated and the most potent saltpetre
- Making right-fitting stone for a gun
- Identifying the right type of charcoal
- Mixing good and less good saltpetre together
- Right weights of mixing gunpowder together, and benefits of grinding it
- How to load a gun
- How to make gun plugs
- Separating salt from saltpetre, making the 'best' saltpetre, purifying saltpetre from walls, what to do if things appear to go wrong, turning raw saltpetre into purified saltpetre
- Preparing sulphur and which one is best
- Making best charcoal

4. A section on the 'inventor'/'discoverer' of gunpowder – Niger Bertholdus (or, Berthold Schwarz).[13] This section is interpolated halfway into the discussions of ingredients at fol. 20r.

---

[13] Much has been written about the role and function of Niger Bertholdus (or Berthold Schwarz) as the discoverer (NB: not the inventor) of gunpowder. Frequently, as in the early sixteenth century, he is described as a 'great expert of the secret art of alchemy' (e.g. Turmair/Aventinus 1522/33 – https://lbssbb.gbv.de/DB=1/SET=5/TTL=1/CMD?ACT=SRCHA&IKT=1016&SRT=YOP&TRM=336894708, 5, 516, 22 (accessed 10 August 2023)). Little evidence is available as to whether or not Schwarz existed; however, almost all *Firework Books* include a reference to Schwarz. The argument that Schwarz may be the placeholder for someone else is supported by the Kassel manuscript 4° Ms. math. 14, where Schwarz (claimed to be a Franciscan) was replaced by Albertus Magnus (a Dominican). For further reference on this, see Chapter 5. For a more detailed summary on the legend of Niger Bertholdus/Berthold Schwarz see Partington, *Greek Fire and Gunpowder*, 91–143, Wilfried Tittmann, 'Der Mythos vom "Schwarzen Berthold"', *Waffen- und Kostümkunde* 25 (1983), 17–30, Franz Maria Feldhaus, 'Was wissen wir von Berthold Schwarz?', *Zeitschrift für Historische Waffenkunde* 4 (1906–8), 65–69, 113–18,

The Leeds *Firework Book*

5. The section on the use of the ingredients:
   - Making gunpowder
     i. Good ordinary powder
     ii. The best powder that 'cannot be spoiled'
     iii. Bringing back powder that 'has been spoiled'
     iv. Bringing saltpetre, sulphur, charcoal together into gunpowder
     v. Separating the three ingredients from each other
     vi. An instruction on the nature of saltpetre
     vii. Making salpratica and purifying salammoniac
6. Instructions on how to fire at night and how to use gunpowder in a siege situation, including how to make wall-breaching powder, and how to shoot down a tower
7. Making powder which 'burns when it gets wet'
   - Making coloured powder
   - Making fire arrows
   - Making powder which makes the shot louder
   - Instructions about the gun dimension and where to position it
   - Instructions on breaking a gun
   - Instructions on loading and firing a gun safely
   - A section on the attributes, moral qualities, skills, and attitudes of a good master gunner. This section is interspersed within the general section on ingredients.[14]
   - Continuation of the section on the ingredients and their uses:
   - Making good tinder
   - Making good 'ball powder'
   - Making 'hidden fire' and 'fire which can be lit quickly'
   - Instructions on buying saltpetre
   - Making oil of sulphur, *'oleum compilatum distillatum'*
   - Bringing back spoiled powder

Hans Jürgen Rieckenberg, 'Berthold, der Erfinder des Schießpulvers. Eine Studie zu seiner Lebensgeschichte', *Archiv für Kulturgeschichte* 36 (1956), 316–22, Kramer, *Berthold Schwarz*, 18–32, and Kramer and Leibnitz, *Das Feuerwerkbuch*, 76–77.

[14] In other versions of the *Firework Book* the sections on the 'discoverer' and the master gunner's attributes often, but not always, follow the Master Gunner's Questions.

Gunpowder Technology in the Fifteenth Century

- Purifying saltpetre
- Firing special types of shots, such as rods, hailstorm, hedgehog
- Firing quickly and accurately
- Firing a gun where water ended up in the powder
- Firing different types of powder and shots such as the use of more than one plug
- Setting fire to waterlogged poles
- Firing accurately and from siege towers
- Making fire arrows
- Setting fire to water, and the use of oil of sulphur and Greek fire
- Checking that saltpetre is of good enough quality, how to test it, and how to make it better
- Making gunpowder for fire arrows, and other purposes
- Turning gunpowder into *Knollenpulver* ('lump powder')[15]
- Making fire arrows for varying purposes
- Emptying a gun
- Firing a glowing ball
- Making tinder
- Hardening an iron tip into a 'house arrow'

Part 1 ends with the phrase '*Et sic est finis*' (fol. 51r) near the bottom of the page, a clear indication that this was an intended end of a seemingly canonical text.

Part 2 follows directly on from Part 1 on the next folio without any specific introduction or explanation, but clearly in a different hand. Compared to Part 1, it is far shorter and it starts with a rhetorical question which is repeated throughout Part 2: 'If you want to make a "courtly art" of' ('*wiltw ein hoflich kwnst mache*', fol. 52r). This part deals with:

- Making an incendiary device for large-scale attacks, longer-ranging, more severe, to smoke out a castle – using a barrel or a wheel hub
- Making a shot which cannot be extinguished and 'kills a hundred men'
- Making 'secret firework'
- Making fire arrows, in four different colours with different attributes
- Making 'hard water': how, and for what purpose

---

[15] See discussion on *Knollenpulver* in Chapter 5 under 'Gunpowder'.

The Leeds Firework Book

- Making and use of 'burnt oil' or *olium petroleum*
- Instructions on cooling down a gun

Part 2 ends with 'This way, you see to take all the precautions that no harm is done to the gun' ('*so scheust dw an alle sorg das der pusche[n] kein schade[n] prengt*', fol. 61r) at the end of the instructions on how to cool down a gun. The text finishes halfway down a page, and it can be assumed that more text was intended to be added at a later stage.

According to informal conversations with curators at the Royal Armouries, it has long been assumed that this part was a unique comment on the earlier instructions in Part 1. In the course of the research for this book, at least one other version of this section of text has been located as part of the manuscript which contains the Strasbourg *Firework Book*. However, the Strasbourg version copies the I.34 text including references to the illustration page numbers without providing any associated illustrations.[16] This suggests that Part 2 of I.34 is not unique as had previously been thought. The likelihood is that I.34 is the older version, copied in full in the Strasbourg manuscript. Nevertheless, it might still be that Part 2 of I.34 was made decades after Part 1 had been produced.

Barter Bailey believes that the recipes were written down when remembered, 'as if the compiler was adding to the collection or improving it as he compiled it, without taking the trouble to go back and eliminate duplication'. However, she admits that the hand 'is a regular copyist's hand not that of a man making a series of scribbled personal notes'.[17] Barter Bailey highlights that a level of contradiction existed between the apparent content of the text and the format of its presentation. It puzzled her that there seemed to have been repetitions, and less of a structure. As the analysis in Chapter 5 will show, there is less repetition than previously assumed, and a clearly discernible structure. At the same time, there are scribal errors and differences from other *Firework Books* which – I would argue – give a much clearer indication of what the text was produced for.

Any Early New High German text contains both regionally specific terminology and highly localized spelling with no orthographical standardization in place, and this text is no exception.[18] The two parts of the text show differences

---

[16] Strasbourg Ms. 2259, fols 30r–36v.

[17] Barter Bailey, 'The Royal Armouries "Firework Book"', 58.

[18] Early New High German has been identified as following Middle High German (where a substantial vowel shift occurred) to be the earliest version of what later became New High German (Thorsten Roelcke, 'Die Periodisierung der deutschen

in spelling and use of terminology. For instance, the two parts show a frequent change of vowels in similar words such as a shift from '*a*' to '*e*' in '*gemaincklick*' (Part 1, fol. 10r) or '*gemain*' (Part 1, fol. 39r) vs. '*gemein*' (Part 2, fol. 60r). Similarly, the shift from '*lassen*' (Part 1) vs. '*loß*' (Part 2) is a shift from an '*a*' to an '*o*'. These vowel shifts are one of the key indicators of regional variations.

The three core ingredients of gunpowder are spelled in a distinctively different way in the text: '*salpetter*' (Part 1) vs. '*salp*' (in Part 2 – almost always abbreviated except for fol. 59v where it is spelled out as '*salpeter*') – indicating a possibly increased familiarization with the ingredient mentioned. Differences can be found in the use of sulphur and charcoal, too: '*swebel*' (Part 1) vs. '*schweffell*' (Part 2), and '*koln*' (Part 1) vs. '*kolle*' (Part 2).

The use of different terms can be both a semantic shift between the times of production of the two texts, or related to different use: for example, '*puchsen pulfer*' (Part 1: fols 1v, 8r, 8v, 13r, 14r, 19r, 21r, 22r, 25v, 29v, 30r, 41v, 46v, 47r, and 48r) compared to '*sisch pulfer*' or '*schiß pulfer*' (Part 2: fols 52r, 52v, 53v, and 54r). Both have been translated as *gunpowder*, but the term *puchsen pulfer* refers to '*powder from the gun*' while '*sisch pulfer*' refers to '*powder which can be fired*'.

Many other differences in spelling can be noted such as '*fewr werk*' or '*fewr*' (Part 1) compared to '*feur werck*' or '*veur*' (Part 2); '*wiltu*' (Part 1) compared to '*wiltw*' (Part 2), to name just a few.

In Part 2 we also find an increased number of abbreviations, where hardly any end-*n* has been written out (see fol. 52r, abbreviations are expanded with text in square brackets). This may indicate someone who writes more frequently, or writes for personal notes, rather than producing something that was primarily intended to be read by others. Also, the phrase '*los dir machen*' (e.g. fol. 52r) appears, which can be translated as 'have made for yourself'. This does not occur in Part 1, and may indicate that the second author was much less hands-on, and more accustomed to instructing others to produce items for him. This may be an indication of the possible changed status of the author and/or scribe.

Following fol. 61v, a total of 22 folios are left blank. Fols 84r–114r contain all the illustrations, all without any accompanying text. These illustrations are described in detail in the catalogue entry of the Royal Armouries. There is a distinct difference between these illustrations and many other related manuscripts from the fifteenth century.[19] Most illustrations in manuscripts ascribed

---

Sprachgeschichte', in Sprachgeschichte, 2.1, eds Werner Besch et al., 2nd edn (Berlin and New York: de Gruyter, 1998), 798–815, at 804–6).

[19] See, for example, the manuscript Munich Cgm. 600, entitled: *Anleitung Schießpulver zu bereiten. Büchsen zu laden und zu beschießen*, which contains images throughout with captions in German vernacular or Latin, or a mixture of both. See Chapter

to the *Bellifortis* or *Büchsenmeister Book* genre tend to be a combination of text and image, and the text is often provided to explain the image in some detail. The text in Part 1 of I.54 makes no reference to the illustrations. In Part 2, there are a number of references to the illustrations at the end of the manuscript as well as to other parts of the text. At least some of the page numbers will have been added at a later stage, seemingly by the same scribe but with different ink (or at a different time), as some numbers appear to be taking up more space than allocated and run into the subsequent text (fol. 54r), while others leave more space than is required (also fol. 54r). On other occasions, the numbers are not on the same line as the rest of the text (for example, fol. 55v).

In particular, fol. 52v refers to 'sheet 95'; fol. 54r refers to 'sheet 79'; fol. 55v refers to 'sheet 95' and 'sheet 96'; fol. 57r lists 'sheet 90' and later refers to 'sheet 90 or 95' (the additional 'v' or 5 is in superscript); on fol. 60r there is a reference to a drawing on 'sheet 90'. On fol. 53v, there is a reference to another sheet, but the actual number has not been completed. The fact that there is a gap in the text implies that it must either have been forgotten by the scribe or it was intended to be completed at a later stage. On fol. 56r the text refers to 'sheet 60 or 90' (additional 'xxx' or 30 crossed out) with once again some more space left behind the numbers. On fol. 57v the text refers to another section 'written on sheet 55'. Fol. 53 r refers to 'sheet 55' which is another section of text with some relevance to the recipe described. Fol. 53r refers to 'sheet 53' with plenty of space still left in the text. This may imply a change of heart by the scribe. The text clearly states 'as you can see on sheet 53' which is not the way that the earlier reference is mentioned (here the author states 'as you can see described at …').

The illustrations (for some examples, see Figures 5, 6, 7) offer a glimpse of the activities carried out by a master gunner – a clearly identifiable figure drawn in almost every illustration as a figure of authority. They can largely be subdivided into three parts: activities in the field (fols 84r–86r, 90r–91r, and 106v), activities in the workshop (fols 85v, 86v–89v), and the remainder of technical drawings. However, as all the illustrations are without captions they are open to interpretation as to what is intended in the depiction. For example, they show some of the insides of the incendiary devices, but do not necessarily provide a comprehensive picture, which has led scholars such as Barter Bailey to explain the illustrations according to their own speculative assumptions, using phrases such as 'apparently intended' and 'what are probably'.[20]

---

1 under '*Bellifortis* and the *Büchsenmeister Book*' for further explanation on the distinction of the genres.

[20] Barter Bailey, 'The Royal Armouries "Firework Book"', 79 and 80.

Fig. 5. Royal Armouries, I.34, fols 90v (above) and 90r (opposite) – in the field (pictures provided by Royal Armouries).

Fig. 6. Royal Armouries, I.34, fols 89v (above) and 86v (opposite) – in the workshop (pictures provided by Royal Armouries).

Fig. 7. Royal Armouries, I.34, fols 85v (above) and 87r (opposite) – in the workshop (pictures provided by Royal Armouries).

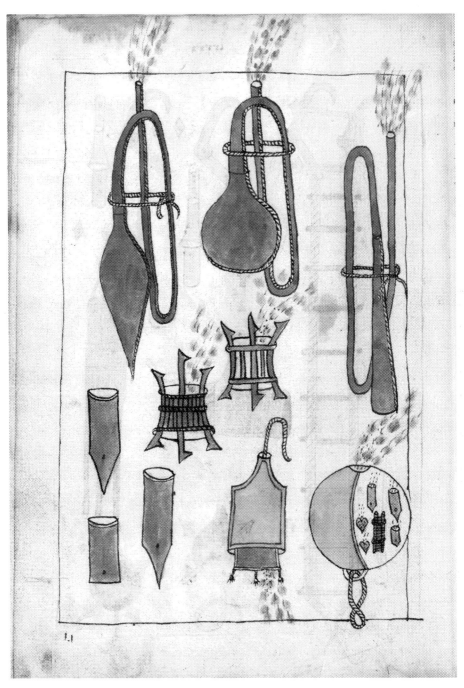

Fig. 8. Royal Armouries, I.34, fols 94v (above) and 95v (opposite) – incendiary devices (pictures provided by Royal Armouries).

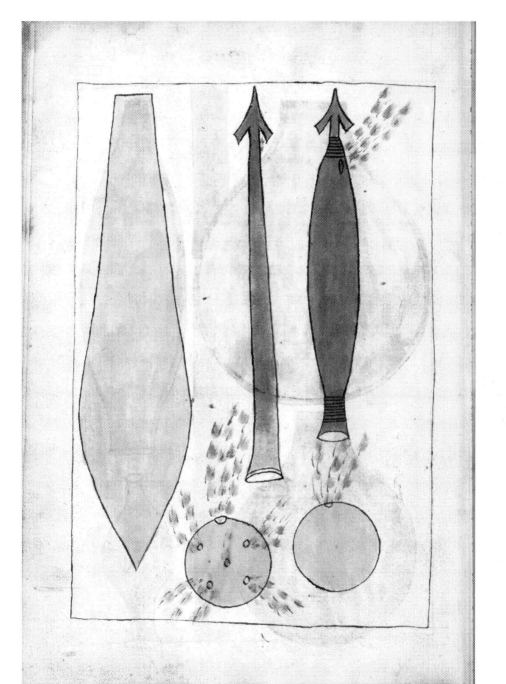

Considerations of authorship and production context of the other manuscripts are covered in Chapters 1 and 5; the ownership history of this manuscript can only be traced so far. Starting from its acquisition in 1950 and working backwards chronologically, I.34 was purchased by the Royal Armouries from the art dealer E. Weil, who, in turn, had acquired it from the Prince of Liechtenstein – the manuscript still contains a book plate '*Ex libris Lichtensteinianis*'. Hassenstein lists it as a copy belonging to the Feldzeugmeister, Ritter von Hauslab-Liechtenstein.[21] This meant it is probably the same manuscript cited by Max Jähns in 1889–91: 'a precious very old manuscript from the library of Hauslab-Liechtenstein (Rossau near Vienna), which has added to it a pyrotechnical book of recipes and an exquisitely illustrated atlas'.[22] Before this, in 1877, some illustrations of the I.34 manuscript pages, then also belonging to the library of the Hauslab family, had been published by Essenwein.[23] Even earlier, in 1868, possibly the same manuscript was listed as the property of Franz Ritter von Hauslab (1798–1883), a polymath who spent his life as soldier, engineer, and cartographer,[24] although where he had acquired it could not be established. It seems that this might be the same manuscript, but this is impossible to prove. Before this date, no further trace of ownership has been found and this is consistent with the ownership of other known copies of the *Firework Book*, as discussed earlier.

Any single manuscript is a complex object and has its own history and provenance. It can contain text, paratext, marginalia, images, annotations, signs of wear and tear, and binding. It was owned over the years, amended, changed, often cut and rebound. The fact that I.34's provenance cannot be pinned down to earlier than the nineteenth century does not mean that it should not be studied. Its study necessitates bringing together a blend of palaeographical, diplomatic, historiographical, linguistic, technical, and archaeological analysis. As the cultural historian Peter Miller says in relation to the study of objects,

---

[21] Hassenstein, *Feuerwerkbuch*, 87.

[22] '… köstliche, sehr alte Handschrift der bibliothek Hauslab-Liechtenstein (Roßau zu Wien), welcher ein pyrotechnisches Rezeptbuch und ein vorzüglicher Bildatlas angehängt sind' (Jähns, *Kriegswissenschaften*, 393).

[23] August von Essenwein, *Quellen zur Geschichte der Feuerwaffen*, 2 vols (Leipzig and Graz: Akademische Druck- und Verlagsanstalt, 1877 [1969]), 111 and B. 1. – dated by Essenwein c. 1430–1440.

[24] Karl Schneider, 'Zusammenstellung und Inhalts-Angabe der artilleristischen Schriften und Werke in der Bibliothek Seiner Exzellenz des Herrn Feldzeugmeisters Ritter v. Hauslab', *Mittheilungen über Gegenstände der Artillerie- und Kriegs-Wissenschaften. Hg. vom K. K. Artillerie-Committé* (Wien: Braumüller, 1868), 123–211, at 126.

what is necessary is 'a scientist's knowledge of materials, a practitioner's knowledge of techniques, and a historian's knowledge of context'.[25] This range of knowledge also applies to the study of this manuscript.

***

This chapter has described the physical attributions of I.34, its format and history, and provided a summary of its contents and structure. The following chapter will provide a transcription and translation.

---

[25] Peter Miller, *History and Its Objects: Antiquarianism and Material Culture since 1500* (Ithaca and London: Cornell University Press, 2017), 16.

4 The Text of Royal Armouries I.34

Editorial Principles

This chapter provides the text and a translation into English of the Royal Armouries manuscript I.34. It is integral to the understanding of the *Firework Book* tradition and I.34's position within it, that the edition and translation are placed in the centre of this book. Only after providing a complete translation is it possible to analyse the content of the *Firework Book* in detail. Before the edition and translation it is important to set out my key editorial principles.

Transcription

In transcribing and translating the *Firework Book* I have tried to replicate the text as it appears in the manuscript. Since no facsimile of the original exists, I have reproduced the transcript of the text according to the principles of the discipline known as Diplomatics, by representing everything as it can be found in the manuscript. The guiding principle of the transcription is to remain faithful to the original, with the intention of providing all the core elements of the original manuscript.

The transcription aims to make the German text as accessible as possible for a reader who is familiar with modern New High German. However, the spelling of the words is taken as in the manuscript and has not been harmonized, in order to enable scholars to observe any linguistically specific features.

The decision was made to retain the page layout of the manuscript text line by line, with any words that were carried over the line allowed to remain. Hyphenation has been included where it is provided in the manuscript.

When obvious scribal errors occur, they are marked in the transcription. Scribal errors, such as word or line repetitions have been included, as have crossings out.

By way of convention, the following rules are observed throughout: vowels *v* and *j* are retained and have not been converted to *u* and *i*, resulting in, e.g., '*vnd*' and not '*und*'.

The Text of Royal Armouries I.34

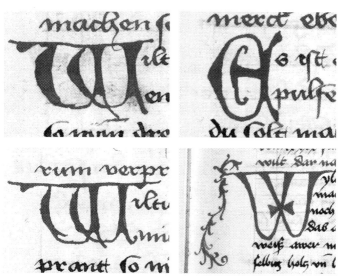

Fig. 9. Royal Armouries, I.34, fols 6r (top left), 14r (top right), 42v (bottom left) and 57r (bottom right) – initials in Parts 1 and 2 (pictures provided by Royal Armouries).

The two colours of the manuscript text are represented in bold for red, and non-bold for brown. Enlarged initials are reproduced in a larger font, but standardized – which is not the case in the manuscript.

Going beyond the diplomatic edition, abbreviations are expanded, added in the text in italics and placed in square brackets.

Diacritic marks have been reproduced, often indicating a lengthening of a vowel, but only when it is clear that they are actual characters and not a scribal oversight or a slip of the pen.

In the interest of ease of reading for a modern audience, the following editorial decisions have been followed:

- Where capitalization exists, it remains as it appears.
- Paragraph spacing has been provided only where indicated in the original.

However, no punctuation has been added unless provided in the text.

Translation

For the English translation I have attempted throughout to translate the prose into a form of English that should be comprehensible to a reader of modern English who has not undergone a specific technical training.

The translation follows the original text as closely as possible, and especially aims to reflect the often monotonous and repetitive sentence structure. This follows the translation theory approach of translating largely '*word for word*' where possible, and only when necessary choosing a '*sense for sense*' approach, as discussed by the translation theorist Susan Bassnett.[1] For instance, one of the most often used words, '*vnd*', is repeated more often than would be usual in an English text. Additions which were deemed necessary for clarification are added in italics and placed in square brackets. In passages where the meaning is unclear, an attempt at explanation has been provided in the translation, referenced in an explanatory footnote.

The translation is intended to be as close to the original as possible, to allow for cross-referencing to the original Early New High German. This results in a very literal translation, and even the sentence structure is only rearranged when required to reflect English grammatical conventions, with the intention of reproducing the 'author's text' as much as possible, while producing a 'relevant translation' as defined by Jacques Derrida.[2]

Modern punctuation and capitalization have been added to ease the reader's task.

Presentation

The transcription and translation are placed side by side to allow for cross-referring and cross-reading where required. However, line numberings have been added to the left of the original text. Any superscripts and textual addition in the original have been added as full lines of text. As Part 2 of the text is written in smaller font in the manuscript, the margins have been decreased in order to keep both text and translation on one page – as in Part 1.

---

[1] Susan Bassnett, *Translation Studies*, 3rd edn (London: Routledge, 2002), 51–57.

[2] *Probable Truth: Editing Medieval Texts from Britain in the Twenty-First Century*, eds Vincent Gillespie and Anne Hudson, Texts and Transitions 5 (Brepols: Turnhout, 2013), 7. A great amount of scholarship has been produced on the theory and practice of translating medieval texts into modern languages, and making them accessible to a modern reader. Most influential in the theoretical framework on translation in recent decades has been the work of Jacques Derrida, and the subsequent translation is indebted to the framework provided by Derrida (see, among others, Jacques Derrida and Lawrence Venuti, trans., 'What is a "Relevant" Translation', *Critical Inquiry* 27:2 (2001), 174–200).

Edition and translation

Royal Armouries I.34 – Part 1

fol. 1r

1   Welch furst grauff her[r] ritter
    knecht oder stet besorgent vor
    iren feinden beligert vnd benot werden in
    slossen festen oder stetten den ist zu vor=
5   auß ain bedürfft das sie haben diener
    die als from vnd vest leut sein das sie
    durch eren willen sel ere leib leben vnd
    gut vnd was in got ÿe verlichen hat
    ee gen iren feinden dar stercken vnd wa=
10   gen dorsten ee das das sie fluchen do
    zu beleiben wer oder ee das sie ichizs=
    auff oder hin geben das zu behalten
    were daz si sich aller poser und ver=
    zagten sachen vnd geschichten schamen
15   vnd als weis leüt seint das sie wissen
    wa man mit schissen werffen an gen

Royal Armouries I.34 – Part 1

fol. 1r

Any prince, earl, lord, knight,
squire, or town who frequently fear that they may
be besieged by their enemies and threatened in their
castles, strongholds, or towns,
they need in advance to have servants
who are reliable[1] and competent people and who
as a matter of honour will commit their souls, lives, bodies, and property
and all that God has given them
against their enemies.[2] And
they [*should*] dare to be bold[3] rather than running away,
to hold their ground rather than
giving up everything[4] that they should keep
where they should be ashamed of all bad and
disheartened matters and events.
And are wise enough people to know
when one can start firing

---

[1] '*from vnd vest*' – often translated as 'pious', generally used without religious connotations (Baufeld, *Kleines frühneuhochdeutsches Wörterbuch*, 96). The religious connotation was introduced with Martin Luther's writing and cannot be applied retrospectively. The definition used here is related to '*rechtschaffend, ordentlich*' (*Frühneuhochdeutsches Wörterbuch Online*, http://fwb-online.de/go/bederblich.h1.4adj_1513870571).

[2] No reference could be traced for '*dar stercken*'; it is possible that this is a scribal error, and that it should be '*dar strecken*' in the sense of 'sacrifice' ('*hingeben, opfern*') or simply '*darreichen*' ('present') (*Frühneuhochdeutsches Wörterbuch Online*, http://fwb-online.de/go/darstrecken.s.3v_1513372249).

[3] '*wagen dorsten*' – both words mean to 'dare' or to 'risk' or simply to 'start' (*Frühneuhochdeutsches Wörterbuch Online*, def. 15, http://fwb-online.de/go/bestehen.s.3v_1513302171), from Middle High German '*türen*'.

[4] '*ichizs*' or '*ichts*' or '*icht*' – positive form of 'nothing' (*Frühneuhochdeutsches Wörterbuch Online*, http://fwb-online.de/go/icht.s.2n_1518601445).

vnd stürmen genotten mocht Das sÿ
dar für wissen zu pawen vnd sich mit
irm zug gen iren feinden auff das
20   gewerlichist zeschicken Sunder an iren
grossen vortail vor den schlossen dar
jn sie besessen sind kain mutwill schar=
müczeln tut vnd an mißhelung vnd

fol. 1v

1   zwaiung in guter freuntschaft vnder ein
ander beleiben jn den sachen nach der weiß
esten rat vnder in handeln[n] vnd welch
furst grauff her[r] ritter oder knecht oder
5   stet haben solich from weiß diener vnd
vest die mugen sich ir wol trosten Doch
bedurffen si beÿ in zu haben leut di ar=
baitten binden vnd mugen als schmid zim=
merleut schůster milner pfister vnd an=
10   der arbaÿter Besunder gut puchsen maist[er]
vnd schuczen do mit si sich behelffen müge[n]
vnd wen[n] das ist das man von guten püchse[n]
maistern guten trost nÿmt so ist ein yedlich
fürst her[re] ritter oder knecht vnd stet bedurf=
15   en das puchsen maister gut maister sind
vnd alle die ol vnd pulfer wol beraiten

and exactly where to start besieging.[5] They
therefore should know how to build[6] and how to handle
their equipment[7] most skilfully against
their enemy. Especially to their
great advantage in front of a castle,
they should not engage in a deliberate skirmish
or other misconduct and

fol. 1v

break a good friendship between two [*people*].
[*They should*] live with each other in a manner which
makes use of the best counsel. And any
prince, earl, lord, knight, squire, or
town that has such competent, wise, steadfast,
and bold servants can rest assured. Nevertheless
they need to have people who are competent workers
and who can work as a smith, carpenter,
shoemaker, miller, baker, or other
workers. Especially [*they need*] good master gunners
and gunners on whom they can depend.
When it is the case that good master
gunners are relied on, then each and every
prince, lord, knight, or squire, and town
is in such need that [*their*] master gunners are good masters.
And [*they*] can prepare all the oils and powder well,

---

[5] '*genotten*' or '*genöten*' – 'to urge, force' (*Frühneuhochdeutsches Wörterbuch Online*, http://fwb-online.de/go/gen%C3%B6t.s.4adj_1514015990). This sentence is not clear in the original, but has been left as a literal translation. It appears to be more a written version of a spoken commentary, an often repeated formula in almost all *Firework Books*, and its meaning is 'ought to hold on to all equipment and personnel instead of surrendering which is bad and disheartening behaviour they should be ashamed of. They should be wise enough to know when to fire and when to attack.'

[6] This is likely to refer to defensive structures, and the role of the master gunner to defend them – in some copies of the *Firework Book* there is an added word or two to highlight this, Dillingen Ms. XV 50, fol. 1r, '*bössywerck vmd brust werî*' (meaning 'bulwarks and gabions'), and in Weimar Manuscript Q 342, fol. 55r, '*für Anläufe, Stürme, Einwerfen*' ('for attacks, advances, and assaults').

[7] '*zug*' or '*zeug*' – collective term for 'things', here 'equipment' or 'train' – not yet captured by *Frühneuhochdeutsches Wörterbuch*.

konnen vnd vi auch andre stuck die nücz
vnd gut sind zu dem puchsen pulfer zu
fewrpfeilen zu fewr kugeln die man wirft
20 zu fewr kugeln die man auß der puchsen
schewst vnd zu andern fewr wercken vnd
sachen die in disem půch das do haist

fol. 2r

1 das fewr we[r]ckpůch her nach geschriben
sten vnd dar vmb das der stuck so vil sind
die ein ẏedlicher guter puchsen maister
konnen sol vnd das sie alle ain maister
5 nit wol bedencken noch in seinem sinne
behalten mag Dar vmb so stet her=
nach geschriben alle die stuck vnd kunst
die ein ẏedlicher guter puchsen maister
kinnen sol vnd wie ainer ain ẏedlich
10 stuck von an gang piß an das end auß
gericht vnd gut bereiten vnd konnen sol
do mit er dan[n] mit der andern leut hilff

and also other things[8] which are useful
and good to be made into gunpowder,
fire arrows, [*and*] fire balls which can be thrown. And [*they can*]
[*also be made*] into fire balls which can be shot out of a gun
and other fireworks and
things which [*are*] in this book, which is called

fol. 2r

the firework book which stands written as follows.
And as there are so many things of
which each good master gunner[9]
should be capable of and which could not all
be well remembered by a master and kept
in his mind; therefore there are written below
all the items and methods[10]
that every good master gunner
should know and how he can make each
item from beginning to end,
and can prepare them well and should be able to do them,
in order that with the help of other people

---

[8] '*stuck*' – could mean anything and everything from 'piece' to 'part', 'element', 'item', or at times simply 'things'.

[9] This could also mean 'gun master' – the word order is debatable. *Frühneu-hochdeutsches Wörterbuch Online*, http://fwb-online.de/go/b%C3%BCchsen-meister.s.0m_1513302890). There is a distinct difference between this and the role of '*Büchsenschmied*' – the smith in charge of the manufacture of a gun (*Früh-neuhochdeutsches Wörterbuch Online*, http://fwb-online.de/go/b%C3%BCchsen-schmied.s.0m_1513341043.

[10] '*kunst*' is a very broad term with many different applicable uses. The *Frühneuhoch-deutsches Wörterbuch*, vol. 8, col. 1830, provides two possibly suitable definitions for '*kunst*': <the following two paragraphs are list items introduced (a) and (b)>

Definition 3: 'knowledge, expertise, insight; also specialist knowledge, training' ('*Wissen, Kenntnis, Kunde, Einsicht [...]; auch 'Gelehrsamkeit, Fachkenntnis*'), or
Definition 4: 'Science; especially, the rules and regulations that are the foundation of art of science, theory, methodology' ('*Wissenschaft; speziell: die einer Kunst oder Wissenschaft zugrundeliegenden Regeln, Theorie, Methode*').

'Method' was deemed the closest approximation in English in this context. The term '*kunst*' is similar to the English use of the term 'art' which similarly underwent a large shift in meanings over the centuries. See Chapter 5 for a more detailed discussion.

**die peÿ im sein ein ÿedlich schloß vest vnd
stat behalten mug vnd von der kunst**

15 **die zu der buchsen gehort geschechen
zwelff frag So beschicht auch über ÿed=
lich frag besunder ein gut vnder rich=
tung vnd lere Die erst frag**

Die erst frag ist ob daz fewr den stein

20 auß der puchsen treib oder der dunst
der von dem fewr get Nu sprechen etlich
das fewr hab die kraft den stain zetreiben.

fol. 2v

1 Ich sprich aber das der dunst hab die kraft
Exemplum ein peispil   Nim[m]e ein pfunt guts
pulfers vnd thu es in ein semig weinfaß

he can hold any castle, stronghold,[11] or
town. Regarding the 'art'
which belongs to the gun there
twelve questions arise.[12] Therefore concerning each
question good[13] information and instructions
are provided. The first question

The first question is whether the fire drives the stone[14]
out of the gun or the vapour[15]
which comes from the fire. Many [*people*] agree
that it is the fire that has the power to propel the stone.

fol. 2v

I say: the vapour has the power
Exemplum, for example:[16] take a pound of good
[*gun*]powder and put it into a solid[17] wine barrel

---

[11] There is a subtle difference between '*schloß*' and '*vest*': it is used as a rhetorical repetition here, '*vest*' relates to any fortified structure large or small.

[12] '*geschechen*' is a verb with multiple meanings such as 'to happen' or 'to occur'. Here the translation of 'arise' was chosen to reflect the causality.

[13] The author often uses terms such as '*gut*', '*recht*' or '*wol*', as well as comparatives such as '*pöß*' or '*pößer*', or superlatives such as '*pester*'. All of these are subjective, emotive terms which could be translated at times into a more technical language of 'accurate' or 'reliable'. However, for the sake of this translation it has been decided to override the sense of the emotive and subject terms and translate it often with a more imprecise 'good'.

[14] 'Projectile', 'round shot', 'stone ball'.

[15] The literal translation here would be 'pressure'.

[16] The author repeats the same words – first in Latin, then in German. The *Frühneuhochdeutsches Wörterbuch* lists under definition 3 '*Beispiel, Verhaltensweise, die anderen zum Vorbild oder (seltener) zur Abschreckung dient; Vorbild, Muster, Lehre*' a range of examples where '*beispiel*' is used in conjunction with '*exempel*' or '*lere/leer/lern*' (*Frühneuhochdeutsches Wörterbuch Online*, http://fwb-online.de/go/beispiel.s.2n_1543441567). For more discussion on the subject see Chapter 5.

[17] '*semig*' – in Freiburg Ms. 362, this term is listed as '*sämig*' – which in turn is interpreted by Kramer as a measurement 'one saum in volume [about 150 litres]' (Kramer and Leibnitz, *Das Feuerwerkbuch*, 22 – no reference provided), Nibler states that 'a clear definition is not possible. Hassenstein's interpretation, on page 43, of it being thick-walled has to be disputed. Kramer uses a measure of c. 150 litres. Most likely is that this relates to a barrel of c. 30–40 litres in size.' ('*Eindeutige Erklärung nicht möglich. Hassenstein S. 43 (sämig=dickflüssig=>dickwandig!) ist zu widersprechen. Kramer. S. 154, führt 'sämig' auf 'Saum', ein altes Hohlmaß von ca. 150 l zurück. Am*

vnd vermach es wol das kein dunst do von
5   komen müg den[n] zu dem widloch do du es
an zindest vnd so du es anzindest so ist daz
pulfer zehant verprunnen vnd pricht der
dunst das vaß

Die ander frag ob salpeter oder swebel
10   die kraft hab den stein zu treiben sprich
ich sie baide dan[n] wann das pulfer enzün=
det wirt in der buchs so ist der swebel
also hiczig vnd der salpeter als kalt das
die kelt die hicz nicht geleiden mag noch
15   die hicze die keltin wan[n] kelt vnd hicz sein
zweÿ wider wertige dinck also mag ir ÿed=
weders das ander nicht geleiden vnd ist
doch ains an das ander nicht nucz zu dem
pulfer zu prauchen

20   Die dritt frag ob ~~ob~~ luczel pulfer beld[er]
ein puchs prech oder weiter schieß

and close it well afterwards so that no vapour
should escape apart from through the touch hole[18] where you
light it. And when you light it the
powder burns immediately[19] and the vapour
breaks[20] the barrel [*apart*].

The second[21] question [*is*] whether saltpetre or sulphur
has the power to expel the stone. I say:
it is both for when the powder is lit
in the gun the sulphur is so
hot and the saltpetre is so cold that
the cold cannot bear the heat nor the
heat the cold,[22] for cold and hot are
two opposing parts[23] which do not tolerate
each other, yet
one without the other [*is*] not useful to
be used for powder.

The third question [*is*] whether a little more powder is likely to[24]
break a gun or [*it*] fires further

---

verständlichsten scheint die Rückführung auf die Traglast eines 'Saum'-Tieres – also ein mittelgroßes, von z. B. einem Maultier tragbares Faß mit etwa 30-40 l Fassungsvermögen.' (Nibler, *Feuerwerkbuch*, 49)).
All of the above assumptions to '*sennig*' are unevidenced and no trace of provenance for this theory could be established. Hence, the more general translation.

[18] '*widloch*' – 'touch hole'.

[19] '*zehant*' – literally 'at hand', 'to hand' – here translated as 'immediately' (Baufeld, *Kleines frühneuhochdeutsches Wörterbuch*, 261).

[20] '*pricht*' means 'break', but presumably implies 'bursting'.

[21] '*ander*' literally means 'other', but as Early New High German does not use the cardinal number 'second', all reference works refer to this as a possible translation.

[22] This is a reference to the medieval concept of 'qualities' which – coming from Greek natural philosophy – was a concept widely accepted and commented on in the fifteenth century in Europe as a natural philosophical core principle. It subdivided nature into four qualities: 'hot', 'cold', 'dry', and 'wet' – deriving from the four elements 'fire', 'earth', 'air', and 'water'. These were seen as the core building stones in nature (*Frühneuhochdeutsches Wörterbuch*, vol. 8, 510–11). See Chapter 5 for more details.

[23] Similar to the term '*stuck*' – as explained above – this could mean anything and everything from 'piece' to 'part' or 'element' or just 'thing'.

[24] '*beld*' – 'soon', 'quickly', or more likely here 'is likely to'.

als ob man die buchsen filt piß an den
kloczen Da sprich ich wen[n] man die puchsen

fol. 3r

1 fult piß an den kloczen so mag das fewr
vnd der dunst nicht weitten gehaben den
schuß zu verbringen piß das daz fewr ain
tail hindersich auf print vnd das pulfer
5 den klocz auf slecht Ist aber die puchs
den drittail piß an den vierden geladen So
mag das pulfer gemainklich ains mals
prin[n]en vnd mag der dunst sein kraft ver=
pringen vnd schust weiter vnd pricht die
10 puchs vil ee den von dan[n] der si fult mittin
gestossem pulfer piß an den klocz

Die vierd frag ob ein linder klocz von
lindem holcz den stein paß treib oder
von hertem holcz als aichein vnd buchein
15 als vil maister prieffen vnd ob die selben

if one fills the gun right up to
the plug.[25] To that I say: if one fills the gun

fol. 3r

right up to the plug, then the fire
and the vapour do not have the width[26] to
carry the shot until the fire has partially[27]
burned down backwards[28] and the powder
has reached the plug. But if the gun
is filled by through the third part up to the fourth part, then
the powder can burn all at once.[29]
And the vapour can use its strength
and fires further and breaks[30] the
gun much more readily than if the gun
was filled with stamped powder[31] right up to the plug.

The fourth question [*is*] whether a lime[32] plug [*made*]
out of lime wood drives the stone better, or, whether
[*one made*] out of hard wood such as oak or beech [*does*],
as shown[33] by many masters. And whether

[25] '*klotz*' – can be any piece of wood for multiple uses (see definition 1 in *Frühneuhochdeutsches Wörterbuch*, vol. 8, 1147).

[26] Presumably here in a less literal sense, to have 'space' or 'room'.

[27] '*ain tail*' – here 'partially'.

[28] '*hindersich*' – here 'backwards' (Götze, *Frühneuhochdeutsches Glossar*, 122).

[29] '*gemein*' – means 'common' (*Frühneuhochdeutsches Wörterbuch*, vol. 6, 828).

[30] This section is not clear in the original. The text implies that it would be better to load the powder chamber only partially, but at the same time it implies that there is a higher risk of the gun exploding or breaking into pieces. It is a positive and negative consequence in one sentence used indiscriminately. One possible explanation is a 'higher-risk' strategy with likely better (or possibly much worse) results.

[31] This is likely a reference about whether to use wet mixed or dry mixed powder. My thanks to Clifford J. Rogers for the suggestion. It certainly seems to suggest a manufacturing process, hence the translation 'stamped' in reference to the stamp mill mentioned later.

[32] '*linder*' – could mean both 'lime', as the type of tree, and the general description of the softness. Therefore, it could also mean 'soft', but here (to compare the wood with oak and beech) it seems more likely to be lime.

[33] '*prieffen*' or '*preisen*' – ambiguous term which could be translated as 'need' or 'show'. This could be seen as equivalent to the common Latin term '*probatum est*' as in 'to demonstrate' rather than 'to have proven'.

klocz kurcz oder lanck dür oder grüen sein
süllen Sprich ich die herten klocz sein nit
gut wann dar vmb sie sein zeherte vn[d]
lassen sich nicht treiben piß auff sein
20   stat vnd behebt den dunst vil paß dan[n]
die herten kloczen Item der klocz sol
nit lenger sein dan[n] er brait seÿ die peste[n]
dürn clocz die man gehaben mag die

fol. 3v

1   mach von dürm erlem holcz Aber die pesten
grünen klocz die macht man auß grünem
erlem holcz Aber die pesten grünen klocz
macht man auß pirckeim holcz als pald
5   es von dem stain[n] gehawen wirt so mach
sie als do vor stat

Die funfft frag ob der stain ver gang
so er hort ligt Sprich ich ye herter
der stain ligt ÿe herter er get also das er
10   gar wol verschopt seÿ daß der dunst do
von nit gen mug So wirt der dunst starck
vnd schewst weit vnd hert

the said plug should be short or longer, dryer or
greener. I say: hard plugs are not
good as they are too hard and
they cannot be driven [*right*] up to its
place. And [*the softer plugs*] retain the vapour much better than
the harder plug [*would*]. Thus, the plug should not
be longer than it is broad. The best
dry[34] plugs one can have [*are those that*]

fol. 3v

one can make from dry alder wood, but the best
green plugs are made out of green
alder wood. But the best green plugs
are made out of birch wood as soon as
it has been cut from the trunk[35] and do this
as stated previously.[36]

The fifth question [*is*] whether the stone goes further
if it lies hard.[37] I say: the tighter[38]
the stone lies the more ferociously[39] it goes. It has to fit
very tightly[40] so that the vapour cannot
escape. This way, the vapour becomes strong
and it [*the gun*] fires far and hard.

---

[34] '*düren*' – can mean both 'dry' and 'thin'. At this point, 'dry' seems more likely in this context.

[35] '*stain*' or '*stam[m]*' – likely to be a scribal error in the original, as in this context it is more likely to mean '*stam*' – 'trunk', rather than '*stain*' – 'stone'.

[36] The author uses conflicting and repetitive statements, by stating first the 'best wood' is 'alder' followed by stating later the 'best wood' is 'birch'. In both cases, the author uses the superlative. It is possible that there may be a question of availability or 'even better use' but the German original does not provide an indication for that.

[37] Presumably meaning 'tighter' or 'better fitting'.

[38] '*herter*' – comparative of 'hart' – literal meaning is 'hard', but also associated with a field of connotations such as 'firm', 'solid', 'heavy', 'strong', 'fierce' or – as here – 'tight'.

[39] While the literal translation is chosen, the meaning here is likely to relate to 'further'.

[40] '*verschoppen*' – here used in the meaning of 'block'.

Die sechst frag ob ^{die} pissen do man den stein
mit verpisset von lindeim oder von

15 hertem holcz sull sein sprich ich welcher
stain gerecht in die puchsen gehort vnd
er nit mer weitin het dan[n] er bedarff
vnd er getrang lugen můß so solt du in
verpissen mit dünnem hertem pissem von

20 aichem holcz Ist aber der stein etwas zu
klein das er nit also getragt ligt so solt
du in verpissen mit dunnen pissen

Die sibend frag ob die selben pissen dick

fol. 4r

1 oder dün[n] sein sullen von dünem holcz sprich
ich das die selben pissen dick oder dün[n]e
sullen sein von dunnem holcz Aber wenn
du den stein do mit verpissest so solt du in
pissen mit aim schrot eÿsen an dem stain

5 ab haw[e]n also das die pissen nit fur den
stain gangen

Die achtend frag war mit man den
stain verschoppen sull das der dunst

Royal Armouries I.34 – Part 1

The sixth question [*is*] whether the wedges[41] which one uses
to wedge in the stone should be [*made*] out of soft[42] wood or
hard wood. I say: [*make sure*] the
stone fits properly in the gun and
it [*the stone*] has not got more girth than it needs
and that it has to fit tightly. Then[43] you have to
wedge it in with thin hard wedges of
oak wood. But if the stone is a little too
small so that it does not fit tightly, then you should
wedge it in with thin wedges.[44]

The seventh question [*is*] whether the same wedges

fol. 4r

should be thick or thin when [*they are made*] out of fir wood. I say:
That wedges shall be thick or thin
[*when they are made*] out of fir wood.[45] But if
you do wedge in the stone with this [*wood*], then make
sure you cut it off with a small piece of iron[46] at the stone
so that the wedges do not
go beyond[47] the stone.

The eighth question [*is*] with what one
should block the stone so that the vapour

---

[41] '*pissen*' – see *Frühneuhochdeutsches Wörterbuch*, vol. 4, 482: in the sense of 'a piece' ('*Brocken, Stückchen*') or more specifically (Götze, *Frühneuhochdeutsches Glossar*, 34) '*bisse*' – '*Keil*' – 'wedge'.

[42] 'lime' – here 'soft'.

[43] In the meaning of 'in that case'.

[44] The last two sentences are contradictions. It has to be either one or the other, and both cannot be right. This must be down to a scribal error.

[45] The 'answer' to this question seems to be a contradiction. It could be read that the author expresses preferences that one would be better than the other, but in the end it does not make that much difference.

[46] See Christa Baufeld, *Kleines frühneuhochdeutsches Wörterbuch. Lexik aus Dichtung und Fachliteratur des Frühneuhochdeutschen* (Tübingen: Max Niemeyer, 1996): '*schrot*' – 'a small, cut-off piece' ('*abgeschnittenes Stück*').

[47] '*fur*' in the meaning of 'in front of' or 'ahead' ('*vor*').

do von gen mug Sprich ich nym wachs
10   vnd wechse ein tuch do mit vnd tu es ein=
fach zu aim sail vnd schopp das mit eim
guten schoppeysen zwischen dem stain vnd
die puchsen auf die pissen so vert es ver.

Die newnd frag ob ain puchs weiter
15   schieß von zweÿerleÿ pulfer dan[n] von
ainerleÿ wan[n] du die puchsen ladest vnd
verschiessen wilt So lug das du habst
zwayerleÿ puluer vnd tu das gut pul=
fer an den poden vnd das pöß dar auff
20   so scheüst du weiter wan[n] mit ainem wan[n]
       das tut die widerwertikeyt baid[er] pulf[er]

Die zehend frag ob der stain den klocze[n]

fol. 4v

1   an rüeren sol oder nit Sprich ich der stein
sol hert an dem kloczen ligen Du solt den
kloczen nemen vnd solt in mit ainem tŭch
bewinden vnd solt den klocz vnter augen
5   prennen das tail das gegen dem stain
gehort vmb das daz er hört werd vnd
lad den stain hört dar an vnd verpiß
vnd verschopp den wol das in der dunst
gemainklich treiben muß

10   **D**ie aylft frag ob das pulfer posser seÿ
zu tun in die puchsen knollen pulfer

Royal Armouries I.34 – Part 1

can escape.[48] I say: take wax
and wax a piece of cloth with it and make it simply
into a rope and stuff it, with a
good ramrod, between the stone and
the gun around the wedge, then it will go far.

The ninth question [*is*] whether a gun fires
further with two types of powder than with
one type. When you load a gun and
want to fire it make sure that you have
two types of powder and put the good
powder at the bottom and the inferior on top:
then you fire further than with one [*type of powder*], as this
is done by the opposing characteristics of the two powders.

The tenth question [*is*] whether the stone should touch

fol. 4v

the plug or not. I say: the stone
should be hard against the plug. You should
take the plug and should wrap it in a piece of cloth
and should – while watching carefully[49] – burn that part
of the plug that belongs next to the stone
so that it becomes hard. And
load the stone tightly against it and push
and wedge it thoroughly so that the vapour must
force it out as usual.[50]

The eleventh question [*is*] whether the powder is better
to put in the gun if it is *Knollenpulver*[51]

---

[48] This may be viewed as a contradiction, as previously the author insists on making sure that the vapour cannot escape. However, in order to enable a projectile to be propelled, there needs to be one direction in which the vapour can escape.

[49] '*unter Augen*' – meaning 'carefully, not leaving it out of one's sight'.

[50] '*gemainklich*' – as in 'commonly', implying that this is the case unless something unexpected happens.

[51] Or, 'lumped powder'. As *Knollenpulver* and corning have a major influence in the development of gunpowder, it was decided to leave this in the original. See Chapter 5 for a detailed discussion on *Knollenpulver*.

oder gestossen pulfer Sprich ich das knol=
len pulfer zwaÿ pfunt mer tun dan[n] ge
stossen pulfer dreÿ pfunt gethon mochten
15 Aber du solt das knollen pulfer beraiten
vnd machen als in disem puch hernach
geschriben stet

Die zwelft frag wie scharrer stain
ein pfunt pulfer mit seiner kraft
20 gewerffen müg vnd was sein recht
trag seÿ Sprich ich ain puchs seÿ groß
oder clein so sol alweg ein pfunt pulfers
ain newn pfundigen stain treiben ist

fol. 5r

1 auch des stains mÿnder so vil get auch
des pulfers ab **Hernach stet geschri=**
ben wie man salpetter sieden sol

Wiltu salpetter sieden So nym starcke
5 laug als hie nach geschriben ist
vnd tu den salpetter dar ain vnd laß den
als lang sieden als man visch seut vnd
geuß in dan[n] ab in ein schon beckin vnd
laß in kald werden und schut die laug
10 wider ab dem salpetter wider in das keslin
vnd laß das sieden piß der halbtail oder

Royal Armouries I.34 – Part 1

or ground powder.[52] I say: two pounds of
Knollenpulver can do more than
three pounds of compressed powder could do.
But you should prepare the *Knollenpulver*
and make it as it is written in this book
below.

The twelfth question [*is*] how one pound of powder
can propel a heavy[53] stone with
its force and what its right weight might be.
I say: a gun may be large
or small and always one pound of powder
should propel a nine pound stone [*ball*].

fol. 5r

If the stone [*ball*] is smaller, then powder will be reduced
as well.[54] **After this is written
how one should boil saltpetre.**

If you want to boil saltpetre take strong
lye as is described later
and place the saltpetre therein and let it
boil for as long as one poaches fish. And
then drain it into a decent basin and
let it cool down and remove the lye
and replace the saltpetre in the small pot
and let it boil until half or

---

[52]   There is little indication about the status of the powder. The original refers to the
fact that the powder was ground, but not that it is still in powder format. A comparative format is required to distinguish it from the *Knollenpulver*. Other *Firework
Books* refer to this powder as *'geräden'* ('powder pushed through a sieve' – Freiburg
Ms. 362), *'gereden'* (possibly 'ground by a wheel' – Dresden Ms. App. 463 or Heidelberg, Cod. Pal. germ. 585 or 502), while others, such as Heidelberg, Cod. Pal. germ.
122, also have *'gestossen'*.

[53]   *'scharrer'* – possible scribal error, as a misspelling. A missing *'w'* would make it *'schwer'* – 'heavy' as it is implied from the context that this term relates to the weight of
the stone. Other *Firework Books* such as Dresden Ms. App. 463 or Freiburg Ms.
362 refer to it as *'swerer'* (fol. 13r) or *'schwärer'* (fol. 74v) – 'heavy'.

[54]   Likely to mean that the smaller the ball, the less powder will be required to propel
it. It is not clear from the original whether there is an assumption that the size of
both reduces in the same proportions.

der viertail ain seüt vnd laß das dann
kalt werden vnd schut es dan[n] aber ab
vnd der[re] dar nach den salpetter vast wol
15   ee du in mischest also solt du guten salpet=
ter leutern der vor zwirunt oder dreÿstunt
geleutert ist worden **Aber wie man
salpetter sieden sol**

Wiltu salpeter leutern einen zentner
20   minder oder mer so nÿm lauter
wasser oder wein vnd tu den salpetter
dar ain also das der salpetter nit weiß
werd vnd daß das wasser ploß ainen

fol. 5v

1   finger fur den salpeter auf gang vnd tu in
über ein fewr vnd so er anfach zu sieden so
tu zu ainem zentner ain lb Salarmoniack
vnd sechs lot spengrüen oder als vil gute[n]
5   galiczen vnd seud in in der leng als do vor
geschriben ist vnd geuß das dan[n] ab vnd
laß den salpetter gesten vnd tu dann das
wasser wider über das fewr vnd seud das
dann aber also lang als vor ainen halben

a quarter has been boiled off. And let it
cool down and pour it off again
and take the saltpetre and dry it well[55]
before you mix it. In this way you can purify good
saltpetre which has [already] been purified twice or
three times. **But how one
should boil saltpetre.**

If you want to purify a hundredweight,
more or less, then take clear
water[56] or wine and add the saltpetre to it
so that the saltpetre does not turn white
and that the water comes to only one

fol. 5v

finger above the saltpetre. And put it
over a fire and when it starts to boil
add to the hundredweight one pound of salammoniac[57]
and six lots[58] of verdigris[59] and just as much [*i.e. the same quantity*] of
stone of Galicia[60] and boil it for as long as has been[61]
stated above and pour it off. And
let the saltpetre rest and place
the water over the fire again and boil
it down as long until [*it reduces to*] one half of

---

[55] '*vast*' – 'strong' (Alfred Götze, *Frühneuhochdeutsches Glossar*, 7th edn (Berlin: de Gruyter, 1967), 73: '*stark*').

[56] '*lauter*' could mean 'clean', or solely 'not diluted with foreign substances, clear' ('*lauteres wasser*').

[57] Salammoniac appears in a number of places in this and other *Firework Books*. There has been some speculation about what it actually relates to and what chemical reaction it would incur. According to Kramer and Nibler, this refers to 'ammonium chloride, NH_4Cl' (Kramer and Leibnitz, *Das Feuerwerkbuch*, 31, and Nibler, *Feuerwerkbuch*, 52).

[58] One '*lot*' equals half an ounce. Imperial measures: 1 pound = 16 ounces = 32 lot; i.e. three ounces.

[59] According to Kramer and Leibnitz, *Das Feuerwerkbuch*, 31: 'basic Cu^{++} acetate', or 'Copper(II) acetate', also referred to as 'cupric acetate'.

[60] According to Kramer and Leibnitz, *Das Feuerwerkbuch*, 31: 'zinc sulphate, $ZnSO_4$' – according to Nibler, *Feuerwerkbuch*, 12: 'most commonly iron or zinc sulphate'.

[61] Scribal error – duplication of '*in*' – or not – could be '*ihn in*' = 'it in'.

10 tail ein vnd tu aber ain pfunt salarmo=
niack her in vnd so es gesüed als vor stet
so schut es dan[n] ab vnd laß es gesten Erst
hast du den aller pessten salpetter den ÿe=
mant gehaben mag besunder so laß in jn
15 dem geschür wol ertrucknen vnd wen[n] du
jn also geleütert hast so schait er sich **Wie
man das weit schüessent pulfer macht**

Wiltu das aller pest pulfer machen
zu ainem weitten schuß so nym[m] iii
20 pfunt salpetters ain pfunt grauß swebels
czwen vierdung koln ain halb saitit arse=
nicu[m] albu[m] vnd stoß das ein clein zusamen=
vnd nÿme ain quertlein guczs gepranczs=

fol. 6r

1 weins vnd ein settet campfer vnd laß es
wider ain ander sieden vnd wenn es kalt
werd so schut es vnder das pulfer vnd stoß
das ab vnd laß es wol trucken so haustu
5 das weit schiessent pulfer so man es fin=
den mag **Aber wie man gut pulfer
machen sol**

Wiltu das aller sterckst pulfer mach
en das nÿemant gemachen kan

it, and add a pound of salammoniac
to it. When it has been reduced as before
pour it out and let it rest.
This way you have the best saltpetre that
anyone could find. Especially if you let it
dry well in the bowl, and when you have
thus purified it, it will separate.[62] **How
to make long-range firing powder.**

If you want to make the best powder of all
to fire a long distance, take three
pounds of saltpetre, one pound of grey sulphur,
two quarters of charcoal, and half a settit[63] of *arsenicum
album*[64] and grind them up together.
Take a quart[65] of good brandy

fol. 6r

and a settit of camphor[66] and bring it
to boil so that it reduces. And when it has cooled down
pour it into the powder [*mixed earlier*] and grind it together
and let it dry well. This way you have
the powder with the longest range you can
find.[67] **But how you make good
powder.**

If you want to make the strongest powder of all
that no one [*else*] can make,

---

[62] There are a number of stages of processes to happen here, but the crucial one is the precipitation. For more details see Chapter 5.

[63] 1 settit = ¼ lot = 4 grams (see fol. 10r, or Kramer and Leibnitz, *Das Feuerwerkbuch*, 40; and also Nibler, *Feuerwerkbuch*, 20 n132).

[64] According to Kramer and Leibnitz, *Das Feuerwerkbuch*, 40, 'arsenic oxide, AS_2O_3', according to Nibler, *Feuerwerkbuch* it is 'AS_4O_6' – but the rationale for either is not explained.

[65] The author uses a diminutive of '*quart*' which could be used as a term of endearment or a sign for brandy to be viewed as precious.

[66] According to Kramer and Leibnitz, *Das Feuerwerkbuch*, 40: '$C_{10}H_{16}O$'.

[67] The challenge with this statement is how this could possibly be verified. The range depends on a variety of different factors, and adding additional ingredients to the basic mixture of gunpowder is unlikely to make much difference.

10	so nÿm[m] drew pfunt salpetters ains pfunt
	grauß swebels zwen[n] vierdung koln als
	vor vnd misch das vnter ain ander vnd
	tu das in ein glesslin vnd laß das den[n] sten
	vnd nym[m] rat Salarmoniack album vnd
15	vnd pulfer vnd tu das vnder ain ander
	vnd das in ein gleslin uber ein gefug fewr
	vnd rwr das vnder ain ander ein halbe stu[n]d
	vnd nÿm[m] starcken gepranten wein vnd=
	schut des ein aÿr schal vol vnder das pul=
20	pulfer in das gleslin vnd rwr es vnter
	ein ander piß das pulfer wider trucken
	werd vnd misch das den[n] vnter ain ander
	vnd stoß das vil wol vnd lad den drittail

fol. 6v

| 1 | der puchsen do mit **Wie man verdorben** |
| | **pulfer wider pringt** |

	Ist ain pulfer verdorben von alter vnd
	ist der salpetter dennoch dar in gut
5	so nÿm[m] das pulfer vnd seud das mit wein
	vnd rwr das vast piß das es sich vor dick=
	en nit wöl lassen rwren vnd tu dan[n] dar
	zu frisch koln als vil du sein bedarfft vnd
	tu das dan[n] in ein guten hare[n]sack vnd=
10	henck den sack dan[n] in ein haisse stuben=

then take three pounds of saltpetre, one pound
of grey sulphur, two quarters of charcoal as before
and mix it together. And
put it into a small glass and let it rest.
Take 'red'[68] *arsenicum album*[69] and[70]
the powder [*mixed earlier*] and mix them together.
And put it into a little glass vessel over a tepid fire
and stir it together for half an hour.
Take strong brandy and
add an egg shell full of it to the
powder[71] in the little glass and stir it together
until the powder dries up again.
And mix it together
and grind it all well and load a third [*of it*]

fol. 6v

into a gun. **How you bring back powder
that has been spoiled.**

When powder has been spoiled because of age and the
saltpetre in it nevertheless is still good,
then take the powder and boil it with wine
and stir strongly until it has thickened
to the point when it cannot be stirred anymore. And add
as much fresh charcoal as necessary
and put it into a good hairy sack[72] and
hang the sack in a heated room

---

[68] The original is 'rat' not 'rot', which does not make sense in this context. Comparison with other *Firework Book* manuscripts shows this error frequently, which indicates a steady copying culture. Just to make it more complicated, Nibler believes it should be 'lot' not 'rot', which was carried through in other copies, but with exceptions such as Munich Clm. 30150 (Nibler, *Feuerwerkbuch*, 55n114).

[69] This is described by Kramer and Leibnitz, *Das Feuerwerkbuch*, 40, as 'white salammoniac [NH_4Cl]'. However, no evidence is provided for this assumption.

[70] Likely scribal error, '*vnd*' repeated.

[71] Likely scribal error, '*pul*' written twice.

[72] A '*hairy sack*', according to the definition provided in the *Frühneuhochdeutsches Wörterbuch*, relates to a 'bag made out of coarse, simple material, and possibly animal hair' (*Frühneuhochdeutsches Wörterbuch Online*, http://fwb-online.de/go/h%C3%A4ren. h2.4adj_1544513501).

piß das das pulfer wol ertrucken **Wie ma[n] poße von ain**
ander schaidet vnd wider
       pringt

Wiltu pöß pulfer von ain an=
der schaiden vnd wider pringen

15   vnd ist auch das gewißest so nym[m] das=
pulfer vnd tu das in ain zwilchein sack
vnd tu wein in ein kesel vnd seud das dar
dar uber gang vnd henck den sack mit
dem pulfer dar ain so get der salpeter

20   in den wein vnd beleibt der swebel in dem
sack vnd schut den[n] den wein ab so er kalt
werd vnd nym[m] den salpetter auß vnd seud
den wein anders vnd tu Salarmoniack

fol. 7r

1   dar zu so schait es sich **Wie man gut fewr=**
kugeln die man auß der puchsen scheust
gerecht vnd gut beraitten vnd dar zu=
machen sol das man die auß der puchse[n]

5   **schießen mug**

Wiltu gar gut fewr kugeln machen
die man auß der puchsen schust so
so nÿm[m] buchsen pulfer als vil du wilt
vnd knit das mit gebrantem wein vnd

10   mach ainen taig dar auß der sinwell seÿ
als ain kugel vnd nÿm[m] dreÿ heslein steb
vnd die stoß důch die kugeln vnd solt die

until the powder has dried well. **How you
separate [*the components of*] bad [*powder*] from one
another and how you bring it [*the powder*] back.**

If you want to separate bad powder
from other [*not bad powder*] and want to bring it back,
then this is the most certain [*way*]. Take the
powder and put it in a cotton cloth bag.[73]
And put wine in a pot and bring it to boil[74]
and hang in it the bag with
the powder so that the saltpetre
goes into the wine and the sulphur remains
in the sack. Then drain the wine and allow it to
cool down. Take the saltpetre out of the wine and boil
the wine once more and add salammoniac[75]

fol. 7r

so that it subdivides itself. **How you make good
fireballs which can be shot from a gun
well and properly and
how you shoot them out
of a gun.**

If you want to make good fire balls
which can be fired from a gun,
take as much gunpowder as you want
and mix it with brandy and
make it into paste as round
as a ball. Take three sticks of hazel wood
and push them through the ball. Wrap the

---

[73] '*zwilchin*' – could be cotton or linen, but more likely in the fifteenth century to be linen; the main advantage is that it is rather thick and strong compared to '*barchant*' – see Note 76; in Götze, *Frühneuhochdeutsches Glossar*, 240: 'of minor quality' ('*aus geringen Stoff*').

[74] '*Seud das dar uber gang*' – while technically the boiling of water is absolute, how to boil water in practice has a range of different levels, and is not always clear to explain. As in present-day general context, people may refer to 'strongly boiling', 'slightly boiling', or 'simmering', which is mirrored in the *Firework Book* text. The author frequently describes it as 'boiling over' or 'boiling hard'.

[75] Kramer and Leibnitz, *Das Feuerwerkbuch*, 39: 'NH_4Cl'.

kugeln über ziechen mit barchat vnd den[n]
in swebel swem[m]en vnd aber uber ziechen
15 mit taig der mit halb salpetter vnd halb
swebel gemischt seÿ vnd uber zeuch das
aber mit dacken vnd zu dem jungsten mal
über zeuch sie mit ludern die zwilchein
sein vnd mit eÿsnem trat crewcz weiß
20 dar über vnd den[n] so swem[m]e die kugeln in
halb swebel vnd halb harcz vnd wenn
sie bereit sein so var mit ainem negwerlein
crewcz weiß ~~dar~~ durch die kugeln vnd

fol. 7v

1   wen[n] du schiessen wilt so por ein lochlein
durch den clocz vnd geleich die lochlein ge=
gen ain ander sechen vnd nÿm[m] dan[n] ain=
kleins rütlein vnd stoß es durch die kugeln
5   vnd durch den klocz ein das pulfer das du
verschiessen wilt das es ein ander geleich
zu sag vnd zund dan[n] die buchs an **Wie**
man ain schreckenden schuß ~~tu~~ schuessen
vnd machen sol das der stain über hun=
10 **dert spring tut wan[n] er von der puchse[n]**
vert

Wiltu ainen schreckenden
schuß tun oder schuessen so nÿm[m]
schrencz pappir vnd leim die auff ander

ball in fustian cloth[76] and then
soak it in sulphur. And wrap the paste
again [*around the ball*] which is a mixture of half
saltpetre and half sulphur and cover it once again
with cloth. And, for the final time, wrap it
with cloth [*made*] out of coarse material.
And wrap iron wire in a crosswise mesh around it
and submerge the ball in
half sulphur and half resin and when
they are ready drive a drill[77]
crosswise through the ball. And

fol. 7v

when you want to fire it drill a hole
through the plug and align the holes
with each other [*ball and plug*]. Take a
little rod[78] and push it through the ball
and through the plug that you
want to fire so that they appear to be
the same [*piece*].[79] And then set light to the gun. **How
you fire a frightening shot
and how you make a stone bounce
over a hundred [*times*] when it comes out of the
gun.**

If you want to make a frightening
shot and fire it, take
shredded paper[80] and glue it together

---

[76] '*barchant*' or '*barchent*' – variety of heavy cloth, made out of cotton (*Frühneuhoch-deutsches Wörterbuch Online*, http://fwb-online.de/go/barchent.s.0m_1543669452).

[77] '*negber*' or '*nebegêr*' – drill (*Mittelhochdeutsches Wörterbuch* von Beneke, Müller, Zarn-ke). See also Nibler, *Feuerwerkbuch*: '*nägberli*' => '*nägborlin*' => '*Nägbor*' = '*Bohrer*' – 'drill', Schmeller, *Bayerisches Wörterbuch*, I, 1733. The modern expression would be '*Nagelbohrer*' (see n. 130, Nibler, *Feuerwerkbuch*).

[78] This could act as a fuse.

[79] Meaning 'appearing to be as one piece'.

[80] Nibler, *Feuerwerkbuch*: '*schrentz bapyr*' = '*schrentz papyr*' => '*Schrenzdeckel: Pappen-deckel aus zusammengeleimtem Fließpapier*', *Bayerisches Wörterbuch*, Vols 1 and 2, ed. Johann Andreas Schmeller (München: Oldenbourg, 1872–77 [2008]), http://publikationen.badw.de/de/022964277.pdf and http://publikationen.badw.de/de/

als groß der clocz sein sol vnd schlach den
15   cloczen nit auff das pulfer vnd auch nit
gar in das ror der puchsen vnd lad den
stain für den kloczen vnd verpiß den stain
die selben pissen schlach ab auff dem stain
vnd verschopp denn den stain mit gehörte[m]
20   tůch vnd richt die puchsen in geleich ge=
leich gewicht vnd zund sie an so last d[er]
stain vnd tut über hundert spring vnd
die buchs sol vorn an dich sein vnd wol

fol. 8r

1   ein geschlagen vnd sol nit für den stain

gen

**Wie man salpetter ziechen sol dz
er gar vil posser wechst den[n] er an den
mauren tut**

5   **W**iltu machen das der salpetter pößer
wechst den[n] an den muren so haiß
dir machen ein rören als groß du wilt
die vol cleiner lochlein seÿ vnd nym[m] wein
staine ain pfunt vnd ain pfunt salcz oder

so that it is as big as the plug is meant to be.[81] And do not drive the
plug flush on top of the powder or also not into the
barrel of the gun. And load the
stone [*ball*] in front of the plug and wedge in the stone [*ball*].
[*Make sure that you*] remove any wedges which are on top of the stone.
And plug the stone tight with hardened
cloth and point the gun level[82]
and light it so that it presses against the
stone. It will bounce over a hundred [*times*][83]
and the gun shall be thick[84] at the front[85] and

fol. 8r

it [*the plug*] should be hammered in properly and should not go
in flush against the stone.

**How you grow saltpetre so
that it grows much better than when it grows
on the walls.**

If you want to cause the saltpetre to grow
better than on the walls, then have made
for yourself[86] a tube as large as you would like
which is full of little holes. And take
a pound of cream of tartar[87] and a pound of salt or

022964287.pdf, II, 609 (both accessed 10 August 2023), and Baufeld, *Kleines früh-neuhochdeutsches Wörterbuch*, 211.

[81] Here the meaning is likely to refer to the size being the same as that of the plug.

[82] Presumably scribal error, repetition of '*geleich*'.

[83] Hundred – no measurement given, is it likely to be a distance or the number of bounces.

[84] Presumed to be '*dick*' – 'thick' – not clear from context. Likely to be a scribal error.

[85] '*dich*' or '*dicht*' – 'close to you' or 'in front' (*Frühneuhochdeutsches Wörterbuch*, vol. 5, 588).

[86] The use of terms in the original comes across as a strong emphasis to say 'have made for yourself' or 'have yourself made', rather than only 'have made'. See Chapter 5 for discussion.

[87] According to *Dictionary of Chemical Technology*, '*Weinstein*' or '*Weinsaures Kalium*' is the equivalent to Potassium Bitartrate, potassium hydrogen tartratec, or KH-$C_4H_4O_6$ – a by-product of winemaking. During fermentation it crystallizes in wine casks, and may appear in wine in bottles.

10	geleich als des weinsteins vnd kalck dreÿ=
	stund als vil vnd ains mans harm der
	wein trinckt vnd mach ain dick muß do
	mit vnd tu es in die rören vnd vnd laß
	es dreÿ tag an der sun[n]en sten vnd geuß
15	an dem vierden tag herwider auß vnd
	henck die rören in ainen koler so wechst
	guter salpetter her auß **Welch specie**
	puchsen pulfer schnel vnd starck macht

	Lebendiger swebel vnd gutes këcksilber
20	mach gewicht gemessen so dan[n] dar
	zu gehort sind baide vast gut zu dem
	pulfer zu weittreibenden schiessen von der
	puchsen **Wie man salpetter gerecht**

fol. 8v

1	**sieden vnd leutern sol**

	Wiltu salpetter sieden vnd gerecht
	leutern so nym[m] lebendigen kalck
	vnd tu den in regen wasser oder in schon
5	wasser vnd laß in sten dreÿ tag so wirt
	ein laug do von die laug nÿm[m] lauter

Royal Armouries I.34 – Part 1

the same as the cream of tartar[88] and three
times the amount of chalk and the urine of a man
who drinks wine. Make a thick paste with these
and put it in the tube and[89] let
it stand in the sun for three days.
On the fourth day pour[90] the contents out
and hang the tube in a cellar and good
saltpetre will grow out of it. **Which ingredients make gunpowder fast and strong.**

Native sulphur[91] and good mercury,
weighed accordingly[92] in appropriate parts,[93] they belong to
[*the powder*] both put together, [*and*] added to the
powder so that the gun fires
a long distance. **How you boil saltpetre properly**

fol. 8v

and purify it.

If you want to boil saltpetre and purify it
Properly, then take quicklime[94]
and add it to rainwater or other pure
water and let it rest for three days, then
it turns to lye.[95] Take the lye, which is proper

---

[88] Possible scribal error; Freiburg Ms. 362 lists only ½ pound of salt – the reference here is a duplication and does not make sense.

[89] Presumably scribal error, repetition of '*vnd*', not translated.

[90] The original German '*geuß*' indicates a decanting action of a liquid, but at this stage the paste would be quite hard and impossible to pour, and the term could simply mean 'empty out'. For purpose of accuracy, the original German intention has been retained.

[91] '*Lebendiger Schwefel*' has also been described as '*Jungfernschwefel*' or '*natürlicher Schwefel*' ('virgin sulphur' or 'native sulphur') – Jacob and Wilhelm Grimm, *Deutsches Wörterbuch von Jacob und Wilhelm Grimm Online* – accessed 10 August 2023.

[92] Presumably a scribal error. '*mach*' could mean a verb 'make'. It is more likely from the context to be '*nach*'.

[93] Presumably meaning 'in equal parts'.

[94] Calcium oxide, CaO – literally 'living limestone'.

[95] Likely to turn into $Ca(OH)s$ – calcium hydroxide, Kramer and Leibnitz, *Das Feuerwerkbuch*, 31.

vnd schon vnd tu den wilden salpetter
dar ain der vor nit gestossen vnd geleu=
tert ist vnd seud in piß das das viertail
10   des wassers einsied vnd spreng den[n] ein
wenig des wassers auff die gelauenden
koln get ein ploß fewr do von so hat es
sein genug vnd geuß den[n] das wasser ab
in ein hilczeins vaß vnd laß es kalt wer=
15   den so vinst du guten gerechten salpetter
an dem grunde **Wie man gar ein mai=**
sterlich nucz gut starck vnd schnel puch=
sen pulfer machen sull

Wiltu gut puchsen pulfer machen
20   das do nucz gut schnel vnd starck
wirt so nym[m] dar zu ein pfunt guczs sweb=
els vnd ain viertail ains pfundes guczs
lindeins kolns von lindem oder von den[n]em

fol. 9r

1   holcze dan an este seÿ gewessen vnd wellest
du des pulfers mer machen so wig die
vorgenanten specie nach gewicht vnd r[er]r
nit dar in aber du tust ein werck das nichczs
5   verfacht vnd merck vast wol ain halber
zentner pulfers zeucht dreyßig pfunt
swebels vnd dreyzehenthalb pfunt kols
vnd dreÿ pfunt spengrüen vnd ein vier=
tail ains pfundes Salarmoniack vnd so
10   vil ains mals man des pulfers mache[n]
wil denn als vor geschriben stet so vil
muß man auch der vor genanten specie
yedlichs nach seinem gerechten gewicht

Royal Armouries I.34 – Part 1

and pure, and add the raw[96] saltpetre
which has not previously been crushed or purified to the lye
and boil the mixture until a quarter of
the water has boiled away. Then sprinkle a
small amount of the water on to some glowing
charcoal. If a blue flame appears, then it has
had enough. Pour the water off
into a wooden barrel and let it cool down
and you will find good and proper saltpetre
at the bottom. **How you make
masterful, strong, and fast gun
powder.**

If you want to make good gunpowder
that can be useful, good, fast, and strong,
then take a pound of good sulphur
and a quarter of a pound of good
lime wood charcoal of a lime tree or from thin

fol. 9r

wood which used to have branches. And if you want to
make more of the powder then weigh up the
aforementioned ingredients as per their weight and mix
nothing in it,[97] as you make a product that does not
weaken.[98] And make sure that a good half
hundredweight of powder is made up[99] with thirty pounds of
sulphur, and thirteen and a half pounds of charcoal,
and three pounds of verdigris, and a quarter
of a pound of salammoniac. As
often as you want to make more of this powder,
as is stated above, you must again take
the same quantity of the above ingredients
each in its correct

---

[96] Or 'wild' – in the sense of unpurified or 'as it can be found in nature'.

[97] Likely to mean that nothing should be added to the mixture.

[98] *'verfachen'* – with the meaning of 'ephemeral', 'evaporate', or 'spoiled', but more likely 'weaken'. The negative used implies that it is powder which is good to be used for a long time without significant loss in quality.

[99] From *'zeugen'* – 'to make, or to bear', but more likely here meant figuratively as 'made up'.

mer nÿemen **Wie man noch ain posser**
15 **puchsen pulfer machen sol**

Wiltu ain gut puchsen pulfer mach=
en das noch pesser vnd stercker
wirt den[n] von dem das do vor geschriben
stet so solt du nÿemem dar zu als vor
20 beschaiden ist vnd gehort dar zu vnd
dar in zu nÿemen ein gut weiß pulfer
das solt du also machen als hie nach=
geschriben stett Nim[m] des gepranten

fol. 9v

1 Campfer der do ist weiß ain tail vnd gebra[n]=
ten salarmoniack das do auch weiß ist vnd
leuchtet als die prawnen stain so die swert
focker haben acht tail vnd tu der czweÿer
5 specie von sublimato vnd merturio dar
zu vnd tu das zu samen in ein morser
vnd stoß das als vast dir mügst vncz es
ein pulfer werd vnd piß das es weiß
wirt vnd ist die aller pest lere die man
10 in ganczer alchamie vinden mag vnd tu
gar wenig von dem pulfer in das daz do
gemacht ist von salpetter swebel vnd

Royal Armouries I.34 – Part 1

proportions.[100] **How you make an even better gunpowder.**

If you want to make a good gunpowder
that becomes better and stronger
than that stated above
then take as before all the ingredients
proportionally and put them together
and take the ingredients and turn it
into good white powder as is written
below. Take one part of burnt

fol. 9v

camphor which is white and eight parts
of burnt salammoniac which is also white
and which glows as the brown stone[101]
that is used by a sword furbisher.[102] Add two
types of *sublimato*[103] and mercury
and place it into a mortar
and grind it together as much as possible until it
become a powder and turns white.[104]
This is the best recipe[105] that can be found in
all of alchemy. Add a little bit of the powder
to the one you made of
saltpetre, sulphur, and

---

[100] This section is a reminder about the nature of this role. The author makes sure to remind the reader that trying out different recipes is not advisable.

[101] Nibler believes this to be a 'sword furbisher's stone' ('*Terminus technicus der Schwertfeger*'), literally a 'brown stone' ('*brauner Stein, [...] der leuchtet*'), citing as reference points Weimar *Firework Book* '*prawn stein*' and the Memmingen text as '*brun stain*', discrediting at the same time Hassenstein's argument that this may refer to a 'stone from a well' ('*Brunnenstein*'), as the term in the two different surviving prints is '*Prunnenstein*' (Nibler, *Feuerwerkbuch*, n. 116). I translated this as 'brown stone' as the actual meaning is unclear.

[102] This connection between a brown stone and sword making may be mirrored in Nibler's suggestion of a possible connection between brown stone and someone involved in the finishing stages of the production of a sword.

[103] $HgCl_2$ – mercury chloride (Kramer and Leibnitz, *Das Feuerwerkbuch*, 43).

[104] This is a very unlikely recipe. Charcoal has the tendency to turn any mixture black.

[105] Or 'instruction'.

koln nach dem als dich die wag lert
ain achten tail ains lotes ist genug in
15   ein pfunt der vor genanten pulfer sal=
petter swebels vnd kolns

Ganner ist gar kestenlich in der appo=
tecken geprenter salarmoniack ist
weiß vnd leich vnd vint man es in der
20   appotecken Salarmoniack der nit geprent
ist der ist an der gestalt als lanter zuck=
er vnd vint man es in der appotecken

fol. 10r

1   Atriment ist swerczlot vnd vint ma[n]
es in der appotecken vitriolum romanu[m]
ist nit kosper vnd vint man es inder appo=
teken Sublimatus mercurius ist zu teutsch
5   geret als vil als kecksilber weisser sweb=
el hat ainen vnder schaid es ist vnter
dem weissen einer pösser dan[n] der ander
Merck vol eben arsenicu[m] spricht zu teutsch
opperment vnd ist nit kosper in der appo=
10   tecken Jaspanicum spricht zu teutsch spen=

charcoal as the scales teach you.
One eighth of a lot[106] is enough for
a pound of the aforementioned powder of saltpetre,
sulphur, and charcoal.

Camphor[107] is very pricey in the apothecary.
Burnt salammoniac is white and
light and can be found in the
apothecary. Unburnt salammoniac
has a structure like purified sugar
and can be found in the apothecary.

fol. 10r

Atramentum[108] is deep black and can be
found in the apothecary. *Vitriolum romanum*
is not precious and can be found in the apothecary.
Sublimatus mercurius which in German means as much as
mercury.[109] White sulphur
is different from other [*sulphurs*], it is among the
white [*sulphurs*] better than others.
Note carefully as well that *arsenicum* is called in German
orpiment and it is not expensive in an apothecary.
Jaspanicum, or in German verdigris,[110]

---

[106] '$\frac{1}{30}$ or $\frac{1}{32}$ of a pound', or according to *Frühneuhochdeutsches Wörterbuch*, vol. 9.1, 1408, '1 lot usually is equivalent to ½ ounce, $\frac{1}{14}$ of a mark, or $\frac{1}{32}$ of a pound of weight' ('*1 Lot entsprach in der Regel einer halben Unze, einem Vierzehntel einer Mark, einem Zweiunddreißigstel eines Gewichtpfundes*').

[107] Other *Firework Books* refer to this as '*gauncy*', '*gani*', '*saucy*', '*aney*', '*sanei*' – but it was decided here to refer to this as 'camphor' (*Frühneuhochdeutsches Wörterbuch Online*, http://www.fwb-online.de/go/kampfer.h2.0m_1513374772).

[108] *Atrimentum*, or *Atramentum*, atrament, or atriment: a black liquid, often used for dyeing leather or in painting. See also reference to 'atramentous' and its definition of 'black as ink'. Partington refers to it as 'ink' (Partington, *Greek Fire and Gunpowder*, 155). It is 'black liquid, mixture or solution of $CuSO_4$ and iron sulfate'. Its use was for medication and as dyeing ink ('*schwarze Flüssigkeit; [...] Gemisch aus $CuSO_4$ und Eisensulfat bzw. deren Hydraten [...], die in Wasser gelöst diese dunkel färben [...] Verwendung als Heilmittel, Schusterschärze (zum Färben des Leders), Tinte*', *Frühneuhochdeutsches Wörterbuch Online*, http://fwb-online.de/go/atrament.s.2n_1543646551).

[109] Earlier in the text, fol. 9v, these were described as two different components.

[110] In German, the origin of verdigris is not from Greece ('from the Middle English *vertegres*, from the Old French *verte grez*, an alteration of *vert-de-Grèce* ('green of

grüen vnd vint man es gar gemaincklick
Item wa man in disem půch vnd in diser
geschrift vint das wert setit das bedeüt
nit anders den[n] ein viertail eins loczs
15   eins ẏetlichen gewichtzs **Wie man sal=**
petter der vor auß geleutert ist vnd=
doch nit genug geleutert ist auff sein
rechte stat gerecht vnd wol zu gutem
salpetter leuttern sol

Wiltu salpetter sieden vnd leuttern
20   der vor auch ainst geleuttert ist
so nym[m] salpetter als vil du sein gehaben
magst vnd tu den in ein guten kessell

fol. 10v

1   vnd leg in eben vnd nym[m]e denn ein helczlein
vnd miß den salpetter wie vil do sein sey
vnd laß vor do sein erzaichet and dem holcz=
lein do stupff ein lochlein vnd wer das
zaichen drei[e]r finger prait über sich auff
5   vnd stupff aber ein löchlein vnd nym[m]
vast guten essich vnd tu als vil dar ein
piß das der essich ge an das ober lochlein
vnd tu dan[n] den kessel uber ein ~~gu~~ gefüg
fewr vnd so es anfach lawen so fewm=
10   den fewm oben herab gar wol vnd so
so erwallen wol so nym[m] galiczen stain
oder augstein vnd leg sein ein stuck dar
ein vnd laß es wol wallen das der wal
sich ~~si~~ ergang vnd rwre es von angeng
15   sitlich vnd so der salpetter über ~~w~~ al aller
ding zergangen seẏ so nẏm dan[n] den kesel

and can be found commonly.
Note that when this book and this
text refers to the measurement 'settit' then this means
nothing else but a quarter of a lot of
any common weight. **How you
turn saltpetre which has previously
been purified, but not enough,
into its right and proper state, and how you purify it
into proper saltpetre.**

If you want to boil and purify saltpetre
which has been purified before [*but not enough*]
then take as much saltpetre as you have of it
and put it into a good pot

fol. 10v

and spread it out and take a wooden stick
and measure the saltpetre how much it is.
Make a hole on the stick[111] where [*the saltpetre*] comes to
and then mark another one
three finger wide above the first,
and make another hole. And take
very good vinegar and add enough for
the vinegar to reach the upper hole
and place the pot on top of a suitable
fire and when it starts to boil then take off
the top[112] from the top. And
when it starts to boil more strongly take some acetate
or white vitriol[113] and add a piece of it
to the mix and let it boil strongly until the boiling
comes to an end. And stir steadily from the beginning.
And when the saltpetre has dissolved
take the pot off the fire

Greece')' – *Oxford English Dictionary Online* 'verdigris', but from Spain (from Middle Latin *viride Hispanum*) and this could be a generic form for 'some things from Spain'. Checked in *Frühneuhochdeutsches Wörterbuch*, no reference found.

[111] Likely meaning to make a mark to measure the amount of liquid.

[112] Likely to be impurities which have risen to the top in the form of froth.

[113] Scribal error, repetition of '*so*'. White vitriol is the historical name for zinc sulphate $ZnSO_4$.

ab vnd stöl in an ein haimliche stat
do es kalt sey vnd do nÿemant wandel
zu hab dar vm das dir nichczs dar ein
20   val vnd hut dich dar vor das dir
nichczs dar ein kom dan[n] das oben geschri=
ben stet vnd so er ein clein weil uber=

fol. 11r

1   schlecht so geuß in ab in ein sauber ge=
schir vnd laß in kalt werden vnd so der
essich erkalt vnd der salpetter so nym[m] den[n]
den kessel vnd geuß den kalten essich
5   lauter vnd schon oben ab so hast du ein
guten geschaiden lautern salpetter vnd
laß den salpetter in dem kessel vnd tu in
zu ainem warmen offen vnd kere in
das er wol erseich vnd ertrucken vnd
10   nym[m] dan[n] den selben trucken salpetter vn[d]
leg in zu ainem offen auf ein ~~lader~~
laderlachen vnd laß in wol dur werden
ÿe durrer er wirt ÿepesser er wirt vn[d]
nÿm[m] jn vnd wirck do mit als do vor ge=
15   schriben stet ein bewerung des salpet=
ters nÿm[m] den rwrstab oder des zergang=
ens salpetters auß dem kessel vnd spreng
das auff die gelawenden koln gibt es
gut frisch zwiczred gaust vnd in et=
20   licher maß plawes fewr so ist der sal=
petter fein vnd gut.

Aber den abgossen salpettern schonen
essich solst du ton in ein schonen

Royal Armouries I.34 – Part 1

and place it in an undisturbed place
where it is cool and where no one passes
so that nothing falls into the mixture.
And be careful that nothing
enters the mixture other than what is stated
above. And when it [*the vinegar*] has boiled[114] for a little while

fol. 11r

then pour it off into a clean bowl
and let it cool down. When the vinegar cools down
and [*with it*] the saltpetre, take the
pot and pour the cold vinegar
pure and good off at the top. And you have
good separated and purified saltpetre. And
leave the saltpetre in the pot and place it
in a warm oven and turn it over
so that it drains and dries. And take
the same dry saltpetre and place it
in an oven on a
leather[115] cloth and let it dry out properly –
the drier it gets the better it will become. And
take it and work it as it has been written
before. Measuring of the saltpetre:
with a whisk or [*some other tool*] take some of the dissolved
saltpetre out of the pot and sprinkle
it on glowing charcoal. If the charcoal gives off
a good, lively, repeated sizzle[116] and if the fire
burns in a blue flame then the saltpetre
is fine and good.

But you should place the removed saltpetre
and the good vinegar in a good

---

[114] Literal translation 'beaten over', meaning that it boiled heavily with liquid spilling over the edge. Checked in *Frühneuhochdeutsches Wörterbuch*, no reference found.

[115] '*lader*' written twice, once crossed out. Presumably scribal error.

[116] '*zwiczred*' – 'twice', or, 'more than once'. '*gausen*' (Jacob and Wilhelm Grimm, *Deutsches Wörterbuch von Jacob und Wilhelm Grimm Online*, 16 vols (Leipzig: Hirzel, 1854–1961), http://woerterbuchnetz.de/cgi-bin/WBNetz/wbgui_py?sigle=DWB, Band 4,1,1, col. 1588 – accessed 10 August 2023) – 'sizzle' ('*aufzischen*'). The translation is leaning towards the figurative image of the action implied.

fol. 11v

1   kesel uber ein gefug fewr vnd den selben
   lassen sieden das der halb tail einseut
   vnd nÿm[m] in denn ab dem fewr vnd tu do
   mit geleich als mit dem vorigen den[n] allein
5   so er gestet so macht du wol den lautern
   essich ab gießen vnd in behalten oder auß
                           schütten

   Ein lere soltu wissen ÿe dicker
   vnd ÿe mer du den salpetter leuterst
   ÿe minder dir des salpetters wirt vnd swint
10   vast aber er wirt wertber wer jm also tut
   der aller konnst vnd pest salpetter den ÿe=
   mant finden noch gehaben mag vnd wirck=
   est do mit fast in andern specieba v[o]n pulfer

   Item wan[n] das ist die kaufleut gewon=
15   **lichen vast in allen sachen damit sie**
   vmb gen vortail suchen wa sie mugen
   vnd do mit ir kaufmanschatz dick ge=
   ringert vnd geswecht wirt also das
   die leut die vmb sie kauffen wen[n]en sie
20   **haben guten kauff gethan so werden**
   sie oft betrogen vnd besunder an dem
   dem salpetter dar vmb stet hernach

fol. 12r

1   **geschrieben stet wa pÿ man in erkennen**
   sol gerechten guten salpetter sein ver=
   mischt mit salcz oder mit aland so vint
   man auch in disem pŭch gar aÿgentlich
5   **beschriben wie man salcz vnd aland vn[d]**

Royal Armouries I.34 – Part 1

fol. 11v

pot on top of a gentle fire. Let the mixture
boil so that it is reduced by half
then take it off the fire and do the same
as the one before. When it appears on its own[117]
then you can pour off the purified
vinegar and keep it or pour it
away

One point you should know:
the thicker and more often you purify the saltpetre
the less the saltpetre becomes and disappears
almost completely. But it also becomes more precious
when you have turned it into the most audacious and best saltpetre
anyone can find and it will react well
with almost all types[118] of powder.

**Note that the merchants normally,
in almost all matters they are dealing with,
seek their advantage whenever they want to
so that their trading capital[119] does not shrink in size
but grows. Then, when the
people who buy from them think they
have made a good purchase, that then they have
often been cheated and especially in[120]
saltpetre. This is why**

fol. 12r

**there is written below how one can recognise when
good and proper saltpetre has been carefully
mixed with salt or with alum. This is why you can find
very accurately described in this book
how you can separate salt and alum and**

---

[117] Meaning that the saltpetre has crystallized. See Smith, *Reports of the HO Group*, mainly from 2013 and 2014, for images on how saltpetre crystallizes.

[118] Not clear about '*speciba*' – it seems to refer to varieties or types, but neither seems to be an ideal translation.

[119] '*kaufmanschatz*' can relate to a wide range of items from 'trading goods' to the overall business. See http://fwb-online.de/go/kaufmanschaz.s.0m_1544289397.

[120] Possible scribal error, repetition of '*dem*' in original – not translated.

**alle vnsaubrikeit von dem salpetter
schaiden vnd leuttern sol**

Ein besunder kunst ist zu salpetter zu
kauffen der nit auff sein stat geleu=
10 tert ist noch geschaiden vnd als
er erst von venedig komen ist Merck
wol man vint salpetter der gemengt
ist mit aland der ist in dem mund we=
der zu pitter noch zu suß kenst du den
15 aland wol von dem salpetter schaiden
so mach du wol das kauffen aber sein
wirt luczel vnd must in doch tewr kauf=
fen vnd verfacht der aland noch des
salcz geleich nicht Es ist wol den kra=
20 mern die den salpetter verkauffen wan[n]
sein wirt vil an dem gewicht aber
luczel an der schaidung vnd leutrung

fol. 12v

1 Man vint auch salpetter der nit gemein
gut ist wan[n] das er ein wenig geseubert
vnd geleutret ist geleich als er new von
dem perg oder stain komen ist vnd der
5 selb zerkennen ist in dem mund gar vast
pitter vnd enpfinst du weder salcz noch
aland dar in den solt du kauffen wann
er lauter seÿ ÿe leuter ÿe pesser wan[n] der
lauter schait sich gern vnd vast wol vn[d]
10 wirt posser zeug dar auß dan[n] auß dem
vorigen Man vint salpetter vnd sol in   ·

Royal Armouries I.34 – Part 1

**all impurities from saltpetre
and how you can purify it.**

It is a special 'art'[121] to buy saltpetre in a state
which has not been purified up to scratch
nor has been separated and has just come
like this from Venice. Note carefully
that you can find saltpetre which is mixed
together with alum and which tastes neither
too bitter nor too sweet when put into your mouth –
if you can separate the alum from the saltpetre
then you may well buy it. But there will
be little of it and you have to buy it dearly.
The alum does not evaporate nor the
salt in the same quantity. It suits the traders who
sell the saltpetre when
it has a lot of weight but little
[*substance*] when separated and purified.

fol. 12v

You will also find saltpetre, which is usually not
good, when it is [*only*] a little cleaned and
purified similar to when it comes fresh[122]
from the mountains or the stone [*quarry*]. And
you can spot it when it is very bitter in your mouth
and you taste neither salt nor
alum in it. You should buy it if
it is purified. The more purified the better as the
more purified [*saltpetre*] can be divided [*from the alum*] easily and quickly
and it turns into better material[123] than
the previous [*kind*]. You can find saltpetre and should look for

---

[121] '*kunst*' has been translated as 'art'. In both languages, these terms have multiple meanings. This will be discussed further in Chapter 5.

[122] 'New' in the meaning of 'fresh' or 'unpurified'.

[123] '*Zeug*' is a general term which could be translated into '*matériel*'; an armoury in German is often described as a '*Zeughaus*', a place where the material for arms and armours is being kept. However, in this context it is more generically used as 'stuff' or 'substance'.

suchen bey prucken der augstain oden
sunst in stainen gehawen vnd lochern
der perg alban feuchten muren die vnder
15   weiln ertrucken vnd uber lang etwen
naß werden **Welch salpetter aller kref=**
tigst ist

Du solt wissent sein mit rechter war
heit das der salpetter der wilt ist
nit als vil kraft vnd macht hat als der
20   salpetter der do wechst in den heusern vn[d]
in den kelrn an den mawrn die vnder

fol. 13r

1   weilen ertrucknen vnd uber etwen lang
wider naß werden vnd wa du haimsche[n]
wol vnd rech leuterst so tut sein ein pfunt
so vil mit seiner kraft vnd küenhait als
5   des wilden salpetters drey lb tun mochten
Wie man in ein yedlich puchsen sie seÿ
clein oder groß die stain hawen sol
das sie gerecht werden

Man sol allweg die weit der puchsen
10   inwendig peÿ dem clocz meßen vnd
denn die form des stains dar nach ziechen
mit einem gewisgen zirckel vnd als man den
stain haut so sol man in hawen das der
zering vmb uber all der form geleich zu
15   ste **Welch specie das kol sterckt das es**
nicht verdürbt

Du solt wissen das atriment sterckt die
koln das sie nit verderben wan[n] das
geschicht vast vnd vil das daz kol an

Royal Armouries I.34 – Part 1

it in quarries, [*where there is*] agate stone,[124] or in
stone quarries and holes
in meadows, on damp walls which sometimes
dry out and which over prolonged periods
turn damp again. **Which saltpetre is the most
potent.**

You should be informed with the real
truth that the saltpetre which is raw does
not have as much power and force as the
saltpetre that grows in houses and
in the cellars on the walls which at

fol. 13r

times are dry and over a time
become wet again. And when you purify [*saltpetre*] from the home
well and good, then one pound
has as much power and audacity[125] as
three pounds of raw saltpetre can have.
**How you make the stone for each gun
whether it is small or big
so that they are right.**

You should always measure the width of the gun
on the inside next to the plug and
then draw the form of the stone accordingly
with a reliable compass. And when you strike the
stone then you should carve it in such a way that
it has the same form all around.[126]
**Which kind of charcoal is the strongest and which
does not deteriorate.**

You should know that atrament strengthens
charcoal so that it does not go off. For it
happens quickly and often that the charcoal in

---

[124] In *Frühneuhochdeutsches Wörterbuch Online*, http://fwb-online.de/go/achat.s.0m_1514384844: 'Semi-precious gem achat' ('*Halbedelstein Achat*').

[125] The use of both of these terms '*kraft*' and '*küenhait*' suggests the personification of saltpetre, giving it personal agency. See also fol. 15r.

[126] This is likely to mean that the stone is intended to be perfectly round so that it fits tightly into the gun.

20 ein puchsen pulfer verdirbt do peÿ atri=
ment nit ist Het man atriment dar zu
getan das es nit verdorben wer dar vmd

fol. 13v

1 so sterckt es das kol **Wie man salpetter
der vor ain mal geleutert ist in dem
andern sieden leutern sol das es sich schen
reinigt vnd schait von allem dem das**
5 **nit zu gehort vnd das nit faulen kan
noch mag wan[n] das es lauter gerechter
vnd guter salpetter wirt war zu du
in brauchen wilt**

Nym colina alis alumen iaspanicun
10 vitriolum romanu[m] vnd salcomnume
vnd leg es in dem andern sieden des sal=
petters vnd das ist vast nucz vnd ist das
alle pest zu dem schaiden des pulfers vnd
das bewere ich also sa comnune das zeucht
15 zu jm vnd tailt sein geleich als salem sil=

gunpowder goes off when it has no atrament,
[*but*] not when one has added atrament
so that it does not go off which thereby

fol. 13v

strengthens the charcoal. **How you purify saltpetre**
which has been purified earlier, which is mixed together
with some other [ingredients], so that it is already
clean and divides itself from everything
which does not belong to it. And it cannot and does not
want to turn mouldy. Then it becomes properly purified
and good saltpetre which you will
need.

Take *colina alis*,[127] Spanish alum,[128]
Roman vitriol,[129] and common salt,[130]
and mix them together with the saltpetre, and let it
boil. Then it becomes very useful and is
the best of all for separating powder – and
I can vouch for that. Take the mixture [*you put*] together
and divided in equal parts. And [*add*] *salem*

---

[127] Not clear what this refers to. One explanation could be that it is a form of *'culinalis'* (meaning: boiled or purified). In Freiburg Ms. 362, fol. 78r this is listed as *'comla'* (likely an abbreviation), translated by Nibler as *'comula'* (no explanation provided). Kramer's translation lists this as 'comla (unidentified)' (Kramer and Leibnitz, *Das Feuerwerkbuch*, 32).

[128] In other *Firework Book* versions, such as Freiburg Ms. 362, fol. 78r, or St Gallen VadSlg Ms. 396, fol. 14v, this is called *alumen Yspanicum* which is interchangeable with *Alumen hispanium*; or *Alumen hispanium* (fol. 34r) or *Alumen gispanium* (fol. 27v, Kunstbuch des Wolfgang Sedelius I, Munich Cgm. 4117, which in turn has been identified as soda or CO_2-water according to Thomas Brachert, *Nachträge und Corrigenda zum 'Lexikon historischer Maltechniken. Quellen – Handwerk – Technologie – Alchemie, München 2001'* (Hildesheim: Hornemann Institut, 2010)).

[129] Copper (II) sulphate, $CuSO_4$.

[130] This section in the Freiburg Ms. 362 is listed on fol. 78r: '*Nym comla vl alume[n] yspanicum bittriolu[m] romonu[m] vnd sal comonie*', which Kramer translates as 'Take *comla* [unidentified] or *alumen yspanium* [Spanish alum, a natural product], *vitriolum romanum* [Roman potash alum], and *sal commune* [rock salt, NaCl]' (Kramer and Leibnitz, *Das Feuerwerkbuch*, 32). This section is only one of two where the rhetorical repetition of *'Wiltu ...'* is omitted and instead starts directly with *'Nym ...'*. These two sections (see fol. 37r) are the longest listings of ingredients.

uestru[m] Alumen zeucht zu jm vnd tailt
sein geleich als alumen den man in den
salpetter legt so man in mert jaspanicu[m]
vnd vitrolun romanu[m] auf haufent ein
20   yetlichs species oder materÿ vnd von den
vorgenanten specien muß es sein wurcken
lauf vnd tailung han vnd weiß in recht[er]

fol. 14r

1   warhait daz diczs nicht felt **Wer gerecht**
vnd gut puchsen pulfer machen wil
der volgt disem nach geschriben capit=
tel nach wan[n] das weist vnd lert gar
5   **verschaidenlich gewiß vnd gewar wie**
man die specie dar auß man das pul=
fer machen sol nach gerechtem gewicht
ÿedlich nÿemen vnd mischen sol das sein
weder zu vil noch zu wenig ist vnd
10   **das das ein gut nucz pulfer dar auß**
werden sol wan[n] es geschicht oft vnd
vil das pulfer unnucz werden wann
man der stuck ains so dargehort zu we=
nig oder oder zu vil nympt dar vmb
15   **merck eben**

Es ist aber ein gewiß ler auff puchsen
pulfer recht vnd gut zu machen
du solt machen ain gewiß gut wag vnd
leg auf ÿedweder tail der wag guten ge=
20   leutterten salpetter als vil du den[n] ÿe wölst
das der salpetter gegen ein ander geleich=
weg vnd nym[m] dan[n] ein tail salpetter ab

fol. 14v

1   der wag vnd leg den selben tail hin vnd
gegen dem beliben salpetter leg auf die wag
ein geleichter wag oder gewicht so vil guczs

Royal Armouries I.34 – Part 1

silvestrum[131] and alum to it and remove it from the powder
in the same way as with alum which one adds to
saltpetre so that one gets more. Jasper
and Roman vitriol bulk up
any ingredient or material. And from the
said elements it has to trigger
an action and a separation. And I know the real

fol. 14r

truth[132] which will not fail you. **Anyone who wants
to make good and proper gunpowder
should follow this chapter written below
as it teaches and instructs
in many ways truly and honestly how
you mix the ingredients out of which you can make
powder each time taking
the right weight. And [*you*] shall mix it
neither too much nor too little and
a good useful powder can come of
it as it happens so often and
frequently that powder becomes useless when
you take too little or too
much of one ingredient. Therefore take good
note.**

These are precise instructions on making gun
powder right and properly.
You should make a good and accurate pair of scales.
Place on either side of the scales as much good
purified saltpetre as you would like
so that the saltpetre at each side weighs
the same. Then take one part

fol. 14v

of the saltpetre off the scales and put it aside. And
place on the [*opposite*] side of the scale to the saltpetre
an equal quantity or weight of good,

---

[131] Origin of term not clear. Could be related to a fir tree ('Pinus Silvestris').

[132] Or, 'for certain'.

Gunpowder Technology in the Fifteenth Century

frisch swebels vnd wan[n] das geschickt so
5 leg den salpetter hin vnd nym[m] dan[n] paiden
tail des swebels vnd tail in jn geleicht ge=
wicht vnd wen[n] das geschicht ♀ so leg ein
tail des swebels hin vnd laß den[n] andern
tail beleiben vnd wen[n] das also geschechen
10 ist dem beliben tail des swebels leg zu an
geleichem gewicht so vil dan[n] ab oder lin=
des kols das nit est gehabt hat vnd nit
mit wasser geschlecht seÿ vnd wan[n] das
also geschechen ist so leg den tail des kols
15 hin vnd den beliben swebel tail gegen ein
ander in geleich gewicht wan[n] das ge=
schicht so nÿm[m] ain tail des swebels in ge=
leich gewicht so vil des obgeschriben
kols so das geschechen ist so nym[m] dan[n] dar
20 nach all ob geschriben tail den salpetter
den swebel vnd das kol vnd misch sie all
vnter ain ander so du ym[m]er pest kast vnd

fol. 15r

1 magst vnd so es also gemischt seÿ so stoß
es vast wol ÿe mer du es stost vnd ÿe clein[er]
das pulfer wirt ye küener vnd schneller
das pulfer vnd laut dester heller wan[n] es
5 an gezunt wirt vnd der[er] das pulfer wol
in ainem guten peckin in einer warmen
stuben vnd sunder hüt dich vor fewr vnd
tu es dem offen nit zu nach wan[n] es em=
pfacht von hicz geleich als von fewr vnd
10 also hastu ein gewiß gewicht wie man
zeug sol auß wegen vnd vach aber an
zu wegen andern gezeug vnd tu geleich
als vor Merck dise ler eben wan[n] sie ist
die gewist lere so sie in diser kunst uber
15 all ist wan[n] welchs zeugs đ mer ist denn
sein sein sol nach diser lere so hastu ain

fresh sulphur. When that is done,
put the saltpetre aside and take both
parts of the sulphur and split it into equal
weights. When that is done, then put one
part of the sulphur aside [*from the scales*] and leave the other
part in place. When that is done,
put the remaining part of sulphur to the
same weight, and take it off. Take lime wood
charcoal which did not have branches and which
has not been made bad with water. When that
is done, put a part of the charcoal
to the remaining part of sulphur to
the same weight. When that is
done, take another part of sulphur of the same
weight as the above described
charcoal. When that is done, then take the
saltpetre, sulphur, and charcoal
described above and mix them all
together as much as you can and are

fol. 15r

able to. When it is mixed together then grind
it well, the more you grind and the finer
the powder becomes, the bolder and faster
the powder and the louder and brighter [*it becomes*] when it
is set alight. Dry the powder well
in a good basin in a heated
room. Be aware of fire and
do not place it too closely to the stove as it may catch fire
through heat as well as the flame. And
in this way you have an exact weight as you have
weighed the material, and after weighing other
material and do the same [*as before*].[133]
Note carefully these instructions as they are
the exact instructions as this an 'art' which exists
everywhere. For if there is more material than
there should be following these instructions, then you have made

---

[133] This could also imply that it means: 'when you are told to use a specific weight of
something, it matters, and makes a difference'.

werck gentzlich vmb sunt gethan vnd
dar zu den zeug ellentlich verdebt vnd
wer dise vor geschribne ler verstet dem
ist sein gen[n]ug **Wie sich der zeug schuck**
von dem stossen

20

Wan[n] du den
zeugt stöst so wirt er vnder ain=

fol. 15v

1   ander verwandelt vnd wirt ein weing
feucht des solt du nicht achten wan[n] es ge=
nug gestossen sey so nym[m] es auß vnd der[re]
es wol so werden groß knollen vnd hebt
5   sich der zeug an einander die knollen laß
beleiben wan[n] der zeug vil mÿnder an den
knollen den[n] ob er clein gestossen wer **Wie**
man ein yedlich puchs sie seÿ groß oder
clein laden sol mit dem puluer klocze[n]
10   **vnd stain nach rechter mensur das es**
der puchsen nicht zu ring noch zu swer
ist

Nach diser lere soltu ÿetlich
buchsen sie seÿ groß oder clein das
15   ror der puchsen messen wie lang
es in wendig seÿ piß an den poden vnd
tail dan[n] das selb meß in funff geleich
tail ain tail sol der klocz sein so er in die=
puchsen wirt geschlagen der ander tail

Royal Armouries I.34 – Part 1

this work a complete waste of time as
the material will be spoiled miserably.[134]
He who understands the above instructions will
know all he needs to. **How the material changes**[135]
when grinding it.

When you then
grind the material it will be

fol. 15v

mixed up and it will become a little
damp which should not concern you. When you
have ground it enough, then take it out [*of the mortar*] and let it
dry out well. Large lumps[136] will form and the ingredients
stick together. Keep the lumps
together. The material with fewer lumps is less good when
the lumps are ground down.[137] **How**
you should load any gun, whether it is big
or small, with powder, plug,
and stone and in the right measure, so that
it is neither too light nor too heavy for the
gun.

According to these instructions you should measure each
gun whether it is big or small. Measure its
length inside the gun
right to the bottom.
Divide this measurement into five equal
parts. One of these parts should be the [*length of the*] plug
as you have to drive it into the gun, another part

---

[134] The whole section sounds like 'weigh it properly, or it won't work', 'precision is crucial'.

[135] '*schuck*' is a challenging term to translate. It implies that the grinding action causes a change in the material, but the origin of '*schuck*' is not clear. In other manuscripts it is referred to as 'changed' ('*schicket*', Freiburg Ms. 362, fol. 81r, or Heidelberg, Cod. Pal. germ. 122, fol. 14r).

[136] '*knollen*' generally refers to 'lumps'. However, in the development of gunpowder, *Knollenpulver* has a major relevance. See Chapter 5 for an overview of the *Knollenpulver* debate.

[137] This could mean that it is beneficial to the quality of the powder if there are more lumps. If there are fewer (or if they are ground down) the powder is less efficient.

Gunpowder Technology in the Fifteenth Century

20   sol wan sten vnd der drittail hinder
  sich hinein sullen geladen sein mit gute[m]
  pulfer vnd dißeler treibt gewiß schuß
  von der puchsen **Wie man puchsen clocz**

fol. 16r

1   **machen sol**

Wiltu klocz machen so nym[m] guczs
  dürs albriß holcz vnd mach sie
  dar auß vnd mach sie da vornen cleiner
5   denn hinden vmb das du ein clocz wölst
  in die puchsen schlachen das er ye getrang=
  er hin ein ge vnd schlach den clocz gar
  mit ainander ein vnd vnd laß nichczs
  auß wendig dem ror so lait sich der stain
10   recht in die puchsen fur den clocz **Wie**
  man salcz von salpetter schaiden söl

Wiltu salcz von salppetter schaiden
  vnd tun so nÿm[m] den salpetter
  vnd wirff jn in ain kalcz wasser also
15   das das wassser nun ploß über den sal=
  petter ge ab du solt den salpetter vor mes=
  sen mit ainen holcz ee du das wasser dar
  ein tust so zerget das salcz vnd beleibt
  der salpetter in der kelt wan[n] der salpetter
20   mag indem kalten wasser mit zergen er
  gestet wol in denn kelt in vnd geuß wasser
  ab vnd laß den salpetter wol erseichen

should be the stone and the third part behind
should be filled with good
powder. This drives a shot properly
from the gun. **How you make gun**

fol. 16r

plugs.

If you want to make plugs then take good
dry white poplar wood and make them [*i.e. plugs*]
out of it. Make them smaller at the front
than at the back, so that the plug can be
driven into the gun, and that it [*the plug*] can be as tightly
inside [*the barrel*] as possible and that you can drive the plug thoroughly
inside [*the barrel*]. Do not let it stick out of
the barrel so that the stone lies
right on the plug in the gun.[138] **How**
you should separate salt from saltpetre.

If you want to separate salt from saltpetre,
and do it [*well*], then take the saltpetre
and throw it into cold water so that
the water just covers the
saltpetre. Measure the saltpetre
with a wooden stick before you add the
water. Then the salt dissolves, and the
saltpetre remains in the pot as the saltpetre
prefers the cold water and it will appear as
crystals.[139] Pour off the water
and let the saltpetre settle and form.[140]

---

[138] There is a difference between the gun, the barrel, and the powder chamber. The
barrel is perceived to be the part of the gun where the ball or stone is kept, while
the powder chamber is the narrower section at the end of the gun. For more details
see Chapter 5.

[139] The original implies a level of creation ('*gestehn*') which incorporates the understanding of some active input rather a mere appearance.

[140] Kramer and Nibler refer to Freiburg Ms. 362, fol. 77r, where it says 'vinegar or
wine' are to be added to the mixture to separate the two (Kramer and Leibnitz, *Das
Feuerwerkbuch*, 30, and Nibler, *Feuerwerkbuch*, 11). The above-listed text does not
mention any additional ingredients other than water.

fol. 16v

1 vnd tu in an die sunne[n] das er wol truck=
en werd so verget sich der salpetter wol
für gut **Aber gar ein gut kunst wie
man wie man das salcz von dem sal=**
5 **petter schaid vnd jm helffen sül das
der salpetter vesch vnd gut wirt**

Wiltu aber salpetter vesch vnd gut
machen das er starck werd so
tu den salpetter in ein kesel vnd tu so vil
10 weins oder essichs dar zu das er aber
ploß über den salpetter gang vnd misch
in vnter ein ander vnd stoß ein rûtten dar
ein vnd miß den wein oder den essich vn[d]
zaichen das geleiche halb vnd seud das
15 auch halbs ein vncz an das zaichen der
rûtten vnd wen[n] du es also seudst so geuß
den[n] wein oder essich ab vnd seich das sau=
ber ab so vinstu den salpetter an dem po=
den in dem kessel der salpetter gestet in
20 dem wasser den solt du nÿeme[n] vnd in
wol derren an der sun[n]en so hastu guten
salpetter **Wie man wein essich oder laug**

fol. 17r

1 **nennet dar nach als salpetter dar
in geleutert worden ist**

Du solt wissen als pald du den salpett[er]
tust in wein oder in essich oder in laug
5 oder in wasser als pald das geschicht
so haissen das die maister dan[n] dar nach
salpetter wasser vnd stost man pulfer
do mit ab wan[n] es kreftigt das pulfer
mer den[n] der wein oder essich **Wie man**

144

Royal Armouries I.34 – Part 1

fol. 16v

Place it in the sun so that it dries
well. This way the saltpetre becomes
good. **But this is a special method to
separate the salt from the saltpetre
and how you help with making
the saltpetre fresh and good.**

If you want to make saltpetre fresh and good
so that it becomes strong then put
the saltpetre in a pot and add enough
wine or vinegar to just
cover all the saltpetre and mix
it together. Push a stick [*into the saltpetre*]
and mix with the wine or the vinegar and
make a mark of half the quantity [*on the stick*]. Boil
it down by half,[141] until you reach the mark on the
stick. And when it has boiled, then pour
the wine or vinegar off. Drain it tidily
and you will find the saltpetre at the bottom
of the pot. Saltpetre forms in
the water, and you should take it and
dry it well in the sun, and you have good
saltpetre. **What you call wine vinegar or lye**

fol. 17r

**after saltpetre has been
purified in it.**

You should know that as soon as you put
the saltpetre into wine or vinegar or lye
or in water, when this is done,
then this is called by the masters afterwards
saltpetre water. And if one uses this to purify[142] the powder
than that the powder is stronger
than the wine or vinegar. **How you**

---

[141] That is, 'the liquid is reduced by half'.

[142] '*abstossen*' in the sense of 'smooth', to remove impurities ('*abhobeln*', '*Unebenheiten bereinigen*'). *Frühneuhochdeutsches Wörterbuch Online*, def. 14, http://fwb-online.de/go/abstossen.s.3vu_1544459265.

Gunpowder Technology in the Fifteenth Century

10 **den aller pösten salpetter machen sol**
vnd salcz vnd aland aller gewist do
do von schaiden

Aalso soltu den aller posten salpetter
machen vnd den alant vnd das salcz
15 do von schaiden nÿm[m] zwaÿ pfunt vnge=
loschens kalcks vnd aïn pfunt jaspanicu[m]
ain pfunt galiczen stains zwaÿ pfunt
salcz vnd mach her auß ein laug von
wein oder von essich vnd laß die laug
20 dreÿ tag sten das sie lauter werd vnd
dar nach tu den salpetten in ain kesel
so vil du wilt vnd tu diser laug dar zu

fol. 17v

1 so vil das die laug ploß uber den kesel ge
vnd misch das als vor geschriben ist vnd
seud das geleich halbs ein vnd geuß es
dan[n] ab so vinstu alant vnd salcz vnd alle
5 vnrainikeit an dem poden in dem kessel vnd
laß das salpetter wasser das so vor ein=
laug ist gewesen kalt werden so gestet der
salpetter als essich die do gefroren sein vnd
wenn er also gestat so schut die laug her=
10 ab vnd trucken den salpetter wol an der sun=
nen so hastu den aller pesten salpetter den
ÿemant gehaben mag man gibt des selben
salpetters der also geleutret vnd gereinigt
wirt ein pfunt vmb ein guldein so gut

Royal Armouries I.34 – Part 1

**make the best of all saltpetres
and [*how to make sure that*] salt and alum will certainly
be separated from it.**

This[143] is how you should make the best saltpetre of all
and [*how to*] make sure that the alum and salt
separate from it. Take two pounds of
quicklime and one pound of *jaspanicum*,[144]
one pound of cupric acetate, [*and*] two pounds of
salt. Turn this into a lye of
wine or of vinegar and let the lye
stand for three days so that it turns into purified [*saltpetre*].[145]
After that put the saltpetre in a pot,
as much as you want, and add to this enough lye

fol. 17v

so that the lye reaches [*the rim of*] the pot.
And mix it as is stated earlier and
boil it down by half. Then pour it
out and you will find alum and salt and all
impurities at the bottom of the pot.
Let the saltpetre water which was the lye
cool down and saltpetre will form
as if the vinegar was frozen. And
when that happens, pour out the lye
and dry the saltpetre well in the sun.
This way you have the best saltpetre which
anyone may have. For a pound of this same
saltpetre which has been purified and cleaned, you pay[146]
a guilder which is how much

---

[143] Presumably a scribal error, repetition of '*a*' – an indication that the rubrics were added at a later stage, and that sometimes the scribe of the text adds the first letter in error.

[144] In Freiburg Ms. 362 this refers to as '*ispantium*' (fol. 77r), translated by Nibler and Kramer as 'verdigris' (Nibler, *Feuerwerkbuch*, 11, and Kramer and Leibnitz, *Das Feuerwerkbuch*, 30). Could also be Spanish alum (see footnote 128), but left in the original, as this assumption could not be verified.

[145] Precipitation process as described above.

[146] The original uses the term 'give', suggesting an exchange economy, but in this context 'pay' seems more suitable.

15	wirt er vnd so vil get sein ab aber ain lb des selben salpetters tut mer den sunst funff pfunt so man in zu zeug berait **Wie man** **salpetter leuttern sol den man erst ab** **den mauren nÿmpt das er gut wirt**
20	**W**iltu newn salpetter leuttern als er erst ab den mauren genumen ist so nym[m] salpetter als vil du sein gehabe[n]

fol. 18r

1	macht vnd leg es in ein keltin vnd schut ein haiß wasser oder wein ist posser den[n] wasser oder essich vnd rwr es vnter ain ander mit ainem stecken vnd laß es kalt werden vnd
5	dar nach geuß das wasser durch ein dick tuch das es lauter seÿ vnd tu es aber uber ein fewr vnd laß es sieden in der maß als man visch seüt vnd seuch es dan[n] aber durch ein dinß důch vnd laß es kalt werden so ge=
10	stet der salpetter zu zapfen vnd schut den wein oder den essich oder das wasser ab vnd laß den salpetter wol trucken werden so wirt er gut aber als man den vorigen leuttert der ist pösser **Ob der salpetter nach dem**
15	**sieden nit gesten wil wa mit man in** **dan zu pringt das er gestet**

	Es kompt vil vnd dick dar zu das der salppetter nach dem sieden nit gesten= wil vnd das geschicht nun ob man vil wei[n]s
20	oder essich oder wasser dar an tut das nit in rechter maß ist als vor beschaiden ist wiltu machen das er geste so nÿm[m] eins

it is worth. It is so good that one pound
of the same saltpetre does more than five
pounds of any other kind when you make it into powder.[147] **How you
purify saltpetre which has just been taken off
walls so that it turns good.**

If you want to purify fresh saltpetre when
it has just been taken off the walls,
take the quantity of saltpetre you have

fol. 18r

and put it in a basin and pour into it
hot water or wine, which is better than water,
or vinegar and stir it. And mix it well together
with a stick and let it cool down. And
afterwards pour off the water through a thick
cloth so that it becomes purified. And put it over
a fire again and let it boil in the same way as you
poach fish. And then pour it out through
a thin cloth and let it cool down and thus the
saltpetre will start to crystalize. And pour off the
wine, or the vinegar, or the water and
let the saltpetre dry out. This is good, but not
as good as that purified by the previous method
which is better. **When, after boiling, no saltpetre
appears and how you can
make it to appear.**

It happens often and regularly that
no saltpetre appears[148] after boiling
and that happens when you have added [*too*] much wine
or vinegar or water to the saltpetre which is not
in the right quantity as is described before.
If you want to make it appear then take

---

[147] Meaning that 'it is five times more powerful than ordinary stuff'.

[148] The German original implies a level of choice such as 'choosing to appear' or 'deciding to appear'.

fol. 18v

1 manß haren der wein getruncken hat vnd ÿe
elter der harm ist so er ÿe posser ist vnd leg
salcz dar ein vnd seud den salpetter als vor
so gestet er wol vnd wirt lauter vnd schön

5 **Wie man den wilden salpetter der do hert
zepft ist reinigen vnd leuttern sol**

Wiltu das salpetter der wild ist auß
den pergen vnd der do hert zepft
ist so lauter vein vnd gut machen als ob

10 er nit zepft wer so nÿm[m] sein als vil du
sein gehaben magst vnd gib in zu malen
in ain mül vnd wan[n] es clein gemalen seÿ
so nÿm[m] jn vnd tu in jn ein kessel vnd geuß
dar an als dich diß půch vor gelert hat

15 vnd rwr es vmb vnd laß es dreÿ tag sten
dar nach tun jn über ein fewr vnd seud
die zwaÿtail ein vnd geuß das übrig
durch ein tůch vnd was in dem tůch beleibt
das seud denn in starckem essich piß das

20 das halbtail ein geseut vnd geuß dann
aber ab vnd laß daz gesten das es kalt
werd vnd geuß das wasser dan[n] do von

fol. 19r

1 so hastu dan[n] schonen salpetter zapfen die
laß trucken werden **Wie man den swebel
beraiten sol daz er zu dem puchsenpulfer
vnd zu allem fewr werck nuczlicher**

5 **kreftiger vnd hicziger wirt dan[n] vor**

Wiltu guten swebel machen so nym[m]

fol. 18v

the urine of a man who has drunk wine, and the
older the urine is the better, and place
the salt in it and boil the saltpetre as previously
and it will become pure and good.[149]
**How you turn raw saltpetre which crystalized hard[150]
so that it is clean and purified.**

If you want to make saltpetre, which is raw from
the mountains and which crystalized hard,
to be very pure and made well as if
it was in icicle form. Take however much you want
and put it to grind
in a mill. And when it is finely ground
then take it and put it into a pot and pour
over it what this book has taught you previously
and stir it and let it rest for three days.
Then place it over a fire, boil it so
that it is reduced by two parts[151] and pour the remainder
through a cloth. And what remains in the cloth –
that should be boiled with strong vinegar so that
half of it is boiled away. Pour it off
and let it rest so that it cools
down and pour the water off it

fol. 19r

and you have nice saltpetre crystals which
can be dried. **How you prepare sulphur
so that it can be used for gunpowder
and for all fireworks which is more useful,
stronger, and hotter than before.**

If you want to make good sulphur then take

---

[149] What is important is that a large amount of urea is produced which is required for the saltpetre process.

[150] The original uses the term '*zapfen*', which is related to icicles or pine cones, but for clarity it helps to give it the description of 'crystals'.

[151] Presumably reducing it so that a third is left.

weissen swebel auß der kram vnd
zerlaß den in ein irdischen geschir[re] das es
zergang vnd nym[m] zu ainem pfunt sweb=
10   els ein lot quecksilbers das mit swebel ge=
tet seÿ vnd rwr das vnter den swebel vnd
dar nach geuß den swebel in guten gepran=
ten wein so wirt er so vil dester trückner
vnd dester hicziger **Welch swebel der**
15   **posser swel ist**

L ebendiger swebel ist der aller pest sweb=
el wan[n] er ist stark vnd gut vnd
schnel zu fewr vnd braucht man sein nit
als vil vnter pulfer als vnter swebel als
20   du mich wol hie nach horen wirst **Wie**
man den aller pesten kol machen sol den
ÿemant machen kan

fol. 19v

1   W iltu die aller pesten koln machen
die ÿemant gemachen kan oder
mag so nÿm[m] weiß denne holcz oder albren
oder lindes holcz das frisch seÿ vnd mach
5   dar auß scheiter vnd der[re] sie in einem bach=
offen vnd verpren[n] sie gar wol zu eyteln
koln vnd beware das daz die die scheiter kein
ast haben vnd nym[m] die koln also frisch
vnd tu sie in ein becklin vnd lesch die mit
10   dem gepranten wein ab vnd stürcz alweg
ein peck über das ander so du die koln leschst
das dich der flamme nit verpren **Wie ma[n]**
zu zunder pulfer das aller pöst kol mach=
en sol das ÿemant gehaben mag

Royal Armouries I.34 – Part 1

white sulphur[152] from the store and
dissolve it in an earthenware dish until
it has dissolved. Add to a pound of sulphur
one lot of mercury which is saturated
with sulphur and stir it into the sulphur.
Then pour the sulphur into good brandy
and it will become much dryer
and even hotter. **Which sulphur is
the best sulphur.**

Native sulphur is the best sulphur
for it is strong and good and
burns quickly. You need not add
as much to the powder as with [*ordinary*] sulphur
as you will hear from me later. **How
to make the best charcoal anyone can
make.**

fol. 19v

If you want to make the best charcoal
anyone could or would like to make,
then take white fir wood or poplar
or lime wood which is fresh. And break it up
into kindling and dry it in an oven
and burn it into proper
charcoal. Be careful that the kindling wood is free of
branch holes. Take the fresh charcoal
and place it into a basin and extinguish it
with brandy. Always place one bowl
over the other to ensure that when you extinguish the charcoal
that the flame does not burn you. **How you
make the best charcoal for priming powder
that anyone has ever made.**

---

[152] It is not entirely clear what is referred to here. Super sublimated sulphur is also
called 'white sulphur of Das', or 'ω-Sulphur', which is an allotrope of sulphur, but
that is a post-medieval commercial product. While the colour of sulphur is mainly
yellow, when exposed to oxygen and moisture it takes on a pale yellow, grey, or
white colour at the surface. The use of the colour here may indicate a lower quality
of sulphur.

15	Das aller pest kol das ÿemant gehabe[n]
	mag zu zunder pulfer wer das mache[n]
	wil der sol nÿemen ein verschlossen tischlach
	das gar wol vnd schon gewaschen seÿ an
	alles stercken vnd sauber ertruckent seÿ vnd
20	ver pren[n] das zu pulfer in ainem irdischen
	haffen vnd lesch es mit nichte[n] du solt dem
	haffen seczen in einen haissen offen oder in

fol. 20r

1	in ein groß fewr das das tischlach dar in
	verprin[n]en müg Du solt auch den haffen
	wol bedecken das der dunst nit do von müg
	das kol ist über als kol **Hernach stet ge=**
5	**schriben wie ein maister hieß Niger**
	Berchtoldus vnd ist gewessen nigrematicus
	vnd ein alchimist zum ersten die kunst
	vnd auß buchsen zu schiessen vnd wie
	er das fand
	Die kunst hat fun=
10	den ein maister hieß niger bertholdus
	vnd ist gewessen ain nigermaticus vnd
	ist auch mit grosser alchamie vmb gange[n]
	sunder als die selben maister mit grossen

Royal Armouries I.34 – Part 1

The best charcoal that anyone may have
for use as tinder powder. Anyone who wants to make
this should take a closed[153] tablecloth
that is in good condition and has been washed
with starch and has been dried cleanly.
And burn this into powder in an earthenware
bowl and do not extinguish it with nothing. And place the
bowl in a hot oven or in

fol. 20r

a large enough fireplace to burn a table cloth
in it. You should also cover the bowl
well so that the fumes cannot escape.
This is better charcoal than other charcoal. **Below is
written how a master named Niger
Bertholdus who was a necromancer
and an alchemist discovered first the method
to fire guns and how
he found[154] it.**

The method was found by
a master called Niger Bertholdus[155]
who was a necromancer and who
also handled major alchemy[156]
such as the same masters who

---

[153] The literal translation is 'closed', but it could imply 'clean', 'unused', or 'folded', or could also be 'starched' or 'tightly woven', or even 'without holes'.

[154] There is a question about the use of the term '*finden*'. '*finden*' may imply an incidental nature of discovery rather than an organized structured approach – which is the same in most other western European languages.

[155] In the *Frühneuhochdeutsches Wörterbuch* in the entry on 'alchemy', reference is made to alchemy's main focus as 'the quest to create gold out of unpurified materials, often with negative connotations' (*Frühneuhochdeutsches Wörterbuch Online*, http://www.fwb-online.de/go/alchimei.s.1f_1519026099). In this context, there is no sense of negative connotation, but instead a seeming level of admiration in the praise of Niger Bertholdus.

[156] The author seems to make a point by using 'major' ('*gross*') as if that provides for a particular kind. It is not clear whether this relates to an actual definition or knowledge or any reader, or whether it is merely used as a rhetorical device. Term not included in *Frühneuhochdeutsches Wörterbuch*, as all Latin terms were excluded.

kunstlichen hoflichen sachen vmb gen mit
15   gold mit silber vnd mit den siben materÿ
also das die selben maister silber vnd gold
von dem andern geschmeid schaiden kün=
nen vnd von kunstlichen varben so sie
mache[n]

Also wolt der selb maister
20   bertholt ain varb prenne[n] zu der sel=
ben varb gehort salpetter swebel vnd
pleÿ vnd ol vnd wen[n] er die stuck in ein

fol. 20v

1   kupfre dinck pracht vnd er den hafen wol
vermacht als man auch tun muß so brach
der hafen zu gar vil stucken er macht auch
groß gancz kupffer heffen vnd verschlug
5   die mit einem grossen eÿsnein nagel vnd
wen[n] der dunst dar von nicht kome[n] mocht
so pracher vnd tetten die stuck grossen scha=
den also tet der vor genant maister berch=
tholt das pleÿ vnd ole do von vnd legt
10   kol dar zu vnd hieß ain puchs giessen vnd
versucht ob man stain do mit gewerffen
mocht wan[n] es jm vor mals türen zer
worffen het also vand er dise kunst vnd
pessert sie etwas Er nam da zu salpet[er]
15   vnd swebel geleich vnd kol etwas mÿnder
vnd also ist die selb kunst seid so wol ge
naw gesucht vnd funden worden das sÿ
an puchsen vnd an pulfer vast gepesert
ist worden als ir an disem puch wol ver=
20   stet **Wie man ein gemein gut pulfer
machen sol von dreÿen stucken**

Wiltu machen ein gemein gut pulfer

deal with the big, artful, and courtly matters,
with gold, with silver, and with the seven materials,
such as the same masters who were able to separate
silver and gold from the other metals
and who could make such artful colours.

And when the same master
Berthold[*us*] wanted to burn a colour – the same
colour which belongs to saltpetre, sulphur, and
lead, and oil –[157] he placed the ingredients in a

fol. 20v

copper pot and sealed the pot,
as you have to, and the pot
broke into many pieces. Then he made a
large copper pot, sealing it shut
with a big iron nail. And
when the steam could not escape,
it broke and the broken pieces [*of the copper pot*] caused great
damage. So, the said Master Berthold[*us*]
took away the lead and oil and added
charcoal. And he ordered a gun to be cast, and
tried out whether one could throw a
stone with it [*the gun*] to demolish towers [*as it has done*] before.
In this way, he discovered this method and
improved it a little.[158] He took saltpetre
and sulphur in equal parts and a little less charcoal
and this is the same method that has been
researched and found to be
better for guns and vastly better for powder
as you can understand well from this book.
How you make ordinary, good powder
with three components.

If you want to make ordinary, good powder

---

[157] This has been interpreted in other *Firework Book* editions as using the ingredients
to make gold. However, this cannot be ascertained from the context. See Kramer
and Leibnitz, *Das Feuerwerkbuch*, 25, or Nibler, *Feuerwerkbuch*, 6.

[158] This is a curious downplaying of the role of Berthold when the author seems to
diminish the achievement to a rather modest scale of improvement.

fol. 21r

1 machen von dreien stucken so nym[m] zeweÿ
pfu[n]t salpetter ain pfunt swebel dreÿ vier=
ling koln vnd stoß die mit gutem wein
ab vnd der[r] es wol an der sunne[n] so wirt
5 es ein gemein pulver **Item is disem nach**
geschriben capittel stet geschriben wie
man das aller pöst puchsen pulfer mach=
en sol das nÿemant mag gemachen vnd
das es nit verdirbt

10 Wiltu das aller pest pulfer machen
das nÿemant gemachen mag
oder kan so nym[m] drithalb zentner salpetter
ein zentner swebel vnd stoß das vnter ein
ander vnd wig es den[n] auß mit einer rech=
15 ten wag vnd nÿm[m] alweg den achtail kols
vnd den dreyßigsten tail salarmonicus den
selben tail salarmonici silitageris vnd
misch vnd stoß das vnder ein ander vnd
nym[m] ÿe zu dreißig pfunt zeugs als vor
20 vnd drew lot demerturis sublimato vnd
ein lot Campfer vnd funff lot arsenicu[m]
vnd tu salpetter wasser dar zu ein wenig

fol. 21v

1 vnd nit zu vil das do von dem salpetter kompt
vnd stoß das da mit ab du solt der stuck

fol. 21r

from three ingredients, then take two
pounds of saltpetre, one pound of sulphur, three
quarts of charcoal and grind them together with good wine.
Dry it out in the sun, and this will
become ordinary powder. **Here in this
following chapter is written how
you can make the best powder of all
that anyone has ever made and
that does not get spoiled.**[159]

If you want to make the best powder of all
that anyone has ever made
or can make: then take three halves of a *zentner*[160] of saltpetre,
one *zentner* of sulphur and grind them together
and weigh on proper scales
and take off one eighth [*of the total*] of the charcoal
and one thirtieth part of salammoniac and the
same part of salammoniac *silitageris*.[161]
Mix and grind it together and
take thirty pounds of each as before
and three lots of *demerturis sublimate*,[162] and
one lot of camphor, and five lots of *arsenicum*.
And [*then*] add a little bit of saltpetre water,

fol. 21v

but not too much of that which comes from the saltpetre,
and then grind it. You should not stir any of

---

[159] In the meaning of 'deteriorate'.

[160] 'Drithalb' = 1.5 *Zentner* (just as in 'anderthalb' being 1½) (*Frühneuhochdeutsches Wörterbuch*, vol. 5, 1471–72, 1 *Zentner* = 100 pounds). An alternative reading could be 'a third of a *Zentner*', which would make the saltpetre content too small for the powder to be functioning.

[161] According to Kramer and Leibnitz, *Das Feuerwerkbuch*, 37: 'Chaucer's *Yeoman's Tale* refers to this as 'bole Armeniac' which he claims can be translated to 'Armenian potter's clay'. Alternatively, it could simply be a measurement or container of a certain size.

[162] Kramer and Leibnitz, *Das Feuerwerkbuch*, 37, refers to this as 'mercury sublimate' (in Freiburg Ms. 362 this is listed as '*Mercurio sublimato*' [fol. 80v]), mirroring Mercury(I) chloride (Hg_2Cl_2) mentioned in other sources.

keins rwren du solt das pulfer in koln las=
sen vnd solt das gar wol derren ist das=

5   du den salpetter wol leuterst vnd die an=
dern stuck auch gut sein so verdirbt diß
pulfer nym[m]er mer **Wie man vordorben
pulfer wider pringt**

Es geschicht vil vnd dick das pulfer
10 von alter poß wirt vnd der kol zu
feuch wirt oder das der salpetter nit
wol geleuttert ist vnd das das pulfer ver=
dirbt dem solt du also wider helffen
du solt nÿemen guten gepranten wein vnd
15 solt in dar in siedem salpetrica vnd sal=
petter geleich vnd solt das pulfer also
mit haissem wein beschütten vnd solt
das darnach stossen gar wol vnd solt
nÿeme[n] in dein hefen vnd solt die fullen
20 wol gestossen vnd solt die hefen wol ver=
machen vnd solt die seczen in ain pack=
offen der nit zu haiß seÿ vnd so das pul=

fol. 22r

1   fer in dem hafen wol trucken worden seÿ
so nym[m] es den[n] herauß vnd stoß das ein=
wenig vnd nit zu vil so kumpt das pul=
fer aller ding wider zu jm selber vnd
5   wirt posser pulfer wan[n] es vor ÿe gewe=
sen ist **Item in disem nach geschriben
capittel vinstu gar ein gut ler vnd
gewiß wie du die drew stuck des sal=
petters swebel vnd kolns wen[n] se ge=**
10 **stossen vnd zu einem puchsen pulfer vn=
der ein ander gemischt sein wider von
ein ander schaist vnd das du yedlichs
stuck besunden von dem andern nympst**

Royal Armouries I.34 – Part 1

the ingredients. You should leave the powder in the charcoal
and you should make sure that it is very dry. Then you have
purified the saltpetre properly and the other
ingredients are also good so that this powder
will never go off. **How you bring
back powder that has been spoiled.**

It happens often and frequently that powder
turns bad from age and that the charcoal becomes too
damp or that the saltpetre has not
been purified properly. If powder has been
spoiled then you can bring it back in this way:
you should take a good brandy and
boil it [*the brandy*] in salpetrica and saltpetre
in equal measures. Then pour
hot brandy[163] over the powder. You should
then grind it very well and should
then place it into bowls and fill[164] them
well ground. Close the top of the
bowl, and place it in a baking oven
which is not too hot. When the powder

fol. 22r

has dried out in the bowl,
take it out of the oven and grind it further
but not too much. This way the powder
will regain all its properties as before and
it will turn into better powder than what it was
before. **Here in the following chapter
you will find good instructions and
knowledge of how you handle the three ingredients
saltpetre, sulphur, and charcoal, when they are ground
and mixed together into gun
powder. How you can separate them from
each other, and how each
ingredient can be used separate from the other**

---

[163] Including the dissolved saltpetre and salpertica.

[164] Possible scribal error, could be '*sullen*'. The most likely intended meaning here
would be 'should have'.

als ee sie zu ainem puchsen pulfer ge=
15 **mischt waren**

Wiltu puchsen pulfer von ain an=
der schaiden also das du den sal=
petter also weißen hast als vor vnd den
swebel den andern weg vnd das kol den
20 dritten weg vnd des yedlichs als frisch
seÿ als es vor ist gewesen So nym[m] pul=
fer als vil du wilt vnd tu das in ein

fol. 22v

1 haissen essich der siedent seÿ also das der
essich ain drittail über das pulfer ge vnd
laß das ein weil sten vnd fewrn den[n] den
kol ab mit einem trechlein der zwischen
5 einem gebelingespannen ist vnd schut des[n]
essich dar nach in einen zwilchen sack so
get der essich dar in so der salpetter zerga[n]g=
en ist durch den sack vnd beleibt der sweb=
el in dem sack wan[n] der swebel mag in kaÿ=
10 nem wasser zergan als der salpetter tut
der swebel mag auch nicht verderben
vnd dar nach so der sack wol erseicht so
er wöll den essich vnd seud in jn der maß
als man visch seut vnd laß den essich dar
15 nach kalt werden vnd laß in gesten vnd
seüch das wasser dan[n] ab so vinstu den sal=
petter in zapffens weiß den swebel soltu
wol erwaschen auß wasser so wirt er als
lauter als vor Aber das pöst schaidwasser
20 in den essich so du in anders erwöllen wolst
so tu dar ein ein pfunt jaspanicu[m] vnd ain
pfunt galiczenstains **Es geschieht oft vnd**

Royal Armouries I.34 – Part 1

as before they were mixed together into gunpowder.

If you want to separate [*the ingredients of*] gunpowder from each
other so that you have saltpetre that
is white as before, and
sulphur goes a different way, and the charcoal the
third way, and each of them is just as fresh
as it was before: then take the quantity of powder
you want and put it in

fol. 22v

hot vinegar which is at boiling point. Make sure that the
vinegar covers the powder by a third part and
let it rest for a while. Burn off[165] the
charcoal with a cloth which is stretched
over a frame, and then pour this vinegar
into a cloth bag so
that the vinegar as well as the saltpetre
goes through the bag, but the sulphur
remains in the cloth bag as sulphur does not
like to dissolve in water, unlike saltpetre.
Sulphur also does not go off.
After all the liquid has gone through the bag,
take the vinegar, and boil it in the same way
as you boil fish. And let the vinegar
cool down and let it rest. Pour off
the water and you will find white
saltpetre crystals. The sulphur you should
wash out of the water and it will be more
purified than before. But the best of all separating water
you can have in the vinegar is
when you add a pound of jaspanicum and a
pound of white vitriol. **It happens often**

---

[165] The broader translation would be 'take off', but it is important that the text insists
on the burning – not clear how that could be achieved.

fol. 23r

1 vil das pulfer unnucz wirt vnd doch
von alter wegen nit werdorben ist
vnd newr der geprech ist der dreier stuck
ain salpetter swebel vnd kol zu vil peÿ
5 den andern zwaÿen stucken ist wie vnd wa
peÿ man wissen mag welcher stuck zu vil
peÿ dem andern ist des wirst du in disem
nach geschriben Capittel aigentlich vnder
weist so stet auch sunst in disem půch
10 geschriben wie man solch pulfer pössern
vnd wider pringen süll

Ob dir ein pulfer vnder dein hant
kompt des zu vil salppetters swebels
oder kols hat ÿeder sechs stuck vnder den
15 dreÿen stucken zu vil wer wilt du wissen
welchs stucks zu vil do ist pren[n] des pul=
fers als groß als ein nuß auf ainem ge=
latten stain warn Aber ist des kols zu vil
so beleiben die koln also roch vnd als ein
20 růß mit grosser unsaubrikeit Aber ist des
swebels zu vil so print der swebel alweg
lancksam dar nach so das pulfer verprint

fol. 23v

1 es seÿ denn das der swebel nit wol gestossen
seÿ
**Was natur der salpetter hat vnd
welcher der pöst ist**

Salpetter der ist von natur kalt vnd
5 trucken in quartu gradu das ist an dem
wierden genant der salpetter wechst auch

fol. 23r

**and frequently that powder becomes useless, not
because it has not been spoiled due to its age, but
rather because one of the three ingredients in the mixture –
saltpetre, sulphur, and charcoal – there can be too much of one
compared to the other two ingredients – as and when
one knows which ingredient is too much
compared to the others. You will find in this
chapter following instructions
how it is written elsewhere in this book
how such powder can be made better
and can be brought back.**

Should a powder come into your hands
that has too much saltpetre, sulphur,
or charcoal: six parts of each of the
three ingredients are too much.[166] If you want to know
which ingredient you have too much of, then burn
a quantity of the powder as big as a nut on a
smooth stone. If the charcoal is too much,
then the charcoal will remain and it will burn
with soot and a lot of impurities. If the sulphur
is too much, then the sulphur will burn
more slowly than the rest of the powder burns

fol. 23v

unless the sulphur has not been ground down
properly.
**What the nature of saltpetre is and which one
is the best.**

Saltpetre is by nature cold and
dry in '*quartu gradu*', that is in the
fourth degree: saltpetre also grows

---

[166] This seems to imply that gunpowder is not of usable quality if one of the three ingredients makes up more than 60% of the overall mixture. This is in direct contradiction to the ratios suggested throughout, where saltpetre makes up between 51% and 72%. This sentence is not repeated in most *Firework Books*, e.g. Bucharest Ms. Varia II, 374, Dresden Ms. App. 463, Freiburg Ms. 362, Heidelberg, Cod. Pal. Germ 787, Munich Cgm. 4902, or Strasbourg Ms. 2259, but it is identical in Darmstadt Ms. 1074 fol. 20r. See also discussion in Chapter 5.

in dreÿ weg er wechst auch an den per=
gen er wechst an dem feld an herten staine[n]
als aland als hert vnd als weiß vnd
10   schat jm kein regen Der dritt salpetter
wescht gern an den mawren vnd in den
kelern die do feucht sein der selb ist auch
der pest Du solt wissen das salpetter in
salcz ist vnd peist vast vnd haist nach
15   latein stain salcz vnd wenn er geleuttret
wirt so haist er nit mer salpetter er haist
saluiter wan[n] er wirt als kalt vnd als
trucken von dem sieden wa in hicz begreift
do mag er nit beleiben von der grossen
20   keltin wegen die er an jm hat der sweb=
el ist von natur haiß vnd trucken vnd
empfacht geren das fewr so mag dann

[bottom margin right] der salpetter

fol. 24r

1   der salpetter nit peÿ der hicz beleiben al=
so ist es auch vmb das quecksilber vnd
vmb etlich stuck mer die kein fewr gelei=
den mugen sunder soltu dich alweg hüe=
5   ten vor dem frischen weisen salpetter **Wie**
man machen sull ein gut salpratica de[n]
man spricht salpratica do mit man alle
pulfer schaut vnd schnelt es seÿ pulfer
von schiessen zu fewrkugeln zu fewr pfeiln
10   **oder zu andern fewrwercken zu prauchen**

Wiltu machen ein gut Salpratica de[n]
man spricht salpertica vnd leüter
jn das saluiter dar auß werd vnd [wen[n]] du das
saluiter dreistund geleutert hast so tu es in
15   einen kesel vnd schut gepranten wein dar
zu das der wein dreier finger hoch über

Royal Armouries I.34 – Part 1

in three different ways, it grows in the mountains,
it grows in the fields, on hard stone,
as alum hard, or as white and
no rain spoils it. The third saltpetre
grows on walls and in
cellars which are damp, and that one
is the best one. You should know that saltpetre is
in salt, and is very corrosive. It is called
in Latin 'rock salt'. When it is purified,
it is no longer called saltpetre but is called
salniter. When it turns cold and dry
after boiling, when it catches the heat, then it does
not like to remain so on account of the great
coldness which it possesses. Sulphur
is by nature hot and dry and
catches fire easily. But
the saltpetre[167]

fol. 24r

the saltpetre does not like to be near the heat
which is why mercury
and other ingredients also do not cope
well with fire. But you should always be
careful about fresh white saltpetre. **How
to make good *salpratica* which
is called *salpratica* with which all
powder is made and which can be used in powder
to shoot fire balls, fire arrows
or to make other fireworks.**

If you want to make good *salpratica* which
is called *salpertica*[168] and which can be purified
into *salnitre*. If you purify
salnitre for three hours, then you put it into
a pot and add brandy to it so
that the wine is the width of three fingers above

---

[167] This note is made at the bottom of the page, most likely as a binding notation as it
is at the end of one gathering.

[168] See Partington, *Greek Fire and Gunpowder*, 155, and Needham, *Military Technology:
Gunpowder Epic*, 353.

den salpetter auf ge vnd tu zu ainem pfunt
saluiter vier lot salarmonarum vnd ein lot
kampfer vnd seud das ~~vnd~~ vnd wenn das
20   ein viertail ein gesotten seÿ so tu es dann
ein clein weil ab dem fewr vnd schut den
wein in ein newn haffen der irdisch seÿ vnd

fol. 24v

1   henck den salpertica an ein sail in ein kalten
keler vnd laß in dreÿ wocken dar in hange[n]
oder sechs wochen so wirt er grob vnd
lancknucz vnd wechst das post dar durch
5   vnd das zartest vnd dar nach so du in dar
gehenckst so ge an dem newnden tag dar
vnd wasch den haffen auß wendig mit
einem haffen vast in ein schon beckin
vnd behalte das wol wan[n] das ist das
10   pöst vnd das sterckst stuck das ÿemant
gehaben kan vnd tut man sein vnder
dreyßig pfunt ein lot doch ÿe me man
sein dar ein tut ÿe pessers alweg wirt
vnd gibt man sein ein pfunt vmb dreÿß=
15   ig s pfunt haller

Wie man guten salpett[er]
an den mawrn ziechen vnd ab nÿeme[n] sol

Wiltu guten salpetter ziechen an den
mawren so schut salpetter wasser
do salpetter in gesoten seÿ in ein feucht
20   mawr in ein keler oder do salpetter gern
wechst die mawr gewint salpetters genug
vnd dar nach so du in ab nÿmpst so spreng

fol. 25r

1   alweg das wasser mit einem wedel an
die mawr das die mawr do von naß werd

the saltpetre. Add to one pound of
salnitre, four lots of salammoniac, and one lot of
camphor. Boil it until
one fourth of the liquid has boiled down. Take
it off the fire for a short while and pour the
wine into a new earthenware bowl.

fol. 24v

Hang the *salpertica* on a rope in a cold
cellar and let it hang there for three weeks
or for six weeks. It will become coarse and
will keep for a long time and it will grow the best
and the softest. And after you let it hang
on the ninth day you can go to it and
wash out the bowl with another
good strong bowl in a suitable basin.
And keep what you get as it is at its best and it is
the strongest that anyone
can have. If you add one lot of this
into thirty pounds, it will be good; but the more you add to it,
the better it will get.
And for one pound you will get thirty
pounds haller.[169]
**How you develop good saltpetre
on the walls and how you take it off [*the walls*].**

If you want to develop good saltpetre
on the walls, then pour saltpetre water
in which saltpetre had rested onto a damp
wall in a cellar or where saltpetre likes
to grow. The wall will gain enough saltpetre.
And after you take off the saltpetre sprinkle

fol. 25r

some more water on to the wall
with a brush so that the wall is wet

---

[169] A '*haller*' is a silver coin minted in the Swabian city of Hall, and is worth half a
penny. Not clear what the meaning of this equation is – other than this produced
very high-quality material.

so wechst es gern

Wie man salarmoniaru[m]
leuttern vnd beraiten sol

5   Salarmoniaru[m] sol man also leuttern
sol nÿm[m] salarmonato als vil du
wilt vnd leg in jn ein saubern kesel
vnd tu guten wein dar zu ÿe zu einem
pfunt salarmonitu[m] ain maß gucz weins
10   vnd seud das drittail ein vnd tu den[n] den
wein her auß vnd laß in kalt werden
so schut den wein den[n] ab dem salarmo=
niorum vnd laß in trucken werden so ist er
berait man gibt unberaiten salarmo=
15   narum ein pfu[n]t vmb sechzehen schilling
haller vnd der wol berait ist ein pfunt
vmb ein guldein **Her nach stet geschri=**
ben ein gar gut heflich stuck wie ~~man~~
ein maister nachczs schiessen sol vnd wis=
20   **sen mag wa er hin geschossen hat**

Eein gar hoflich gut kunst die
hernach geschriben stet als du gern

and it will grow nicely.

**How you purify salammoniac
and how you prepare it.**

Salammoniac can be purified like this: you
should take *sal ammonato*[170] as much as you
want and place it in a clean pot.
Add good wine to it, for each
pound of salammoniac add a measure of good wine.
Boil it down by a third, and pour off
the wine and let it cool down.
Pour the wine off the salammoniac
and let it dry, and it is purified.
Unpurified salammoniac costs
sixteen shillings and a haller per pound
and if it is prepared well it will be worth
a guilder for one pound.[171] **Below is written
a very 'courtly' advice[172] how
a master can fire at night and how he can know
how to aim his fire.**

A[173] very good, 'courtly' method which
is described below:

---

[170] There are a number of different spellings of this ingredient. However, it is likely to refer to salammoniac. Kramer (Kramer and Leibnitz, *Das Feuerwerkbuch*, 49), believes it is 'raw salammoniac' or NH_4Cl. In other *Firework Books*, e.g. Freiburg Ms. 362, fol. 85r, Dillingen Ms. XV 50, fol. 22v, this is listed as '*salarmoniack*' (see also *Büchsenmeysterei. Von Gschoß, Büchsen, Puluer, Salpeter vnd Feuerwerk etc.*, Strassburg: Christian Egenolph, 1529 – subsequently referred to as Egenolph 1529, 34).

[171] One guilder equals 24 shillings. One shilling equals 12 pennies. This section is copied in many other *Firework Books*, e.g. Freiburg Ms. 362, fol. 85r, Dillingen Ms. XV 50, fol. 22v, New York Spencer Collection Ms. 104, fol. 37v, and Heidelberg, Cod. Pal. germ. 122, fol. 22v. In all of these sections the stated value stays the same without adjustment for inflation, even in the case of the Dillingen manuscript or in the sixteenth century printed editions, which have been dated to be from the 1460s or 1529 respectively.

[172] '*heflich*' or '*hoflich*' has been translated as 'courtly' throughout. This does not mean it refers to a courtier or people actually based at, or employed by, a court. Rather, it refers to a skill or knowledge which could be put to good service in a courtly context. It clearly has an aspirational connotation, and it is mentioned on three different occasions in Part 1. See Chapter 5 for a discussion on this.

[173] Scribal error in original. Repetition of '*e*'.

fol. 25v

1 wölst wissen wa hin du zu nachczs scheüst
so nym[m] zechen pfunt harcz ein pfunt vnst=
lit vnd zerlaß das in einem kessel vnd
tunck den stein dar ein vnd nym[m] ein pald
5 dar auß vnd wirf in jn ein puchsen pul=
fer das verhangt vnd verwigt sich in
das harcz vnd die puchsen dar nach mit
ladest vnd den stain mit guten laudern
verschoppen vnd scheuß wan[n] du wilt so
10 sichst du den stain prin[n]en du darfft den
stain nit an zinden wan[n] er get selber
prinnent von der puchsen wan[n] du die
puchsen an zint hast **Es ist zu wissen**
wan[n] das ist das man frome fürsten herre[n]
15 **ritter knecht vnd stet oft vil vnd zu ma[n]ge[n]**
mal als gar versampt bezogen vnd beli=
gert sind worden Also das sie sich dar
vor nit gewist haben zu hüeten vnd auch
solch leut peÿ in nit hetten noch die zu
20 **in pringen mochten durch der kunst**
weishait rat vnd hilff das sie iren fein=
den wider sten vnd sich ir auff enthalten

fol. 26r

1 **mochten vnd wan[n] auch laider oft schein=**
berlichen ist das den[n] manig from fürst
ritter vnd knecht vnd stet oft swerlich
engolten haben vnd des zu verdorbenlich
5 **ein schaden komen ist vnd der wirdig**
adel der dem hailigen römischen reich

Royal Armouries I.34 – Part 1

fol. 25v

if you would like to know how you fire at night
then take ten pounds of resin, one pound of cheap tallow,[174]
and melt it in a pot. Dip
the stone into it and take
it out again shortly afterwards, and throw it into
gunpowder. The gunpowder sticks to and joins the resin.
When you load the gun subsequently
push the stone back and tightly with good
cloth. When you fire it,
you will see the stone burning.[175] You will not
have to light the stone as it burns
by itself out of the gun when you have
lit the gun. **It is known that**
when honest princes, lords,
knights, squires, or towns often and frequently and
at various times have suddenly been attacked or
besieged. And that they did not
know how to protect themselves and they did not have
such people with them nor could they bring anyone
who through method,
wisdom, counsel, could help them to withstand
their enemies and could be with them.

fol. 26r

Unfortunately, it is also often the case that these
have often not been compensated well by the prince,
knight, squire, or town, which is
why – as a result – they have
come to dreadful harm. The worthy
nobility who are there to strengthen

---

[174] In Nibler '*Unschlitt*', or '*vns{t}lit*' = '*inßlat*' => '*Unschlitt*' (Nibler, *Feuerwerkbuch*, 54 n137); in Kramer, 'Cheap tallow' – no reference provided (Kramer and Leibnitz, *Das Feuerwerkbuch*, 49). The *Frühneuhochdeutsches Wörterbuch Online* refers to it as '*unstlit*' in the entry on candles (*Frühneuhochdeutsches Wörterbuch Online*, http://fwb-online.de/go/kerze.s.1f_1514210227). Defined as the lowest quality of butchered animal product.

[175] This helps the gunners to provide some sense of direction, distance, and perspective – something that is still done in modern artillery.

zu sterck vnd dienst geordnet vnd von
got selber gewirdigt ist Dar durch et=
wen[n] geschmecht vnd getruckt worden

10 ist Dar vmb so rat ich allen fürsten
herren rittern vnd knechten vnd stetten
die do stet vnd vesten haben in ganczen
trewen das sie sich bewaren vnd fursech=
en mit köst vnd gezeug den sie alweg

15 haben in iren vesten vnd schlossen salpett[er]
vnd swebel vnd ander specie die zu puch=
sen pulfer vnd fewrwercken gehören als
in disem puch dar vor vnd hie nach ge=
schriben stet vnd sunder das sie haben

20 solch holcz in gutem haw gehawen vnd
an ein trucken stat gelert das du nach
diß püchs lere nucz vnd gut seÿ vnder

fol. 26v

1   das pulfer zu den cloczen hinder den stain
vnd zu den puchsen do mit man die stain
verpiset vnd ~~d ist~~ das ist dar vmb zu tun
ob ÿemant durch urstumpft bezoge[n] vnd

5   beligert wurd da er doch peÿ hett do
mit er sich seiner feint erweren mocht
Dan[n] der also beligert wirt ~~sein~~ vnd sein
feind das veld getrawen in zu haben so
fachen sie mangerleÿ an do mit sie in

10 wollen gewinnen vnd dar vmb stet in
disem nachgeschriben Capittel ob ein furst
herr ritter oder knecht oder stet sein vein=
de so nachent hi zu gerüst hetten das
sie jm an die mawr komen weren mit

15 laczen oder schürme[n] vnd layttern an
stussen zu schürme[n] wolten wie ein ÿed=
licher furst her[r] ritter oder knecht oder
stet ir schloß vest oder stet sturmhals

Royal Armouries I.34 – Part 1

the Holy Roman Empire and considered to
be worthy by God himself have been
shamed and defeated.
Therefore, I advise all princes,
lords, knights, squires, and towns
which have towns or castles in all
honesty that they should preserve and seek
out such food and supplies at all times
in their castles and strongholds: saltpetre
and sulphur and other ingredients required
belonging to gunpowder and fireworks as
are described in this book beforehand
and later. Especially that they have
such wood well chopped and in a
dry store so that it can be used for
these gun instructions and that it is good

fol. 26v

within the powder, on the plug, behind the stone,
and in the guns which are used
to fire the stone. That is so that
anyone who has been attacked through *urstumpft*[176] and
besieged, he has with him someone
who can defend him against an enemy
when he is also under siege and when his
enemy is in the field, then to have such [*knowledge/person*]
try various things so that they
want to win and therefore there is written later
in this chapter whether a prince,
lord, knight, or squire or town have
made preparations against their enemy so that
they can come to the walls with
cats and screens and ladders with the
intention to take it, [*just*] as any
prince, lord, knight, or squire or
town in a castle, stronghold, or town can withstand

---

[176] No meaningful translation for this term could be found. It could be that it relates
to 'guile', 'sheer power', or even 'core' (from the etymological sources of '*ur*' = 'origin'
and '*stumpf*' = 'trunk'), or something more generic such as 'craft'.

wol behalten vnd iren veinden wider
20 **sten mügen**

S[o] vor dir ligt es seÿ in einer vesten
oder in einer stat vnd man an die

fol. 27r

1 mawr komen wer mit gutenn schürme[n]
oder mit laczen vnd man an die mawr
mit leütern stöst oder pricht vnd du ꝺ sein
in wendig nit wissend pist wa man auß
5 wendig an stöst oder pricht so nÿm[m] einen
würffel vnge in wendig zu der mawr
vnd leg in in die mawr ÿe auff den ne=
sten stein vnd wa der wurffel auff springt
do prich gegen in durch die mawr auß
10 Nim[m] aber vor hin dreißig pfut harcz
dreÿßig pfunt salpetters swebels vnd
koln alles wol gestossen in das ze[r]lassen
harcz vnd mach pallen dar auß als
groß als die öpfel vnd zünd sie an vn[d]
15 wirff sie zu in die außwendig in der mawr
sein so prinne[n] die paln vnd gewinnen
also grossen dunst vnd rauch vnd print
auch also ser das dir dein feind keinen
schaden tun mügen piß du aber die
20 puchsen geledst vnd also mag sich ein
yedlicher wol erweren vor kaczen vnd
schürmen vnd sein schloß vest vnd stat

fol. 27v

1 oder stürm hab behalten Merck wol eben
vnd bewar dich mit köst vnd zeug vnd
fromme[n] leuten denn manig vest sein ver=
lorn worden vnd die leut dar in gefange[n]
5 dar vmd das sie ~~sich~~ sich nit virsechen

Royal Armouries I.34 – Part 1

**their enemy and they hold their
position.**

When he [*the enemy*] is in front of you, whether you are in a castle
or a town and when he has come

fol. 27r

to the walls with good screens
or with cats,[177] and he hits the walls
with ladders and breaches them while you
are inside without knowing what is happening
outside and whether it breaches [*the walls*], then
take a single die within the walls
and put it on the wall. On the nearest
stone the die falls onto
there will the wall break down.
Prepare before then thirty pounds of resin,
thirty pounds of saltpetre, sulphur, and
charcoal all well ground and mixed with
the resin. Make this into balls the size
of apples and set them alight
and throw them beyond the wall.
The balls will burn and give off such a lot
of steam and smoke and they will burn
so much that no enemy can cause
you any harm until you have loaded your
gun. That is how anyone can
protect themselves against cats and
screens and their castle, stronghold, or town

fol. 27v

can withstand such an attack. Note carefully
to prepare your food and supplies and
that many reliable people lost strong castles
and the people inside were captured
only because they have miscalculated

---

[177] A cat was a wooden structure, a form of siege tower, which was used to protect an
attacker at a siege from enemy attack. Possible images of this kind of cat can be
found in I.34 illustrations at fols 91r and 91v.

hetten mit kost vnd zeug vnd auch des
halb nit haben mochten piß man sie entret=
tet oder ir feind mit guten taidingen do
von geweist hetten **Item in disem hernach**
10 **geschriben capittel stet geschriben wie**
man ein tureren nÿder schiessen sol vnd
wie man in beschiessen sol das man
in mit wenig schüssen als wol nider
scheust als mit vil schussen

15 **W**iltu einen turen nider schiessen
auff ainen hauffen so lug das
du habst ein guten quaderaten vnd
ein rechte mensur vnd auch ein gute
puchs vnd das du sie ladest mit sweb=
20 el puchsen cloczen die pi[e]chein sein vnd
die stain die du schiessen wilt solt du
pinden mit guten eÿsneÿn reÿffen die

fol. 28r

1 crewczweiß uber ein ander gange[n] vnd
lug das du ein gerechte mensur habst
zwaier man hoch an dem turen von dem
ertreich vnd alle die schuß die du tust die
5 du all neben einander ab vnd scheuß nit
hocher noch nider[er] so erschelt er vnd er=
wegt sich der turen vnd velt behend ni=
der den[n] ob du sunst zwaÿhundert schüß
dar an test **Item wenn das ist das man=**
10 **ges man[n]es feind sich fur sein stat vest**

Royal Armouries I.34 – Part 1

food and supplies and they could not
keep hold of them until they could fight off the siege
or their enemy was turned away by good
deeds.[178] **Here in this chapter**
written below there is written how
you can shoot down a tower and
how you should shoot at it so
that you can bring it down with a few shots
rather than with many.

If you want to reduce[179] a tower
to rubble, then see that
you have a good quadrant and
good measuring skills[180] as well as a good
gun. You should load the gun with sulphur
gun plugs which are covered in pitch and
the stone you want to fire should be
tied with good iron rings which

fol. 28r

are placed in a crossways fashion over one another. And
make sure that you have the right measurement
of the height of two men at the tower from the
ground upwards and that all shots you fire
should be able to land next to each other and neither
higher or lower, then the tower will be hit,
will move, and will fall down as quickly
as if you had otherwise fired two hundred shots
at it. **Here when you have the**
enemy with many a man who is laying in siege to one's

---

[178] Disputed in various forms. Nibler calls it '*Tading*' or '*Taiding*' = '*Gerichtsverhand-lung, Richterspruch*', Schmeller, *Bayerisches Wörterbuch*, I, 585. Göttingen 2° Cod. Ms. philos. 64, fol. 132r, '*tadingen*' = 'deeds'. *Frühneuhochdeutsches Wörterbuch Online* refers to it as 'dispute', 'decision', or 'achieve' (*Frühneuhochdeutsches Wörterbuch Online*, http://fwb-online.de/go/teidingen.s.3v_1513765010).

[179] The literal translation of the original is 'shoot down'.

[180] Can have a variety of meanings, most likely a generic term for 'measure', referring to the ability for the measurer to take care (*Frühneuhochdeutsches Wörterbuch Online*, http://fwb-online.de/go/geometer.s.0m_1514540582).

Gunpowder Technology in the Fifteenth Century

oder stet legen vnd sünst mangen feind
hat die auff secz haben wie sie jm ein
schloß abgewinnen mochten es seÿ
mit an lauffen des morgens als man
15 frw auff schleulst reit oder get des
nachtes mit steigen Dar vmb stet
hernach geschriben in disem Capittel
wie ein man ein fewrwerck mach vn[d]
auß werffen sull do mit er sich wol
20 versechen mag doch wenn er das
fewerck auß geworffen hat vnd
hin nach sich uber auß weschen wil

fol. 28v

1 so sol er ein ren[n]tarsch for fur auß bitte[n]
vnd sich do mit bedecken für geschoß
dann manig man ist sein vmb das
leben komen das er sich ploß vnd un=
5 gewaffent seins haubtzs sich ꝫ beschen[n]
wolt dar vor sol sich ein ÿeder from[m]er
man hueten

So man vor dir ligt es seÿ in einer
vest oder in es seÿ in ainer stat vnd
10 du sichst das sie dir zu nachent an die
mawr rüsten oder gangen oder ob man
nit vor dir ligt oder ob dich sunst ge=
dunckt man seÿ zu deiner vesten geschlich=
en So nym[m] speiß glas ain pfunt harcz

town, castle, or stronghold.[181] And any kind of enemy
that can besiege you, and who can capture
your castle, be it
at the beginning of the morning
as you ride early to the castle, or be
it at night with ladders. Therefore there is written
in the following chapter
how a man can make a firework and
use it, with which he can cause a
lot of harm. But when he has thrown
the firework [*outside the castle*] and
afterwards he wants to 'wash his [*hands*] of it',[182]

fol. 28v

then he should request a protective shield[183]
and he should cover himself with it from the fire
which causes many men to
lose their lives as you are unprotected and
go unarmed against their howitzers
which is what any decent man should try
to avoid.

If someone besieges you in a
castle or be it in a town, and
you find that they get ready to come closer to
your walls, or, if you are not
under siege, but you think that
someone has come close to your defensive structures
then take *speiss glass*,[184] one pound of resin,

---

[181] Unclarity about '*stat, vest vnd stet*' in original – appears to be a rhetorical expression, but includes the same stem of 'town' twice. The text also switches the subject from 'you' to 'he' and back again, making it unclear whether the fireworks are part of the offensive or defensive.

[182] Metaphorical expression with the meaning of 'not admitting responsibility or sense of guilt for any of the consequences', or more generally 'avoiding the consequences'.

[183] '*renntarsch*' translated as '*Kampfschild*' – a protective shield used in tournaments, used as a protective device.

[184] Also described as '*spießglaß*' (Freiburg Ms. 362, fol. 79v) or '*spießglas*' ('Dye nachuolget vonn Büchen geschoß, Pulver, Fewerwerck …,' as appendix to *Flauii Vegetii Renati vier Bücher der Ritterschaft*. Augsburg: Stainer, 1529, 91r–101v – printed in

15	drew pfunt swebels ain pfunt salpetters
	ein pfunt koln vnd mach dar auß sin=
	wellin kugilin vnd mit wercken soltu in
	zu same[n] knetten vnd wen[n] du sein be=
	darfst so wirff ein kugelein hin auß
20	das print gar lang vnd auch gar laut[er]
	vnd leucht schon das du wol sichst ob
	ÿemant her zu ge oder nit sie were[n] auch

fol. 29r

1	auch zu prenne[n] **Wie man ein wun=**
	derlich pulfer machen sol das selb
	pulfer auch die art hat wa man es
	hin legt da es truchen leit so enprent
5	**es von jm selber nicht aber wenn dar**
	auff regent oder beschut wirt so enprint
	es do von

	Wiltu ein gut pulfer machen das
	gar wunderlichen ist leg es sech=
10	zehen wochen auff ein dach oder wa du
	wilt alle die weil vnd es trucken leit so
	print es nit aber als pald es dar auff
	regent oder man es beschüt so print es
	gar grymlichen vast also solt du es mach=

three pounds of sulphur, one pound of saltpetre
one pound of charcoal, and turn this into
round balls.[185] Knead all of it together with old cloth.
If you need to
throw one ball outside
that burns a long time and is louder
and shines brightly so that you can be sure whether
someone has come close or has not,

fol. 29r

also[186] to burn. **How you make miraculous**
powder, the same
powder which has the ability, when you
put it down and it is dry, not to
burn by itself. But when
rain falls on it, or it is shot at, then it starts to
burn.

If you want to make good powder that
is quite marvellous, then put it on
a roof, or where else you want, for sixteen weeks
so that it is allowed to dry and it
will not burn until rain
falls on it or until it is shot at. Then it burns
grimly and quickly. To make it you should

Hassenstein, *Feuerwerkbuch*, 202 – in the following called 'Stainer 1529') which
was interpreted by Nibler as a 'group of ore (metal sulphide)' ('*Spießglanz, arten-*
reiche Gruppe von Erzen (Metalsulphid)') (Nibler, *Feuerwerkbuch*, 202). Kramer believes it is 'antimony sulphide, Sb_2S_3' but there is no evidence provided as to why
this would be the case (Kramer and Leibnitz, *Das Feuerwerkbuch*, 54). It could also
be a mere container, a 'glass for something', but from the context it is more likely
to be an ingredient.

[185] In Freiburg Ms. 362, fol. 79v: '*sibentzig kugelin*'; in Heidelberg, Cod. Pal. germ. 122,
fol. 26r: '*sibitzig*', in Stainer 1529, 202: '*sibentzig kugeln*'; or in Göttingen 2° Cod.
Ms. philos. 64, fol. 132v: '*sibentzig*'. No reference found for '*sinwellin*', but it is most
likely that it refers of the quantity or shape.

[186] Repetition of '*auch*', presumed scribal error – not translated.

15	en Nym[m] saluiter vnd funff salp hirntis z
	itar bonel z ß vnd pulfer das vnder ein
	ander vnd nym[m] einen weissen kysling
	stain vnd prenne den zu ainem kalck
	vnd stoß den ungeloschen kalck wol vn[d]
20	tu z des kols dar zu vnd dreier pfeng=
	nig swer campfer vnd temperier das
	wol vnter ein ander vnd laß es wol

fol. 29v

1	trucken werden **Wie man ein gut weiß puch=**
	sen pulfer machen sol

Wiltu machen ein gut weiß pulfer so
nym[m] ain pfunt salpetters vnd ein

5	pfunt swebels ain halb pfunt salbonis oder
	albranne vnd der[r] das wol in einem hafen
	vnd stoß das vnter ein ander zu pulfer wiltu
	dan[n] das es vast weiß vnd starck werd so tu
	salarmoniarum vnd campfer nach gewicht dar
10	vnder als vor geschriben ist so hast du ein
	gut weiß pulfer **Wie man rot puchsen pul=**
	fer machen so

Wiltu machen ein gut rot pulfer so
nym[m] aber geleich gewicht vnd

15	salpetter vnd swebel vnd nym[m] anderhalb

Royal Armouries I.34 – Part 1

take *salniter*,[187] and five *salpetre hirntis*,[188]
half a pound[189] of *itar bonel*[190] and powder [*mix*] it
together. And take a white pebble
stone and burn it to chalk.
Grind the quicklime well and add
a pound of charcoal to it and three pennys'
weight of camphor and mix it
together well and let it dry

fol. 29v

out well. **How you make good
white gunpowder.**

If you want to make good white powder:
take one pound of saltpetre and one
pound of sulphur, one half of a pound of sandalwood[191] or
white poplar wood. Put all of it into a bowl
and grind it together into powder. If you
want to make it very white so that it becomes strong then add
salammoniac and camphor as weight to it
as is stated above. Then you have good
white powder. **How you make red
gunpowder.**

If you want to make good red powder, then
take equal weights of
saltpetre and sulphur and take one and a half

---

[187] Alternative term for 'saltpetre', possibly making some judgement on purity.

[188] No meaningful translation could be established for this term. '*Hirntis*' appears to be a genitive, probably related to 'saltpetre'.

[189] '*z*' abbreviation for pound; '*ß*' abbreviation for 'semi', 'half'.

[190] No meaningful translation suggestion could be established. It could be that this may be a scribal error for '*carbones*' => 'charcoal'. In Heidelberg, Cod. Pal. germ. 122, fol. 26v, it is '*i car bones z*' and broken after '*car*' at the end of the line.

[191] The author uses a range of different spellings, but from the context it is likely that it refers to 'sandalwood'. Sandalwood has the reputation of being very fragrant for a prolonged period of time. Arguably, in this instance it is used as a colorant to make the powder red – sandalwood is used as a common colouring ingredient in cooking and dyeing (see Chris M. Woolgar, 'Medieval Colour and Food', *Journal of Medieval History* 44 (2018), 1–20, at 15). However, it is less clear why the red colorant is mentioned in a section making 'white' powder, which may be a transmission error.

vierdung rotzs sandels vnd mal das so du
ym[m]er cleiner magst oder kast vnd stoß dise
stuck gar wol zu samen in einem morser
vnd wiltu es vast starck han so tu dar=

20   vnder als vor geschriben stet **Wie man ein**
plaw puchsen pulfer machen sol

Wiltu ein plawb pulfer machen so nÿm[m]

fol. 30r

1   salpetter als vor geschriben stet vnd tu
korn plomen dar zu vierthalb lot ein halb
pfunt sulsarboni holcz vnd stoß dise stuck
gar wol vnter ein ander so wirt es plaw

5   knoln vnd laß dann die knollen vast wol
trucknen so hastu plaw pulfer sarbonim
fur den kol vnd sterck das pulfer als vor
Wie man ein gel puchsen pulfer machen sol

Wiltu ein gel pulfer machen so nym[m]

10   aber salpetter swebel ein geleich
gewicht als vor vnd nym[m] ein halb pfunt
spicandi vnd stoß das auch wol vnder
einander vnd wilt du es starck haben
so nym[m] die stuck dar zu die du vor mals

15   dar zu genomen hast du solt wissen das
dise stuck nicht als genczlich vnd als
schnel mugen sein als die pulfer mit den
koln die sein wol als arck Auch ist zu
wissen das manig ꝫ pulfer gar starck vn[d]

20   stercker ist dan[n] ob es sunst gar vast wer
nun von den dreien stucken **Wie man die al=**
ler pösten fewrpfeil machen sol die ÿema[n]t

quarters of red sandalwood which you can grind as
finely as possible. Grind these
ingredients together thoroughly in a mortar.
If you want to have it very strong then add to it
what has been described before. **How you
make blue gunpowder.**

If you want to make blue powder, then take

fol. 30r

saltpetre as is stated above and add
cornflowers to it. One quarter of a lot, one half
of a pound of sandalwood and grind these ingredients
well together so that it becomes blue
knollen [or, lumps] and then let the *knollen* dry out
and you have blue powder of sandalwood
for the charcoal and strengthen the powder as before.
How you make yellow gunpowder.

If you want to make yellow powder, then take
saltpetre, sulphur, both in equal
measures as before, and take half a pound
of spikenard[192] and grind them together well.
And if you want to have it strong,
then take the ingredients and grind them together
as you have done before. You should know
that these [*powder*] recipes are not as complete and as
fast as the powder with the
charcoal which is very strong. Also you have to
know that plenty of powder is not strong and
it is stronger when it comes
from just the three ingredients. **How you make
the best of all fire arrows which have ever**

---

[192] '*spicanardi*' according to Hassenstein, *Feuerwerkbuch*, 40, has been translated as '*in-
dische Narde, eine gelbe Blume*', or '*Speik*' – no reference provided.

fol. 30v

1 **gehaben mag**

Wiltu die pösten fewr pfeil mach die
ÿemant gehaben mag so nym[m] v
pfunt saluitter vnd ein pfunt swebel ein
5 halb pfunt kols vnd stoß das ineine[m] mor=
ser gar wol vnder einander vnd tu olio
benedicto vnd gepranten wein dar vnder
als vil als sein genug ist vnd mach eine[n]
taig dar auß vnd knit des taigs an die
10 pfeil als vil du sein haben wilt vnd tu
die an eine[n] stecken in eine[n] warme[n] offen dz
es wol ertrucken vnd der[r] Dar nach nym[m]
in her auß vnd schab vnd formier in mit
einem messer als er sein sol vnd uberzeuch
15 in mit einem cleinen saubern tuch vnd be=
wind in mit faden wol vnd swem in jn
swebel merck eben **Wie man über laut**
schiessent pulfer schuß tun mug

Wiltu einen uber lauten schuß tun
20 so leg ein vas zwischen den clocz
vnd das pulfer vnd tu ein tröpflein queck=
silbers jnnen zu dem widloch ein so clopft

fol. 31r

1 er laut uber vast wiltu gar gewiß schuß
tun die gewer sein so lug das du aller erst
wissend seÿ wie ver es tragen muge wie
vil des pulfers seÿ wie swer der stain seÿ
5 gegen dem pulfer vnd die clocz geleich vn[d] eins

fol. 30v
been made.

If you want to make the best fire arrows
which have ever been made: take five
pounds of salniter, and a pound of sulphur, one
half of a pound of charcoal and grind them
together in a mortar and add *oleum*
benedictum[193] and brandy to it
in sufficient quantity. Make it into
paste and knead the paste around
an arrow as big as you want to have it. Put it on
a stick and place it into a warm oven so
that it dries well. After it has dried take it
out [*of the oven*] and sharpen its tip with
a knife as it should be and cover it
with a small clean cloth and wind
some string around it and note to soak it in
sulphur. **How you can**
make overly loud powder shot.

If you want to create an overly loud shot,
then place a hair between the plug
and the powder and add a drop of
mercury into the touch hole. This makes it

fol. 31r

bang very loudly. If you want to make certain that your shot
is reliable then make sure that you firstly
are well informed as to how much it can carry, how
strong your powder is, how heavy your stone is
in relation to the powder, and whether your plugs are equal [*in size*] and

---

[193] '*Oleum benedictum*' could literally just be 'blessed oil'. It has been referred to as being various substances, 'also called *oleum philosophorum* or *oleum laterium*', which would make it 'Oil of brick', and described as 'a clear red oil, the result of pyrolithic distillation of olive oil' (Kramer and Leibnitz, *Das Feuerwerkbuch*, 58), or 'mixture containing oil and tar' ('*Teerölgemisch*', Nibler, *Feuerwerkbuch*, 30). Partington assumes this to be 'a light coal-tar fraction (*Teeröl, Benzol*)', but also raises doubts as to what exactly it may have been (Partington, *Greek Fire and Gunpowder*, 156). As the term cannot be confirmed, it was decided to leave it in the original.

holcz sein vnd die pisen geleich sein vnd ge=
leich getriben werden vnd das die puchß
gewiß stand vnd das sie sich nit entrüste
also da die clocz geleich getriben sind das
10   sÿ nicht für das ror auß gangen vnd nit
für das ror ein getriben werde Mit sunder
hüt dich das die puchs auff recht stand
vnd auff recht lig das ein rad ein halms
nit hocher ste wan[n] das ander Vnd wen[n]
15   du die puchsen mit diser lere also geladest
so kanst du keinen schuß fellen **Ain frag**
in welcher maß ein puchs sein muß die
aller weitzt scheust vnd die antwürt

dar über

Aber tut der maister
20   ein frag jn welcher maß ain puchs
sein muß die aller weiczt schüst Antwurt
wen[n] ein puchs ein venediger zentner scheüst

fol. 31v

1   die scheust aller weitest **Ain andre frag**
von der puchsen

Aber ein andre frag ob die puchs
weitter schieß die cleine ror haben
5   oder grosse ror sprich ich welch puchs ror
hat das das ror funff clocz lang sein die
puchsen sein die pesten wan[n] die kurczen
mugen nÿndert hin geschiessen **Aber ein**
frag wie die puchs aller past lige

10   **E**in frag ob die puchs paß hert lige
oder lind sprich ich wenn sie hert
ligt so spricht hertes wider hertes vnd
mag nit gesten dar vmb sol man die
puchsen in lindes holcz legen Man sol
15   auch hinder die puchsen pleÿ giessen y zweir
vinger dick vmb das daz sie ainen linden
stoß haben Man sol sie nit tieffer legen
wan[n] ains halms prant über das halb=

out of the same wood. The wedges need to be the same,
and need to be driven the same way, your gun
needs to stand firmly and must not be able to move.
When you have driven in the plugs, [*make sure*] that they
do not stick out at the front of the barrel and that they are not driven in
too deeply. Especially, you have to be
careful that the gun stands straight and
sits level so that one wheel is not a blade of grass
taller than the other. If you load a gun
following these instructions
no shot should miss. **A question on
what the dimensions of a gun have to be that
fires the longest distance and the answer
to it.**

But if a master asks
the question what the dimensions of a gun
have to be to fire the longest distance then answer
that when a gun fires a Venetian hundredweight

fol. 31v

then it fires the longest distance. **Another question
about the gun.**

But to the other question whether a gun fires a longer
distance which has a smaller barrel or
a larger, I say: the gun barrel
that is five plugs long is
the best of the guns. If they have to
be shorter, they shoot less far. **But to the question
how best to place a gun.**

To the question whether a gun is better
placed on a harder or a softer base, I say: if it is on a hard base
and hard against hard, it is not good and
should not be. That is why you should
place the gun on lime [*or soft*] wood. Behind
the gun you should pour some lead, two
fingers thick so that it can hit something
soft. You should not place it lower than
when one blade of grass burns over a half

tail in so ligt sie maisterlichen wol **Wa**
10 **mit man ein yedlich puchsen sie sey groß**
oder clein prechen mag

Wiltu ein puchsen prechen wie groß

fol. 32r

1 wie starck sie seÿ so nym[m] dreierleÿ gutes
pulfers vnd lad einen drittail der puch=
sen do mit vnd schalch einen pu^echein clocz
dar ein vnd vermach den stain mit gute[m]
5 pissen ze ring vmb all vmb vnd tu queck=
silber oben zu dem widloch ein so pricht
sie an zweifel **Aber wie man ein puchsen**
prechen sol

Aber zu dem selben
lad die puchsen geleich als vor vn[d]
10 necz das pulfer an dem clocz vnd schüt dan[n]
zu dem widloch wein hin ein vnd tu das
pulfer hin ein dar auff vnd zind sie an et
fragit
Wie man ein puchs laden vnd an=
zinden sol das man do von komen mag an
schade[n]

15 **S**o du ein puchsen geladest vn[d]
du sie beschiessen wilt so nÿm[m] ein pfre=
men vnd stoß in durch das widloch hin ein
piß auf den poden durch das pulfer ab
vnd hab das zund pulfer peÿ dir dem man
20 do spricht paulums currasiue vnd see es

Royal Armouries I.34 – Part 1

part.[194] Thus it will sit expertly. **How you can break[195] any gun whether it is big or small.**

If you want to break a gun however

fol. 32r

strong it may be, then take three parts
good powder and load a third of the
gun with it and drive a beech plug
into it. And seal it with a stone and with
wedges all around the stone and add mercury
into the touch hole, then it will break
without fail. **How you break**

a gun.

But [*add*] to the same
load as before and
wet the powder near the plug and pour
into the touch hole wine and add
powder to it and light it. And
I ask:

how do you load a gun and light it so that you can get away without harm.

When you have loaded a gun and
when you want to fire it, then take an
awl[196] and push it through the touch hole
right to the bottom through the powder.
And have the tinder powder with you which
is called *paulum currasine*.[197] Make sure to put it to

---

[194] Not clear what this refers to.

[195] This could also be translated as 'burst', implying that it would render a gun useless and unable to be repaired.

[196] 'Pfriem' (*Frühneuhochdeutsches Wörterbuch Online*, http://fwb-online.de/go/pfriem. h2.0m_1514157328).

[197] The translation for this term could not be established. Other *Firework Books* refer to this section as '*pulvris guvrasine*' (Freiburg Ms. 362, fol. 84r) or '*puluris curasine*' (Strasbourg Ms. 2259, fol. 6r) which has been interpreted as 'priming powder' (Nibler, *Feuerwerkbuch*, 54n123). Kramer translates this as '*pulvris dura sine*' without

dem prinnenden nach vnd tu sein so vil=
dar ein das du das widloch füllest wann

fol. 32v

1   die pösen pulfer sein gar haiß vnd scharpf
vnd an zinden das pulfer behend in der puch=
sen vnd ob das pulfer inder puchsen verdor=
ben wer so hilf im das pulfer das es pis=

5   sen muß du solt aber treg pulfer auf die
puchsen vnd das zuntloch legen auf das
an zünd pulfer vmb das daz du do uon
kumen mugst du solt dich hietten das du
nym[m]er das selb gut pulfer auff dem wid=

10   loch an zundest an das treg pulfer das
soltu alweg nur an zinden **Item disem
nachgeschriben Capittel was waffen vnd
guter gewonhait ein yedlicher puchsen
maister an jm haben sol vnd auch maß**

15   **kunst erkennen sol**

Dise stuck gehören einem ẏedlichen puch=
sen maister zu das er sie an jm hab
Des ersten sol er got eren vnd foderlichen
vor augen haben vnd in forcht dan[n] ander

20   raißleut vnd wenn er mit der puchsen oder
mit dem pulfer vmb get so hat er seine[n]
grossen feind vnder handen vnd also muß

fol. 33r

1   er alweg driueltig sorg haben Er sol sich
auch beschaidenlich mit der welt halten
mit er do wandelt Er sol auch beherczter
sein vnd manhaft vnd sol sich auch trest=

5   lich in kriegen stellen wann man grossen

Royal Armouries I.34 – Part 1

the burning [*powder*] and add to it
as much as fills the touch hole when

fol. 32v

the bad powder is not hot or fiery.
And light the powder speedily in the
gun and if the powder has been spoiled in the
gun. What helps you is that the powder should be biting,[198]
then you should carry the powder to the
gun, place it on the touch hole on to the
tinder powder so that you can get away
with it. You should be careful
never to light the good powder on the touch
hole. The slow powder
you can always light. **Here this
chapter written below [*lists*] which arms and
good habits should be part of any master
gunner who wishes to learn
the method.**

This part is what each master
gunner has to have within himself.
Firstly, he should honour God and keep Him foremost
in his eyes, and respect other
travellers. And when he handles a gun or
powder he has his
great enemy in his hands. He

fol. 33r

always has to be three times more careful. He should be
modest within the worldly [*status*]
he is in. He should be steadfast
and manly and should provide comfort
in war where he also can draw great

---

any translation or explanation provided (Kramer and Leibnitz, *Das Feuerwerkbuch*,
44).

[198] From the German '*beissen*', which is likely to refer to the acidic nature of the powder (*Frühneuhochdeutsches Wörterbuch Online*, def. 3, http://fwb-online.de/go/pas-
sen.s.3v_1513616100).

trost von sölchen leuten nympt Dar vm[m]
sol er sich tröstlich vnd beschaidenlich hal=
ten dan[n] ander reissig leut Der maister
sol auch künne[n] schreiben vnd lessen wan[n]
10   er kund anders der stuck nicht behalten
die zu diser kunst gehore[n] es sey mit dissul=
ieren seperiern sublimiern oder conuertiern
vnd manig ander stuck die dar zu gehore[n]
Dar vmb muß ein maister die geschrift
15   kunnen Er sol auch all stuck die so her zu
gehören es sey von wilden oder zame[n] sach=
en oder von swebel konnen beraitten von
erst uncz an das end Er sol auch alles
das kunnen ordiniern zu vesten erckern
20   oder mawren fur kaczen schirme[n] fur angan
vnd was dar zu gehört Er sol auch dreÿ
dinck wissen von dem tragman vnd mensure[n]

fol. 33v

1   er sol sich auch erberklichen vnd frumckliche[n]
ziechen mit wortten oder mit wercken peÿ
den leuten vnd sol besunnen sein zu allen
zeitten vnd zu allen ~~zeit~~ stund besunder
5   sich hueten vor trünckenheit **Item wie
sich ein ÿedlich puchsenmaister halten sol
so er mit pulfer vmb get das es jm kein
schaden tun mag**

Item wie ein maister sich halten sol
10   so er mit pulfer vmbget das jm das
pulfer keinen schaden pringt wann der
dunst [vn[d]] der dampf ist ein rechte vergift
dem menschen vnd ist auch vnder den
dreien stucken salpetter swebel vnd kol

comfort from these people. For that reason, he
should behave modestly and comfortingly, more so
that other travelling people. The master should
know to write and to read as
he could not retain the details
that belong to this method; be it dissolving,
separating, sublimating, or converting,
and the many elements it takes.
That is why the master must know how
to write. He also [*must know*] all the parts,
whether it is the wild or tame[199] elements
or the sulphur preparation,
from the beginning to the end. He should also
know how to coordinate matters, in castles,
in alcoves, or in walls, for cats, shields, and for advances[200]
and all that comes with it. He should also know three
things about the loads and the measures.

fol. 33v

He should behave honestly and reliably
with words and deeds towards
other people. He should be calm at all
times and at all hours. He should be especially
careful to avoid drunkeness. **Here [*is written*] how
any master gunner should behave
when handling powder so that it does not cause him
any harm.**

Here [*is written*] how a master should behave
when handling powder so that the
powder does not cause him any harm as the
steam and vapour are real poisons
to humans. And even if out of the
three parts, saltpetre, sulphur, and charcoal,

---

[199] As an opposite to 'raw' or 'wild', and could equally be translated as 'raw' or 'processed'.

[200] For the attack ('*an gan*'), to advance, to 'set alight'. It could be that this may refer to the chemical element Manganese (which would not make sense from the context) or (largely contextually) a mangonel, but as three minims are unlike to have been omitted, it was left as a more general translation.

15	keins sunderbar dem menschen schedlich
	er gesein zu niessen vnd wan[n] sie vnder
	ein ander komen vnd getempert werden
	so schaden sie dem haubt vnd dem hercz=
	en vnd besunder so feült es die lebern
20	Der aller grest schad dar an ist ist der
	dunst oder der tampf der do von dem
	verprun[n]en pulfer gat wiltu dich dar=

fol. 34r

1	vor hueten so lug das du nit nüechter
	do mit vmb gest vnd huet dich vor wein
	das du sein nit zu vil trinckst du solt
	linde kost niessen wan[n] wenn du zu vil
5	mit dem gezeug vmb gangst so gewinstu
	gern das getwang vnd du solt die vil
	zimlichen niessen abentzs vnd morgens
	vor essich vnd aÿre hut dich was aber
	feucht vnd kalt ist das macht du wol
10	niessen vnd was hert vnd trucken seÿ
	vor dem soltu dich hueten **Wa ein yedlich=**
	er puchsen maister aller sicherst sten mug
	so er die puchsen auß lassen wil

	Wann du ein puchsen auß laden wel=
15	lest so soltu wissen das du ny[n]dert
	sicher pist dann du standest über ort
	das ist auf zehen schrit von der puch=
	sen zwischen dem podem vnd der feÿtte[n]
	der puchsen **Wie man ein gute[n] zunder sie=**
	den sol

20	**W**iltu einen guten zunder
	sieden so nÿm[m] die vorgenanten
	laug die man pulfert zu dem salpetter

fol. 34v

1	vnd sich schneid den zunder dar ein vnd
	schneid in auff sechs sturck vnd pulfer

none of them are uncommon and harmful to humans
when they are consumed. When they come
together and are mixed together,
then they are harmful to the skin and the
heart, and it especially fouls the liver.
The biggest damage from it is the
steam or the smoke that comes
from the burnt powder. If you want to

fol. 34r

protect yourself from it, then make sure that you are not handling it on an empty
stomach, and be careful about wine
so that you do not drink too much. You should
take in mild food for you are handling the
ingredients frequently. You may find that you get
stomach cramps. You should eat moderately
in the evenings and in the mornings
abstain from vinegar and eggs. Moist
and cold [*food*] you can consume well.
You should be aware of what is hard and dry
and you should avoid it. **How any
master gunner position is the safest of all
when the gun is emptied.**

If you want to empty a gun
then you need to know that you are never
safe unless you stand at a place
which is ten steps away from the gun
between the floor and the side
of the gun. **How you make good
tinder.**

If you want to make good tinder
then take the aforementioned
lye which was made when the saltpetre was turned into powder

fol. 34v

and cut pieces of tinder into it.
Cut it into six pieces[201] and grind it

---

[201] '*sturck*' is presumably a scribal error, more likely to be '*stuck*'.

vnd stoß in so hastu guten zunder **Wie
man gar gut kugel pulfer machen sol**

5   **I**tem du solt neme[n] zweÿ pfunt salpetters
ein pfunt swebels ein vierdung koln
vnd zerlaß den swebel in ainem tegel
vnd schut den salpetter vnd die koln wol
gestossen dar in vnd zeuch eine[n] grossen
10   vaden dar durch das werden die aller
pesten swebel kercze[n] die ÿemant gehabe[n]
mag auch laß es kalt werden in dem te=
gel so hastu das kollen pulfer das man
vinden mag **Welch zunder der aller
15   aller pest ist**

Item nuß pawme[n] zunder ist der aller
peste zunder vnd der prunstigst zunder
den ÿemant gehaben mag **Wie man
ein verborgen fewr machen sol auff
20   zwen dreÿ oder vier funfft sechs siben
oder acht tag das es dann erst enprint
vnd flam[m]et**

fol. 35r

1   **W**iltu ein fewr verporgen han auff dreÿ
vier oder acht tag so nym[m] zweÿ tail jotono
mris ein tail harcz ein tail wachs ii tail sal=
petter ein vierdling weiß dennes holcz vnd

Royal Armouries I.34 – Part 1

into powder. Then you have good tinder.[202] **How you shall make good ball powder.**

Here you should take two pounds of saltpetre, one pound of sulphur, one quarter of charcoal and let the sulphur melt in a pot.
And add the saltpetre and the charcoal by grinding it well and pull a large piece of string through it, and this becomes the best sulphur candles which anyone can ever have. Let them cool down in a pot and you have [*the best*] *Knollenpulver* you can find.[203] **Which tinder is the best of all.**

Here, tinder from a nut tree is the best of all tinder and the fastest burning tinder anyone can have. **How you make a hidden fire in two, three, or four, five, six, seven, or eight days that only starts to burn then and catches fire.**

fol. 35r

If you want to keep a fire hidden for three, four or eight days, then take two parts *jotomris*,[204] one part of resin, one part of wax, two parts of saltpetre, one quart of white wood from a fir tree, and

---

[202] This section does not make sense. Compared to other *Firework Books* there seems to be a line or two missing, and this could be a scribal error. Other *Firework Books* state in this section that 'the tinder should simmer for six hours, and then it should be allowed to dry, and then it should be pulverized' (Freiburg Ms. 362, fol. 87r).

[203] It appears most likely that the scribe made an error here, and conflates 'ball powder' and '*Knollenpulver*'. In Heidelberg, Cod. Pal. germ. 122, 31r, this section is in the same sequence as I.34, but instead of '*kugel pulfer*' it mentions '*knollen puluer*' while stating the same end product '*Knollenpulver*'.

[204] A translation for this ingredient could not be established. This component is an addition compared to other *Firework Books*, e.g. Freiburg Ms. 362, fol. 87r. In Heidelberg, Cod. Pal. germ. 122, fol. 31v, '*rötömil*', Heidelberg, Cod. Pal. germ. 502, fol. 34r, '*ytotomrl*', and Dillingen Ms. XV 50, fol. 26v, '*jetams*'. In other *Firework Book* copies this section is missing completely, e.g. Dresden Ms. App. 463.

Gunpowder Technology in the Fifteenth Century

5   zelaß das vnder einander vnd zeuch eine[n]
langen zachen dar durch vnd zund ab vn[d]
laß es dann wider ab das es nit lauter
prün[n]e vnd das es sich nach vnd furpaß
muß schmelczen vnd wart wann die glock
10   schlach das du es an zündest vnd nÿm[m]
eben war wie ver es in einer stund prünne[n]
mug das maß behalt vnd zaichen den
zachen mit dem meß als lang er seÿ vn[d]
recht wie vil der meß seÿ als vil stund
15   prunnet auch diser zach vnd zu welcher
stund du gern ein fewr habest so heb
in swebel kerczen dar an so hastu ein fewr
du solt einem zachen vmb ein stecken win=
den das er nach ein ander abschmelcze[n] muß
20   **Wie man ein fewr machen sol das einer**
tregt an groß bekimernuß ainem halben
oder ganczen tag vnd nacht vnd das er

fol. 35v

1   **auf dem selben fewr ein swebel kerczen**
an zunden mag wan[n] er kompt an die
statt do er fewr prauchen wil

W iltu ein höflich fewr machen so
5   nym[m] groß mist pinczen in gutem
als in den weiern vnd in den mosern stat
vnd schut die pinczen in guten wein dar
in salpetter gesoten seÿ vnd nÿm[m] die her=
auß vnd trucken die pinczen an der sunne[n]
10   vnd zeuch jm die groben ausser haut ab vn[d]
hab in an ein prinenden koln das er das

Royal Armouries I.34 – Part 1

let it melt together. Drag a long
piece of string[205] through it and light it.
Put it out so that it does not burn
further, and smoulders bit by bit and
melts. And wait when the bell
tolls so that you light it and take
note how far it has burned in an hour.
Take the measure and make a
mark which is as long and
straight as any measurement would be for many
hours with a wick, and for any
hours you may want to have fire.[206]
Put sulphur candles to it and this way you have fire
that has a wick which you can wind around a stick
so that it can melt one after the other.
**How you make a fire that you can
carry with great care one half or a
full day and night and**

fol. 35v

**with the same fire you can light sulphur
candles when you arrive at the
city where you need the fire.**

If you want to create a 'courtly' fire,
then take large mixed reeds which are good
as they stand in the ponds and in the marshlands.
Put the reeds into a good wine in which
saltpetre had been dissolved. Take them out,
and dry the reeds in the sun.
Peel off the outer skin and
place them in burning charcoal, so that they

---

[205] Two possibilities: a) 'hook' ('*Zacken*') – less likely through context; or b) more likely to be 'string' or 'wick' (def. 2, *Deutsches Wörterbuch von Jacob und Wilhelm Grimm Online* – accessed 10 August 2023 – particularly used in Bavarian context).

[206] This is using two separate time measurements: first, using the bell chiming to measure one hour; second, using the wick to measure multiples of the hour in order to have a time-sensitive fuse.

empfacht du tregst einer spanne[n] lanck
ein meil wegs weren vnd wen[n] du wilt
ein fewr machen oder haben so hab ein sweb=

15 el kerczen dar an so hast du fewr **Ein be=
sundre gute lere auff salpetter zu kauf=
fen der erst von venedig komen ist das
man an dem kauff nit betrogen werd**

Wiltu ein besundre ler halben auff

20 salpetter zu kauffen als er von venedig
kompt so du kompst über ein geschür mit
salpetter so stoß die hand dar ein vnd wirt

fol. 36r

1 sie naß so wirt er nit gut beleibt sie aber
trucken so wirt er gut **Aber wie man salpett[er]
kauffen sol**

Aber salpetter verkauffen versuch in mit

5 dem mund ist er reß pitter vnd gesalcze[n]
so ist er nit gut ist er aber piczenlich vnd
suslich vnd vast übel so ist er gut **Aber wie
man salpetter kauffen sol**

Aber salpetter zu kauffen der zapfent vn[d]

10 gelat salpetter ist gut aber der rauch=
zapfent salpetter ist nit gut rauch gemaln[er]
salpetter ist nit gut **Indisem nach geschribe[n]
Capittel stet gar aÿgentlich geschriben wie
man gut swebel ol machen sol das nucz vnd**

15 **gut wirt vnd alles fewrwerck vnd besunder
vnder alles pulfer denn es hiczigt vnd sterckt
vnd hehelt alle stuck für verderben war
zu man es praucht**

Royal Armouries I.34 – Part 1

catch fire and can be carried a span[207] long and for
a mile on the road. And if you want to
make a fire, or to have one, then have a sulphur candle
ready to have a fire. **A special
instruction on how you buy saltpetre
which has come from Venice so that you are not
being defrauded at the purchase.**

If you want to have special instructions on
how to buy saltpetre as it comes from Venice:
if you come across a dish with
saltpetre put your hand it it and if

fol. 36r

if it is wet then it is not good; if it stays
dry then it is good. **But how do you buy
saltpetre.**

But if you want to sell[208] saltpetre try it in your
mouth. If it is quite bitter and salty,
then it is not good. If it is, however, sharp
and sweet and almost sickening then it is good. **But how
do you buy saltpetre.**

But if you want to buy saltpetre which is icicle shaped and
smooth saltpetre, [*then*] it is good saltpetre. But smoky,
icicle shaped saltpetre is not good, ground, smoky
saltpetre is not good. **In the chapter written
below is actually written how
you can make good oil of sulphur[209] that is useful
and good for all fireworks and especially
for all powder. As it is hot and strong
and moves all parts, make sure it does not get spoiled
as you may need it.**

---

[207] The measurement of the New High German '*Spanne*' as a length of hand was only
defined later (in 1618 – *Deutsches Wörterbuch von Jacob und Wilhelm Grimm Online*
– accessed 10 August 2023).

[208] In German, 'buy' and 'sell' are the same word field, '*kaufen*' and '*verkaufen*', something that may be less clear in English.

[209] Or, 'sulphuric acid'.

Gunpowder Technology in the Fifteenth Century

20
Also soltu swebel öl machen nym[m] sweb
el wie vil du wilt vnd stoß in gar
wol vnd tu dar zu salsparatu[m] auch wol
gestossen vnd wol gemischt vndereinander

fol. 36v

1
vnd schüt dar zu accetu[m] benedistillatu[m] vnd
vnd laß es wol sieden in eine[m] verdeckten
haffen piß das der haffen wol trucken werd
vnd tu das in ein co[n]turbit vnd ain alambte
5
dar auff vnd leuter das gar wol vnd
secz das auff ein offelin auff die aschen
vnd mach ein gefug fewr piß es auch
tropflin vnd mach dar auß ein groß fewr
das du kainen dunst mer sechst do von
10
gen Diczs öl ist auch gut zu medicinas
vnd ist auch gut zu dem pulfer vnd
gibt dem pulfer kraft vnd behelt es für
verderben Item nym[m] kampfram z i petrali
z iii arsenicu[m] et decarbonibus vite oleum
15
sulpuntis ay et ii vnd tu das in ainen
haffen vnd vermach das wol mit einer
bastet z tu essich dar zu bene distillatis

Royal Armouries I.34 – Part 1

And when you want to make oil of sulphur then take
as much sulphur as you want and grind it well
and add to it *salsparatum*,[210] grind it
well and mix it well together.

fol. 36v

Add to it *accetum bene distillatum*[211] and
let it boil well in a covered
pot until the pot has dried out well.
Place it into a cucurbit,[212] and put an alembic
on top of it, and let it purify well.
Place it in an oven on ashes
and make a moderate fire until it
starts to drip. Then turn it into a large fire
until you cannot see any more steam coming
from it. This oil is also good as medicine
and is good for powder. And it
provides strength to the powder, and protects it
from getting spoiled. Take 1 pound of camphor, 3 pounds of petroleum,
arsenicum et decarbonibus,[213] *vite oleum*
sulphuris,[214] each at 2 pounds. Place it in a
bowl and seal it well with a
paste.[215] Add vinegar and distill it well

---

[210] Possible scribal error; likely to be 'salpraticum' (see, for example, Dillingen Ms. XV 50, fol. 27v, or Freiburg Ms. 362, fol. 87v).

[211] The addition of '*bene*' may imply that 'distilled oil' ('*acceto distillato*') may even be sold in different forms, with this version being of higher quality.

[212] In other *Firework Books* this is referred to as an '*alempt*' (Freiburg Ms. 362, fol. 87v) or '*kukurbit vnd alent*' (Stainer 1529, 33), or '*kachibit*' (Dillingen Ms. XV 50, fol. 27v) = something related to a '*Destillierkolben*', or '*kupfferin beckin*' = copper pot (Nibler, *Feuerwerkbuch*, 29); or 'cucurbit' as base unit to an alembic.

[213] The precise nature of this ingredient is unclear. Freiburg Ms. 362 refers to the ingredients at this stage as '*arsenicum de carbonibus*' (fol. 87v) which is mirrored in the Stainer print (Stainer 1529, 33).

[214] It is unclear what this ingredient is intended to be. Freiburg Ms. 362 refers to the ingredients at this stage as '*vite oleum sulfuris*' (which is mirrored in Stainer 1529 as '*vitriolum sulphur*', and in Dillingen Ms. XV 50 (fol. 27v) as '*vitriolum sulphuris*'.

[215] Other *Firework Books* refer to this as '*pedast*' (Freiburg Ms. 362, fol. 87v) or '*petast*' (Dillingen Ms. XV 50, fol. 27v) = '*Destillierhalm*'. The suggested translation 'paste' here is based on the original word used.

vnd prenn aquam fortem herauß **Wie**
man das aller pest oleu[m] co[m]po[m]itu[m] distillatu[m]
20   **machen sol zu welcherleÿ fewrwerck das**
praucht wenn das enprint so print es so
grimlich vast das es nyemant erleschen

fol. 37r

1   **kan noch mag all die weil es zeug hat**

Nym[m] mirram ellectam z i thuris menstis
pistis ay et sublimatu[m] argentu[m] vinu[m]
in campfram z i arsenicu[m] z i in salarmo[n]iarum
5   z v i salpratica z iii in hebratica z ii saluiter
z v salphir vinu[m] z v ꝙ aquam vite mensu=
ram ß vnd tu dise stuck vndereinander wol
gestossen vnd tu dar zu i mensis olie oliue
et distillabitur z iii vinu[m] distillatis vnd
10   lug das kein fewr dar zu kum oder es
mocht nÿemant erleschen dan[n] mit aschen
also hastu das pest oleo co[m]positis distillatis
Wie man verdorben pöß pulfer wider pringt
vnd es jm wern sol

and you will have burnt out *aqua forte* as a result. **How
you make the best oleum compomitum distillatum**[216]
**which you need for many fireworks. You
need it for lighting it because it burns so
fast that no one can or would want to extinguish**

fol. 37r

it nor would want to as it contains material.[217]

Take 1 pound of mirram ellectam, thuris menstis
pistis, and *argentum sublimatum*, wine in camphor,
1 pound of *arsenicum*, and 1 pound of salammoniac,
and 6 pounds of *salpratica*, 3 pounds of *hebratica*, 2 pounds of *salnitre*,
and five pounds of *salphir vinum*, and 5 pounds of *aqua vita mensuram*.
And put all these ingredients together, grinding them
well. Add to it 1 pound of *olie oline et
destilibatur* and 3 pounds of distilled wine. Make
sure that no fire gets to it, or no
one could extinguish it. In the ash
you have the best *oleo compositis distillatis*.[218]
**How you bring back spoiled, bad powder
and how it can become new again.**

---

[216] It is not clear what this term refers to. It is a section not found in most other *Firework Books*.

[217] The implication is that this is highly flammable, and adding water to it would make the fire burn more vigorously.

[218] It was not possible to establish a meaningful translation for the ingredients without additional information and context. This section is not replicated in many other *Firework Books*. The two notable exceptions are the Dillingen Ms. XV 50 (fol. 27v):
Nym mirram cloctam vi thwe mestr pict aii z solimatu[m] argintu[m] vinu[m] pita-mpffan z I chr z senitu z I salarmoniack z vi salpartica z I pi hebrayca ß vr tu dise stark vnder ain ander wol ge stossen vn[d] tŭ dar zŭ ain meß oliu[m] oline + disstillabitum z iii vrtu[m] distillate[m] vn[d] lŭg das kain für dar zŭ komen mŭg oder es möcht nieman erlöschen denne mit aschen. Also haust du das aller best oleu[m] co[m]paitu[m] distil-latu[m].
and Darmstadt Ms. 1074 (fol. 33v):
Nym mirvram clertra[m] zi thuris menstis pistis ay et sublimate[m] argentu[m] vinu-u[m] in campfram zi arsenic[m] zi in salaram[n]iak z vi salpratica z iii inhebratica z ii salniter z x salphir vinu[m] z v aqua[m] vite niefirra[m] ß vn[d] diese stuck vntter einandr wol gestossn vnd ihn darzu 1 mensis olie iline et distillabi[tur] zm vnu[m] dis-tillate[um] vnd lug daz chain fewr darzu kum oder es mocht niemant erlesche[e]n dann mit aschn also hast du das peßt oleu[m] conport[is] distillat[um].

Gunpowder Technology in the Fifteenth Century

15 So du ein pulfer schaidest vnd du es
wider vndereinander temperiern wilt
so nym[m] zwaÿ pfunt salpetters vnd ein lb
als er dir indem sack beliben ist vnd nucz
das also her auß als vil sein dan[n] ist vnd
20 tu weder swebel noch kol dar zu vnd stoß
das ab cum acceto distillato vnd laß das
gar wol trucke[n] an der sunne[n] vnd tu con

fol. 37v

1 uortaniu[m] dar zu so hastu gut pulfer er=
nert von dem pössen **Aber wie man sal=**
petter leuttren sol

 Wiltu salpetter leuttern als du wol
5 waist so nÿm[m] in vnd schlach in
durch ein reittern vnd was in der reittern
beleibt das seud in harn der von wein
seÿ gemacht als lang als man visch
seut vnd geuß in dann ab vnd laß in
10 sten piß er kalt wirt Zu dem andern
mal so seud in in wein als vor Zu dem
dritten mal so seud in in acceto distillato
als vor Zu dem vierden mal sued in
in vino distillato als vor Und also hastu
15 saluiter p[rae]p[ar]at[us] In quartu gradu doch schut

Royal Armouries I.34 – Part 1

When you separate the powder and you
want to mix it together again,
then take two pounds of saltpetre and one pound[219]
which has remained in the bag. Take
as much of it as possible and
add neither sulphur nor charcoal to it and grind
into it *acceto distillato*[220] and let it
dry out well in the sun and add

fol. 37v

conuortanium[221] to it, and you have good powder
renewed from bad. **But how you shall
purify saltpetre.**

If you want to purify saltpetre as you know
well, then take it and put it
through a sieve.[222] What remains in the sieve
boil in urine which has been made from wine
as long as you would boil a fish.
Pour it [*the reduced liquid*] off and let it
rest until it has cooled down. The second time,
boil it [*the saltpetre crystals*] in wine as before. The
third time, boil it [*as above*] in *acceto distillato*[223]
as before. The fourth time, boil it
in *vino distillato*[224] as before. And thus you have
salniter praeparatus in '*quartu gradu*'. Make sure

---

[219] Likely scribal omission; must have been sulphur and charcoal.

[220] Kept in its original as it is not certain what this refers to. Hassenstein refers to it as 'distilled vinegar' ('*Tropfessig*'; *Essig, der durch tropfweises Destillieren gereinigt ist*, Hassenstein, *Feuerwerkbuch*, 39) and others followed (e.g. Nibler, *Feuerwerkbuch*, 9, and Kramer and Leibnitz, *Das Feuerwerkbuch*, 28). It certainly seems to be an ingredient known to any practitioner.

[221] Not clear what this term refers to. In other manuscripts it is described as '*confortium*' (Freiburg Ms. 362, fol. 82v), '*confortatiuum*' (Stainer 1529, 28). Kramer interprets this as a 'reinforcer' (Kramer and Leibnitz, *Das Feuerwerkbuch*, 40).

[222] '*reiter*' can be defined as 'a coarse sieve, especially used for sifting wheat' (*Deutsches Wörterbuch von Jacob und Wilhelm Grimm Online* – accessed 10 August 2023).

[223] Presumably here 'distilled vinegar', but it is not clear what the benefit would be.

[224] Presumably here 'distilled wine', but it is unclear what chemical reaction this would cause.

alwegen des salpetters wasser gar wol
Wie man stangen auß auß puchsen schiessnn
ssol

20

Wiltu stangen oder pfeil auß
der puchsen schiessen sol so lad
die puchsen dreÿ tail mit pulfer vnd
mach ein linden clocz auß leim als der
clocz zu der puchsen sein sol vnd spicz die

fol. 38r

1

stangen als sie für den clocz gehört in das
ror vnd schlach oben ein hülczein zweck
zwischen die puchsen vnd die stangen vn[d]
mach ein stůl der sich hoch oder nider

5

laß treiben vnd leg den[n] die stangen dar
auff das sie der puchsen geleich sech so mag
dann die stang geleich von der puchsen
gen vnd wann du sie geladest so zund sie
an vnd lauß sie lauffen **Wie man einen**

10

hagel schiessen sol

Wiltu einen hagel schiessen so mach
eine[n] herten clocz der vmb das
halbtail kurczer seÿ dan[n] er prait seÿ vn[d]
lad den geleich an die puchsen vnd lad

15

vier stain i[te]m den cloczen das sie den cloczen
nit an rwre[n] vnd schlach wol gepranten
~~wein~~ leim dar ein der mit porris mit vierol

that you pour away the saltpetre water.[225]

How you fire rods out[226] **of**
guns.

If you want to fire rods or arrows out
of guns, then you should load
the guns with three parts of powder and
make a soft plug out of clay so that the
the plug sits [*tightly*] in the gun.[227] Sharpen

fol. 38r

the rod which has to be in front of the plug, and put it into
the barrel. Drive in a wooden twig
between the gun and the rod and
make a rest which can be raised or lowered
and place the rod onto it
so that it stays level with the gun. This
way the rod can leave the gun level
and when you have loaded it, light it,
and let it run. **How you fire a**
hail of shot.

If you want to shoot a hail of shot, make
a plug of hard wood which
is half as short as it is wide. And
load it tightly in the gun. Then load
four stones ahead of the plug so that they
do not touch it. And add well burned
clay[228] which has been enriched with *porris*,[229]

---

[225] This presumably refers to the water in which the saltpetre crystals were formed.

[226] Repetition of '*auß*' – appears to be a scribal error – not translated.

[227] This presumably is a reference to its size and shape.

[228] Scribal error in original – crossed out. Translates as 'wine'.

[229] In Freiburg Ms. 362 the German original is '*porf*' (fol. 88r), in Dillingen Ms. XV 50, fol. 28r, it is '*porris*', and in the Stainer print as '*porren*' (Stainer 1529, 34), and not even Kramer suggests a translation (Kramer and Leibnitz, *Das Feuerwerkbuch*, 58).

vnd mit salcz vnd mit puppilln[n] saft wol
gepert seÿ vnd stoß den[n] vil stain die in
20   der maß sein als die aÿr oder grosser vn[d]
vermach es dan[n] aber mit dem vor gena[n]te[n]
leim piß das die puchs vol werd vnd

fol. 38v

1   schlach sie mit einem tribel vast wol auff
einander vnd lug das du die puchs ver=
sorgest das nichczs vor ir seÿ vnd auch
in gut noch nucz noch behender seÿ **Wie**
5   **man einen igel schiessen sol vnder eim folk**

Wiltu einen igel schiessen vnder
eim folck von vierhundert stucke[n]
vnd nach dem vnd die puchs ist so lad
die puchsen gar starck mit eine[m] pu^echem
10   clocz vnd haiß dir ein eÿsnein plochlein
fur den clocz machen als der clocz preit seÿ
vnd haiß dir machen so uil eÿsner starck
Wie man auß der puchsen behendlich vnd
gewiß vnd gewer lern schiessen sol

with *vierol*,[230] with salt, and with *poplar juice*.[231]
Then, drive in more stones
which are of the same size or bigger and
seal it with the aforementioned
clay so that the gun is full and

fol. 38v

hit it with a rammer tightly together.
Be careful that the gun does not have
anything in front of it and that it is looked
after, and in working condition. **How
to fire a hedgehog**[232] **into a crowd.**

If you want to shoot a hedgehog into a
crowd of four hundred people,
depending on the gun, then load
the gun tightly with a beech
plug. And have a small iron sheet made
for the plug which is as wide as the plug,
and have made as many as you have iron pieces.[233]
**How to fire quickly and accurately
and how to learn to fire a gun.**

---

[230] The term used here is unclear but it most likely relates to a particular type of oil. In the Freiburg manuscript the German original is '*vyel*' (could just mean 'oil') (fol. 88r) and it is not listed in the Stainer 1529 print.

[231] Kramer suggests 'virgin's milk – calomel Hg_2Cl_2 as preservative', but how this conclusion was reached is not explained in detail (Kramer and Leibnitz, *Das Feuerwerkbuch*, 58). In Dresden Ms. App. 463, fol. 62r, '*Pappel safft*' ('juice of poplars') and in Freiburg Ms. 362, fol. 88r, '*pupillen safft*' ('juice of pupilla'). In Stainer 1529 this is transcribed as 'leeks' and 'juice of poplars' ('*Porre*' and '*Pappelsaft*', Hassenstein, *Feuerwerkbuch*, 74). The meaning of the addition is not clear. One other suggestion could be from '*purpul*' or '*purpur*' – from 'purpura' – the colour 'purple'. This would provide a reason for this addition as it would dye the powder purple.

[232] Kramer translates this as 'grapeshot' (Kramer and Leibnitz, *Das Feuerwerkbuch*, 58) – which makes sense from the context, but could not be substantiated from the original word.

[233] Compared to the Freiburg manuscript, the text here seems to be incomplete. Freiburg Ms. 362 contains two more lines which explains this section in more detail: fol. 88r: '*als denn verschiessen wilt vnd lad die hart für das blächlin das vor dem klotzen ist*', which could be translated in relation to the above as 'which you can fire. Load them tightly to the plate where the plug is'.

Gunpowder Technology in the Fifteenth Century

15 **W**iltu behend vnd wol lern schies=
sen so nym[m] stain geleich in die
puchs gehoren vnd swem den in harcz
vnd in wachs vnd lad die puchsen mit
leinn vnd mit den[n] staine[n] vnd mit pis=
20 sen an stopfen vnd also machtu behend
schiessen benesencio **Wie man auß der
puchsen schiessen mag mit wasser an pul**

fol. 39r

1 **pulfer also das das wasser das pulfer
verwischt vnd als weit vnd als starck
mit scheust als mit pulfer**

Wiltu mit wasser schiessen das du
5 dann kain pulfer prauchst vnd
stercker vnd weitter scheust dan[n] ob du das
pest pulfer hest das ÿe gemacht ward
so nym[m] salpetter vnd distiller das zu was=
ser vnd den swebel auch zu öle vnd salar=
10 moniarum auch zu wasser vnd nym[m] oleum
benedictum auch dar zu nach gewicht
als du wol hern wirst wann du das was=
ser zu same[n] pringen macht so nym[m] sechs
tail salpetter wasser zwaÿtail swebel=
15 wasser zwaÿtail salarmo[n]iarum zwaÿtail
deoleo benedicto vnd lad die puchsen
vast mit cloczen vnd mit staine[n] vnd geuß
dise wasser in die puchsen ain zechen tail
vnd zünd sie an mit zucken das du do
20 von komen magst vnd luge das die
puchs vast starckt seÿ mit disen wassern
scheust du mit einer gemaine[n] puchsen

Royal Armouries I.34 – Part 1

If you want to learn to shoot well and quickly,
then take a stone which is the same size as the
gun and soak it in resin
and in wax. And load the gun with
clay and the stone, and fill it up with
wedges, and you can shoot quickly
and very well.[234] **How you
fire a gun with water**

fol. 39r

**in the powder when water has got
into the powder and you can fire it as far and as strongly
as if with [dry] powder.**

If you want to fire with water so that you
do not need any powder [at all], and to
fire more powerfully and further then you would with the
best powder that was ever made:
take saltpetre and distill[235] it to water
and the sulphur to oil, and salammoniac,
and also to water. Also take *oleum
benedictum* which you have weighed
as much as you want to hear. In order to bring the
water together, take six
parts of saltpetre water, two parts of sulphur
water, two parts of salammoniac, two parts of
oleum benedictum. And load the gun
tightly with a plug and with a stone and pour
this water into the gun, up to one tenth of a part [*of the gun*].
Light it it with tinder so that you
can get away. Make sure that the
gun is very strong. With this water
you can fire with a common gun

---

[234] The word in the original is '*benesencio*', and it is presumed that it is a misspelling of
'*beneficio*'.

[235] Possible scribal error. More likely to mean 'dissolve'.

fol. 39v

1 ob dreÿ tausent schrit weit es ist aber
gar köstenlich **Wie weit man schieß von
gemaine[n] oder zu geleu[er]ten starcken pul=
fer schiessen mag**

5 **E**in gemainer schuß von der puchs
vnd von pulfer ist funfzehen hun=
dert schrit weit oder in der selben maß
aber von gelautterte[n] pulfer funffvnd=
zwainczig hundert schrit weit **Das ma[n]**
10 **kainer puchsen getrawen sol wie sie ist**

Aber ein andre ler sich das du kainer
puchsen nichczs getrawst sie seÿ
clein oder groß vnd sie sey beschlagen
der nicht sie seÿ übel oder wol geladen
15 wie die puchs seÿ so hu^{e}t dich nichtzs dest[er]
mÿnder dar vor Auch lug wen[n] du sie
ladest das kein eysen das ander rwr wan[n]
das pulfer mocht villeicht do von enzindt
werden **Wie man ein gut confertet mach=**
20 **en sol das zu allem fewr werck gar gut**
                    vnd nucz ist

Nÿm[m] ein pfunt geschla=
gens wasser pleÿ dreÿ pfunt sweb

fol. 39v

up to three thousand paces but
this is rather costly. **How far you fire
with common or with purified, strong
powder.**

A common shot from a gun
with [*common*] powder goes fifteen hundred
paces, or, with the same measurements
from purified powder twenty-five
hundred paces. **That you
should never trust a gun as it is.**

But other instructions [teach] you that you
cannot trust any gun: whether they are
small or large; whether they have been repaired;
whether they have been loaded badly or well.
Whatever state a gun is, do not take less care
about it. And make sure when you
load it that no iron touches any other as
it may set the powder
alight. **How you make good paste**[236]
**which is useful and good for all
fireworks.**

Take one pound of 'beaten water'[237]
three pounds of lead, nine

---

[236] Kramer translates this as 'intensifier' without explanation (Kramer and Leibnitz, *Das Feuerwerkbuch*, 59), while Nibler describes it as 'strengthener' ('*Verstärkungsmittel*', Nibler, *Feuerwerkbuch*, 31). It is likely to be something which improves some of the quantities of the powder, but it is unclear that the word states this, hence translated into 'paste'. Other *Firework Books* refer to this as '*conforcet*' (Freiburg Ms. 362, fol. 88v) and '*confort*' (Dillingen Ms. XV 50, fol. 29r).

[237] Not clear what 'beaten water' refers to. Kramer interprets this as '*geschlagenes wasser* [urine]' (Kramer and Leibnitz, *Das Feuerwerkbuch*, 59), while Nibler interprets it as 'lukewarm water' while providing some critical commentary. He doubts Kramer's assumption that this could relate to urine, and wonders whether it could refer to the temperature of water, thus translates it as 'lukewarm water' ('*Kramer vermutet hier "abgeschlagenes Wasser", also Harn, aber es ist offen, ob der Ausdruck um 1400 gebräuchlich war, und was Harn im Rezept soll. Schmeller kennt (ab-)schlagen in diesem Sinne nicht! Denkbar ist auch "geschlages wasser" = "überschlagenes Wasser" => lauwarmes Wasser.*' (Nibler, *Feuerwerkbuch*, 57).

fol. 40r

1 els newn pfunt salpetters ein pfunt salar=
mo[n]iarum arsenicum ß mercuriu[m] sublimatu[m]
ein pfunt vnd leg die in einem hafen wol
gestossen vnd tu dar zu pawmöl das es
5 ploß über die materÿ auff gang vnd
vermach den̶ hafen wol mit gepran=
tem leÿm das der dunst nit do von müg
vnd tu den hafen über ein gefug fewr
vnd laß in als lang ob dem fewr vnd
10 prich in auff so ist er worden Item trück=
en es ein manet an der sunne[n] so vil vnd
du sein prauchen wilt das übrig laß
in dem hafen Item hu^et dich das vnder
zehen pfunden nit mer nempst den[n] sechs
15 lot vnd besunder zu fewr pfeiln vnd
zu fewr kugeln ist es die pest kunst
die ÿemant gehaben mag **Wie man**
auß einer puchs etwen vil clocz mit aine[m]
anzünden schiessen sol vnd das ÿedlich
20 **clocz sein besunder clepsi tut vnd doch**
mit mer dan[n] zu mal an gezundt wirt

Wiltu ein clocz puchsen beschiessen mit

fol. 40v

1 sechs oder zechen cloczen sie sein eysnein
oder pleyein vnd ÿe ein stuck nach dem
andern get so tu zu dem ersten als vil
pulfers in die puchsen als lang die clocz
5 sein vnd schlach den cloċz auff das pulfer
vncz das sie vol werd es sol ein ÿedlich
clocz ein durch geng plöchlein haben

fol. 40r

pounds of sulphur, one pound of saltpetre, and a pound of
salammoniac, *arsenicum*, and *mercurium sublimatum*.
Put them all into a bowl, and grind
them well. Add to it some tree oil so that it
covers the ingredients. Seal
the pot well with burned
clay so that no steam can escape from it.
And put the pot into a moderate fire and
let it stay for some time on the fire.
Break it open and it is done. Let as much as you want
dry in the sun for a month.
The remainder you can keep
in the pot. Be careful that out of
ten pounds you do not take more than six
lots. Especially for fire arrows and
for fire balls this is the best 'art'
which anyone may want to have. **How you
fire many plugs out of a gun with one
light, and each plug
has its special clap.**[238] **And you have
more than you require to set it alight.**

If you want to fire a plug gun[239] with

fol. 40v

six or ten plugs which are made out of iron
or lead, and one piece goes off after the other,
then first add to the gun as much
powder as the plug is long.[240]
Drive the plug onto the powder
until it fits tightly. Each
plug should have a small piece of metal

---

[238] In the meaning of a 'loud bang'.

[239] Kramer asserts that this refers to a 'type of charge', not a 'type of gun' (Kramer and Leibnitz, *Das Feuerwerkbuch*, n. 16). However, not every gun takes this kind of load – they also need to be lit from the front. See Leng, *Anleitung Schiesspulver*, 104–5, and in Smith and Gnudi, *Biringuccio*, 425–28, where they are described as fire tubes.

[240] Meaning 'the same amount of powder as the plug is wide'.

das das fewr von einem durch das ander
gen müg Die plochlein sullen in der maß
10 groß sein als ein spindel spicz vnd laß
pulfer durch die löcher vnd stoß ein
swebel kerczen dar ein vnd zünd es an
so clopft einer nach dem ander piß das
die pichs ler wirt **Wie man einen pfal**
15 **in einem weg verprennen mag wie tieff**
er stet

Wiltu einen pfal verprenne[n]
in einem weg wie tieff er stet
so [nym][m] ludern vnd necz die in oleo benedicto
cu[m] aqua saluiter als vor indisem půch
20 stet vnd bewind das pfal mit disen
ludernd vnd scheusch einen prin[n]enden
fewr pfeil in ainen pfal so enzunden die

fol. 41r

1 ludern vnd prinne[n] all die weil vnd sie
clein feuchtein von dem wasser gehaben
mag wann die lauttern haben vmb den
pfal gar vast gepunden and er erst
5 wan[n] sie prinnen in dem wasser wol auf
vier und zwainczig stund ee das wol=
len verprinnen die feuch schlech alweg
von dem wasser and das fewr an den pfal
piß das er verprint **Wie man auß ainer**
10 **puchsen gewiß schuß schiessen sol**

Wiltu auß einer puchsen schiessen ge=
wiß schüß so sich das du den erste[n]
schuß nit zu hoch schiescht oder du macht

Royal Armouries I.34 – Part 1

so that the fire can go from one through to
the next. The pieces of metal should have a hole
the size of the tip of a spindle, and this lets
the powder through the holes. Insert a
sulphur candle and set it alight.
This way one knocks one after the other until
the gun is empty. **How you
burn down a pole**[241] **on a path however deep
it stands.**[242]

If you want to burn down a pole
on a path however deep it stands
then take some cloth and wet it [*the cloth*] with *oleum benedictum*
and salniter water as has been described in this book above.
And wrap these cloths around the
pole and shoot a burning
fire arrow at the pole. And it [*the arrow*] lights

fol. 41r

the cloth and all of it [*the pole*] will burn as it
is a little wet from the water.
The cloth has to be tightened
neatly around the pole. It will
burn away completely in water after
burning four and twenty hours.
The fire is driven away
by the water but the fire stays with the pole
until it has burned down.[243] **How
to fire an accurate shot from a gun.**

If you want to fire a shot out of a gun
accurately then make sure that the first
shot is not too high or you may

---

[241] This relates to a wooden 'pole, post, stake', but there is insufficient context to determine what function the pole has at this point.

[242] Kramer suggests that this could be translated as a pole in a 'pool', 'pond', or 'ditch' (for all, in their function as 'waymarker'). However, this cannot be evidenced from the context (Kramer and Leibnitz, *Das Feuerwerkbuch*, 59).

[243] The assumption here is that the fire is not extinguished completely but keeps burning due to the very wet pole.

komen pald in kainem mer Auch soltu
15 wissen die gewicht des stains vnd des clocz
vnd des pulfers vnd sein kraft solt du
wol wissen was es tragen mag als du
wol hast in disem půch Wiltu sicher
vor der puchsen sten das sie dir kein
20 laid tu so lug des ersten das du in dem
namen gottes nicht schiest **Wie man
fewr stain auß einer pleienden oder werck**

fol. 41v

1 **in ein fest stat wffen sol**

Wiltu fewr stain auß ainer pleien=
den oder werck weffen so nym[m] de[n]
stain als in das werck oder das pleÿ
5 gewerffen mag vnd swem[m] in in sweb=
el vnd in harcz vnd wirff in dan[n] in
puchsenpulfer vnd mit den zwilchein
tu^echern über var den stain oder über=
zeuch in vmd swem in aber in swebel
10 vnd in harcz vnd nym[m] vnd wirff in
dan[n] aber in puchsenpulfer vnd nym[m]
denn barchat tuch vnd stoß es in den
swebel vnd harcz vnd über zeuch den
stain aber do mit vnd see oben an ein
15 clein puchsen pulfer dar auff die weil
das tuch naß ist vnd wen[n] du den
stain werffen wilt so leg zunder hartz
dar an vnd zund das wan[n] du dan[n]
das werck laust lauffen so print es
20 in dem seckel vnd tut vast grossen
schaden in vesten vnd in stetten **Wie
man gar gut fewr pfeil machen sol**

Royal Armouries I.34 – Part 1

not make another one. Also you should
know the weight of the stone and the plug
and the powder and its power. You should
know well what it can cope with as you
have had described in this book. If you want
to stand safely in front of the gun so that no harm
will come to you, make sure first of all that you do not fire
in the name of God. **How you throw
a fire stone from a gabion or from a siege tower into**

fol. 41v

a fortified town.

If you want to throw a fire stone
from a gabion or from a siege tower, then take
the stone you want to throw from a siege
tower or a *pley*.[244] And soak it in sulphur
and in resin and put it into
gunpowder. And brush a cotton
cloth over the stone or polish
it and soak it once again in sulphur
and in resin and take it and put it
into the gunpowder again. And take
fustian cloth and put it into the
sulphur and the resin and wipe
the stone with it. Make sure that a
little gunpowder stays on it as the
cloth is wet. And when you
want to throw the stone, add tinder resin
to it and light it. When you let
the siege tower do its work, it burns in its
bag and causes great
damage in castles and in towns. **How
to make a really good fire arrow.**

---

[244] Seems more likely to be referring to a short form of '*pleienden*' for 'gabion', and
not lead ('*Blei*'), as the stem may suggest. The use of a shortened form may imply
a familiarity with siege devices by both the author and any potential reader. Nibler
interprets these as 'incendiary devices which were projected via slings', but that
does not seem to be clear from the original (Nibler, *Feuerwerkbuch*, 32).

fol. 42r

1   **W**iltu gar gut fewr pfeil machen so
nym[m] dreÿ pfunt salpetters ein pfunt sweb=
els ein halb pfunt kols vnd stoß das zu pul=
fer vnder einander vnd bint das pulfer zu
5   samen mit geprantem wein vnd mach den[n]
ein clein stecklein auß parchat tůch als
lang als der pfeil seÿ vnd tu den taig in
den sack vnd stoß den pfeil dar durch vn[d]
verpind in mit einem vaden hinden an
10   vnd vornan vnd swem es in swebel oder
in harcz vnd laß es trucken werden so hast
du gar gut fewr pfeil **Wie man macht
das sich wasser enzundet**

   Wiltu machen das sich wasser en=
15   zundet so nym[m] unerloschen kalck
vnd laß vil swebels an der wag vnd
auß der materÿ mach ein dach vnd spreng
dar auff wasser so enzünt es sich vnd
geuß öl dar auff so ɉ list es **Wie man**
20   **swebel öl machen sol**

   Wiltu machen swebel öl das dir
zu starckem fewr pulfer gut

fol. 42v

1   seÿ vnd nucz so nym[m] aÿr tottern die hört ge=
soten sein vnd stoß die in einem morser gar
wol piß das sie werden als ein schmalcz so
nym[m] dan[n] lebendigen swebel wol gestossen
5   vnd durch ein tůch gesaigt vnd misch es
durch ein ander vnd rüer es vast das es
ein materÿ werd vnd tu es dann in ein

Royal Armouries I.34 – Part 1

fol. 42r

If you want to make good fire arrows then
take three pounds of saltpetre, one pound of sulphur,
one half of a pound of charcoal, and grind it together
into powder. Bind the powder together with
brandy and make a
small bag out of fustian cloth
which is as long as the arrow. And put the paste in
the bag and punch the arrow through and
tie it with a piece of string at the back
and the front. And soak it in sulphur or
in resin and let it dry out, then you have
a very good fire arrow. **How you
make water set itself alight.**

If you want to make water that sets itself
alight, then take quicklime
and leave a lot of sulphur on the scales.
And make a pile out of these and sprinkle
water on it.[245] This will set it alight. And
pour oil on it to extinguish it. **How
you make sulphur oil.**[246]

If you want to make sulphur oil that is
good and useful for strong fire powder

fol. 42v

then take egg yolks which are hard boiled
and grind them in a mortar
until they become like lard. Then
take the native sulphur which has been ground well
and has been passed through a cloth. And mix them
together and stir it strongly, so that it
becomes one consistency and put it into a

---

[245] Assuming that it is the same quantities of quicklime and water. However, this is not made clear in the text. Quicklime, or, Calcium oxide (CaO), is highly flammable, reacting with water.

[246] It is not clear what sulphur oil is intended to be or is meant to achieve. Sulphur cannot be dissolved in oil. As the recipe does not list quantities there is not enough context to recreate the recipe.

kurbs vnd pren[n] es auß zu ol als du wol
waist **Wie man ein fewr machen sol**
10   **do mit allexander das lant agarono=**
      rum verprant

Wiltu fewr machen do allexander
mit das lant agarrenoru[m] ver=
prant so nym[m] palsam ein pfunt gloriat
15   ein pfunt öl vnd ayr funff pfunt lebend=
igs kalcks zehen pfunt vnd reib den kol
mit dem öl das es ein confet werd vnd
bestreich dan[n] den stain do mit oder kraut
oder was fruchtig seÿ das enzünt sich
20   mit der materÿ von dem ersten regen
der dar auff kompt vnd verwiest es
als sampt vnd spricht aristotiles das

fol. 43r

1   das fewr zehen jar werhaftig seÿ **Wie ma[n]**
     ein fewr mache[n] sol wen[n] der regen dar auff
     kumpt das es sich selber enzündent

Wiltu ein fewr wann der regen dar
5   auff kompt das es sich enzundet
nym[m] lebendigen kalck vnd ein wenig gu=
merabicum vnd swebel vnd linsad öl vnd
das mach alles mit ein ander das es ein
materÿ werd vnd mach dar auß ein pild
10   vnd spreng dar auff wasser so enzünt es
sich vnd mit der selben materÿ machtu

cucurbit[247] and burn it into oil as you know
well. **How you make a fire
which was used by Alexander to burn
the land of Agaronorum.**[248]

If you want to make the fire with which Alexander
burnt the land of Agarrenorum,
then take a pound of balsam, a pound of oil of turpentine,[249]
a pound of oil, five pounds of eggs,
and ten pounds of quicklime. And grind charcoal
together with the oil [*mixture made above*] so that it turns into a paste.
And spread it over the stone, over the plants,
and over all that is fruitful so that it catches fire
with this mixture at the first rain
which falls on it and it becomes
one. And as Aristotle says that

fol. 43r

the fire truly burns for ten years. **How you
make a fire which lights itself
when rain falls on it.**

If you want to make fire which lights itself
when rain falls on it then
take quicklime, and a little
gum arabic, and sulphur, and linseed oil, and
mix it all together so that it turns into one
consistency. Make a sample from it[250]
and sprinkle water on it and it will start to
burn. With the same mixture you can

---

[247] Augsburg manuscript, III, 1.2º.44, fol. 48r: '*kukerbit*'.

[248] This is presumably a reference to Greek fire. This section has been added in some *Firework Books*, referring to it as '*Agarranora*' or '*Aggarorum*', e.g. Munich Clm. 30150, fol. 145r, and Dillingen XV 50, fol. 30v. It was not possible to ascertain what land this term relates to. It is one rare reference to a historical context and requires the audience to have an understanding of who Alexander was, and why or how to set fire to a country.

[249] The Kassel manuscript 4º Ms. math. 14 refers to it here instead as 'turpentine, which is called people's resin' ('*terbentin, dz feisr luter hartz*', fol. 41v).

[250] *Frühneuhochdeutsches Wörterbuch Online*, def. 6, '*Beispiel*' (*Frühneuhochdeutsches Wörterbuch Online*, http://fwb-online.de/go/bild.s.2n_1513344239).

229

wol ein yedlich hauß verprennen wann
der regen dar auff get

Wie man ein fliegend fewr machen sol das
do fert in die höch vnd verwiest was es
                    begreift

15

Wiltu machen ein fliegend
fewr das do fert in die höch wa
du wilt so nym[m] ain tail coloflinia das ist
kriechisch harcz vnd zwaÿ tail lebendigs

20   swebels vnd dreÿ tail saluiter das reib
alles gar clein vnd reib es dan[n] mit eine[m]
cleinem linsad öl oder loröl das es dar in

fol. 43v

1   zergen das es ein confet werd vnd tu das
in ein estain ror die lang seÿ vnd gee dan[n]
vnd zünd es an so vert es wa du das ror
hin kerst vnd wüst was du begreifest mit

5   dem fewr **Wie man gar ein starck fewr**
pulfer machen sol

Wiltu machen ein starcks fewr pulfer
so nym[m] alkitram das ist gloriat vn[d]
swebel vnd öl vnd aÿr tottern auß geprant

10   das nym[m] als mit ein ander geleich tailung
vnd rest das in ainer pfannen gemainklich
peÿ dem fewr ob einen koln das es ein con=
fet werd vnd nym[m] dar zu das viertail
wachs dar vnder das es sich mit einander

15   misch als ein materÿ vnd tu es dann in

Royal Armouries I.34 – Part 1

burn down any house
when rain falls on it.
**How you make flying fire
which flies up in the air and drives away
everything near it.**

If you want to make flying
fire that flies [*high*] up in the air when
you want it to, then take one part of *coloflinia*,[251] which is
greek resin, two parts live
sulphur, and three parts salniter. Grind it
together finely and add to it a
little[252] linseed oil or laurel oil so that they melt together

fol. 43v

and become a paste. Place it
in a stone gun[253] which is long. Go ahead
and light it and it flies where you point the barrel
to. And now you know what to do with
this fire. **How you make really strong fire
powder.**

If you want to make strong fire powder
then take liquid tar, which is oil of turpentine,
sulphur, oil, and egg yolk which have burnt out.[254]
Take equal parts
and place them in a pan together
next to a charcoal fire. [*Mix it*] so that it turns
into a paste. Then add a quart of
wax to it and mix it together so that it becomes
one consistency. And then place it into

---

[251] No exact modern translation could be traced. Heidelberg Cod. Pal. germ. 562 refers to it as '*colosania Dz ist kriechisch hartz*' (possibly 'kolophonium which is Greek resin' – see Nibler, *Feuerwerkbuch*, n. 253: '"colosania" => "colofania" => *Kolophonium als "kriechisch hartz" ist ziemlich sicher im Vergleich mit "callofonna" in Cpg 562, 4")*'; Kassel 4° Ms. math. 14 refers to it as 'Greek tar' ('kriechisch pech'), fol. 42r.

[252] In the meaning of 'little quantity'.

[253] This could be a '*Steinbüchse*', and would be one of the first times that the term was mentioned. See Chapter 5 for more details.

[254] No explanation as to what that means. Nibler and Kramer also do not comment. This could simply suggest older eggs.

einrinden plat die wol gestrichen seÿ mit
öl vnd vmb vach es mit wachs vnd wen[n]
du es nüczen wilt so leg die materÿ an ein
stat das es luftig seÿ vnd wen[n] der wint
20 dar zu get so wirt es priment vnd ver=
wiest alles das das es begreift vnd ist
das man wasser dar auff geust so gewint

fol. 44r

1 es tetlich flammen vnd wa man die materÿ
also berait auff ein holcz schreibt do enzint
es sich von der sunnen wann es die hicz
begreift vnd verprent es alles **Wie man**
5 **versuchen so das salpetter gut seÿ vnd recht**
       geleuttert seÿ

Wiltu versuchen ob
salpetter gut seÿ vnd recht ge=
leutert so nym[m] sein ein wenig vnd leg
es auff ainen gluenden koln print es dan[n]
10 schon auspringen vnd das er nit über
sich praczelt so ist er gut vnd gerecht
Wie man salpetter versuchen sol ob er mit
salcz gefelscht seÿ oder nicht

Wiltu salpetter versuchen ob er mer
15 salcz in jm hab oder nit oder ob
er nicht mer gefelscht seÿ so nym[m] sein als
groß als ein halbe welsche nuß vnd leg
es auff ainen gelwenden koln oder auff
ein prant der wol gelwe print er denn
20 schon auff dem prant also wol vnder sich
so ist er gut vnd gerecht praczelt er aber
sich als der salcz in ein fewr wirft das

fol. 44v

1 ist ein zaichen das er nit wol geleutert
ist vnd mer salcz da peÿ ist **Wie man sal=**
petter an fewr versuchen sol

Auch mocht man salpetter wol ver=

Royal Armouries I.34 – Part 1

a calf's bladder which has been coated with
oil, and seal it with wax. When you want
to use it, take the mixture to an airy place
and when the wind gets
into it, then it will burn. And it
will spread to everything it touches. If
you pour water onto it then it will burst into

fol. 44r

actual flames. If you spread the mixture thinly
on wood then it will start to burn
by the action of the sun when heat gets
to it and everything will burn. **How you
ascertain that saltpetre is good and has been
purified well.**

If you want to ascertain
whether saltpetre is purified
well and properly then take a little and place
it onto glowing charcoal. If it starts to
burn straightaway and if it does not
spit, then it is good and proper.
**How you find out whether saltpetre has
been adulterated with salt or not.**

If you want to find out whether saltpetre
contains more salt or not, or whether
it is no longer adulterated with salt then take
as much as half of a walnut and put
it on top of glowing charcoal or on
a fire that burns well and yellow. If it
burns straightaway on the fire on its own
then it is good. But if it sizzles,
as if some salt was thrown into the fire, then this

fol. 44v

is a sign that it is not well purified
and that it contains more salt. **How you
try out saltpetre without a fire.**

You may also try out the saltpetre

5   suchen an fewr wer salpetter nem
     als groß als ein welsche nuß vnd tu das
     in ein schußelein das nit schmalczig seÿ
     vnd geuß dar an ein weing lauters=
     wasser das kalt seÿ vnd laß es dar in
10   sten ein cleine weil vnd saig dan[n] das
     wasser ab vnd versuch es jn dem mund
     ist es vast gesalczen vnd hat der salpetter
     vast abgenomen das sein vil mÿnder
     ist dann vor das get von salcz zu ist sein
15   aber nit vil minder worden denn vor
     so ist er gut vnd gerecht **Wie man sal=**
     petter leuttern sol der vor auch geleuttert
     ist vnd doch nit auff sein recht stat ge=
     nu[n]g ist

20   **W**iltu salpetter leuttern der dich nit
     gut dunkt vnd der doch vor
     geleuttert ist so nym[m] ein kesel vnd mach

fol. 45r

1   den gar schon das kein schmalcz oder nichcz=
     it vaistes dar an seÿ vnd tu dar ein pru[n]=
     nen wasser vnd laß es warmen das=
     dich dunck es wöl schier an heben zu sie=
5   den vnd schut den salpetter dar ein vnd
     laß in sitlich sieden das er nit uber lauff
     Hat er auch schawm das macht du wol
     herab werffen mit einem schonen leffel
     wann er zwen well oder dreÿ tut so nym[m]
10   ein saubers holcz vnd stoß das dar ein vn[d]
     tropfe die tröpflein auff ein gelwende koln
     oder auf ein prant prinnen die tropfen
     die von dem holcz wallen so hat er sein
     genung Auch mochst du es sust wol ver=
15   suchen wann du nÿmpst vier helmlein

Royal Armouries I.34 – Part 1

without a fire. Take as much saltpetre as the size
of a walnut and put it
in a bowl which is not greasy[255]
and pour over it a little pure[256]
water which is cold and let it
rest for a while. Then drain the
water and try it in your mouth.
If it is very salty, then it has less
saltpetre or it has lost some [of the saltpetre] it had
before, as this comes from the salt.
But if it is not much less than before
then it is good and proper. **How you purify
saltpetre which has already been purified
but is not yet in the right
state.**

If you want to purify saltpetre which does not
appear to you to be good even after it has been
purified, then take a pot and make

fol. 45r

sure that it had no lard or anything
with fat in it and add some water from a
well. Warm it gently,[257] so that
it seems to you that it will soon start to
boil and add the saltpetre to it.
Let it boil gently so that it does not boil over.
If there is froth then you can skim
it off with a good spoon.
When it has welled up two or three times then take
a clean piece of wood and dip it into the pot and
drip a drop onto a glowing piece of charcoal
or onto a fire. If the drops
which come from the piece of wood flare up then it is
[*purified*] enough. You may also want to try
taking four or five pieces

---

[255] In the meaning of 'free of lard'.

[256] Could be 'distilled' or 'clean' – not clear from the context.

[257] Presumably by placing it on a heat source, not specified here.

oder funffe vnd stiest die in den kesel vn[d]
ließ die tropflein auff ein hosen vallen
oder sunst auff ein wullin tuch würden
denn die tropflein an dem tuch als eyß=
20   tropflein so het er sein aber genug Dar
nach laß den kessel uber schlachen das
er kalt werd vnd saig dann das wasser

fol. 45v

1   durch ein zwifach leine tuch oder durch
eins das dick seÿ vnd saig in in ein schone
beckin wer sein aber als vil so saig in in
ein schön schaff oder in ein weite prenten
5   dar ein macht du wol legen ł vier helcz=
lach oder fuffe vnd secz es do nÿemant
dar zu gang vnd laß es sten zwenn tag
vnd nacht so sichst du wol ob es sich
an hat gehenckt vnd gesammet so saig
10   dann das wasser ab in ein sauber geschir
vnd nym[m] den salpetter vnd trucken den in
eim peck oder wer sein als vil so tu es
auff ein lëderlachen so wirt er gut vnd
gerecht hüt dich all zeit vor schmalcz
15   Dar zu nym[m] das ander wasser das du
abgesoten hast vnd seud es ander weid
in eine[m] kessel vnd tu ein geleich als
vor hernach geschriben stet was dann
dar an beliben ist das samet sich das
20   du es auch vinst **Wie man salpetter leut=
tern sol der roch abgenumen wirt vnd
nit geleuttert ist**

of straw and dipping them into the pot.
Then let the drops drip on your hose
or elsewhere onto a woollen piece of cloth.
If the drops on the piece of cloth become like drops of
ice then it has boiled enough. After
this let the pot be set aside so
that it can cool down. And drain the water

fol. 45v

through a double linen cloth or through
one that is thick. Drain it into a nice
bowl which is big enough for everything you drain –
a nice bucket[258] or a wide barrel.[259]
In it you place four pieces of
wood, or five, and place it [*the container*] in such a way that no one
has access to it and let it stand for two days
and nights. This way you can see whether it has
formed and collected. Then drain
off the water into a clean bowl.
And take the saltpetre and dry it in
a pot, or – if there is a lot – put it
on a leather cloth and it will be good and
proper. Be careful at all times not to add
any grease. Take the second water which
you have drained off, and boil it once more
in a pot. Do the same as
has been described below. What
remains is all that
you can get. **How you purify
saltpetre which has been taken off raw and
has not been purified.**

---

[258] A '*scheff*' or '*scheffel*' is a container, often made out of wood, especially used for cereals (*Deutsches Wörterbuch von Jacob und Wilhelm Grimm Online* – accessed 10 August 2023).

[259] A '*brente*' is defined as a 'wooden container, especially for milk, cured meat, fish, or wine' ('*hölzernes Gefäß, besonders für Milch, gesalzenes Fleisch, Fisch, Wein*', *Frühneuhochdeutsches Wörterbuch Online*, http://fwb-online.de/go/brente.s.1f_1513373142) – this statement refers to two types of containers, the second one bigger, more like a tub.

fol. 46r

1   **W**iltu salpetter leuttern der roch ist
   der abgenomen ist vnd nit geleuttert ist
   so nym[m] ein scharpf laug oder tu aber
   kalck in ein schaff vnd geuß wasser dar
5   zu vnd rier es vmb mit einem stecken
   als ein kalkas vnd laß es stan über nacht
   so wirt es dester leuter vnd tu das in
   ein schen[n] kessel vnd wen[n] es warm wirt
   so schüt den salpetter dar ein vnd laß
10   in wol sieden vnd greiff mit einem lef=
   fel an den poden was stain dar in sein
   die sam[m]en sich an den poden die tu her
   auß vnd schawm in wol vnd lug das
   er nit über gee vnd das nichczs schmalcz=
15   igs dar zu kom Wenn du versuchen
   wilt ob er sein genug hab so stoß ein
   holcz dar ein vnd trewff es auff ein ge=
   lwenden koln print es denn so hat er
   sein genug oder versuch in mit eim
20   helmlein an eim tuch wirt es dann tropf=
   lein als eÿß so hat es sein aber genug
   so laß es kůlen vnd saig es durch ein

fol. 46v

1   dick leine tuch oder durch ein filczhut in
   ein peckin were sein aber als vil so seich
   in in ein schenß schaff oder in ein prente[n]
   vnd laß sten aine[n] tag vnd ein nacht dz
5   man es nit rier vnd leg oben dar ein ein
   wenig helczlach vnd lug dann dar zu
   ob es sich gesamet hab vnd an gehenckt
   hab hat es sich nicht angehenckt vnd

Royal Armouries I.34 – Part 1

fol. 46r

If you want to purify saltpetre which is raw
and has been taken off[260] or which has not been purified,
then take a sharp[261] lye or put
chalk in a bucket[262] and add water to
it. Stir it with a stick
like chalk and let it stand overnight.
This way it will become purer. Put it [*the mixture*]
in a nice pot and, when it has warmed up,
pour the saltpetre into it and let
it boil strongly. Reach to the bottom
[*of the pot*] with a spoon. Whatever stone[263] has
collected at the bottom [*of the pot*] take it
out. Let it froth and make sure
that it does not boil over and that nothing
greasy can get to it. When you want to find
out if it has been enough dip a
piece of wood into it and drip it onto
some glowing charcoal. If it burns then it is
enough. Or, try it out with a
piece of straw on a piece of cloth. If a drop
turns into ice then it is enough.
Let it cool down and drain it into a bowl through

fol. 46v

a thick linen cloth or through a felt hat.
If there is a lot then drain it
into a nice bucket or into a barrel
and let it stand one day and one night. [*Make sure*] that
you do not stir it but add
a few pieces of wood to it.[264] Have a look whether
something has formed and attached [*to the lattice*].
If it has not formed and

---

[260] In the sense of 'scraped off' – no physical description of 'off where' provided.

[261] This presumably means 'strong'.

[262] As before – larger container (see Note 273).

[263] This presumably means 'grit' or other 'impurities'.

[264] '*helzlach*' contains the collective suffix '*lach*' which means a small quantity.

gesam[m]et so laß dennoch ein tag vnd ein
10   nacht sten vnd saig dan[n] das wasser
ab in ein sauber geschir vnd trucken
den salpetter in aim schenen peck auff
einem offen oder auff einer lederlachen
vnd nym[m] das wasser das du abgesoten
15   hast vnd seud es anderwierd vnd laß
es lenger sieden denn vor vnd tu nü ge=
leich als du im vormals gethan hast
Was dann dar in ist das sammet sich
das du es auch vinst **Wie man puchsen**
20   **pulfer machen sol zu puchsen oder zu**
fewrpfeilen

Wiltu pulfer machen
zu puchsen oder zu fewrpfeilen

fol. 47r

1   so stoß den salpetter besunder vnd mal
in als clein das er sich reden laß durch
ein engs siblein als ein pfeffer sib macht
du das nicht gehaben so nym[m] einen wei=
5   ten peitel vnd peutel ~~v~~in dar durch in
ein schaff vnd was in dem peutel beleibt
oder in dem sib das stoß anderweid piß
du es als hin durch peuteln mugst vn[d]
tu den gebeutelten salpetter besunder vn[d]
10   tu den swebel auch besunder vnd laß
ÿedlichs besunder den salpetter vnd den
swebel vnd die kol **Wie man ein gemein**
puchsen pulfer machen sol

Wenn du wilt ein gemain pulfer
15   machen so nym[m] vier pfunt od[er]
vier gewicht salpetters vnd nym[m] zwaÿ
pfunt swebels vnd ein pfunt koln das

Royal Armouries I.34 – Part 1

Collected, then let it stand for a [*further*] day and
night. And drain off the water
into a clean bowl and dry
the saltpetre in a nice bowl on
the oven or on a leather cloth.
Take the water you have poured
off and boil it again and let it
boil for longer than before and now do the
same as you have done before.
What is left in it, will form itself,
for you to find. **How you make gun
powder for guns or for
fire arrows.**

If you want to make powder
for guns or fire arrows

fol. 47r

then grind the saltpetre thoroughly and grind it
so finely that it runs through
a fine sieve such as a pepper sieve.
If you do not have one of these, then take a broad
bag[265] and pour it [*the saltpetre*] through it
into a bucket. Grind what remains in the bag
or in the sieve again until
you manage to get it [*all*] through the cloth.
And keep the bagged saltpetre separate.
Do this carefully to the sulphur [*too*] and keep
the saltpetre and the
sulphur and the charcoal carefully.[266] **How you make common
gunpowder.**

If you want to make common powder
then take four pounds or
four weights of saltpetre and take two
pounds sulphur and one pound of charcoal and

---

[265] This refers to '*peutel*' (as is likely from other texts, e.g. Freiburg Ms. 362, fol. 80v:
'*wyten roggen bütel vnd büttel in da durch*' = '*rogken peytel* => '*Roggenbeutel*' which is
hung at the bottom end of a sieve in milling to sieve out impurities) (*Frühneuhochdeutsches Wörterbuch Online*, http://fwb-online.de/go/beutel.s.0m_1513517452).

[266] Presumably meaning 'separately'.

haist ein gemain pulfer misch es wol
durch einander das pulfer ist gut auff
20   den kauff vnd mag man es wol geben
für ein gut gemain pulfer **Wie man ein
pesser pulfer machen sol einem pider man**

fol. 47v

1   **auff sein schloß**

Wiltu machen ein pesser pulfer
einem piderben man[n] auff sein
schlosch oder hauß der do sprich mach
5   mir ein gut pulfer so nym[m] funff pfunt
salpetters vnd zwaÿ pfunt swebels vn[d]
ein pfunt koln vnd misch es wol durch
einander das wirt ein gut pulfer **Wie
man ein pulfer machen sol das noch**
10   **stercker scheust**

Wiltu machen stercker pulfer
das noch stercker scheust wen[n]
der ains so nym[m] sechs pfunt salpetters
vnd zweÿ pfunt swebels vnd ain pfunt
15   kols das wirt ein gut starck pulfer vnd
scheust weit **Wie vil man der dreier stuck
salpetters swebels vnd kol ir yedlichs
auff das swerst gewicht vnd nit mer
zu einem pulfer genemen mag**

20   **A**uch mocht man wol ein pulfer
machen das man nem ein pfunt
koln vnd zweÿ pfunt swebels vnd siben=

[bottom margin right] **thalb lb**

Royal Armouries I.34 – Part 1

this is called common powder. Mix it together
well and the powder is good to
be sold and can pass as
good common powder. **How you
make better powder for an honest man**[267]

fol. 47v

in his castle.

If you want to make a better powder
[for] an honest man in his
castle or house who says: 'make
me a good powder'. Take five pounds of
saltpetre and two pounds of sulphur and
one pound of charcoal and mix it together
well [*and*] then it will be good powder. **How
to make powder which fires even
stronger.**

If you want to make an even stronger powder
that fires more strongly than
the others, then take six pounds of saltpetre,
two pounds of sulphur and one pound of
charcoal. This makes a good strong powder and
fires long distances. **How much can you take
of the three ingredients of saltpetre, sulphur, and charcoal
before it gets too heavy and cannot
be made into powder any more.**[268]

If you want to make good powder
then take a pound of
charcoal, two pounds of sulphur, and seven and
[bottom margin right] a half pound[269]

---

[267] This could be 'upstanding man' or 'man of integrity' – from the twentieth century onwards, the term '*biedermann*' obtained negative connotations – there is no such reference in *Frühneuhochdeutsches Wörterbuch Online*, http://fwb-online.de/go/biederman.s.0m_1513801728.

[268] The term 'heavy' is used in the sense of 'imbalanced' here. The issue of ratios has long been a question of scholarly debate. See Chapter 5 for more details.

[269] This note is made at the bottom of the page, most likely as a binding notation as it is at the end of one gathering.

fol. 48r

1 thalb pfunt salpetters nit mer was man
mer salpeters nem zu so vil swebels vnd
koln das wer nit gut wann es sunst ein
starcks gucz pulfer ist **Wie man ein puch=**
5 **sen pulfer herter vnd zu reschnn knollen**
pulfer machen sol

Wiltu ein puchsen pulfer machen
herten wann du es dann schon
gemischt durch ein ander vnd wol von
10 welcher michlung du es gern[n] hast so tu
sein ein ainen grossen morser als vil als
oder in ainem stampf als vil du dar in
gehaben macht vnd begeuß das mit
guten wein essich vnd stoß das wol vn=
15 dereinander mit einem hulczeim klupfel
vnd mach das also feucht mit dem es=
sich das es sich zu samen trucken laut
vnd pallen wie groß du dann die pul=
fer kugeln wilt machen dar nach nym[m]
20 ein gleschten swebel vnd tiff tegelin

fol. 48r

a half pounds of saltpetre – no more
saltpetre than this [*should be added to*] so much sulphur and
charcoal as this would not be good. It is otherwise
a strong good powder. **How you make gun
powder harder**[270] **and into strong**[271] *Knollen
pulver.*

If you want to make gunpowder
to be harder when you have already
mixed it well together into
the mixture you would like.
Put as much as [*you want*] into a large mortar
or into a stamp mill[272] as much as you want
to have. Add to it
good wine vinegar and grind it together
well with a wooden pestle.
Make it damp with the vinegar
so that it can be dried together.
You can make powder balls as large
as you would like. Take
extinguished sulphur[273] and a deep pan[274]

---

[270] It is not clear what the scribe means when he describes the powder as 'harder'. It is most likely that it would make it more resilient to external influences.

[271] '*Resch*' often refers to 'fast' and 'speedy'; in this context it is more likely to refer to 'strong' or 'fresh' (see def. 2, *Deutsches Wörterbuch von Jacob und Wilhelm Grimm Online* – accessed 10 August 2023).

[272] Such as the one depicted on fol. 87r (see Figure 7, right).

[273] This may be a reference to '*getötetem*' or '*gelöschtem*' sulphur. Reference to Christoph Entzel's *Traktat von metallischen Dingen*, 1608, or Franz August von Wasserberg's *Chemische Abhandlung vom Schwefel*, 1788; or, even, in much earlier text such as the fourteenth-century Konrad von Megenberg, *Buch der Natur* '*Lebendiger Schwebel – erleschter oder toter Swebel*' – available as an edition in *Konrad von Megenberg: Das buch der natur*, ed. Franz Pfeiffer (Stuttgart: K. Aue, 1861), https://archive.org/details/dasbuchdernatur00pfeigoog/page/n548 – accessed 10 August 2023. Alternatively, this could be a scribal error, as other manuscripts list a number of different containers in which the powder can be mixed together, e.g. Freiburg Ms. 362 refers to it as a 'small glazed bowl' ('*verglest sinwel*' (fol. 80r)). If the latter was the case, '*swebel*' would be a scribal error.

[274] 'Container which can be placed into the fire' – could also be 'crucible' but unlikely in this context (see '*Tiegel*' – *Deutsches Wörterbuch von Jacob und Wilhelm Grimm Online* – accessed 10 August 2023).

oder ein nepflein oder ein krupfre schal
vnd truck es also naß dar ein als der

fol. 48v

1   als der einem keß in einem napf deucht
  vnd stre es dann um[m] auff ein pret so get es
  gern auß der pulfer kugeln macht du mach=
  en als vil als du pulfers hast Ist es in hais=
5   sem sumer so mag man die kugeln wol der=
  ren an der sunne[n] were des nit so müst ma[n]
  sie derren in einer stuben die müst man senf=
  tigklich ein haiczen vnd müst das tun auff
  zehen tag Die kugeln sol man dann neme[n]
10   vnd sol sie legen in ein dür vaß oder in ein
  dür legel vnd secz es an ein trucken stat
  do es nit feuchtin hat Das pulfer nimpt
  nit ab vnd ist gut wie lang es wert
  vor allen dingen So man das pulfer
15   trucket in der stuben oder su[n]st so sol mal
  sein wol hüetten vor fewr vnd vor liecht
  wan[n] es kind nyemant erretten es geschech
  grosser schad **Wie man fewrpfeil machen
  sol die gut sein**

20   **W**iltu machen gut fewr pfeil so mach
  secklach von parchat vnd nym[m] pul=
  fer das do gemacht seÿ vnd scheub es in die

fol. 49r

1   secklach so du hertest mugest vnd pind es
  zu vmb vnd vmb mit zwifachem faden
  so du hertest mugest vnd nym[m] ein eÿsen
  ain swebels oder das gefiert sey das als

Royal Armouries I.34 – Part 1

or a small dish or a copper bowl
and press it into as wet [*as possible*] as if[275]

fol. 48v

you were putting cheese into a dish.
Then turn it upside down on a wooden board and it
comes out easily. Make as many powder balls
as you have powder. If it is a hot
summer, then you may want to dry your balls
in the sun. If it is not, then you have to
dry them in a [*heated*] room. You must warm
them up slowly and you have to do this over [*a period of*]
ten days. You can take the [*dried*] balls
and place them in a dry barrel,
or in a dry store. Put it in a dry place
where it is not damp. The powder
will not deteriorate, and it is good as long as it lasts.
Of all things, if you dry the powder
in the heated room or elsewhere, then be
very careful about fire and about light
as no one can be saved and it could cause
great harm. **How you make fire arrows
which are good.**

If you want to make good fire arrows, then take
a fustian bag and take the powder
that has been made and push it into

fol. 49r

the bag to get hard and tie it
around it with a double thread
so that it hardens. Take a [*piece of*] iron,
which is round[276] or four-cornered, which should

---

[275] Repetition of '*als der*', most likely to be scribal error – not translated.

[276] The literal translation here implies 'sulphur' but that is most likely to be a scribal
error. In other versions of the *Firework Books* this is referred to as a '*synbel*' or '*sinwel*'. Stainer 1529, 235, '*synbel*' = '*sinwel*' => '*rund*', Schmeller, *Bayerisches Wörterbuch*,
II, 291 – see Heidelberg Cod. Pal. germ. 122, fol. 44r, and Göttingen 2° Cod. Ms.
philos. 64, fol. 143v: '*sinwel*'.

247

5 groß seÿ als das pfeil eÿsen vnd stoß es
do mitten durch das secklein nach der leng
vnd scheub das eysen do hin ein vnd über
zeuch in mit swebel so hastu einen guten
pfeil **Wie man fewr pfleil machen sol** ~~wie~~
10 **wie lang sie ligen das sie nit rostig werde[n]**

Wiltu fewr pfeil machen die do lige[n]
wie lang du wilt so pich die eÿsen
das sie nit rostig werden so ligen sie wie
lang du wilt **Wie man fewr pfeil machen**
15 **sol die sich selber an zünden wann sie kome[n]**
an die stat do sie hin geschossen werden

Wiltu fewr pfeil namchen die sich sel=
ber enzünden die man nit anzun=
den darff so nym[m] zunder schneyd in als preit
20 als zwen helm sein vnd zwaier zwercher
vinger lanck die scheub vornan in das seck=
lein do das eÿsen her auß get nach der

fol. 49v

1 leng das es das pulfer erlang so enzint es
sich selber wann du wilt **Wie man ein**
puchsen auß lassen sol die lang gelegen
ist vnd nicht lassen wil

5 **H**ast du ein puchsen die geladen ist die
lang gelegen ist vnd nit auß wil
gen so nym[m] ein lad eÿsen vnd treib die ku=
geln hin ein paß oder den klocz vmb ein
zwerchen ~~vinger~~ halm oder mer vnd
10 rawm das widloch mit einem griffel
vnd see ein gut pulfer dar ein vnd zind
es an so get es **Wie man ein gluend ku=**
geln auß einer puchs schiessen sol das

Royal Armouries I.34 – Part 1

be as big as an arrow iron, and push it
right through the bag lengthwise,
and slide the iron into place.[277] Cover it [*the bag*]
with sulphur and you have a good
arrow. **How you make fire arrows which
can be stored for a long time and do not turn rusty.**

If you want to make fire arrows which can be stored
for as long as you want, then cover the iron in pitch so
that they do not get rusty, and they can be stored for as
long as you want. **How you make fire arrows
which catch fire themselves when they reach
a town when they are fired at it.**

If you want to make fire arrows which catch
fire themselves and which do not need to be set
alight, then take tinder, cut it as thick as
two straws and two small fingers'
breadths long, push it into the front of the bag
where the iron comes out lengthwise

fol. 49v

so that the powder catches fire by itself
when you want it to.[278] **How you empty
a gun which has been lying around for a long time
and should not be fired.**

If you have a loaded gun which has been
lying for a long time and [*the charge*] does not want to come out[279]
then take a loading iron and push in the
ball a little. Or, move the plug
by [*the size of*] a small piece of straw or more.
Clear the touch hole with a stick
to see that good powder can get it and light it
as well as it goes. **How you fire
a glowing ball out of a gun which**

---

[277] It is not entirely clear what action is intended to be done here.

[278] The implication is that you would have to light the fuse before firing, but this is not stated here.

[279] As in 'cannot be fired'. '*auslassen*' implies a wide range of possible actions, but it does not necessarily suggest 'letting off'.

249

sie verprent war an sie geschossen wirt
15   **in holcz werck**

W iltu ein pleÿ puchsen laden so lad
es mit einer kugel vnd haiß dir
machen ein eÿsne kugeln die gerecht dar
ein seÿ vnd leg ein nassen hader auff die die pleÿ
20   kugeln vnd haiß die eÿsneÿn kugeln vast
gelwend machen vnd leg sie mit einer
zangen in die puchs auff den hadern das

fol. 50r

1   tůst du wol an allen schaden vnd zind es
an was dann die kugel beriert von holcz
do es innen steckt das verprint als **Wie**
man guten zunder machen sol

5   W iltu machen guten zunder so nym[m]
buche swem vnd haw die ausern
rinden herab vnd nym[m] glut vnd aschen als
die aÿmrigen das da vast vnder ein ander
glwt vnd nym[m] ein haffen vnd scheid

**will burn when it hits a
wooden structure.**

If you want to load a lead gun[280] then
load it with a ball. And have
an iron ball made which is the right size
and put a wet piece of cloth[281] on the lead
ball and heat up the iron ball so that it almost
glows and put it in the gun with
some tongs, in front of the other,

fol. 50r

and this will cause all the damage. Fire it [*the gun*],
and any wood the ball touches,
or gets stuck into, will burn. **How
you make good tinder.**

If you want to make good tinder, then take
beech sponge,[282] and cut off the outer
bark, and take embers and ash as they
are glowing[283] which almost glow together.
Take a bowl and split

[280] 'Lead' presumably refers to the ball and not the gun, similar to the term *Steinbüchse*.
Alternatively, it could relate to a gun on a gabion (see fol. 41v).

[281] This is the same as in the Göttingen 2° Cod. Ms. philos. 64, fol. 144v: '*hadern*'; or
the Heidelberg Cod. Pal. germ. 122, fol. 44v: '*hadern*'. See *Frühneuhochdeutsches
Wörterbuch Online*, http://fwb-online.de/go/hader.h1.0m_1513543590.

[282] It is not clear whether this refers to bark, a particular fungus, or to the beech wood
soaked in some particular substance. However, the fungus – as it is described in
German as a sponge – seems more likely.

[283] In Stainer 1529, this section refers to '*einmeerung*', and Nibler in his synoptic comparison of Freiburg Ms. 362 and Stainer 1529 argues that '*einmeerung*' = '*aimern,
emmern*' => 'hot ash', 'embers' ('*heiße Asche*', '*Glut*'), as also referred to by Schmeller,
Bayerisches Wörterbuch, I, 75, who has referenced this for Munich Cgm. 4902. Hassenstein, *Feuerwerkbuch*, 77, translates it as 'bucket' ('*Eimer*') which seems to be
incorrect. Heidelberg Cod. Pal. germ. 122, uses '*Vnd nim die glüt vnd aschen als die
aÿmrigen Das das vast vnder ain ander glüt*' (fol. 45r) just as Göttingen, 2° Cod. Ms.
philos. 64, which describes it as '*vnd nÿm glut vnd aschen als die aymrigen das da fast
vnd ainand[er] glut*' (fol. 145r). Following the etymology of '*ember*' it would refer to
the '*ammer*' (def. 2) in relation to 'a spark glowing underneath ashes' ('*unter der Asche
glühender Funke*', *Frühneuhochdeutsches Wörterbuch Online*, http://www.fwb-online.
de/go/ammer.h2.1f_1515305643).

10	den swam zu stuckweiß als prait als
	ein hand vnd eins vingers dick vnd schüt
	es in den haffen vnder die aÿmrigen der
	glut vnd leg ein lecke schwam dar auff
	vnd ein leg der koln vnd aber ain leg des
15	swams vnd tu es als oft piß das der ha=
	fen vol werd vnd geuß dar über ein was=
	ser das oben dar über ge vnd teck in zu
	vnd secz in hin vnd laß in sten auff zehen
	tag vnd wenn er nit wasser hab so
20	vil in wider vnd nym[m] in vnd wasch in
	auß rein vnd sauber das kain asch oder
	kot dar in seÿ vnd reüch in an einen va=

fol. 50v

1	den vnd henck in auf zu dem offen oder an
	ein sunnen vn[d] laß in wol trucken das er dür
	werd **Wie man zunder machen sol**

Wiltu in aber gern haben das er

5	nicht riech oder schmeck so nym[m]
	sein als vil als du sein wilt vnd leg in
	in einen essich vnd laß in dar in ligen ein
	tag vnd nacht vnd henck in auf vnd laß
	in trucken so wirt er gut **Wie man ein**
10	**eÿsne tüll zu einem haußpfeil herten sol**
	das er als hert wirt als ob er fein stech=
	lein wer vnd auch als nucz auff platen
	harnasch vnd ring harnasch als ob er
	stechlein wer vnd also macht du auch
15	**wol da mit herten welcherleÿ du wilt**
	das eÿsen ist

the sponge into pieces the width
of a hand and one finger thick.
Put them in a bowl into the glowing part of the
embers and place a sponge on top of it.
Add more charcoal, and more sponge,
and repeat this until the bowl
is full. Pour water
over it until it overflows and cover it.
Store it away and let it stand for ten
days. When it runs out of water, then
refill it again. Take it out and wash it
clean and tidy so that no ash
or dung remains in it. Tie it with string

fol. 50v

and hang it over an oven or put it in the
sun and let it dry out well until it is [*completely*]
dry. **How you make tinder.**

If you would like to have it that
it [*the tinder*] does not smell or taste, take
as much as you want and place it
into a bowl of vinegar and let it rest in it
for one day and one night. And hang it up and let
it dry and it will be good. **How you harden
an iron tip into a house arrow**[284]
**so that it becomes so hard like a thin
stick and also can be used against plate
armour and mail armour
like a knife. And make [*it*] also
as hard as you like
so that it is like iron.**

---

[284] It is not clear what is meant by the term 'house arrow' (*Haußpfeil*). Plenty of speculative interpretations are offered, from Hassenstein's 'an arrow that can be fired at
a house' (*gegen ein Haus zu schießender Pfeil*, Hassenstein, *Feuerwerkbuch*, 77) to
Nibler's admittedly hypothetical explanation that it relates to an arrow, the head of
which was fastened in a more secure way to be able to be fired effectively against
'plate or mail armour' (*Platten und Ringharnische*, Nibler, *Feuerwerkbuch*, n. 270).

Gunpowder Technology in the Fifteenth Century

Wiltu herten ein eÿsne tül zu eine[m]
hauß pfeil geschmit oder was
du gern wilt so nym[m] ein kraut das haist
20   verbena etlich haissen es eÿsen kraut vn[d]
das hat plaube plomlein Das selb ist
das recht vnd das sol man nemen mit

fol. 51r

1   dem stengel vnd mit dem kraut als es do
stat vnd sol es stossen in einem morser
dar nach sol man es auß trucken durch
ein tuch als vil du mugst vn[d] tu das wasser
5   in ein glaß dar nach nim als vil wassers
als vil du sein nemst zu bedurffen zu der
hert vn[d] als vil mans harn der nit warm
seÿ geleicher weis als vil als gens vnd
misch vn[d] rier es durch ein ander vn[d] nach
10   ostern so ma[n] die ecker praucht so vint man
wirm die haissen egerling die sein clein
vn[d] haben groß köpff macht du der geha=
ben so truck sie auß vn[d] tu das selb wasser
vn[d] er das hert wasser vn[d] wen[n] du es herte[n]
15   wöllest so soltu es nit rot lassen werden
dz es nit zu haiß werd vnd stoz es dann
als ver du es herte[n] wilt in das wasser

If you want to harden an iron tip to become a
sharpened house arrow,[285] or what
you would prefer. Take a herb that is
called *verbena* or is commonly called 'iron herb' and
which has blue flowers. The same is
the right one.[286] And you shall take it at

fol. 51r

the stem and with the herbs as it
stands and grind it in a mortar.
Afterwards you press it through
a cloth as much as possible and you put the
water [*of the liquid*] in a glass flask. Afterwards you take as much water
as you think is necessary for it to
harden and as much man's urine that is not warm
in the same manner, the same quantity as the other[287] and
mix it and stir it together. And after
Easter when you prepare the fields you find
worms which are called '*engerling*' which are small and
which have large heads. You can catch them
and dry them out and place them in the same water
and before the water hardens. And when you want it to
harden, then do not let it turn red,
that it does not get too hot. And plunge it into water
because you want to harden it.

---

[285] Alternatively, this could be read as '*geschundet*' (Göttingen 2° Cod. Ms. philos. 64, fol. 145v) – '*schinden*' – to 'skin' or 'strip' or here 'sharpen'. Other *Firework Books* refer to this as 'forged' ('*geschmidet*', Stainer 1529, 36).

[286] Verbena or vervain is a genus in the family Verbenaceae. It has been commonly used in medicine, herbalism, and folklore since Egyptian and Roman times (*The Encyclopedia of Herbs and Herbalism*, ed. Malcolm Stuart (London: Orbis, 1979), 279). It has been referred to as a 'wonder drug' with multiple uses, one of them being the 'ability to harden iron – a claim made by Paracelsus' (Francis B. Brévart, 'Between Medicine, Magic, and Religion: Wonder Drugs in German Medico-Pharmaceutical Treatises of the Thirteenth to the Sixteenth Centuries', *Speculum* 83 (2008), 11 n22.

[287] '*als vil as gens*' refers here to '*als vil als yenes wasser*' (Göttingen 2° Cod. Ms. philos. 64, fol. 146r, or Stainer 1529, 42), or in Heidelberg Cod. Pal. germ. 122, fol. 45v and 46r, '*als vil als gens wassers*'. Etymologically, it appears that this derives from '*jenes*' – 'the other'.

vn[d] laß die hicz vo[n] im selber wider vergen
piß das es gotfarb fleck gewin[n] so küel es
20   wider in der selben hert vn[d] laß es do peÿ
beleiben liestu es gar plaube werden so
wird es gar waich Et sic est finis

And let the heat come off from itself
until it gets gold-coloured blotches.[288] Then cool it
down again in the same hardening [*water*]. But if you let it
turn blue, then it becomes
soft. And here is the end.

---

[288] Nibler suggests that something must be missing as it would need to be heated up again, before cooling it down (Nibler, *Feuerwerkbuch*, n. 277). From the context it is not clear how he reached that conclusion.

Royal Armouries I.34 – Part 2

fol. 52r

1 **Wiltw ein hoflich kwnst mache[n] vo[n] eine[m] feur das**
einer tawsent an einem stwrm ab treibt ab ma[n] vor
eine[m] slos oder stat stwrme[n] wolt so merck dÿ her noch
geschribe[n] kapitell wi dws mache[n] solt vo[n] welche[m]
5 **zeug wn gewicht je mer ma[n] mit waser dar auf**
gewst je wnsicher di lewt dar pei sint

W iltw dise vor geschribe[n] veu[e]r mache[n] so
~~w~~ volg disem noch geschribe[n] kapitell noch
wi dw das feur werck fasen solt vn[d] vo[n] welche[m]
10 czeug das vinst dw her nach geschribe[n] czw[m]
ersten am an vang so los dir mache[n] ein veslein al[s]
gros dw eß hawe[n] wilt das einer wber ein maur[n]
oder czine[n] geverfe[n] mag da mit ma[n] ein stwrm[m] ab
treibt vn[d] loß dirs vo[n] holcz dick mache[n] vn[d] woll gepunte[n]
15 das es an dem bwrf nit czw vall vn[d] piche[n] mer merck
wi dw den czeug vase[n] sollt der do ein das vaß gehort

nim ein geleiche wog un[d] leg auf das ein teill	v	lb
am gewicht vn[d] auf das ander teill der wog	v	lb
salp[eter] vn[d] nim den den salp[eter] ~~he~~her ab vn[d] wig	iii	lb
salp[eter] salcz nim den das salcz her ab vn[d] wig	i	lb

20

Royal Armouries I.34 – Part 2

fol. 52r

**If you want to make a 'courtly art'[1] of the fire[*work*],[2] which
will fend off a thousand in an attack, [*or*] to make an attack
in front of a castle or a town, then note the
written chapter below: what you should do, which
ingredients and what weights [*to use*], the more water you
pour onto it, the less safe people are with it [*i.e. when handling it*].[3]**

If you want to make the fire[*work*] indicated above, then
follow the chapter written below:
how you should handle the firework, and about which
ingredients [*to use*] – you will find that in what is written below.
First, to begin with, have made a small barrel
as big as you would like it, so that you can throw it
over a man and over the battlements to fend off an
attack. Have a thick piece of wood made and tie it well together
so that, when you throw it, it does not fall apart. Note
how you gather the ingredients which have to go into the barrel.

Take a well-balanced pair of scales and put onto one side	5	pounds
of weight and on the other side of the scales	5	pounds
of saltpetre. And take the saltpetre off and weigh	3	pounds
of saltpetre salt.[4] Then take the salt off [*the scales*] and weigh	1	pound

---

[1] The expression '*hoflich kwnst*' has been translated as 'courtly art' throughout Part 2.
'Courtly' refers to a skill and knowledge which would be of relevance at court. It has
(as mentioned in Part 1) an aspirational aspect; the fact that it appears more often
in Part 2 may indicate that this aspiration was more pronounced at the time of
production of Part 2. '*kwnst*' or '*kunst*' refers to 'art' and itself has multiple meanings.
For a discussion of these terms see Chapter 5.

[2] The original often refers to it as 'fire' ('*fewr*' or '*feur*'), but this reference is usually
related to 'firework'. For this reason, this has been changed throughout the text.

[3] The explanation about the use of water is not very clear. It could be that this is a
metaphorical expression known to the reader, or an expression which could be related to the processes and ingredients (in neither case would water help the process
of producing good quality gunpowder). It could also be that petroleum and resin
cannot easily be extinguished with water alone.

[4] Not sure what the author meant by an ingredient 'saltpetre salt', as the main state
for saltpetre is in crystallized form like salt. This raises the question of what state
the main ingredient 'saltpetre' is meant to be in.

Gunpowder Technology in the Fifteenth Century

schwefells nim den schweffell ab vn[d] wig mer   ii lb
gwcz sisch pulferß vn[d] nim das pulfer ab vn[d] wig   i lb
gemalle[n] faul[n] puche[n] holcz das vinst dw her nach geschrib[en]
wi dws male[n] solt vn[d] itliger czeug sol klein gestosen
25   sein sam woltz dw pulfer dar auß mache[n] vn[d] misch
den rein vnter ein ander vn[d] nim ein weicz spen sip
vn[d] rid den czeug dar dwrch das es sich mit ein
ander vor ein vn[d] wen das geschit so loß wnter
dem stamfp stossen so wirt es dester pesser vn[d] wen

fol. 52v

1   das geschit so nim den selbe[n] czeug vn leg ein leg
ein das vaß vn[d] nim vn[d] mach vo[n] alte[n] seille[n] czoche[n]
geflochte[n] eins vinger dick vn[d] seud in salp[eter] auf ein
stwnd vn[d] loß den trucke[n] an der swne[n] oder ein der
5   stwben vn[d] schwem si den in harcz vn[d] geus ein weng
oliw[m] pretoliu[m] wnter das harcz das oll vinst dw her
nach geschribe[n] wan das fewr bwrt dester herber

Royal Armouries I.34 – Part 2

of sulphur. Take off the sulphur and then weigh   2 pounds
of good gunpowder. Take the powder off and weigh   1 pound
of ground-up rotten beech wood which you will find described below
how to grind it. All the ingredients should be ground together finely
if you want to make good powder out of them and mix
them together well. And take a wide,[5] tautly strung sieve[6]
and force the ingredients through it so that they are mixed well.
And when that is done [*i.e. mixed well*], then grind [*the mixture*]
in a stamp mill[7] – the more, the better. And when

fol. 52v

that is done, then take the same 'thing' [*i.e. the mixture*] and put it
into a barrel. And take and make out of old bits of rope a wick[8] which is
braided and one finger thick.[9] Boil it in saltpetre for an
hour and let it dry in the sun or in a
warm room. Then soak it in resin and add to
the resin a little *olium petroleum*[10] – which you will
find described below. When the fire burns strongly[11]

---

[5]   Not clear whether this refers to the mesh size or the size of the sieve itself.

[6]   Not clear what '*spen*' refers to. It could be the name of a sieve (size unclear), or a reference to its material. No reference was traceable regarding its use, size, format, or function. It could even relate to the density of the sieve.

[7]   The stamp mill is depicted on fol. 87v. The main function of the stamp mill is grinding the mixture and mixing it, not compressing. The illustration at fol. 87v shows both an hourglass (suggesting the need to do the grinding for a minimum amount of time) and the master gunner standing at the side supervising the grinding. He also has a specific tool in his hand which could be understood to be aiding in the task (see Figure 7, right).

[8]   '*zoche*' can be a range of different items: stick, string, and also wick or fuse ('holzscheit, knüppel, or Stock', but also 'docht, lunte, zündstrick', *Deutsches Wörterbuch von Jacob und Wilhelm Grimm Online* – accessed 10 August 2023). Here translated as 'wick', as it is mainly aimed to burn and not act only as a fuse.

[9]   Ordinarily, rope would be twisted. To braid or plait rope means that it is slightly less flexible, but has more integral stability.

[10]   It is virtually impossible to trace what exactly '*olium petroleum*' refers to. From the context, it is likely to be a form of petroleum, and that the tautological use of the term was a rhetorical aid, perhaps emphasising that it was petroleum of good quality.

[11]   It is not clear what is the purpose of the reference about the fire. It could be that the resin may benefit from warming up (e.g. softening it to ease mixing with the other ingredients).

Gunpowder Technology in the Fifteenth Century

wn[d] leg der selbe[n] czoche[n] awf das vor genant pulfer
ein leg vn[d] wider ein leg pulfer vn[d] leg dÿ leg alß

10   lang piß das vaß auf das halb teill vol burt vn[d]
loß dir den mache[n] kegell vo[n] murbe[n] eise[n] alß dw her
nach gemolt vinst an dem lxxxxv plat wi si sein swle[n]
vn[d] las si mit gwte[n] sisch pulfer in aller der moß
alß ein pusche[n] vn[d] leg ir ein das vaß das auf das halb

15   teill gefult ist alß vil dwr habe[n] x oder xx dar nach
alß dw daß fewr dester wnsicher habe[n] willt vn[d] leg
den deß vor genante[n] pulferß dar auf vn[d] ein leg czoche[n]
vn[d] leg dÿ leg alß lang piß das vaß vol burt vn[d]
czu oberst leg ein wenig sisch pulferß vo[n] deß an czwnte[n]

20   wege[n] vn[d] slach den das vaß czw vn[d] mach an den
czu geslage[n] pode[n] pei v locher mit eim negber eins
finger groß vn[d] czunz da pei an wan dw darft dich
nicht forchte[n] vn[d] loß an gen[n] vn[d] auch nicht czu lang
das eß nit auf dÿ kegell prin wan eß schlug dir

25   den halß ab vn[d] burß das faß den hin ab an den
stwrm so host dw dÿ pesten stwrm feur do nimant
sicher pei ist

Royal Armouries I.34 – Part 2

put the same braided rope on the aforementioned powder
in [*the barrel*], and add a layer of powder and a layer [*of rope*]
until the barrel is half full. And
have a ball[12] made for you out of soft iron[13] as you
can find drawn later on sheet 95[14] how it should be.
And fill it [*the iron ball*] with good gunpowder in the same way as [*you would*]
for a gun.[15] And put it [*the ball*] into the barrel which is filled
half full, and add [*a further*] ten or twenty [*balls*]
if you want to have the fire[*work*] be more unsafe.[16] And put
the aforementioned powder on top of it and add the braided rope.
And put them one on top of the other until the barrel is full to the top.
Right on top put a little gunpowder so that it can be lit more easily.
And hammer the barrel closed and make five holes[17] in the
sealed bottom with a drill,[18] each one
finger wide. And when you light it you must have
no fear. And you must let it catch alight, but do not wait so long
that it burns down to the ball, otherwise it will knock
your head off and will burst the barrel. Then take it to the [*front of the*]
attack, and thus you have the best attack fire[*work*] from which no one
is safe.

[12] Early New High German does not distinguish between 'cone' (in New High German '*Kegel*') and 'ball' (in New High German '*Kugel*'), but it is more likely to be 'cone' than 'ball'. For consistency reasons, however, it will be translated as 'ball'. The original term could be either singular or plural; plural is used here, as subsequently the verb indicates more than one ball.

[13] The German could imply brittle or soft, referring to the status of the iron, its flexibility and physical characteristics.

[14] The insert of a sheet number is in different coloured ink and is probably a later addition as the number is slightly longer than the space provided. This could refer to both fols 95r and 95v. Both folios depict fire arrows and some of their contents (see Figure 8).

[15] One possible assumption here may be that this is related to the compressing of gunpowder (which needs to be compressed, but not too much).

[16] Likely to mean 'aggressive', or even 'deadly' or 'lethal', as 'unsafe' must apply to the opponents.

[17] Likely referring to these holes as 'touch holes' – not specified in the text.

[18] See I.34, fol. 7r, as well as related footnote 77.

fol. 53r

1 **wiltw ein hoflich kwnst mache[n] das auch czwm stwrm**
dint vn[d] heist ein stwrm fewr vn[d] ist nimat sicher dar
pei hwndert schrite[n] on geferlich so folg disem noch
geschribe[n] kapitell noch vn[d] wen dws wase[n] wilt alß
5 **dw her nach geschribe[n] vinst so ge weislich da mit**
wmb vn[d] vor sich dich vn[d] ander leut das eß sich
nicht enczwnt wan groß schwede[n] da vo[n] mochte[n]
kwme[n] vn[d] den leute[n] dy helß ab schlug

Wiltw dise vor geschriben feur werck mache[n]

10 so volg disem noch geschribe[n] kapitell noch wi | | |
dws mache[n] solt vn[d] von welche[m] gewicht des | | |
czewgs czu erste[n] loß dir mache[n] ein vaß vo[n] dicke[m] | | |
holcz vn[d] woll gepunte[n] alß vor wen das geschit so nim | | |
ein geleiche[n] wog die geleich vn[d] recht sei leg auf ein teill | | |
15 der wog alß dws wege[n] wilt am gebicht | viii | lb
vn[d] leg den der gege[n] auf das ander teill | viii | lb
salp[eter] vn[d] leg den salp[eter] ab vn[d] leg auf dy wog | iiii | lb
am gebicht vn[d] leg auf das ander teill wog | iiii | lb
schweffell vn[d] leg den schweffell ab leg auf wog | ii | lb
20 am gewicht vn[d] dar gege[n] auf das and[ere] teill | ii | lb
gestosser kolle[n] vn[d] nim di kolle[n] ab vn[d] leg auf | i | lb
am gewicht auf dy wog der teill eins gege[n] | i | lb

gestosen harcz vn[d] wig den mer ein lb des vor genant[en]
puche[n] faulen gemalle[n] holcz das her nach geschribe[n] stet
25 an dem lv plat da dw den rauch geschribe[n] vinst
da vinst dw wi dw das holcz male[n] solt losse[n] vn[d] nim
dÿ stwck alle[n] czw same[n] vnd misch dwrch ein ander awer
dw must itlich stuck vor rein stosse[n] vn[d] rede[n] sam wolst

fol. 53r

**If you want to make a 'courtly art' for attack
and which is called attack fire[*work*], and which is dangerous
and no one is safe [*within*] a hundred paces, then follow the
chapter written below. And if you want to know how,
you will find it below. And treat it with caution
and be careful for yourself, and for other people, so that it
does not catch fire. This can cause a large amount of damage
and which knock off the people's heads.**

If you want to make the firework described above
then follow what is written in this chapter [*as to*] how you
should make it, and the weight of [*each of the*]
ingredients. First have a barrel made of thick
wood which is tied[19] together well. When that is done, then take
a well-balanced pair of scales which are good and level. Place on one side
of the scales, when you are ready to weigh it, 8 pounds in weight.
And put on the other side against it 8 pounds
of saltpetre. And take off the saltpetre and put on your scales a weight
of 4 pounds and put on the other side 4 pounds
of sulphur. And take off the sulphur and put on the scales a weight of
2 pounds, and put on the other side 2 pounds
of ground charcoal. And take off the charcoal and put on a weight
of 1 pound, and on the other side, against it, 1 pound of
ground resin. Then weigh up, furthermore, one pound of the aforementioned
ground-up rotten beech wood which is described below
on sheet 55.[20] There you will find the description of the smoke,[21] and
there you will find how you have to have the wood ground. And put
all the ingredients together and mix them thoroughly. But
you have to grind any small pieces down properly if you want

---

[19] The original implies 'tied', but it is not clear whether it is the material used that is
referred to, or any particular part of the barrel.

[20] This number does not refer to an illustration, but to a later description in the text.
This is the only time the author makes this reference to another part of the text, and
not (as happens more frequently) to an illustration in a later folio. This may imply
that the text contained previously known elements of text, and is not a continuous
record of an experiment.

[21] Not clear what 'smoke' this is. One possibility is that this may be related to the
white dust of rotten beech wood.

Gunpowder Technology in the Fifteenth Century

30 dwu[n] pwlfer dar auß mache[n] vn[d] wen das geschit so
nim ein weicz spen sip vn[d] rid den czeug dar dwrch
das er sich verein vn[d] nim den ein nab vo[n] eim wagner
di do gancz sei las an pede[n] orte[n] dar an lege[n[ii ring

fol. 53v

1 vo[n] aich gerte[n] gemacht vn[d] loß in auß pore[n] vn[d] alß hoch
alß das vor geschribe[n] vaß das der pode[n] fur mug vn[d] slach
den grosser ort der nab wnte[n] czw mit eim aiche[n] klocz vn[d]
verpor in rein vn[d] mach ein kreuz kerbe[n] an den verslage[n]
5 pode[n] vmb des wille[n] wen den stock ein das vaß seczt das
er sich dester e enczwnt mer por dwrch den klocz ein czwnt
loch piß an das pulfer vn[d] nim den den selbe[n] stock vn[d] vaß
in voller sisch pulfer auf das herczt vn[d] slach ein klocz dar
fur vn[d] verpor in alß vor vn[d] nim den vn[d] se ein das vor
10 geschribe[n] vaß an den pode[n] ein wenck sisch pulfers vn[d] secz
den stock dar auf ein das vas vn[d] loß dir mache[n] kegell
di hinte[n] spiczig sent alß dw gemolt vinst an dem____
plat vn[d] loß vo[n] murbe[n] eise[n] mache[n] vn[d] lanck das dws vo[n]
awsen dwrch das vas slecht piß an den stock awer dw

Royal Armouries I.34 – Part 2

to make fine[22] powder out of it. When that is done, then take
a wide, tight sieve and force the ingredients through it
so that they become one. And take a wheel hub from a wagon builder
which is complete [*in one piece*].[23] Have two rings

fol. 53v

made from oak twigs placed onto it at both ends. And have [*a hole*] drilled as long
as the aforementioned barrel so that it comes through the bottom. And force
an oak plug into the larger end of the wheel hub. And
make sure it fits tightly.[24] And make a cross groove in the sealed
end so that when you place the stick[25] into the barrel
it catches light more easily.[26] And drill through the [*oak*] plug a touch
hole until you reach the powder. And take the same stick and fill
it full of gunpowder up to the top. Hammer a plug onto
it and tighten it as before. And take it and make sure that the
barrel described earlier has a little bit of gunpowder at the bottom. And insert
the stick into the barrel. And have made for you balls
which are pointed at the end as you find painted on sheet____.[27]
And let them be made of soft iron and [*let them be*] long enough for you
to [*reach it*] from the outside through the barrel up to the stick. But beforehand

---

[22] The literal meaning is 'thin', but it is likely that it is used in the sense of 'fine' or 'finely ground'.

[23] In the sense of 'not broken' as one piece of wood. There is a variety of possible interpretations of this. It could either relate to a wheel hub which has not yet had the spokes (or their holes) added to it. In this way, it would have more structural integrity (important for an incendiary device). Alternatively, it could refer to a wheel hub which is completely finished (with holes, and possibly also with spokes) which would give the wheel hub additional channels for any explosion to escape through.

[24] The original implies a drilling or twisting motion to check that it fits tightly.

[25] This could relate to what, from the sixteenth century onwards, has been known as a '*linstock*'. However, the context is not very clear. The use of the definite article implies that the author may not need to tell the reader what the stick is. It is most likely that the stick acts as a fuse or as a stabilizing element.

[26] The implication here is that the sealing of the end of the wheel hub means that any powder inside would be in a more confined space, and thereby more powerful and effective.

[27] Space for folio number left but not inserted, which looks like a scribal omission. It is possible that the author refers to fol. 89r or fol. 89v, but with some reservations; another possibility is that the page was never drawn (or was forgotten by the artists), which is the reason why it had been left blank.

15	must vor durch das vaß locher pore[n] als dick di kegell
	sint vn[d] lad di selbe[n] kegell in aller der mos alß ein hant
	pusche[n] e dws hin ein slecht vn[d] nim den der vor genant[en]
	alte[n] seill der czoche[n] in salp[eter] gesote[n] vn[d] harcz geswemt vn[d] leg
	ein leg vmb den stock vn[d] des vor genante[n] pulferß vo[n] viii
20	teil salp[eter] gemacht ein leg auf di czoche[n] vn[d] awer ein leg
	czoche[n] vn[d] leg di leg alß lang piß das vaß vol burt vn[d]
	leg czw oberst ein wenig schiß pulfer vn[d] slach den das
	vaß czw vn[d] mach durch den pode[n] pei v locher eins
	finger groß da czunt pei an vn[d] saum dich nit lang wan
25	dws von dir werfe[n] wilt so hast du dÿ peste[n] slachent fewr
	da nimant sicher pei ist am stwrmen

fol. 54r

1 **wiltw awer ein hoflich stwrm fewr mache[n] das vill**
mer schwede[n] da vo[n] kwm dan vo[n] den vor genante[n]
fewre[n] wan si sint stercker vn[d] herber

Wiltu dise her nach geschribe[n] feur werck mache[n]
5 so volg disem noch geschribe[n] kapitell noch alß dw
hore[n] bwrst czw[m] erste[n] nim ein nab als vor vn vaß
dar ein gut sisch pulfer auf das herczt vn[d] mach vnte[n]
dwrch den verschlage[n] klocz ein czwt loch vn[d] ein kreucz kerbe[n]
awer dw scholt den stock vor rain pinte[n] losen[n] mit gute[n] ringe[n]
10 mer wen dw den stock halbe[n] gelade[n] hast so leg dar ein ain
geladen[n] kegell als dw her nach gemolt vinst mit czencke an

Royal Armouries I.34 – Part 2

you have to drill holes in the barrel the size of the balls.[28]
And let the same balls [*be made*] the same size as you need for a hand
gun. Before you hammer it in, take the
old rope pieces described earlier which were soaked in saltpetre and resin, and put
then bit by bit around the stick. And take the said powder of 8
parts of saltpetre and put it on the pieces of rope. And place
those pieces of rope into the barrel until the barrel is full. And
place on top a little gunpowder and seal the
barrel shut. And make five holes one finger wide
to set it alight at the bottom [*of the barrel*]. And do not wait too long before
throwing it away from you. This way you have the best striking fire[*work*]
that no one is safe against when attacking.[29]

fol. 54r

**But if you want to make a 'courtly' attacking fire[*work*] which causes
much more damage, as it is stronger and more severe
than the aforementioned fire[*work*].**

If you want to make the firework described below
then follow this chapter written below as you will
hear.[30] First, take a wheel hub as before and fill it
with good gunpowder up to the top. And make a touch hole
through the sealed plug[31] and make a cross groove.
But before [*this*] you should have made the [*bundle of*] sticks tied with good rings;[32]
add more [*rings*] when you have loaded the [*bundle of*] sticks half [*way*]. And
put a loaded ball into it [*the bundle*] as you find drawn later – jagged as on

---

[28] The literal translation is 'as big as the balls are'.

[29] It is unclear what exactly the recipe is trying to achieve. The key terms used, such as barrel, hub, rope, powder, and stick, are very generic, and unless the context is known they can be very ambiguous.

[30] This is a rare reference which may refer to the usage of this text, giving the impression that it was more likely to have been read out and presented orally instead of being read in silence.

[31] The original implies a hitting or beating action, but for clarity it is changed here to 'seal'.

[32] The assumption here, supported by the illustrations depicted on fol. 89r, is that this stick is not a single stick, but rather a bundle of sticks. This is not made clear in the text, but it would explain the illustrations and the actions described.

Gunpowder Technology in the Fifteenth Century

dem lxxxviiii plat vn[d] secz den stock ein das vas awer dw solt
an pode[n] des faß sisch pulfer ton das sich der stock da von
enczwnt mer los dir mache[n] eise[n] mit feder[n] di dwrch das

15 vas gen an den stock vn[d] ause[n] vernagelt um des wille[n] das
sich der stock nit werrwckt vn[d] mach de[n] stock owe[n] czw mit
eim aiche[n] klocz vn[d] verpor in genau alß vor mer e dw de[n]
stock ein das vaß seczt so se an poden vnter den stock gucz
pulfer das sich der stock enczunt wen das geschit so nim

20 alte auf getrifelt seill vn[d] seud in salp[eter] vn[d] loß trucke[n]
vn[d] nim stein als groß dÿ hwner air vn[d] vmb wint
di stein mit den alte[n] saille[n] vn[d] tauf si ein schwefell
vn[d] aß pallent sol si in pulfer vn[d] swem si den in pech
vn[d] auß dem pech wehent in das hernach geschriben

25 weiß pulfer das czw dem rauch gehort vn[d] nim den
der vor genante[n] czoche[n] in salp[eter] gesote[n] vn[d] in pech geswemt
vn[d] leg ein leg auf den pode[n] des vaß vn[]d ein leg des
vor genante[n] pulfer vn[d] das vo[n] viii teil salp[eter] vn[d] vo[n] iiii
teill swefell vn[d] vo[n] ii teill kolle[n] vn[d] i teill harcz i teill

30 faul puche[n] gemalle[n] holtz das pulfer hast dw an dem
liii   plat vn[d] auf das selbig pulfer ein leg der vm
bvnte[n] stein vn[d] wider czoche[n] vn[d] wider stein vn[d] leg

fol. 54v

1 vn[d] leg die leg alß lang piß das vas vol bwrt awer
dw magst woll der vor genante[n] spiczige[n] gelade[n] kegell
vor ein den stock slache[n] alß wil dw bilt wmb des wille[n]
das ma[n] dester vn[d] sicher dar pei ist vn[d] leg czw oberst ein

5 wenig gwcz sisch pulfers vo[n] des an czwnte[n] wege vn
slach das vas czw vn[d] mach an pode[n] pei v locher alß vor

Royal Armouries I.34 – Part 2

sheet 89.[33] Place the [*bundle of*] sticks inside a barrel. But you should put [*some*] gunpowder at the bottom of the barrel so that the [*bundle of*] sticks catches light from it. Furthermore, have made for yourself an iron with feathers[34] which goes through the barrel to the [*bundle of*] sticks and which is nailed on, so that the sticks do not move anymore. And seal off the [*bundle of*] sticks on the top with a piece of oak wood and drill [*a hole*] exactly as before. And before you place the sticks in the barrel, put at the bottom underneath the stick good powder which allows the sticks to be lit. When that is done, take old unravelled rope and soak it in saltpetre and let it dry. And take a stone as big as a chicken egg, and wrap the old rope around the stone, and soak it in sulphur. And as quickly as possible put it in powder, and soak it in tar, and from the tar[35] take the white powder described below which is part of the smoke. And take the said rope, soaked in saltpetre and in tar, and put it into the bottom of the barrel. And add the aforementioned powder, and that of 8 parts of saltpetre, and of 4 parts of sulphur, and 2 parts of charcoal, and 1 part of resin, [*and*] 1 part rotten ground beech wood. [*This is*] the powder you have on sheet 53.[36] And into the same powder add coloured stone around it and more rope and more stone and

fol. 54v

continue to do so until the barrel is full. But you can put the aforementioned pointed loaded balls to the [*bundle of*] sticks as much as you would like. The reason is that it is better and safer that way. And put on top a little good gunpowder so that you can light it, and seal the barrel shut, and make five holes in the bottom as before.

---

[33] As previously, the page number reference is in different ink, but appears to be in the same hand. This page reference is not entirely clear. From the context, the section could apply to both fols 89r and 89v, but also to fol. 88v.

[34] What the original implies with 'feathers' is not clear. One possibility is that the iron is made as thinly as a feather, and in the form of a hollow tube, thus acting as a fuse.

[35] It is not clear at this point what the term '*wehent*' relates to. The word is related to 'wind' and it may be a reference to the stench of tar. Not translated in this instance.

[36] This appears to be in the same hand and similar ink, but the scribe left some space after the number. This could imply that the page number was meant to be longer when the original text was written.

wiltw awer ein pesre kwnst mache[n] vo[n] einem rawch
das ein ma[n] mocht ein her ab treibe[n] an eim stwrm
da ma[n] stwrme[n] wolt oder aus eine[m] sloß reuche[n] das
10 **di dar ine[n] kein geschick mochte[n] hawe[n] noch mit ir**
wer czw verkvme[n] mochte[n] zu wer vn[d] merck dise her
nach geschribe[n] kapitel

W iltw dise[n] vor geschribe[n] rawch mache[n] so volg
disem noch geschribe[n] kapitell nach czw ersten loß
15 dir mache[n] ein veslein alß vor vo[n] starcke[m] holcz vn[d]
woll gepwnte[n] vo[n] des werfe[n] wege[n] vn[d] wen das
geschit so nim ein geleiche[n] wog vn[d] leg auf das ein teill
iiii lb gewicht vn[d] nim den dar gege[n] auf das and[er] teil
iiii lb salp[eter] vn[d] nim vn[d] leg den salp[eter] ab vn[d] leg auf
20 ii lb am gebicht vn[d] leg den auf das ander teill
ii b schweffell vn[d] nim den schwefell ab vn[d] leg auf
ii lb am gewicht vn[d] leg auf das and[er] teill d[er] wog
ii lb gestose[n] harcz vn[d] durch ein sip gerede[n] leg ab nim
i lb am gewicht vn[d] leg auf das and[er] teill d[er] wog
25 i lb salp[eter] salcz nim das salcz ab vn[d] vn[d] leg auf
i lb am gewicht vn[d] leg auf das ander teill
i lb gemale[n] faulz puche[n] holcz awer dw must
itlig vor klein stose[n] sam wolß du pulfer dar auß
machen vn[d] merck wi dw das holcz malle[n] solt losen

fol. 55r

1 wn[d] male[n] czw[m] erste[n] nim fawl puche[n] holcz das awf
dem stock erfawlt sei vn[d] an der farb weiß mer nim
den das selbig holcz loß dwn schneide[n] vn[d] dar nach rein
dere[n] vn[d] dar nach vnter dem stamfp stossen wn[d] las dar
5 nach malle[n] wn[d] wen das alß geschit so misch den czeug
vnter ein ander vn[d] rid in durch ein weicz sip vmb dez

Royal Armouries I.34 – Part 2

But if you want to make a better 'art',[37] of a smoke,
which you use to drive away an attack, [*or if*]
you want to attack. Or, [*if*] you want to smoke out a castle so that
those inside [*the castle's inhabitants*] have no chance to
defend themselves [*against it*]. And note this in the
chapter written below.

If you want to make the said smoke, then follow
the chapter written below. First, have
a barrel made which is of strong wood and
well fastened together so that it can be thrown. And when this
is done, then take a well-balanced pair of scales. And add to one side [*of the scales*]
4 pounds of weight, and add against it to the other side
4 pounds of saltpetre. And take the saltpetre off, put it down and place
2 pounds of weight, and add to the other side
2 pounds of sulphur. And take the sulphur off and place [*on the scales*]
2 pounds of weight, and add to the other side of the scales
2 pounds of ground resin which is driven through a sieve. Take it off and take
1 pound of weight and add to the other side of the scales
1 pound of saltpetre salt. And take off the salt and place
1 pound of weight. And add to the other side
1 pound of ground-up rotten beech wood.[38] But you have to make
sure that all the parts are finely ground if you want to make powder out
of it. And note how you should grind down the wood:

fol. 55r

first, grind the rotten beech wood which has
rotted on the stick [*i.e. on its branches*], and which is white in colour. Take
this wood and let it be cut. And then let it
dry and after that have it ground in the stamp mill. And let it all be
ground. And when it is all done, then mix the ingredients
together and run [*the mixture*] through a wide[39] sieve so that

---

[37] As described before, '*kwnst*' can refer to a range of issues, and in this case it is more
likely to refer to 'device' or 'technique'. To keep the imprecise nature of the original it
is left as 'art'.

[38] This recipe is missing charcoal. It could be that this is a scribal error, or that charcoal
was the one ingredient which was so commonly available that they would not need to
specify it in the recipe. This hypothesis may be unlikely, considering the other details
in the recipes provided.

[39] This could mean 'big in size' or 'coarse' – but it is not clear from the context.

Gunpowder Technology in the Fifteenth Century

wille[n] das es sich vor ein vn[d] nim ein ol krugell vn[d] faß
vol das eß loß sei vn[d] musterß wi eß tut ob eß gerecht
sei welch czw sacz czw vil oder weng sei dar nach richt

10 dich vn[d] nim den der vor genante[n] czoche[n] vo[n] alte[n] seille[n]
in salp[eter] gesote[n] vn[d] har geschwemt vn[d] nim des vorgnant
weise[n] pulferß vn[d] leg ein leg ein das vaß eins czwere[n]
vinger dick vn[d] der czoche[n] ein leg vn[d] wider deß
weise[n] pulfer ein leg vn[d] wen dw das vaß auf das

15 halb teil gefast hast so leg dar ein der vor genante[n]
gelade[n] kegell pei x vn[d] des weise[n] pulfer ein leg dar
auf vn[d] wider czeche[n] vn[d] leg dÿ leg alß lang piß das
vaß vol burt vn[d] slach den das vaß czw vn[d] dw vor
czw[m] oberst ein leg sisch pulfers vo[n] des an czwute[n] wege[n]

20 vn[d] mach dwrch den poden pei v anczunt locher vn[d]
loß den wol an gen e dws auß y burfst
wiltw awer ein hoflich kwnst machen vo[n] eine[m] fewr
das dw well awß einer pwsche[n] schise[n] magst
da mit dw ein itlig slosch awß fewren magst

25 **das eß nimat ab gelesche[n] mag wan di kwgel**
schlog hwndert di helß ab

W iltw dise ver geschribe[n] sischent feur machen
so volg disem noch geschribe[n] kapitell noch wi
dw dise fewr werck mache[n] solt vn[d] vo[n] welche[m]

fol. 55v

1 czeug vn am an vang so nim dy weite[n] der puschen
dar awß dw das feur sische[n] wilt wn[d] nim de[n]n stein
dester kleiner vmb des willen wan di kugel bwrt mit
harcz wber czog als dw her nach geschribe[n] vinst dar

5 wmb must dw der kugel enpfor losse[n] vn[d] loß dir den kugel

Royal Armouries I.34 – Part 2

it all mixes together. And take an oil flagon[40] and fill it to the top [*with the mixture*],
so that it is loose [*i.e. not compressed*] and is just like it has to be. You should be
careful that each component is not too much or too little. Make sure you follow
this. And take the aforementioned piece of rope from old rope
which has been soaked in saltpetre and floats [*i.e. reached saturation point*].
And take the aforementioned white powder and place it in the barrel one big[41]
finger thick, and add the [*soaked*] piece of rope. And on top of that put more of
the white powder. When the barrel has been
filled halfway, then add the said
loaded balls. And add the white powder on top
and on top of this add more pieces of rope. Keep doing this until the
barrel is full. Seal the barrel shut, but before that
put some gunpowder on top [*of the barrel*] so that you can light it.
And make five touch holes at the bottom and
let it be lit well before you throw it [*towards the enemy*]
But if you want to make the 'courtly art' of fire[*work*]
which you can fire out of a gun
so that you can set light to any kind of castle with fire[work]
which no one can extinguish, and the ball will
knock off the heads of a hundred [*men*].

If you want to make this fire[*work*] described which you can shoot [*out of a gun*]
then follow this chapter written below on how you
should make this firework, and out of which

fol. 55v

ingredients. In the beginning, take the width of the gun
you want to fire. Take a stone
which is a little smaller [*than the barrel*] as the ball will be
covered with resin as is described below. When
firing you have to let the ball escape.[42] Have made for yourself balls

---

[40] This is likely to refer to the container, but not to any oil being required.

[41] The origin of 'zwere' or 'zawere' is not very clear. The dictionary references only relate to
a verb 'zweren' as 'to stir' ('*verrühren, mischen*', *Frühneuhochdeutsches Wörterbuch Online*,
http://www.fwb-online.de/go/anzweren.s.3v_1513721470) which would not fit in this
context. It is more likely that this is a version of 'heavy' ('*schwer*') – see also at subsequent folios, also for '*zavere*'.

[42] It is not clear what this relates to. The word refers to 'rise', 'escape', or 'slip out' – which
would make sense when referring to a ball coated in resin. Alternatively, it could relate
to 'arise'.

Gunpowder Technology in the Fifteenth Century

fwrm di ine[n] hol sint vn[d] vo[n] murbe[n] czeug un[d] ein gute[n]
dicke[n] vn[d] loß locher auf den seite[n] dar ein furme[n] alß
weit das di kegell dar ein gen vn[d] alß dw her nach
geschribe[n] vinst vn[d] aber ein loch in di kugel geen
10   dem pulfer sack wm des wille[n] das sich di kugell
enczwnt vn[d] wen das alß geschit so loß dir kegell
schmide[n] vo[n] murbe[n] eise[n] alß gefurmt vinst an dem
lxxxxv plat gemolt an der feur kugell vn[d] faß den
ein di kegell gucz sisch pulfer vn[d] lad di kegell in
15   alle der moß alß ein hant pusche[n] vn[d] leg auf das
czwnt loch gucz czwnt pulfer vn[d] vmb wincz mit
hanf werck ein czavere[n] halem dick auf das herczt
vn[d] tauf si in lebentig schwefell den vinst dw ein
der apentecke[n] vn[d] vinst an dem lxxxvi plat wi dw
20   in mere[n] sollt vn[d] ge weislich da mit wm[m] wen dw
di kegell taufen wilt das der schwefell nit prine[n]
wert wan eß schlwg dir den halß ab vn[d] wen das
alß geschit vn[d] nim gafer auch ein der apentecke[n] alß
vil dw wilt der kugell mache[n] vn[d] kweck silber vn[d] faß
25   der czweier stwck itligs ein ~~geß~~ genß veder voll
vn vor machs genau mit wasch vn wm wincz

fol. 56r

1   auch mit hanf werck vn[d] wint alcwege[n] ein feder gafers
wn[d] ein feder kweck silberß czu same[n] vn[d] tauf si den auch
in schwefell vn vor sich dich vor feur we[n] das alß geschit
so merck wi dw den czeug mache[n] solt nim ein leg auf
5   iiii lb an gewicht vn leg aud das ander teil der gege[n]
iiii lb salp[eter] vn[d] nim den salp[eter] ab vn[d] leg auf di wog
ii   b   am gewicht vn leg auf das ander teill wog

to fire which are hollow inside and of brittle material. They have
to be of good thickness. And have made for yourself some holes at the side,
wide enough so that the ball can be put inside as you find
described below. But make a hole in the ball
[*for*] the powder bag in order that the ball
is lit. And when this is done, then have forged for you a ball,
formed out of brittle iron, as you find drawn on
sheet 95 as a fire ball. And fill the
ball with good gunpowder and load it
all to the level as it is [*required*] for a hand gun. And place good gunpowder
on the touch hole and wrap around it some
hemp which has the thickness of a heavy piece of straw. Press it together
and drip onto it native sulphur as you find it
in an apothecary and which you can find on sheet 86.[43] [*It shows*] how
to make more of it and how to handle it carefully when you
drip it on the balls so that the sulphur does not catch fire as
this could knock your head off. And when that
has been done and take camphor,[44] also from the apothecary, as
much as you want to make a ball as well as [*taking*] mercury.[45] And then take
two small pieces each which fill a goose[46] feather.
And seal it [*the feather*] thoroughly with wax and wrap it

fol. 56r

also[47] with hemp and wind the feather of camphor
around the feather of mercury. And soak them both
in sulphur. Be careful [*to stay away*] from fire when this is done.
Then note how to make the ingredients: put on [*the scales*]
4   pounds   of weight and put on the other part against it
4   pounds   of saltpetre and take off the saltpetre and add to the scales
2   pounds   of weight and put on the other part of the scales

---

[43]   This most likely refers to fol. 86v. However, it is not very clear what the reference to
an illustration adds in the understanding of the text.

[44]   This can also spelled as '*gaffer*' or '*gaffran*' ('*Kampfer*', *Frühneuhochdeutsches Wörterbuch Online*, http://www.fwb-online.de/go/gaffer.h2.0m_1514701431).

[45]   It is likely that the implied action is to cover the ball with mercury, but that is not
explicitly stated in the text.

[46]   Scribal error, crossed out of misspelling of '*genß*'.

[47]   The use of 'also' could imply a repeated motion of layering the tasks, but that is not
explicitly stated in the text.

	ii	lb salp[eter] salcz vn[d] leg das salcz ab vn[d] leg auf wog
	ii	lb am gebicht un[d] leg aud das ander teill wog
10	ii	lb schweffell vn[d] nim de[n] schwefell ab vn[d] leg aber
	ii	lb auf am gewicht vn[d] auf das ander teill wog
	ii	lb sisch pulfer vn[d] nim das pulfer ab vn[d] leg auf
	ii	lb am gewicht vn[d] auf das ander teill der wog
	ii	lb lauter gestosen harcz vn[d] leg das harcz ab nim
15	i	lb am gewicht vn leg der gege[n] auf di wog
	i	lb faulß gemale[n] puche[n] holcz vn[d] solt itlig[s] klein

lose[n] stose[n] vn[d] malle[n] sam wolstw sisch pulfer dar auß mache[n]
vn[d] misch den rein wnter ein ander vn[d] ridcz dwrch
ein weicz sip das es sich vorein vn[d] wen dws den vase[n]

20 wilt so ge weislich da mit wmb das eß sich nit enczunt
wan eß slwg dir den halß ab czu[m] erste[n] wen dw an fast
czw vase[n] so mim gucz schiß pulfer das dwr sei vn[d] faß
ein dy kugell auf das virteill vn[d] hert nim den der
vor genante[n] gelade[n] kegell di in schvefell geswemt sint pei

25 x vn[d] faß ein di kugell vn[d] tail si geleich ein mit eim holcz
vn[d] nicht mit eim eiße[n] da hwt dich vor vn[d] nim dÿ ii
feder mit dem gafer vn[d] kweck silber leg si auch hin ein
wan das dut den schade[n] nim den den ob geschribe[n]
czeug den dw gemacht hast vo[n] iiii gebicht salp[eter] vn[d] fwl

30 di kwgell voll auf das herczt awer dw magst auch
wol oliwm pretoliu[m] dar wnter ton das vinst dw
das vinst dw an dem ~~lxxxx~~plat her nach geschribe[n]

fol. 56v

1 so wirt das feur dester herber vn[d] czu oberst alß sich
di pusche[n] vn[d] dÿ kugel gege[n] ein and[er] enczunte[n] soll so
faß ein dy kugell zu oberst ein finger dick gwt sisch
pulfer awer das wer das gewist das dw das czunt

Royal Armouries I.34 – Part 2

2	pounds	of saltpetre salt and take off the salt and put on the scales
2	pounds	of weight and put on the other part of the scales
2	pounds	of sulphur and take off the sulphur and put
2	pounds	of weight and on the other part of the scales
2	pounds	of gunpowder and take off the powder and place
2	pounds	of weight and on the other part of the scales
2	pounds	of ground resin and take off the resin. Take
1	pound	of weight and put against it on the scales
1	pound	of rotten ground beech wood. And you should grind it

all down finely and pound it if you want to make gunpowder out of it.
And mix it well together and press it through
a wide sieve so that it comes together. And when you want to handle
it, then treat it carefully so that it does not catch fire
as it could knock your head off. Firstly, when you want
to use it, take good gunpowder which is dry and fill
your ball by a quarter and let it go hard. Then take
the said, loaded ball which has been soaked in sulphur roughly
ten times.[48] And take the ball and split it evenly with a piece of wood,
and not with an iron, of which you must be cautious. And take the two
feathers with the camphor and the mercury, place them inside [*the ball*] –
that will cause all the harm. Then take the ingredients
written above which you have made of four weights[49] of saltpetre and fill
the ball up to the top. But you may also
want to add *olium petroleum* to it which you find
described on sheet 60 below.[50]

fol. 56v

The fire[*work*] becomes more severe, most importantly, when
the gun and the ball together set each other alight.
To do so, place a finger width of good gunpowder
on top of your ball. But who would have known that the touch

[48] It is not clear what this refers to. It is likely to be a time period, but it was not possible to ascertain its length. *Frühneuhochdeutsches Wörterbuch* refers to '*pei*' as 'approximately', 'somewhat' (def. 20 and 23: '*annähernd, ungefähr*', *Frühneuhochdeutsches Wörterbuch Online*, http://fwb-online.de/go/bei.h2.7pr_1514510828).

[49] The manuscript does not mention pounds at this instance, and it is not clear from the context whether it could be another weight measure.

[50] Folio number in same size lettering, seemingly from the same hand, but written with a colour of ink different to the surrounding text. The point refers to the section at the top of fol. 60r making 'a courtly art of burnt oil'.

Gunpowder Technology in the Fifteenth Century

5   loch der feur kugell her auß kerest vn[d] lwczt di kwgell
       vn[d] vor damese[n] in aller der moß alß ein stein vn[d] raumest
       das czwnt loch der pusche[n] vor ewen ein das dir di
       pusch nit versaget wan es wer ein erweit di vor nicht
       wer vn[d] czunt den di kugell vore[n] in der pusche[n] an oder
10   im werck dar auß dw das fewr sische[n] wilt vn[d] loß dÿ
       kwgell wol an gen wen das alles geschit awer mer dw
       solt vor di feur kwgell in harcz sweme[n] wen dws gefast
       hast vn[d] e dwst ein di pusche[n] leczt ein fart oder iiii
       moll nim ein kesell czw slach dar ein lawter harcz
15   vn[d] vnschlig vn[d] des her nach geschribe[n] oliw[m] petroliu[m]
       vn[d] probirß awf eim spon ob eß czech sei ist eß gerecht
       so swem den dy kwgell ich wil dir mer ein wnter
       scheid gewe[n] ab dw wolst dwrch ein gewalt mit der
       kwgel sischen alß dwrch ein maur czwische[n] rigell gemaurt
20   so loß dir wber di kugell ii ring schmide[n] eins halbe[n]
       czwerhe[n] finger dick vn[d] czweier finger prait kreucz
       weiß das das czwut loch dwrch dy ring ge der kugel
       vn[d] ausen czwische[n] di ring sisch pulfer vn[d] mit hanf
       werck weczoge[n] vn[d] den in dem vor genante[n] harcz
25   geswemt vn[d] ge weislich damit vm das dir kein feur
       ein den keselell kum waa eß keme[n] groß schwede[n] da w[m]
       dw macht auch wol gwt feur pfeil w[o] dem czeug mache[n]

fol. 57r

1   **wiltw awer ein hoflich kwnst mache[n] vo[n] einem heim**
       lichen feur das heist heimlich das einer czw wegen
       prengt das einer pei im treit oder eine das ma[n]

Royal Armouries I.34 – Part 2

hole of the fire ball has to be turned outside.[51] And you light the ball
and from 'damesen'[52] in all their sizes as a stone. And clear out
the touch hole of the gun each time so that the
gun does not fail. Should it do so, do not widen
it [*the hole*]. And then light the ball beforehand in the gun or in
the firework where you want to fire from. And let the
ball develop well[53] when all this is done. But
soak the fire ball long in resin when you have filled
it and before you put it into the gun. A fourth[54] or four
times take a cauldron and place into it a lot of resin
and melt it [*together with*] the *olium petroleum* described later.
And try on a piece of wood whether it has thickened and is ready and right,
then soak the ball. I want to give you more [*details*] to
tell them apart than as you will find out by the force with which
the ball fires through a wall or between tiled walls.
Have two rings forged on the ball, one small
half a finger thick and one two fingers wide. Make a cross
where the touch hole goes through the ring into the ball.
From the outside between the rings [*place some*] gunpowder and
cover it with hemp material. Soak it in the resin described earlier
and do that carefully so that no fire
gets into the cauldron as it would cause great harm. This way
you can make good fire arrows from the ingredients.

fol. 57r

**But if you want to make the 'courtly art' of a secret
fire[*work*] that is called 'secret' [*because it is a secret*] as one can manage to
achieve, which you can have with you, or one that you**

---

[51] It is not clear what this refers to. It is likely that this is suggesting an additional fuse
to reach the touch hole.

[52] It is not clear what this refers to. It could be a locality, a stage in the process of
loading the gun, or even a verb.

[53] In the sense of 'to start' (def. 3: '*seinen Anfang nehmen, beginnen*', *Frühneuhochdeutsches Wörterbuch Online*, http://fwb-online.de/go/angehen.s.3v_1514047428).

[54] The origin of '*fart*' is not entirely clear in this context. It would be a version of
'fourth' ('*viert*', *Frühneuhochdeutsches Wörterbuch Online*, http://fwb-online.de/go/
gepr%C3%A4cht.s.2n_1513289500).

sein nit ine[n] burt in moß eins tramers es sei in har

5 **schnur oder in nodel pein oder prot das ma[n] sein**
nit schmeckt das winst dw her nach gemalt an
dem lxxxx plat gemolt in welcher furm dwß mach
wilt dar nach richt dich

Wyltw dise[n] her nach geschribe[n] heimlich feur

10 mache[n] so volg dise[n] nach geschribe[n] kapitel
noch czv[m] erste[n] nim eins puche[n] faulle[n] holcz
das auf dem stock erfault sei vn[d] an der varb
weiß awer nus pau[m] holcz wer auch gut vn[d] nim daß
selbig holcz vn[d] loß ~~dwn schneide[n] vn[d] dere[n] vn dar nach~~

15 ~~wnter dem stamfp stosse[n]~~ klein schneide[n] das eß in ein neue[n]
hafe[n] mug gen vn[d] faß den hafe[n] voll vn[d] nim ein neue[n]
stwrczen vn[d] vor streich den hafe[n] genau das kein dwnst
da vo[n] mug kwme[n] vn[d] mach dar wm ein gelut vo[n] kolle[n]
auf vi stwnd das eß czw kolle[n] verprin vn[d] deck den

Royal Armouries I.34 – Part 2

**do not have to set alight. It is the size for a '*tramer*',[55] be it 'strand
of hair', or 'needle bone',[56] or '*prot*'[57] which you cannot
taste. You will find it drawn later at
sheet 90[58] in the form you want to make it
then you should follow [*this*].**

If you want to make secret fire[*work*] as is described below,
then follow the chapter written below.
First, take some rotten beech wood
which has rotted on the stick and which is white
in colour, but some walnut wood would also be fine. And take
the same wood and let it be[59]
cut thinly so that it fits into a new
bowl. And fill up the bowl and take a new
lid and seal the bowl so firmly that no smoke
can come out of it. And place it into some embers from charcoal
for six hours so that it burns into charcoal. Then lift the cover

---

[55] There is little evidence for what this could refer to. It clearly relates to a familiar item in size. The *Bayerische Wörterbuch*, vol. 1, 567, lists as '*dreom*', '*drommeter*', or '*trempeter*' as 'arrow' ('*Pfeil*'). Scheller's *Bayerisches Wörterbuch* (cols 661–62) refers to '*tremel*' or '*dremel*' as a 'piece of stick which could be used as a level' ('*Stangenstück, das als Hebel dienen kann*'), i.e. a crowbar. The verb '*tremen*' refers to 'wedge out', indicating a possible reference to a tool in a workshop. Either could be a possible fit within this context.

[56] 'Needle bone' ('*Nadelbein*') is described by Grimm as a 'box for needles made out of bone' ('Nadelbüchse aus Bein', *Deutsches Wörterbuch von Jacob und Wilhelm Grimm Online* – accessed 10 August 2023). Most needles at that time were made out of bone.

[57] The sequence of these words is not clear. It seems a sequence of various domestically known items of uncertain size and use. In this context it appears to refer to smaller sizes. The only reference to the lemma '*prot*' is related to 'bread' (*Frühneuhochdeutsches Wörterbuch Online*, http://fwb-online.de/go/brot.s.2n_1513846425), but it is not clear what this should relate to. One theory is that could be 'as small as breadcrumbs' but that seems quite speculative.

[58] Fols 90r and 90v depict the actions of the master gunner in the field (see Figure 5).

[59] Deleted text not added in translation: 'cut thinly and let it dry out and grind it thereafter in the stamp mill'.

Gunpowder Technology in the Fifteenth Century

20 hafe[n] auf vn[d] lesch di kolle[n] ab mit schell kraut wasser
ab vn[d] deck den hafe[n] wider czw das kein dwnst da vo[n]
mug vn[d] nim di selbe[n] kolle[n] auß vn[d] loß si klein stosse[n]
vn[d] dwrch ein heres sip gerede[n] so hast dw dÿ pesten
kole[n] an rauch vn[d] schmack wen das alleß geschit so heb
25 den wider an vn[d] kauf di peste[n] leinwet so dws gefinde[n]
magst vn[d] schneid si al preit alß dw her nah gemolt
vinst an dem lxxx^{v}x plat vn[d] nim den vn[d] neß czw alß
dy hor flechte[n] einß vingerß lanck vn[d] faß dar ein der
ob genante[n] gestose[n] kolle[n] auf das herczt vn[d] ne den

fol. 57v

1 wider czu vn[d] faf awer ein alß vor vn[d] ne[m] vn[d] faß alß
lang piß du der schnur hast auf v oder vi od[er] x stwnd
alß vil dwr hawe[n] wilt du solt di stwnd vor lege[n] vn[d]
an streiche[n] d dws auß geist den diß do prauche[n] vn[d]
5 lege[n] vm deß wille[n] das si nit vor kwrczt dar vnter

of the bowl and extinguish the charcoal with greater celandine[60] water.[61]
Cover the bowl again so that no smoke can come out of it.
Take the charcoal from it and let it [*the new charcoal*] be ground finely
and run it through a hair sieve,[62] and you have the best
charcoal which smells and looks good.[63] When all this is done,
pick it up again. And buy the best canvas[64] you can find
and cut it lengthwise as you find drawn
on sheet 90 [*or 95*].[65] Then take and wet two
hair plaits, one finger long, and pour the above mentioned
ground charcoal onto it until it is fully covered. And sew it

fol. 57v

up and soak it as before. And sew it and soak it for a lengthy
time until you have a string [*of them*] for five or six or ten hours,
depending how much time you have. You should put them in front of
the fireplace and paint them. Pour away all that [*the liquid*] you do not need. And
place [*them*] so that they are not crossed over each other,[66] and

---

[60] '*Schellkraut*', or '*Schellwurtz*', refers to '*chelidonium maius*', or 'greater celandine' or 'tetterwort', a herbaceous perennial commonly used in herbal medicine as a mild analgesic. It contains sap which at first is yellow, but on exposure to air turns a red colour (Heinrich Marzell, *Frühneuhochdeutsch Wörterbuch der Deutschen Pflanzennamen* (Leipzig: Hirzel, 1943), vol. 1, 923–25). John Gerard's *The herball or Generall historie of plantes* (1597) states that 'the juice of the herbe is good to sharpen the sight, for it cleanseth and consumeth away slimie things that cleave about the ball of the eye and hinder the sight and especially being boiled with honey in a brasen vessell' (Maud Grieve, *A Modern Herbal: The Medicinal, Culinary, Cosmetic and Economic Properties, Cultivation and Folk-lore of Herbs, Grasses, Fungi, Shrubs, & Trees with All Their Modern Scientific Uses*, Volume 1 (New York: Dover, 1971), 179 – see also *Deutsches Wörterbuch von Jacob und Wilhelm Grimm Online* – accessed 10 August 2023, 'chelidonium', mostly 'chelidonium maius').

[61] This is likely to refer to some liquid with acidic properties, probably greater celandine soaked or diluted in water, or distilled.

[62] A 'hair sieve' implies a thin sieve; this is not a term previously used, but is used again on fol. 58r.

[63] The literal translation means 'in smoke and taste'.

[64] This is likely to refer to some form of fabric. '*Leinwat*' is described in the *Frühneuhochdeutsch Wörterbuch* as 'canvas material, cloth' ('*Leinwand als Stoff, Tuchmaterial*', *Frühneuhochdeutsch Wörterbuch Online*, http://fwb-online.de/go/leinwat.s.1fn_1518829027).

[65] This is more likely to be 95, but even then neither conclusive nor hugely helpful.

[66] To prevent them sticking together after they had dried.

Gunpowder Technology in the Fifteenth Century

werde[n] mit der varb an czu steiche[n] di her nah geschrib
stet wen das geschit so nin parchat vn[d] loß dir secklich
mache[n] alß dw gemolt vinst eß sein czofp oder nodel pein
oder andre dinck dy eim kromer czw stend dar nach

10 richt dich wn[d] merck den wi dw den czeug mache[n] solt
der ein di parchet muster gehore[n] dar da an feure[n] soll
czw[m] erste[n] nim ein geleiche wog vn[d] leg auf am gebicht
vi lb vn[d] aud das ander teill da gegen dem gebicht
vi lb salp[eter] vn[d] nim den salp[eter] ab vn[d] leg auf dy wog

15 ii lb am gewicht vn[d] dar gege[n] auf das ander teil
ii lb schweffelß vn[d] nim den schweffell ab vn[d] leg auf
i lb am gebicht vn[d] leg auf das and[re] teil der wog
i lb salp[eter] salcz vn[d] nim das salcz ab vn[d] leg auf
i lb am gebicht vn[d] leg auf das ander teil wog

20 i lb linter kolle[n] vn[d] leg di kolle[n] ab vn[d] leg aud am geb
i lb vn[d] auf das ander teill gege[n] dem gebicht
i lb gestosse harcz das lauter sei vn[d] leg harcz ab leg auf
i lb am gebicht vn[d] auf das ander teil dar gege[n]
i lb gemalle[n] puche[n] faule[n] holcz alß dw vor geschribe[n]

25 vinst an dem lv plat wu dws male[n] solt losse[n] vn[d] loß de[n]
itlig klein stesse[n] sam wolstu pulfer dar auß vn[d] misch den
rein unter ein ander vn[d] ridcz dwrch ein weicz sip das

fol. 58r

1 eß sich vorein vn[d] loß vnter dem stamf stosse[n] vn[d] ful dÿ seck
lein vo[n] parchet gemacht auf das herczt der dy czofp
oder di nodel pein vn[d] czw oberst ein wenig gucz sisch pulfer
des geleiche[n] ein di schnur mit kolle[n] gefast an den ort alß

5 dws czw same[n] burst nee[n] vn[d] nim den der schnur alß lanck

Royal Armouries I.34 – Part 2

paint them with the colour which is described below.
When that has been done take fustian[67] and have made for yourself
little bags which you can find drawn. They are 'plait'[68] or 'needle bone'
or other things as used by a merchant.[69] Follow
this and note how you have to make the ingredients
which are put into a template made out of the fabric and which can be set alight.
First, take a well-balanced pair of scales and put on them

6 pounds of weight and on the other side against the weight
6 pounds of saltpetre and take off the saltpetre and place on the scales
2 pounds of weight and against [it] on the other side
2 pounds of sulphur and take off the sulphur and put on
1 pound of weight. And put on the other side of the scales
1 pound of saltpetre salt. And take off the salt and put on
1 pound of weight. And put on the other side of the scales
1 pound of lime wood charcoal and take off the charcoal and put on one side
1 pound and on the other side against the weight [put]
1 pound of ground resin which is pure. And take the resin off and put
1 pound of weight and on the other side against
1 pound of ground-up rotten beech wood as you find written

on sheet 60 above. You should let this be ground and let it
be pounded into small pieces to make powder of it. And mix it
well together and put it through a wide sieve so that

fol. 58r

it comes together[70] and have it ground under the stamp mill. And fill the little bags,
made from fustian, until they are full, either [with] the 'plait'
or the 'needle bone'. On top add a little good gunpowder
which is equally surrounded with the cord and charcoal at the point
where you have to sew it up. And take from a cord which is as long

---

[67] As in Part 1, this is more likely to refer to a form of coarse wool (*Frühneuhochdeutsches Wörterbuch Online*, http://fwb-online.de/go/barchent.s.0m_1513750868).

[68] Not entirely clear what this refers to. It looks like the terms relate to domestic items of different shapes and sizes. One possible speculation is the reference in the *Althochdeutsches Wörterbuch* where 'cosp' is referred to as 'clasp' ('*Klammer, Verbindung*', *Althochdeutsches Wörterbuch Online* – accessed 10 August 2023). It could also relate to a 'plait' ('*zopf*') as stated later in the text.

[69] From the context it looks likely that these refer to different sizes which may have been known at the time.

[70] This is likely to be read in the sense of 'mixing well'.

dw di stund lege[n] wilt vn[d] stoß ein dÿ vor genante[n] parchet
mister vn[d] neß czu haufe[n] vn[d] wen das geschit so merck wi
dws an streiche[n] solt das im der rauch vn[d] schmack vor ge[n]
das ma[n] sein nit schmeckt so dws heimlich ein lege[n] wilt

10   merck ewe[n] czu[m] erste[n] nim gaffer ein der apentecke[n] auf
ein lot vn[d] geschelt mandell kere[n] wan der gafer let sich
nit stosse[n] vn[d] nim alwer broß vn[d] auf ein achteill lb
gestosse[n] sandelß der durch ein hereß sip gerede[n] sei aber
czipreß holcz wer auch gut vn[d] tu den di stuck czu same[n]

15   in ein glese[n] hafe[n] vn[d] geuß dar an schelkraut waser vn[d]
deck den hafe[n] czu auf iiii tag vn[d] geuß den mer schelkraut
waser dar an vn prante[n] wein vn[d] stoß in eim morser
vn[d] czwings dwrch ein tuch vn[d] nim meng vn[d] deß durch
czwnge[n] waserß vn[d] mach ein varb vn[d] los warm werde[n]

20   vn[d] ein wenig leim waserß das di varb nit ab ge[n] vn[d]
streich den di feur an vn[d] loß trucke[n] so hastu gute heim
liche feur on[n] rauch vn[d] schmack
wiltw gwt feur pfeil mache[n] di gech prinen so
volg disem noch geschribe[n] kapitel noch merck wi dw

25   **den czeug mache[n] solt vn[d] vo[n] welche[n] gebicht streich**
si rot an mit leim farb . . gr . . cza . . kutber

Royal Armouries I.34 – Part 2

as an hour is laid,[71] and push into the aforementioned fustian
template and wet it thoroughly.[72] When that is done, note that
you need to paint it so that the smell and taste[73] is gone [*from it*]
so that you cannot taste[74] it and so that it can be stored in secret.
Therefore, note first to take camphor from the apothecary, about
one lot, as well as peeled almond kernels, if the camphor cannot be ground
on its own. And take half a shoot[75] and for an eighth of a pound of
ground sandalwood[76] which has been filtered through a hair sieve. But
cypress wood would also be good. And then put all the ingredients together
in a glass bowl and add greater celandine water. And
cover the bowl for four days and pour more greater celandine
water into it as well as brandy. Grind it in a mortar
and force it through a cloth and take a bit of the
forced-through water and make [*this into*] a colour. And let it warm up
and [*take*] a little clay water so that it does not lose the colour and
then paint the fire[*work*] and let it dry out. Then you have good secret
fire[*work*] in smell and taste.
**If you want to make a good fire arrow which burns battlements, then
follow this chapter that follows. Note how you
shall make the ingredients and of which weight, paint it
red with clay colour . . . Rare . . . Precious.**[77]

[71] Not clear what this expression refers to.

[72] The literal meaning is 'in a pile', but a figurative meaning can be 'plentiful' or 'often'.

[73] Literally, the terms used are 'smoke' and 'taste', but the expression seems to refer to
the appearance.

[74] It is more likely that this refers to the smell, but to distinguish from the section
before, 'taste' was left in the translation.

[75] The reference for this is '*Sproß*' or '*Knospe*' (*Frühneuhochdeutsches Wörterbuch Online*,
http://fwb-online.de/go/bros.s.0m_1513594193).

[76] 'Sandalwood' (Latin: '*Santalum*') is very heavy and has a strong fragrance which it
retains longer than most other woods. It is also used as a colouring agent in dyeing
processes and in cooking (Woolgar, 'Medieval Colour and Food', 2–3). This means
that this reference may indicate odour and visual appearance as ways to distinguish
the arrows from each other.
'*Sandalum Album*' produces sandalwood oil, distilled from the wood (*A Dictionary of Plant Sciences*, ed. Michael Allenby, 3rd edn (Online, 2013), http://www.
oxfordreference.com/view/10.1093/acref/9780199600571.001.0001/acref-
9780199600571-e-6037# – 10 August 2023).

[77] These fragments of text are unique in this text. Often, the scribe finishes lines
halfway and continues to fill the rest of the line with decorations. However, in this

$$W\text{iltw dise vor geschribe[n] feur pfeill mache[n]}$$

so volg disem kapitell noch wi duß mache[n] solt

czw[m] erste[n] loß dir mache[n] eise[n] einß halbe[n] such

30   lanck alß dw ein disem puch gemolt vinst wi si sein

fol. 58v

1   swlt gestalt vn[d] vo[n] dem peste[n] eise[n] vn[d] nim den parchet

vn[d] loß dir secklich schneide[n] in der furm[m] alß dw gemolt

vinst an dem plat wi preit vn[d] lanck dws schneide[n]

solt vn[d] loß si an dem rauche[n] ort czu same[n] neen

5   vn[d] eng vn[d] ker si den wmb das di net hin ein kwm

vn[d] vaß si den deß her nach geschribe[n] czeugs voll

vn[d] auf das herczt vn[d] nim den ein wog vn[d] leg auf

viii lb   am gebicht vn[d] der gege[n] auf das and[er] teil

viii lb   salp[eter] vn[d] nim den salp[eter] ab vn[d] leg auf

10   iiii lb   am gebicht vn[d] leg auf ander teill d[er] wog

iiii lb   schweffell vn[d] leg den schwefell ab vn[d] leg auf

ii   lb   am gebicht vn[d] auf da and[er] teill wog

ii   lb   linter kolle[n] leg kolle[n] ab vn[d] leg auf wog

i   lb   am gewicht auf das and[er] teill d[er] wog

15   i   lb   des vor genante[n] faule[n] gemalen holcz vn[d]

loß itlig klein stosse[n] sam wolst sisch pulfer dar auß

mache[n] vn[d] misch den wnter ein ander vn[d] rid durch

ein weicz sip das eß sich vorein vn[d] loß den dy eise[n]

an schweste[n] vn[d] stoß geleich dwrch di vor gefult

20   secklein vn[d] pincz obe[n] vn[d] vnte[n] hart czw vn[d] wen

das geschit so hert si den in dem hernach geschribe[n]

hert waser do hab den pfeill ein auf das lengst

das einer macht ein pater noster spreche[n] vn[d] loß

den trucke[n] an der swne[n] oder stwbe[n] vn[d] hucz vor

25   feur vn[d] streich den rot an mit der leim farb

vn stoß dien einß czwere[n] daume[n] lanck in schwef

vn[d] so hast dw di peste[n] feur pfeil di nimat macht

Royal Armouries I.34 – Part 2

If you want to make the fire arrow mentioned above
then follow this chapter how you should make it.
First, have made an iron [*arrow*], one which is half as
long as you find drawn in this book, where its

fol. 58v

shape is shown, and it is made from the best iron. And take the fustian
and have yourself cut some bags in the shape as you find drawn
on sheet[78] where you find how wide and long you should cut it.
And let it be sewn together tightly in the smoky place.
And turn it inside out so that nothing can get inside.
And fill it up with the ingredients described below
until they are full. And take a pair of scales and put on [*it*]

8   pounds   of weight and against [*it*] on the other side
8   pounds   of saltpetre and take off the saltpetre and put on
4   pounds   of weight and put on the other side of the scales
4   pounds   of sulphur and take off the sulphur and put on
2   pounds   of weight and put on the other side of the scales
2   pounds   of lime wood charcoal. Take off the charcoal and put on the scales
1   pound   of weight, on the other part of the scales
1   pound   of the wood from rotten ground as described earlier and

let it be ground finely as if you would want to make gunpowder out
of it. And mix them together and run them through
a wide sieve so that they become one. And take your iron [*arrow*]
which is heavy and push it through the filled
small bag. And tie it at the top and bottom tightly. When this is
done, harden it with the hard water
described below. Place the arrow [*in the water*] for as long
as one can say the *Pater Noster* and let it
dry in the sun or inside, but be careful about
fire. And paint it red with clay paint
and push it into sulphur for a moment with a heavy thumb
and then you have the best fire arrows which anyone can make.

---

context what looks like decoration also includes some words, or fragments thereof,
which are included in the translation.

[78]   No page number or gap for a page number is provided, but it is likely to be fol. 87v.

fol. 59r

1 **wiltw awer grot fewr pfeil mache[n] so folg dise[n]**
nach geschribe[n] kapitell noch vn[d] di sint nit alß
gech als di vor genante[n] vn[d] streich plo an vn[d] faß
in alle der moß alß vor

5 Wiltw di vor geschriben feur pfeil mache[n] so
merck czw erste[n] im an fang loß dir feur
pfeil eise[n] schmide[n] alß vor vn secklich vn faß
das noch geschribe[n] pulfer dar ein awer eß burt
andeß am gebicht czw gen dan for leg auf di wog
10 vi lb am gebicht vn[d] auf das ander teill der wog
vi lb salp[eter] vn[d] leg den salp[eter] ab vn[d] leg auf wog
ii lb am gewicht vn[d] auf das ander teil d[er] wog
ii lb schweffell vn[d] nim den schweffell ab vn[d] leg auf
i lb am gewicht vn[d] auf das ander teil auf wog
15 i lb linter kolle[n] vn[d] nim di kolle[n] ab vn[d] leg auf
i lb am gebicht vn[d] legeg auf das ander teill
i lb gemale[n] faule[n] puche[n] holcz vn[d] loß itlig vor
klein stosse[n] sam wolst sisch pulfer mache[n] vn[d] misch de[n]
rein vnter ein ander vn[d] loß vnter dem stamfp stose[n]
20 vn[d] faß den alß vor vn[d] streich an so hastu gut feur
pfeil di lanck sam prine[n]
wiltw awer gut feur pfeil mache[n] so merck ebe[n]
vo[n] velche[n] czeug dwß vasen solt vn[d] streich sy prau[n]

Wiltw di vorgeschribe[n] feur pfeil mache[n] so vaß
25 in alle der moß alß vor mit den eise[n] vn[d] secklein
awer der czeug muß an der wog anderß wern[n]
czu erste[n] nim ein geleiche wog vn[d] wig vi lb salp[eter]
vn[d] ii lb schweffelß i lb salp[eter] salcz i lb linter kolle[n] i lb
gestose[n] lawter harcz das klein gestese[n] sei vn[d] vn[d] misch

fol. 59v

1 wnter ein ander vn[d] hert si ein dem noch geschribe[n]
hert waser vn[d] halcz dar ain alß lang einer mocht
ein pater noster spreche[n] vn[d] loß den trucke[n] vn streich

Royal Armouries I.34 – Part 2

fol. 59r

But if you want to make a great fire arrow, then follow this chapter written below – and they are not as quick as those previously mentioned. And paint them blue and fill them all using the measurements as before.

If you want to make the fire arrows mentioned above then
note first, to begin with, have yourself [*made*] a fire
arrow forged from iron and a cloth bag. And put
the powder together as described below. But it is proper[79] to
check the weight and place on the pair of scales

6	pounds	of weight, and add to the other side of the scales
6	pounds	of saltpetre. And take the saltpetre off and place on the scales
2	pounds	of weight, and add to the other side of the scales
2	pounds	of sulphur. And take the sulphur off and place on the scales
1	pound	of weight, and add to the other side of the scales
1	pound	of lime wood charcoal. And take off the charcoal and place on the scales
1	pound	of weight. And add to the other side
1	pound	of ground-up rotten beech wood and have it ground

into small pieces, in the same way as gunpowder is done. And mix it
together. And have it ground together in the stamp mill
and fill it up as before and paint it. Then you have a good fire
arrow which burns slowly.
**But if you want to make good fire arrows, then note
which ingredients you should know and paint them brown.**

If you want to make the fire arrows described before, then take
all the measures as before with the iron and the cloth bag,
but the ingredients on the pair of scales have to be different.
First, take the same pair of scales and weigh up 6 pounds of saltpetre
and 2 pounds of sulphur, 1 pound of saltpetre salt, 1 pound of lime wood charcoal,
1 pound of ground pure resin which has been finely ground. And mix

fol. 59v

it together and harden it in the hard water
described below. Keep it in it [*the water*] as long as it takes you
to say the *Pater Noster*. Let it dry and paint

---

[79] '*eß burt*' in the sense of 'to be appropriate', 'to be proper' (Definition 3: '*sich gehören, gez-iemen; notwendig, üblich sein*', *Frühneuhochdeutsches Wörterbuch Online*, http://fwb-on-line.de/go/geb%C3%BCren.s.3v_1513310169).

si mit der varb an prau[n] vo[n] des gemerck wege[n]

wiltu awer feur pfeil mache[n] di auf das lengst
prine[n] vn[d] streich si swarcz an vo[n] deb gemerck wege[n]

Wiltw awer feur fpeill mache[n] auf das lengst
czw prine[n] so merck vn[d] loß dir eise[n] mache[n]
alß vor vn[d] fase[n] mit alle[n] dinge[n] vn[d] herte[n]
so nim iii lb salp[eter] iii lb schwefell i lb linter kolle[n]
vn[d] mach dar auß den czeug czu de feur pfeille[n]
wiltw ein hwbsche kwnst mache[n] von eine[m] hert waser
dar inen dw eine[n] itligen feur pfeil herte[n] must wa[n]
dw des nit tust so ist der feur pfeill vor nichte vn[d]
magst auch wol pulfer dar ine herte[n] wan es vor
dirbt nit vn[d] wirt dester peser vn[d] nimt nit ab

Wiltw dise vor geschribe[n] hert mache[n] so merck
ewe[n] nim xxx moß esig vn[d] wig dar gege[n]
alß schwer salpeter vn[d] nim v lb gemalle[n]
wait asche[n] auf ein moß schel kraut waser
vn[d] iii teill lawter waserß ii lb pilsen some[n] vn[d] schut
di stuck all zw same[n] in ein kessell vn[d] loß side[n] auf
ein firtel stund vn[d] nim den den vor genante[n] feur
pfeil den dw gemacht hast e dw in mit der farb
an streicht halt in ein den kessell alß lang einer
macht ein pater noster spreche[n] vn[d] loß den rein truck
vn[d] streich den mit der leim farb an wer aber das
di hert ab wolt neme[n] so nimst lauter waser vn[d] mereß
si **vn[d] halt di kunst vor porge das dus nit lerst das**
das si nit gemei wert wa[n] eß ist nit zu gerote[n] zu feur
pfeille[n] wan er leit l gar das er nit vor durbt

it with the colour brown so that you can remember them.
**But if you want to make fire arrows which burn longer
then paint them black so that you remember them.**

But if you want to make arrows so that they
burn the longest, take note and have made for yourself some iron
as before and gather together with all the things and harden them.
Then take 3 pounds of saltpetre, 3 pounds of sulphur, 1 pound of lime wood
charcoal and make the material for the fire arrow out of it.
**If you want to make a 'pretty art' of hardening water[80]
in which you have to harden any kind of fire arrow. If
you do not do this, then the fire arrow becomes useless. And
while you may have powder hardened inside, it will
not go off, and it will get better, and will not get worse.**

If you want to make the hardening [water] described earlier, then note
therefore to take 30 measures[81] of vinegar and weigh against it
the same amount of saltpetre. And take 5 pounds of ground
white ash to a measure of greater celandine
and 3 parts of pure water, 2 pounds of fungi spores. And pour
the ingredients all together into a pot, and let it simmer for
a quarter of an hour. And take the aforementioned fire
arrow which you have made, before you paint it
with colour, put them into a pot for as long as
you would take to say a *Pater Noster*. And let them dry thoroughly
and paint them with the clay colour. If that does not
harden them, then take purified water and add to
it. **And keep this 'art' secret so that you do not teach what
is not meant for everyone, when it is not advisable to have fire
arrows, when they work[82] and when they do not go off.**

---

[80] This reference to '*hert waser*' could refer to a particular type of water, or to what the water achieves. From the context the translation intends the latter, as the process would harden the arrows, which in turn would help their use in combat. See Chapter 5 for more details.

[81] '*moß*' or '*maß*' can be translated into a range of different types of measurements, all of them measuring volume. See *Frühneuhochdeutsches Wörterbuch Online*, http://fwb-online.de/go/bechermas.s.2n_1513585950 and http://fwb-online.de/go/aufhaufen.s.3v_1513609850.

[82] '*Etwas leiden*' can be understood with a positive connotation of 'permitting, enabling' (def. II, 2 'gestatten, erlauben', *Deutsches Wörterbuch von Jacob und Wilhelm Grimm Online* – accessed 10 August 2023).

fol. 60r

1 **wiltw awer ein hoflich kwnst mache[n] vo[n] oll geprant**
vn[d] heist oliw[m] pretoliu[m] vn[d] ist gut czu alle[n] feurwerck

W iltw dicz vor geschribe[n] ol prene[n] so volg
disem noch geschribe[n] kapitel noch wi dus
5 mache[n] solt czu erste[n] nim ein neue[n] glesen hafe[n]
grab in ein di erde[n] das er mit dem prort
ii vinger wber di erde[n] ge nim ein neue[n] lauge[n] hafe[n]
der an dem pode[n] locher hab vn[d] secz in ein den glese[n]
hafen mit dem pode[n] alß dw gemolt vinst an dem
10 lxxxx plat vn[d] for streich in rein mit har laim do man
mit fwrmt vn[d] leg den auf den poden ein den locheret[n]
hafen auf ein firdug lebentig schweffell den[n] mer
vnter anderm schwefell wiß wi dw eitell lebentige
schweffell ii lb vnter vii lb gemein scheffel vn loß
15 in vnter ein ander czu gen vn[d] geuß in den auß das
heist lebentiger schwefell wan i lb dut alß vil alß
swnst v lb vn[d] wen das geschit so leg ein hant foll
schwel kraut mit den burczell ein den hafe[n] auf den
schweffell vn[d] wasch vor rein vn[d] nim ein kraut mit
                                    heist metron [superscript text in same hand]
20 burczell vn[d] wasch auch rein des nim auch alß vill
alß deß schelkraut vn[d] nim den kimg holcz das do gron

fol. 60r

But if you want to make a 'courtly art' of burnt oil
which is called *olium petrolium* and which is good for all fireworks.

If you want to make[83] this oil described above, then follow
this chapter written below on how to
make it. First, take a new bowl, made out of glass,
bury it in the ground so that its rim
is two fingers above the soil. Take a new bowl filled with lye
which has holes in the bottom and place in the glass
bowl with its bottom as you can find drawn at
sheet 90.[84] And spread on it clay mixed with hair[85] which
is used to shape it. Put into the bottom of the
bowl with holes a quarter part of native sulphur which is whiter
than the other sulphur. Put 2 pounds of native
sulphur into 7 pounds of common sulphur and let
it come together. Pour it out, and it is
called native sulphur where 1 pound is enough for as much as
5 pounds otherwise. And when this has been done, put a handful of
greater celandine with its roots into the bowl on top of the
sulphur. Wash it properly and take the herb [*greater celandine*],[86] which
is called '*metron*',[87]
[*its*] roots and wash it well. Then take as much as the
greater celandine and take pine[88] wood which is green

---

[83] The original uses 'burn' ('*prene[n]*') which could be a reference to the production process. The context implies a state of purification of the oil.

[84] The number is added in a different colour ink, same hand. It is not clear what this refers to on fols 90r and 90v (see Figure 5).

[85] This presumably refers to clay mixed with hair to strengthen it.

[86] This is what the text refers to, but it is only called by the generic term 'herb'.

[87] No reference could be traced for this. It could be a scribal error of spelling, or a local name which is no longer known or recorded.

[88] This could also be read '*kung*'. It is not clear from the context what this refers to. It requires a type of wood, but the term could be either an adjective (related to size, colour, shape, etc.) or a compound noun (a specific name or a more generic term similar to 'royal wood', i.e. high-quality wood). More likely, however, is that it is a scribal error and was intended to read '*kien*', i.e. pine wood ('*Fichte*', *Frühneuhochdeutsches Wörterbuch Online*, http://fwb-online.de/go/kien.s.0m_1518844486).

Gunpowder Technology in the Fifteenth Century

sei alß klein das eß ein de[n] hafe ge awer wacheltrein
holcz wer pesser vn[d] auf das holcz leg auf ein hant vol
lauter gestose[n] harcz vn[d] aber schel kraus vn[d] metron
25 vn[d] holcz vn[d] mach di leg alß dws an gefang
hast piß der hafe[n] vol burt nim ein neue sturczte[n]
vor streich den hafe[n] mit dem vor genante[n] laune[n]
vn[d] mach dar vm ein gelut mit kolle[n] vn[d] loß di gelut
ab prine[n] vn[d] prich den den haffe[n] auf vn[d] raum in

fol. 60v

1 den auß vn[d] laß den haffe[n] sten vn[d] leg in aller der
moß ein alß vor vn[d] steich wider czu vn[d] pren ein fart
oder iiii stund alß vil dw des olß hawen wilt vn[d] must
den noch czwir prene[n] vn[d] wen dw das erst wider
5 ein seczt auf das halb teill des hafens so leg auf das holcz
vn[d] nim ein lot mekwriu[m] swplimatu[m] leg auf holcz das
vinst ein der apentecke[n] vn[d] ful den den hafe[n] volent
czu mit den kreuter vn[d] holcz vn[d] harcz vn[d] leg di leg
alß lang piß dw den hafe[n] erfulst vn[d] vor streich in
10 alß vor mach dar vm ein gelut auf ii stund vn[d]
vn[d] prich den hafe[n] auf vn[d] raum in auß alß vor vn[d]
secz czw[m] leczte[n] mol ein alß im an fang mit dem schvefel

and so small that it fits into the bowl – but '*wacheltrein*'[89]
wood would be better.[90] And put on the wood a lot
of ground resin and greater celandine and '*metron*'
and wood and put them in one after the other as you have started
until the bowl is full.[91] Take a new lid,[92]
fill up the bowl with the said alum.[93]
And make some embers with charcoal and let the embers
burn down. And break open the bowl and clear it

fol. 60v

out. Let the bowl rest, and add into it all the
measures as before, and seal it again, and burn it a 'quart',
or four hours for as long as you want to have oil. And you
will let it burn twice, and you have to bring it back
to one part of the bowl, then place a piece of wood on it
and take one lot of *mercurium sublimatum*, which you can
find in an apothecary, to the wood, and fill the bowl completely
with herbs and wood and resin. And place one on top of the other
until the bowl is full. And cover[94] it
as before and make warm embers for two hours. And
break open the bowl and clear it out as before. And
place it for the last time as in the beginning with sulphur

---

[89] No reference could be traced for this type of wood. It is not even clear whether it relates to a particular type of tree or a usage of the wood. For example, see '*Wachtelholz*', which is described in Grimm as a 'piece of wood used to fold collar shirts' ('ein Holz, das dazu dient, den Hemdkragen zu fälteln', *Deutsches Wörterbuch von Jacob und Wilhelm Grimm Online* – accessed 10 August 2023).

[90] Presumably this implies some interaction with resin, but this is not made clear in the text.

[91] It is possible that this process is referring to layering, but this is not entirely clear in the text.

[92] In the *Frühneuhochdeutsches Wörterbuch Online*: '*gekleiberte Sturzen*' refers to a form of a bucket; it implies a wooden container brought together with glue or iron ('*Gefässe, Trichter, in die oder mit denen Flüssigkeit gegossen wird*') or in the sense of a 'lid' ('*Topfdeckel*', *Frühneuhochdeutsches Wörterbuch Online*, http://www.fwb-online. de/go/b%C3%BCtner.s.0m_1519240106).

[93] Likely to refer to 'alum' ('*Alaunen*', *Frühneuhochdeutsches Wörterbuch Online*, http:// www.fwb-online.de/go/alaun.s.0m_1513751058).

[94] In the sense of 'smooth', 'seal', 'cover' ('*abstreichen*', def. 9 and 10, *Frühneuhochdeutsches Wörterbuch Online*, http://fwb-online.de/go/abstreichen.s.3vu_1513744469).

Gunpowder Technology in the Fifteenth Century

vn[d] di czweirlei kreuter vn[d] holcz piß auf das halb teill
des hafenß vn[d] nim auf i lb oliu[m]prettoliu[m] ein d[e]r
15 apentecke[n] secz mit der pusche[n] ein den hafe[n] vn[d] fwll in
follent czu mit den kreuter vn[d] holcz vn[d] harcz vn[d] mach
dar vm ein gelut vn los ab prine[n] vn[d] prich den
hafe[n] auß vn[d] raum auß vn[d] heb den vnter[n] hafe[n] auß
der erden so hast dw das pest ol czw mancher lei fe[u]r
20 wercke dw mach auch wol mit lein ol mere[n]
wiltw awer ein hoflich kunst mache[n] vo[n] einem
waser da mit dw ein itlig pusche[n] mit ab kelten
mast ab dir so vill schwß dest das dir di pusch
erhiczest das du kein schwsß dorst ton so volg
25 **disem noch geschribe[n] kapitell noch**

Wilt disß vorgeschribe[n] waser mache[n] so volg
disem nach geschribe[n] kapitell noch czu erste[n]
nim xxv lb weinstein xv lb wait asche[n]
der gemalle[n] sei xl lb salp[eter] salcz schut das

fol. 61r

1 czw same[n] in ein neusch schaf vn[d] misch vnter ein ander
vn[d] nim den der hefe[n] dar auß die meschingslacher gise[n]
oder di rot schmit vn[d] faß in den vol des gemiste[n] czeug
vn[d] vn[d] secz in ein wint offen dar ine[n] di rot schmit gisse[n] vm[b]
5 mach dar wmb ein glwt vo[n] kolle[n] vn[d] loß prine[n] auf ii
stwnd vn[d] stoß wnter weille[n] ein den hafe[n] mit eim
eisen das eß sich hin noch secz vn[d] schwt den auß dem

and two types of herbs and wood until you have filled the bowl halfway.[95] And take 1 pound of *olium petroleum* from the apothecary, and place it into a pot with a brush.[96] And fill it up completely with the herbs and wood and resin. And place embers around it and let it burn down. And break open the bowl and clear it out. Lift up the lower pot from the ground, and you have the best oil for all types of firework to which you can also add linseed oil.

But if you want to make a 'courtly art', of a water with which you can cool down any gun which has been fired a lot so that the gun has become so hot that you cannot fire from it anymore, then follow the chapter written below.

If you want to make the water written about above, then follow this chapter written below. First, take 25 pounds of cream of tartar, 15 pounds of white ash which has been ground, [*and*] 40 pounds of saltpetre. Put it

fol. 61r

all together in a new barrel and mix it together. And take all that is left [*and*] pour into a brass tray or [*one*] which is from a brass smith. Take all the ingredients mixed together[97] and place them into a wind oven,[98] one which is used by a brass smith to smelt.[99] Get embers from the charcoal and let it [*what is in the oven*] burn for two hours. And stir it occasionally in a pot with an iron [*poker*] so that it finally settles down. Then pour it out of

---

[95] This action seems to imply that the process applied here is a reduction of liquid, but it is unclear what it would achieve with *olium petroleum*.

[96] '*puschen*' is used throughout the text to stand for 'gun' ('*Büchse*'). However, this would not make sense in this context. It is more likely to refer to a 'brush' (from '*busch*', *Frühneuhochdeutsches Wörterbuch Online*, http://fwb-online.de/go/busch.h1.0m_1513568092).

[97] German original unclear.

[98] The term '*offen*' is written in the manuscript in superscript, and appears to be written in the same hand, which suggests that the author added it after reading the text again. This most likely refers to a fireplace or forge with the added possibility of air supply to make the embers as hot as possible (as a blacksmith would use).

[99] The literal meaning of '*giessen*' is to 'pour', but it is more likely that it refers to the brass smith's action here.

Gunpowder Technology in the Fifteenth Century

5 hafe[n] vn[d] secz der hefe[n] alß lang ein alß vil dw deß
waserß hawe[n] wilt vn[d] loß den prene[n] in der moß alß
10 den prante[n] wein vn[d] geuß den in gleser vn mach
di geleß genau czu vn[d] wen dws prauche[n] wilt ab
dir ein pusch haiß burt das dw nit gesische[n] mocht
so nim des geprante[n] waserß vnter ein halbe[n] aimer
vn kul die pusch da mit ab so scheust dw on alle sorg
15 das der pusche[n] kein schade[n] prengt

Royal Armouries I.34 – Part 2

the pot and keep the remainder for as long as you want
to have the water. And let it burn[100] with a measure of
brandy and pour it into glasses, and seal the
glasses well as you will need it when
your gun will get so hot that you cannot fire it anymore.
Then pour the burnt water into half a bucket[101]
and cool down the gun with it. This way, you see to it that all the precautions
[*are taken*] that no harm is done to the gun.[102]

[100] Here this implies having it 'reduced' or 'concentrated'.

[101] This could either imply the size of the bucket, or that it is a bucket which is half-filled with water.

[102] Text ends halfway down one page.

5 Analysis of the Text

Rainer Leng describes the *Firework Book* as a 'recipe collection of chemical knowledge'.[1] He mentions this in order to distinguish it from related manuals, such as the *Büchsenmeister Books*, all of which developed their own momentum in relation to distribution, use, and functionality. Berg and Friedrich are more specific, describing it as an 'instruction for making saltpetre, gunpowder, and various incendiary devices'.[2] They also single out the *Firework Book* as the first extant publication which collates practical knowledge related to a technical profession written in German, or any other vernacular European language – even if it was not the earliest it would have been among very few others. This chapter shows that it is far more than a 'collection of chemical knowledge'. Following on from the edition and translation just provided, it gives a detailed analysis of the content of the *Firework Book*. Analysis will begin with the structure of the *Firework Book* and its key sections, discussing in particular the Master Gunner's Questions, the master gunner's core attributes, key terminology, and then in more detail the bulk of the *Firework Book*'s recipes.

The majority of the *Firework Book* text consists of a wide range of recipes and notes, with seemingly little discernible structure and some repetition. This range implies that the book was not meant to be read from cover to cover, but instead to be used in its individual sections, and that it was helpful to have more information provided, even if it was repeating an earlier section. It is less clear, however, why their order changes from copy to copy.

Gerhard Kramer (1996 and 2001) is very specific in his analysis of the *Firework Book* composition, distinguishing between what he calls earlier and later sections, which he refers to 'strata'. In total, Kramer subdivides the *Firework Book* into three stages of writing:

1   Produced around 1380: The Master Gunner's Questions and the core components on the ingredients and the powder (in I.34 this equates to fols 2r–20r, and fols 20v–25v, fols 29r–32v, and fol. 34r).

---

[1]   Leng, *Anleitung Schiesspulver*, 12.

[2]   Berg and Friedrich, 'Wissenstradierung', 170.

2 Produced around 1400: The 'Preamble', the 'invention' of gunpowder, and the gunner attributes, and the epilogue (in I.34 this equates to fols 1r–2r, fols 20r–20v, fols 25v–29r and fols 32v–34r).

3 Produced before 1432: 'postscript' (in I.34 this equates to fols 29r–32v, fols 34r–51r).[3]

The difference in format of the *Firework Book* (where the earlier stages are a very close match to most copies in sentence structure, word selection, and rhetorical devices; the later sections with less coherence and looser structure) led to the assumption that 'the second section was added in a later production stage'.[4] However, the text produced in all the *Firework Book* manuscripts which have been viewed continues without interruption, and does not indicate a break in the production stages.

It would indeed be useful to discern the chronological development in the *Firework Book* text. However, Kramer fails to provide any substantiating evidence for any of these assertions. There is little to be gained in looking for earlier or later sections of the *Firework Book*, as it quickly enters speculative territory. It is more likely that the first few folios of the text would have formed the better-known sections, while the latter stages are not sufficiently different to give any indication of a change in technology, language, or style of writing. The basis for speculation thus appears slender.

I.34 contains more than what has traditionally been viewed as a *Firework Book*. While the first 51 folios are similar in many copies, Parts 2–4 (second text part on fols 52r–61v, the blank section on fols 61r–83v, and the illustrations on fols 84r–115r) contain further recipes and instructions, which give some indications of users and practitioners of the *Firework Book*. More beneficial than the above divisions is a detailed analysis of content and terminology.

Royal Armouries I.34 Part 1

The Preamble

A clearly distinguishable feature of all *Firework Books* is their opening statement. Starting with the introductory phrase 'Any prince, earl, lord, knight,

---

[3] Kramer and Leibnitz, *Das Feuerwerkbuch*, 10–12, and Kramer, *Berthold Schwarz*, 98–120, where more explanations are provided for the subdivisions; however, the argument is incomplete, and cannot be fully reconstructed. It largely revolves around speculation as to whether one should be regarded as written before another without explanations of the choice of dates.

[4] Berg and Friedrich, 'Wissenstradierung', 219.

squire, or town who frequently fear that they may be besieged by their enemies
…'. This sets the tone for the public reason for the intended use of the *Firework Book*.[5] It is a phrase that does not change in any of the *Firework Books*, and reminds the reader that there is a threat which requires planning and foresight. It will have had a clear recognition factor to a reader or audience – something that becomes even more clear when read aloud. After the introductory phrase, the preamble defines the position of the Master Gunner in a late medieval (largely urban) context, and sets out what follows.

The Master Gunner's Questions and Attributes

As explained in Chapter 1, the traditional sections of the *Firework Book* form a relatively regular pattern, with a preamble, the Master Gunner's Questions (usually 12), a section on the discoverer of gunpowder, and a section – which in I.34 is later in the text than in most other *Firework Books* – related to the skills and attributes of a master gunner, followed by a list of individual recipes and advice on ingredients, gunpowder, handling cannons and other incendiary devices. The reason for a section on skills and attributes is because the gunner's observation of these outer signs will indicate their inner state. In the context of fifteenth-century morality, how a person behaves is an indication of their professionalism and ethical outlook. A master gunner has to be able to read and write; he also had to be of the right temperament and aptitude, which provide a moral code to which he should adhere – thus showcasing the close relationship between etiquette (personal comportment and behaviour) and ethics.[6] It mentions that a good master gunner should fear God, and display courage and pragmatism. Furthermore, it relates to the master's ability to lead a balanced lifestyle (not over-indulging in alcohol or in specific foods), and to be of moderate temperament. The value and importance of listing these qualities is debatable. It is not clear whether they should be viewed as similar to twenty-first-century health warnings about 'not eating fatty foods' or 'binge drinking', and thus representing a reaction to such behaviour being widespread, or whether they are more of a reassurance for anyone selecting a new

---

[5]   'Welch furst grauff her[r] ritter knecht oder stet besorgent vor iren feinden beligert vnd benot werden …' (Leeds, Royal Armouries, I.34, fol. 1r).

[6]   The *Firework Book* clearly shows markers of emerging professionalism, e.g. a standard of conduct, a system of training, and a sense of keeping one's knowledge within their professional community. This subject has been discussed in various fields, in most detail within the medieval medical profession. See Toby Gelfand, 'The History of the Medical Profession', in *Companion Encyclopaedia of the History of Medicine*, eds William F. Bynum and Roy Porter (London and New York: Routledge, 1993), 119–50.

Analysis of the Text

apprentice by considering these moral and general attributes for safe handling of gunpowder.[7] In I.34, this section comes relatively late in the text (fols 32v ff.) – while most *Firework Books* have this section near the beginning, after the general introduction in the preamble – but all copies of the *Firework Book* contain the same core elements. It could be seen as a link to the introductory sections in the preamble of the *Firework Book* and appears to read as though it were an insurance device; having spelled out the key attributes of a master gunner, any users of the text would not have any comeback should they behave differently from the instructions expressed in the text.

The Master Gunner's Questions follow a strict rhetorical principle which is different from the style applied in any of the later pieces of text in the *Firework Book*. They usually contain the 12 questions, stating whether and how:[8]

1   the fire or the gas drives the projectile out of the gun;

2   sulphur or saltpetre provide the strength to the shot;

3   a projectile flies further with more or less powder;

4   a plug should be softer or harder;

5   a stone should sit tightly or loosely in the gun;

6   wedges used should be made out of soft or hard wood;

7   wedges should be thinner or thicker;

8   the projectile is sealed most effectively in the gun;

9   mixing powders increases the power of a shot;

10   a projectile should touch the plug in the gun;

11   ground powder or *Knollenpulver* is stronger; and

12   to find the most advantageous proportions of powder quantity and projectile weight.

These questions address the core elements of gunpowder artillery; they do not address tactics or subtle differences, but highlight the basics: from how to load and fire the gun to core observations of powder in the period. As early as 1889–91, their importance was acknowledged by Max Jähns, who referred to

---

[7] See Rainer Leng, 'Gründe für berufliches Töten. Büchsenmeister und Kriegshauptleute zwischen Berufsethos und Gewissensnot', in *Der Krieg im Mittelalter und in der Frühen Neuzeit: Gründe, Begründungen, Bilder, Bräuche, Recht*, ed. Horst Brunner, Imagines medii aevi 3 (Wiesbaden: Reichert, 1999), 307–48, at 318–20, and Leng, *Ars belli*, vol. 1, 201–2.

[8] There are occasionally exceptions to the 12 questions, e.g. Berlin manuscript germ. fol. 710a only lists ten questions, and Berlin manuscript germ. Quart. 1187 lists only 11 questions.

Gunpowder Technology in the Fifteenth Century

the 12 Master Gunner's Questions as the epitome of gunpowder artillery of the fifteenth century.[9]

The questions have consistently been referred to as a 'catechism', akin to religious teachings, according to the way the rhetorical question is followed by an explanatory answer.[10] This style, directly addressing one actual or imagined individual in a one-to-one teacher–pupil relation, is a familiar rhetorical format which was used in a wide range of instructional and didactic texts.[11] It must have been such a familiar context that it continued to appear in the probably later *Büchsenmeister Books*. These questions are highly formulaic and became a standard of artillery training into the seventeenth century.[12] They were also carried through into the English language, as, for example, in the 1647 publication of *The Gvnners Glasse*, which lists the instructions of an experienced gunner to an apprentice.[13] This rhetorical style of questions and answers provides a good indication of the use of the *Firework Book* as a teaching tool. Within the subject field it follows in the footsteps of Theophilus's *De diversis artibus* in the twelfth century, a text which provided detailed insight

---

[9] He describes it as the '*artilleristische Schibolet des 15. Jahrhunderts*' which literally translates into the 'shibboleth for artillery in the fifteenth century' (Jähns, *Kriegswissenschaften*, 386), meaning an *in-group* tool that distinguishes members of a group from outsiders. Later, Jähns elevates the Master Gunner's Questions to describe them as having 'transmitted for one and a half centuries the kernel of artillery knowledge' ('*durch anderthalb Jahrhundert den Kern des artilleristischen Wissen überliefert hat*', Jähns, *Kriegswissenschaften*, 395). He also refers to a sign of *Firework Books* being updated over time, and claims that questions 6 and 7 (related to the wedges) were changed in later *Firework Books* when gunpowder artillery had changed, and the lengthening of a gun, made out of one piece, improved the accuracy to such an extent that wedges were no longer required (Jähns, *Kriegswissenschaften*, 397). Unfortunately, this observation could not be verified as the later version referenced ('*Manuskript des Berliner Zeughauses von 1454*') has been lost since Jähns's survey was produced.

[10] Jähns, *Kriegswissenschaften*, 395, Schmidtchen, *Bombarden, Befestigungen, Büchsenmeister*, 179, or Leng, *Ars belli*, vol. 1, 199.

[11] This includes the medical model of the Salernitan questions and the later scholastic university model. See Brian Lawn, *The Salernitan Questions: An Introduction to the History of Medieval and Renaissance Problem Literature* (Oxford: Clarendon Press, 1963), especially 92–112, for its use in the vernacular texts.

[12] One example mentioned by Jähns is the *Kunstbüchlein von Geschütz und Feuerwerk*, published by De Bry in 1619 (Jähns, *Kriegswissenschaften*, 395).

[13] See William Eldred, *The Gvnners Glasse* (London: T. Forcet Boydel, 1646/47), *Early English Books Online*, https://go.openathens.net/redirector/leeds.ac.uk?url=https://www.proquest.com/books/gvnners-glasse-vvherein-diligent-practicioner-may/docview/2264183063/se-2 (accessed 10 August 2023).

308

Analysis of the Text

into the techniques used for a wide range of material arts which has been recorded to be used for teaching and which it structures in dialogue format, but without the inclusion of didactic questions and answers.[14]

Key Terminology

One major challenge throughout the entire 61 folios is the lack of clarity about key ingredients and terminology used – both in the original and in translation. Producing a translation has made this lack of clarity even more apparent, and has highlighted shortcomings in previous studies of the *Firework Book*.

Core terms such as 'gun' (*'puchse'* or *'püchse'*), 'barrel' (*'ror'*), 'powder' (*'puluer'* or *'pulfer'*), and 'plug' (*'clotz'*, *'klotz'*, or *'klotzen'*) all require explanation. While these elements may appear obvious, modern scholars often allow their knowledge of later periods to influence their understanding of what was actually going on in this field in the fifteenth century.

Hence, where the *Firework Book* refers to a 'gun', this is to be understood as the entire piece which is loaded with powder and a ball without any specification as to whether this may have included the carriage. Apart from two exceptions, on fols 31v and 41r, the *Firework Book* does not specify the size, format, mounting, and firing of the gun, and no description is given as to the length or size of barrel. Nor is there is any indication as to the range of the gun, which was not a priority in early gunnery;[15] in the fifteenth century, guns were used at relatively short range as direct shots.[16]

What is called the 'barrel', on the other hand, I understand to be the part of a cannon in front of the 'powder chamber' or 'chamber of the gun'. The chamber of the gun itself is the part in which the gunpowder charge is placed. It is sealed by the 'plug' which normally needs to be rammed into the barrel to be entirely inside it, sitting flush with its end. The 'barrel' is also often called the 'chamber'. 'Powder' is used as a generic term for a mixture of ingredients which are brought together as described in detail. There is, however, no indication about the consistency of the powder, whether flour, lumped, *Knollenpulver*, or some other form.

---

[14] Theophilus focuses in particular on painting, glassmaking, and metalwork. The author's name is likely to have been a pseudonym used by Roger of Helmarshausen, a Benedictine monk, metal worker, and goldsmith. His main work, *De diversis artibus*, was often published, copied, and translated from its original Latin (*Theophilus. On Divers Arts*, eds John G. Hawthorne and Cyril Stanley Smith (New York: Dover, 1979), xv–xviii).

[15] Smith and DeVries, *Artillery of Burgundy*, 211.

[16] Glenn Foard and Anne Curry, *Bosworth 1485: A Battlefield Reconsidered* (Oxford: Oxbow, 2013), 136.

Gunpowder Technology in the Fifteenth Century

The 'plug' is referred to on 60 separate occasions. In most cases it refers to the piece of wood used to seal the end of the barrel with the powder. In one case it is referred to when firing a 'plug gun' ('*Klotzbüchse*').[17]

Dealing with these terms in English (and Early New High German) is a challenge. The terms might appear straightforward, but they leave scope for interpretation. The same applies to the term '*Büchsenmeister*' which, for the purpose of the translation, has been rendered as 'master gunner' or 'gun master', to distinguish between the head of a gun troop and someone skilled in handling guns. The modern German term '*Büchsenmeister*' implies that the master gunner has an input into the manufacturing process, while in a fifteenth-century context all references of '*puchsen maister*' (or similar) seem more related to the Early New High German term '*Konstabel*', describing an individual in charge of the handling of an artillery piece, and later a title as a non-commissioned officer in an artillery unit. The *Frühneuhochdeutsches Wörterbuch Online* definition of '*Büchsenmeister*' was changed after my discussions with the editorial team to exclude 'maker of guns', as all references refer to the role of the person in charge in situ, and no references are related to the production of guns.[18] There is a distinct difference between this and the role of '*Büchsenschmied*' – the smith in charge of the manufacture of a gun.[19]

Similarly, caution is needed when referring to guns or ammunition. For example, what can be understood by a '*Steinbüchse*' ('stone gun')? It is largely a post-medieval term to describe a particular type of gun – but may receive its first mention in this manuscript on fol. 43v ('*estain ror*'). Other *Firework Book* manuscripts refer in this section to '*aichin ror*' (Dillingen Ms. XV 50, fol. 31r), '*aicheny rören*' (Stainer 1529, 35), or '*eychne rören*' (Egenolph 1529, 41), which would imply 'made out of oak', interpreted by Nibler and others as a scribal error.[20] As Heidelberg Cod. Pal. germ. 562, fol. 4r lists it as '*eysenn rör*', it has generally been interpreted as 'iron'. Only Darmstadt Ms. 1074, fol. 31r copies

---

[17] See Leng, *Anleitung Schiesspulver*, 104–5, Smith, *Reports of the HO Group*, mainly 2002 and 2003, and early sixteenth-century Biringuccio (in *The Pirotechnia of Vannoccio Biringuccio*, eds Cyril Stanley Smith and Martha Teach Gnudi (New York: Dover, 1990), 425–28) for references to this technique, which was commonly used against horses, but does not fire long distances.

[18] *Frühneuhochdeutsches Wörterbuch Online*, https://fwb-online.de/go/b%C3%BCchsenmeister.s.0m_1513302890.

[19] *Frühneuhochdeutsches Wörterbuch Online*, https://fwb-online.de/go/b%C3%BCchsenschmied.s.0m_1513341043.

[20] The term used in Nibler's edition is '*eisern*', meaning 'iron' (Nibler, *Feuerwerkbuch*, 60).

Analysis of the Text

the I.34 wording with *'esten ror'*. Other manuscripts, such as Freiburg Ms. 362, omit this section completely.

The term 'stone gun' is generally used to describe a gun which fired one or more stone projectiles, before iron or lead shot became the standard. It can be seen in parallel with the chronological material culture periods (such as 'bronze age' or 'iron age'), which have been retrospectively applied to people living in particular times. Most German scholarship refers to the seminal works by Schmidtchen, which provide an overview of the *Steinbüchsen* type.[21] His research was built on a century of scholarship investigating this terminology by Essenwein, Jähns, Romocki, Rathgen, and Feldhaus.[22] However, this does not mean that a *Steinbüchse* would only fire stone projectiles. Stone, lead, and iron were all used as ammunition, as often composite shots were 'made out of more than one material'.[23] Cast iron only came to be used frequently in the 1470s.[24] The research work led by Glenn Foard at the battlefield site of Bosworth has shown a large amount of ammunition of varying sizes, much of which contains iron or lead.[25] Projectiles which had been entirely made out of stone rarely register in the archaeological survey.[26] This transitional phase is reflected in the terminology used in the *Firework Books*. The terms 'stone' (*'stein'*) or 'ball' (*'kugel'* or *'kegel'*) are all used, but it is not clear whether the material they are made of is always known to the author (or even relevant).[27]

---

[21] Brought together in Schmidtchen, *Bombarden, Befestigungen, Büchsenmeister*, 12–82, and in subsequent publications by the same author.

[22] Their major outputs on this topic are von Essenwein, *Quellen zur Geschichte der Feuerwaffen*, Max Jähns, *Handbuch einer Geschichte des Kriegswesens von der Urzeit bis zur Renaissance*, 2 vols (Leipzig: F. E. Grunow, 1878–80), and Jähns, *Kriegswissenschaften*, Romocki, *Geschichte der Explosivstoffe*, Bernard Rathgen, *Das Geschütz im Mittelalter* (Berlin: VDI-Verlag, 1928), and *Feldhaus, Technik der Antike und des Mittelalters*.

[23] Smith and DeVries, *Artillery of Burgundy*, 247.

[24] Smith and DeVries, *Artillery of Burgundy*, 253.

[25] Foard and Curry, *Bosworth*, mainly chapter 7, and especially 147–49.

[26] Stone projectiles cannot be detected by metal detectors, but only recognized by being viewed (through shape, size, petrology, or some combination of the three) by a trained archaeologist. On a former battlefield such identification is necessarily limited to items on the surface, while further uncertainties are introduced where projectiles have been changed in shape by firing, impact, or later plough damage.

[27] 'Stone' is used throughout, e.g. in the Master Gunner's Questions, and fols 7v, 13r, 15v, 16r, 20v, 25v, 26v, 27v, 31r, 32r, 38r, 38v, 39r, 41r, 41v, 42v, and 43v. *'Kugel'* or *'kegel'* appears less frequently in fols 1v, 7r, 7v, 28v, 34v, 40r, or 50r.

'*Kugel*' is more often used in relation to ancillary incendiary devices such as fire balls.

The text also uses a range of seemingly standard technical terms which may not always be easily explained. A term such as '*stuck*' – meaning 'elements', 'parts', or simply 'thing' – is a collective term similar to the English 'stuff' ('*zeug*').[28] It is unclear whether this is a deliberately broad term, or whether an experienced practitioner would know to which item it refers.

The author is prone to using some rather imprecise technical terms. One example is on fol. 6v: '*Seud das dar uber gang*' (the literal translation for this would be 'heat until it boils over'). The author frequently uses terms such as 'boiling over' or 'boiling hard', an expression which would literally be translated as 'beaten over'. This implies that the water was heated to such a temperature that liquid spilled over the edge. Excess energy input (e.g. a high or hot flame) will make the conversion of water to steam at the bottom more aggressive.[29]

As this text was written before the emergence of more widespread technical instructive texts, terms such as '*schaiden*' were not yet defined. This seemingly simple term has been translated as 'to separate', 'to break down', or 'to subdivide', and is used to describe a number of different stages in saltpetre production. Historically, the term came to be a specific chemistry expression by the eighteenth century.[30] While there may not have been an authorized vocabulary in the fifteenth century, nevertheless there was the need to describe what action took place. For the translation, this provided a challenge not to become too technical, or more figurative, but rather to convey what actually seems to be happening.

The author uses a wide range of measurements, which were by no means completely standardized, and sometimes related to actual numerical descriptions; e.g. what is a quintal?[31] Does the time at which the *Firework Book* was

---

[28] 'Arsenal' translates into German as '*Zeughaus*', which literally means 'the house of stuff'.

[29] Technically, the temperature of boiling is absolute, but – to use cooking terminology – this instruction may refer to the difference between a slow boil or simmer (gentle bubbles) and a full rolling boil (a continuous rapid boil), cf. https://www.oed.com/view/Entry/167013?redirectedFrom=rolling+boil#eid25217662 (accessed 10 August 2023).

[30] See Definition II. A. 1) a) *Deutsches Wörterbuch von Jacob und Wilhelm Grimm Online* (accessed 10 August 2023).

[31] A quintal was often referenced as measurement and is an historical unit of mass, often defining 100 units of pounds or kilograms, but it had not yet been standardized. See Harald Witthöft, 'Maß und Regio – Herrschaft, Wirtschaft und Kultur. Von aequalitas, Einheitlichkeit und langer Dauer', *Jahrbuch für Regionalgeschichte*

Analysis of the Text

written make a difference? Sometimes it mentions different sizes of barrels, pots, and sieves which – without context – are often too speculative to reconstruct.[32] It is not clear how much credence can be given to the accuracy of the measurements and weights provided (see also the section on the use of balancing scales below). What is likely, though, is that the proportion would be adhered to as stated. Debate among twentieth- and twenty-first-century gunpowder technologists has shown that adding some ingredients, such as camphor, or a wide range of different woods for charcoal, does not make any actual difference in efficiency, but it is likely that there would be a psychological effect of making the user feel better/more likely to be successful, or even an aesthetic one by virtue of it looking/smelling/feeling more pleasing.[33] It is important, too, that adding these ingredients does not make matters worse, so 'why not' do it?[34]

Sometimes particular types of tree have become the name for a specific type of wood (or vice versa) such as '*linder holtz*' – this is both soft wood (as the description of a generic characteristic of the wood) and 'lime wood' (as the definition of a particular type of tree). In German, the term '*Linde*' is the name of the tree, as well as an adjective which could be translated as 'soft', 'mellow', 'calm' – often used in a figurative context.

In two instances, I.34 lists monetary values: fol. 17v states that 'saltpetre which has been purified and cleaned' would be worth 'a guilder'; the other case is on fol. 25r where unpurified salammoniac is listed as costing 'sixteen shilling and a haller per pound', while the costs of purified salammoniac would rise to 'a guilder for one pound'.[35] Strikingly, in neither instance does the

---

und Landeskunde 24 (2006), 49–75, at 49–51, or Jessica Dijkmann, *Shaping Medieval Markets: The Organisation of Commodity Markets in Holland, c. 1200–c.1450*, Global Economic History Series 8 (Leiden: Brill, 2011), 203–13. At the same time, the difference of measures may not have had such an impact on the recipes as long as the ratio of the ingredients stays the same.

[32] It was only in the early nineteenth century that measurements of volume were standardized in Bavaria (even later for other parts of Germany). In the fifteenth century, measures were largely local, and the terminology and actual sizes varied substantially, with various attempts for harmonization made. See, for example, Witthöft, 'Maß und Regio', 54–59.

[33] See, for example, Smith, 'Gunpowder Chemistry', 157–58.

[34] Many of these experiments can be tested in modern laboratory conditions, while others – such as the adding of mercury to the touch hole – would be harder to restage for reasons of health and safety.

[35] See Freiburg Ms. 362, fol. 84v, Dresden Ms. App. 463, fol. 50r, Heidelberg Cod. Pal. germ. 122, fol. 22v; and Dillingen Ms. XV 50, fol. 22v.

Gunpowder Technology in the Fifteenth Century

value of the equivalent change in other copies of the *Firework Book*, but they are changed in the first printed version in 1529.[36] Assuming that the surviving *Firework Books* were produced over a period of more than 100 years, even modest estimates would require an adjustment for inflation or regional price fluctuations.[37] This suggests an interrelation between the surviving *Firework Books*, and may well indicate a limited actual usage. However, fossilization of prices also occurred in other kinds of texts from the later Middle Ages. It could have been viewed as being too complicated to adjust, and thus the text was left as it was for ease of use, with the assumption that local recalculations were expected.[38]

Ingredients and Recipes

The major part of the *Firework Book* (including of Royal Armouries I.34) is a listing of various instructions and recipes in relation to gunpowder artillery. In total, I.34 Part 1 contains 112 instructions, which can be subdivided into the four main categories: ingredients, gunpowder, guns and techniques, and auxiliary incendiary devices. Inevitably, there are some overlapping cross-references, and sometimes a section combines dealing with recipes, ingredients, and other instructions.

The core ingredients of gunpowder are saltpetre, sulphur, and charcoal. Out of the 42 subsections on ingredients alone in I.34's Part 1, 26 relate to aspects of saltpetre, with the majority on purifying saltpetre (ten sections), buying saltpetre (four sections), acquiring saltpetre and making it usable (four sections), making stronger or better saltpetre (three sections), and distinguishing different qualities of saltpetre (three sections). The making of saltpetre was

---

[36] See Freiburg Ms. 362, fol. 77r, Dresden Ms. App. 463, fol. 23r, Heidelberg Cod. Pal. germ. 122, fol. 16r; and Dillingen Ms. XV 50, fol. 10r; this is different to the first printed text, in Stainer 1529, which alters both the quantity produced and the monetary value. Instead of one pound, the printed version refers to 'one hundred-weight ('*zentner*')' which would be worth the equivalent of a florin.

[37] The groundbreaking work by Thom Richardson on medieval inventories of the Tower Armouries, 1320–1410, lists the emergence of gunpowder manufacture in the Tower of London as early as 1333 (Richardson, *The Tower Armoury*, 175–77.). By the 1370s the production has been recorded on an ever-increasing scale from then onwards (Richardson, *The Tower Armoury*, 177–90). This clearly was in reply to an increase in demand, with the costs increasing for all the ingredients required.

[38] See, for example, Peter Spufford, *Handbook of Medieval Exchange* (London: Royal Historical Society, 1986), xxiv.

Analysis of the Text

complex: as the HO Group research has shown,[39] to make saltpetre requires the addition of urine to animal waste-enriched soil over a prolonged period of time, in order to make potassium nitrate, followed by a process of filtering and reduction through boiling.

From a twenty-first-century perspective, it is virtually impossible to establish what the exact ingredients would have been, or their level of purity and strength. While we may have a modern equivalent to the medieval name, it is by no means a like-for-like equation – that the modern element is the same as the medieval. The same applies to its purity and its chemical composition. This in turn raises questions about whether it is possible to recreate these compositions, and if so whether the results of these experiments will be subject to a not dissimilar level of uncertainty.

The prominence of sections on saltpetre production and purification suggests that the producer of the *Firework Book* may not have been experienced in the extraction of saltpetre (and may only have known about it secondhand). While he may well have heard some details on how it could be extracted or where it came from, it appears that all that is provided are assumptions which record hearsay ('from stables, mountains, or otherwise' in fols 8r, 12v, 18v, and 23v), rather than the actual experience of producing it himself, thereby giving us the impression that the author did not fully understand how the process worked.

The section on how to grow saltpetre in stables or on walls (fol. 8r) has been the subject of repeated experiments and could not be recreated. It has been discredited by scholars as producing the wrong type of salt.[40] It is most likely that, if the author of the *Firework Book* had known how to make saltpetre, he would have written it down. Significantly, this differs from the refining stages, which have been proven to be working recipes and can be recreated.[41] Taken

---

[39] Smith, *Reports of the HO Group*, mainly reports from 2013 and 2014. The HO Group: Medieval Gunpowder Research started in 2002 and has been instrumental in investigating the compositions and properties of medieval gunpowder and associated materials. All reports of the group's findings can be found at https://ahc.leeds.ac.uk/downloads/download/35/fields_of_Conflict or https://www.middelalderakademiet.dk/krudt-og-kanoner (both accessed 10 August 2023).

[40] Geoff Smith, 'Medieval Gunpowder Chemistry: A Commentary on the Firework Book', *Journal of the International Committee for the History of Technology* 21 (2015), 147–66, at 149–50, Emmerich Pászthory, 'Salpetergewinnung und Salpeterwirtschaft vom Mittelalter bis in die Neuzeit', *Chemie in unserer Zeit*, 29:1 (1995), 8–20; or Wilfried Tittmann et al., 'Salpeter und Salpetergewinnung im Übergang vom Mittelalter zur Neuzeit' (online publication, 2017), http://www.ruhr-uni-bochum.de/technikhist/tittmann/4%20Salpeter.pdf (accessed 10 August 2023).

[41] Smith, *Reports of the HO Group*, mainly reports from 2013 and 2014.

Gunpowder Technology in the Fifteenth Century

together, these facts suggest that users of the *Firework Book* would generally not have made their own saltpetre, but would have acquired it from elsewhere. When it was for sale it may have been a product called 'saltpetre', but it may not have been very good quality (being contaminated with impurities) – hence the need for testing its taste (needs to be tangy) and placing one's hand into a barrel of saltpetre, which needs to come out dry (on account of its hygroscopic nature). Before saltpetre production techniques were developed across Europe, the only option of acquiring saltpetre was to buy it (as stated on, e.g., fol. 36r). The fact that the text warns about saltpetre being adulterated with other salts gives an indication of the value of saltpetre and its retail attributes. It appears that it would still be more economical to use relatively expensive ordinary salt (sodium chloride, NaCl) and mix it in with saltpetre to bulk it up.

There is a historiographical debate on the consistency of saltpetre, arguing whether saltpetre had to be potassium nitrate (KNO_3) or could possibly also be calcium nitrate ($Ca(NO_3)_2$).[42] The textual evidence provided by the *Firework Books* provides no further insights. Experiments by the HO Group have shown that when saltpetre has been adulterated with ordinary salt there comes a point at which the mixture ceases to work in the same way as saltpetre alone; the question of whether it could be mixed with other nitrates could not be proven.[43]

Compared to sulphur and charcoal, saltpetre seems to be the most problematic ingredient, or the one that can be modified the most with the hope of improving it. This may explain why the text refers to the nature of saltpetre (fol. 23v), and the various attempts and ways of purifying it (fols 17r ff. and fols 44v–46v). It would also explain the repeated testing of saltpetre in different ways in three recipes (fols 44r–v), and the references to derivatives of saltpetre (such as salpratica (fol. 24r) and saltpetre salt (fols 16r–v).

One surprising placing of a section, which seems out of context, is on fol. 37r, on 'bringing back' spoiled or bad powder. This is likely to have been a regular task of a master gunner. This section includes a small insertion on how to purify saltpetre. In other *Firework Books* the insertion on how to deal with

---

[42] On the debate on KNO_3 or $Ca(NO_3)_2$ see Tittmann et al., *Salpetergewinnung*. See also Smith, *Reports of the HO Group*, mainly from 2004. Kramer claims to have been able to recreate it, but failed to provide evidence for this (see Kramer, 'Feuerwerkbuch: Importance', 45–56). See also Anthony De Reuck, 'The Nature of Saltpeter in the *Firework Book*,' *Journal of the Ordnance Society* 20 (2008), 5–10.

[43] Smith, *Reports of the HO Group*, mainly from 2002, 2003, 2012, and 2013. Tittmann states that the HO Group may have proved something that cannot be proven (Tittmann et al., *Salpetergewinnung*, 4). However, no such claim has been made in any of the works of the HO Group.

Analysis of the Text

spoiled powder appears much earlier in the text in a section on improving saltpetre. It is not clear why it is added at this stage; it could have resulted from a scribal oversight, the writer thus being forced to add a core element out of context at a later stage. The fact that it refers to the term '*in quartu gradu*' gives it an additional gravitas to imply that it is a section that must not be forgotten.[44] In other *Firework Books* this section is listed with other purifying techniques.[45] It is likely that the author had forgotten to add it earlier, and then remembered that it needed including here – even when the sections before and after are not relevant. This may in turn suggest how the *Firework Book* was produced: it was written down from memory, or dictated by someone, and the section order depended on the ability to memorize.

Compared to saltpetre there are very few sections on sulphur (purifying – fol. 19r) and charcoal (fols 13r and 19r–v), or making sulphur oil (fol. 42v) – although their production stages are unclear, possibly suggesting that the author did not understand what he was copying or writing down.

The *Firework Book* includes a list of additional ingredients to be added to gunpowder (see, for example, fols 5v and 6r), often in rather small quantities. It is debatable whether they made any difference. It could be that they provided a psychological effect in that the addition of something precious and rare could seem to make gunpowder even more special and impactful. These 'special' ingredients include brandy, camphor, salammoniac, mercury, salniter, urine, and a range of unidentifiable substances. Many post-medieval records continue to refer to the ingredients mentioned, but are not specific about their

[44] In the second century, the Greek philosopher, physician, and surgeon Galen presented the principle of 'degrees' of strength or primary qualities of medical substances, which was further developed by Arnaldus de Villa Nova in the late thirteenth century. One of its core principles relates to the interaction of ingredients in recipes. This also appears in a cookery context, where every substance is categorized as hot, cold, dry, or wet. See Joel Kaye, *A History of Balance, 1250–1375: The Emergence of a New Model of Equilibrium and its Impact on Thought* (Cambridge: Cambridge University Press, 2014), especially 210–22. It seems highly likely that this concept would have been known to a reader with a certain level of education.

[45] See Freiburg Ms. 362, fol. 76r, Dresden Ms. App. 463, fol. 19r, or Dillingen Ms. XV 50, fol. 8r. However, Heidelberg Cod. Pal. Germ. 122, fol. 34r, includes it at the same location in the text as in I.34.

consistency or purity.[46] Discussions among modern gunpowder experts have failed to provide conclusive evidence.[47]

The author uses about 20 ingredients as Latin terms, often without translation, such as *arsenicum album, atrimentum, sublimata mercurius,* and *salpertica.* It is likely that these ingredients relate to:

- *Arsenicum album*: a white substance, core ingredient used in medicine[48]

- *Atrimentum,* or *Atramentum,* atrament, or atriment: a black liquid, often used for dyeing leather or in painting. See also reference to 'atramentous' and its definition of 'black as ink'[49]

- *Opperment*: orpiment, an arsenic sulphide mineral widely used in medicine and painting; this is referred to by Partington as 'arsenic mineral'[50]

- *Sublimata mercurius*: sublimate mercury[51]

- *Salpertica*: compound of saltpetre and brandy, camphor, salammoniac, added to powder in the belief that it 'quickens and strengthens all powders'.[52]

However, all these terms have been subject to intense debate amongst gunpowder experts, and there is no comprehensive agreement about their precise chemical properties and consistency.[53] Just as the purity of saltpetre is ques-

---

[46] See Biringuccio, in Smith and Gnudi, *Biringuccio,* 403–16, Partington, *Greek Fire and Gunpowder,* 324–29, or George Plimpton, *Fireworks: A History and Celebration* (New York: Doubleday, 1984), 188. By the seventeenth century, powder started to be standardized, and authors such as Babington (1635 [2018]) no longer refer to the core ingredients of gunpowder.

[47] For some suggested explanations see Kramer, *Berthold Schwarz,* 145–50, Kramer and Leibnitz, *Das Feuerwerkbuch,* 72–76, Blosen and Olsen, *Bengedans,* 121–27, Alfred Geibig, *Die Macht des Feuers – Might and Fire* (Coburg: Kunstsammlung der Veste Coburg, 2012), 7–10, and Smith, 'Gunpowder Chemistry', 157–58. However, most of the points made seem to be hypotheses which require detailed testing. It seems clear that there is still a large amount of research to be done to clarify to what extent and in what form an addition of any of these ingredients would increase the performance of a gun.

[48] Partington, *Greek Fire and Gunpowder,* 362.

[49] Partington refers to it as 'ink'. Partington, *Greek Fire and Gunpowder,* 155.

[50] Partington, *Greek Fire and Gunpowder,* 284.

[51] Partington, *Greek Fire and Gunpowder,* 152.

[52] Partington, *Greek Fire and Gunpowder,* 155.

[53] See, for example, Smith, 'Gunpowder Chemistry', 157–58.

tioned in the *Firework Book*, it is likely that these ingredients would refer to a 'semantic field' of components, rather than to one single component.[54]

It is most likely that these were standard supplies to be found in an apothecary's shop, but identifying them exactly proves to be virtually impossible. The spellings have been compared to other *Firework Books*, but even in modern editions of other *Firework Books* the modern translation of the ingredients, and any assumption of their chemical composition, is done only with a level of uncertainty and speculation. Any modern editions of *Firework Books*, published in German or English, appear to have been driven by editors with a background in the fields of chemistry, and the decisions on terms used is based on what should have worked rather than what information the text provides.[55] without any suggestion that the chemical formula is not in the main text. Tests by the HO Group have shown (more to be carried out in 2023–24) that the basic recipe of gunpowder is sufficient in almost all contexts to achieve an explosive effect.[56]

Gunpowder

Plenty of scholarly discussion has taken place on the form and consistency of gunpowder.[57] While the quality and status of the ingredients for gunpowder are important, so are the texture and appearance of the powder itself. The *Firework Book* provides some helpful pointers, but falls short of a comprehensive answer. In total, 29 sections in I.34 relate to various elements on gunpowder.

They can be grouped into subsections on:

1 Making and preparing powder including ratio of ingredients used (fols 6r, 8r, 14r, 15r, 20v, 22v, 39v, 46v, 47r, and 47v)

2 Regenerating powder that for one reason or another has deteriorated (fols 6v, 21v, and 37r),

3 Specialist types of powder (coloured, ball powder, and *Knollenpulver* – fols 29r, 29v, 30r, 34v, and 48r), and

---

[54] See, for example, Maxwell-Stuart, *A History of Alchemy*, x.

[55] Kramer and Leibnitz, *Das Feuerwerkbuch*, 43, where 'sublimato' is translated as 'mercury chloride, $HgCl_2$

[56] Smith, *Reports of the HO Group*, especially reports from 2002, 2003, and 2020.

[57] An overview can be found at DeVries and Smith, *Military Technology*, 144–45, and Smith, *Rewriting Gunpowder History*, 55–69, as well as Hall, *Warfare in Renaissance*, 67–87, Partington, *Greek Fire and Gunpowder*, 323–29, or for a more in-depth analysis of various aspects see Buchanan, *Gunpowder: History of Technology*, and *Gunpowder, Explosives and the State: A Technological History*, ed. Brenda J. Buchanan (Aldershot: Ashgate, 2006).

Gunpowder Technology in the Fifteenth Century

4   'Very good', 'better', 'stronger', 'louder', 'even better', 'miraculous', 'the best', and 'the strongest' powders (fols 8v, 9r, 21r, 29r, 30v, 47r, and 47v).

Subsection 1 deals with a wide range of powder preparation recipes and the importance of balancing all the core and supplementary ingredients. It is the largest subsection within the powder sections, and provides a number of different recipe mixtures. It prescribes that common powder should be at a ratio of 57% saltpetre : 14% charcoal : 29% sulphur (fol. 47r), while basic powder should be at a ratio of 53:20:27 (fol. 20v), the best powder at 57:5:38 (fol. 21r),[58] while even stronger powder should be at 67:11:22 (fol. 47v). The maximum ratio of powder before it stops working (described as 'too heavy') is 71:10:19 (fol. 47v).

Gunpowder ratio comparison table

	Fol.	Proportions	Saltpetre	Charcoal	Sulphur
Wide firing	5v	67:11:22	3 lb	2 quarts	1 lb (grey)
Good	6r	67:11:22	3 lb	2 quarts	1 lb (grey)
Strong and fast	8v	71:6:24	(3 lb)	1 quart	1 lb (good)
Even better	9r	71:6:24	(3 lb)	1 quart	1 lb (good)
Basic	20v	53:20:27	2 lb	3 quarts	1 lb
Best	21r	57:5:38	150 lb	12.5 lb	100 lb
Miraculous	29r	as before			
Loudest	30v	add hair and mercury when firing			
Common	47r	57:14:29	4 lb	1 lb	2 lb
Better	47r	62.5:12.5:25	5 lb	1 lb	2 lb
Even stronger	47v	67:11:22	6 lb	1 lb	2 lb
Heaviest	47v	71:10:19	7.5 lb	1 lb	2 lb

[58]   The fact that the recipe advises adding to the 'best' powder 1 lot of camphor, 2 times 3.5 pounds of salammoniac, five lots of *arsenicum*, three lots of *demertius sublimato* and a little saltpetre water seems unlikely to make a substantial difference to its effectiveness (fol. 21r). However, this is a research topic worth testing under modern scientific conditions.

The subsection includes a section on how to separate out powder into its key components, which is an unlikely recipe, but might be necessary in extreme circumstances (fol. 6v). Recipes such as the one on how to make gunpowder for guns and fire arrows (fol. 46v) again have a strong focus on the saltpetre component, here especially the grinding of it.

Subsection 2 lists instructions for the regeneration of spoiled gunpowder. This would be the bread-and-butter activity of a gun master, as time, weather, or transporting gunpowder will always adversely affect it. However, it is not explained at what point a master gunner could work out whether a specific powder or one of its core ingredients has deteriorated (the main way of doing so is to fire it). An experienced gunner might be able to use his skills to compare look, taste, and storage or transportation to previous experiences, but none of the instances are explained here.

Subsection 3 on various special powders raises a number of questions. Almost all *Firework Books* refer to the colouring of powder, but it is not clear how the colouring would have worked. While the added ingredient would indeed help to colour things blue, yellow, red, or white, the predominant colorant would be charcoal, which almost inevitably would make everything black; that is, unless charcoal was not added to the powder until later in the process. In a stress-infused combat position the colouring (as well as scenting – as could be suggested with the very potent scent of sandalwood) could give the firing side an important advantage, saving precious seconds to go for the right mixture without losing valuable time.[59]

It is less clear what 'ball powder' (*'kugel pulfer'*, fol. 34v) refers to. This can only be explained as a scribal error, where the author wrote *'kugel pulfer'* while meaning *Knollenpulver*.[60] *Knollenpulver* is an early version of what later was to become a much more standardized corned powder, which in turn developed into serpentine powder. Corned and lumped powder are crucial in the development of early gunpowder artillery, and scholars have long discussed the development of powder in the fifteenth and sixteenth centuries.[61] As Bert Hall explains: 'one fundamental fact that affects the ballistics of all gunpowder

---

[59] See Robin A. Donkin, *Between East and West: The Moluccas and the Traffic in Spices up to the Arrival of Europeans* (Philadelphia: American Philosophical Society, 2003), 111–14, on the many uses of sandalwood, including as a sensory *aide memoire*.

[60] Even at the end of this section it is no longer described as 'ball powder' but rather 'kollen pulver', which only omits one consonant to make it 'knollenpulver'. See for comparison, Heidelberg Cod. Pal. germ. 122, fol. 31r.

[61] See Bert S. Hall, 'The Corning of Gunpowder and the Development of Firearms in the Renaissance', in *Gunpowder: History of Technology*, ed. Brenda Buchanan,

Gunpowder Technology in the Fifteenth Century

weaponry is how quickly powder burns'. The way to regulate this in later gunpowder technology was to control the 'grain size of gunpowder', which was called 'corning'.[62] While 'corning' is not understood to have existed before the middle of the fifteenth century,[63] the *Firework Book* provides a predecessor of 'corning' in its *Knollenpulver*. Hall describes this powder as substantially more 'durable, and resistant to spoilage' and he uses the term 'lump powder'.[64] It was produced by carefully grinding all the ingredients and mixing them before wetting the mixture with water or brandy to form lumps. These lumps were dried carefully without exposure to open fire or sparks. The difference between *Knollenpulver* and corned powder is that *Knollenpulver* is much more crumbly and can fragment into irregular particles which could risk falling apart further and turning into flour, and thus losing any kinetic advantage of the powder being in lumps. The fact that the eleventh question of the Master Gunner's Questions specifies the existence of *Knollenpulver* shows its importance and widespread use.[65]

Subsection 4 (about different levels of powder) is of particular interest. The comparatives ('better', 'louder', or 'stronger') or superlatives ('best' or 'strongest') are subjective terms. Without modern scientific equipment it is not possible to measure strength in a meaningful way, whether a shot was better or worse (it would also require a scale of measuring its effect as 'more or less lethal', 'more or less impactful', and so on). The range and impact of a shot varied hugely, and was dependent on a wide range of factors. It could be that certain mixtures were more suitable for particular circumstances and contexts.

87–120, for a detailed discussion on corning and *Knollenpulver* and its kinetic properties (see also Smith, *Rewriting Gunpowder History*, 65–69).

[62] Hall, *Warfare in Renaissance*, 68.

[63] Occasional corning was first recorded in 1407–1411 (Hall, 'Corning of Gunpowder', 89, and 'Gunpowder and Early Gunpowder Weapons', 123). The date has been moved gradually earlier, from the mid- to the early fifteenth century (see Rathgen, *Das Geschütz im Mittelalter*, 109–36). Early debates on corning often relate to the sieve sizes being used. Corning is understood to increase substantially the efficiency and effectiveness of gunpowder. See Jähns, *Kriegswissenschaften*, 401, Romocki, *Geschichte der Explosivstoffe*, 182–85, Henry W. L. Hime, *Gunpowder and Ammunition: Their Origin and Progress* (Waltham Abbey: Royal Gunpowder Mills, 1904), 182, Partington, *Greek Fire and Gunpowder*, 154, Hall, 'Corning of Gunpowder', 87–106, Smith, *Rewriting Gunpowder History*, 65–69, and DeVries and Smith, *Military Technology*, 153. 'Corned powder' was believed to have been too strong for early guns, which is why Hall only lists its widespread use in the sixteenth century (Hime, *Gunpowder*, 183–84, and Partington, *Greek Fire and Gunpowder*, 154).

[64] Hall, *Warfare in Renaissance*, 71.

[65] The production of *Knollenpulver* is described on fol. 34v.

The mention of these subjective terms, however, also has another function. As stated above, it could be used for psychological effect, making the gunner (or his employee, employer, or patron) think that it was 'better' or 'stronger', therefore giving them a psychological boost in combat; it could thus be viewed as a marketing tool. Of particular interest is the section on 'louder shot'. This directly relates to the 'fear factor' that gunpowder artillery had on the battlefield or at a siege.[66] While it would be impossible to hit everyone with a shot, everyone would hear (and possibly smell) the gun fire and this would inevitably have an effect in battle. As far as could be ascertained, the instructions for these shots may not necessarily make them 'better' or 'stronger', but by adding an extra level of work in the powder production it would easily have made the producer *believe* that it added something extra to the powder and its use. Part 2 adds to the psychologically beneficial effect in two recipes (fols 55v and 57r) which do not make much practical sense to a twenty-first-century reader. The author mixes a range of different balls and ingredients, but does not explain consistently what the end result is, nor how the ingredients need to be put together to achieve it. Of interest here are the two headings ('one hundred heads', and 'secret art'). Both imply a level of bragging or boasting along the lines of other marketing ploys mentioned above, as nothing could either be verified or disproven.

The *Firework Book* contains many references which relate to good salesmanship; these include the preamble (equivalent to a twenty-first-century insurance advertisement), and the instructions on the attributes and behaviour of a good master gunner. Thus, the master gunner is presenting a range of options for using gunpowder technology in both defence and offence to any potential employer. This element of choice, arguably, explains the sections on a wide range of powder options, such as 'good', 'better', or 'the best', as stated above, since what is best will strongly depend on the purpose and context.[67]

In the section on 'common', 'better', and 'even stronger' powder (fols 47r and 47v) the crucial change is the ratio from 57% saltpetre to 14% charcoal and 29% sulphur for the common powder (57:14:29) to 62.5:12.5:25 in the

---

[66] While there is little evidence of this being reported in the fifteenth century, there are records for it in the sixteenth century, e.g. the Cortés expeditions in Mexico made specific use of gunpowder artillery to frighten indigenous people (Matthew Restall, *Seven Myths of the Spanish Conquest* (Oxford: Oxford University Press, 2004), 139–40).

[67] This theory was first put forward by Schmidtchen, *Kriegswesen*, 30, as an 'advertising method to inform potential employers about their range of skills and expertise' ('... *in Sinne eines Werbeeffekts, zur Information potentieller Auftraggeber bezüglich ihrer Fähigkeiten* ...').

'better powder', and 67:11:22 in the 'even stronger' powder. With modern mixtures based on a 75:15:10 ratio,[68] the 'even stronger' mixture comes closest to this. One possible reason for this generally low saltpetre ratio is the higher cost of saltpetre; but this argument is not very convincing as the costs for sulphur would be equally high, because sulphur was the ingredient which most depended on purchase and an existing supply route (sulphur was imported from Italy or Iceland, but its purification process was relatively straightforward). However, if the technique of producing saltpetre had not been developed, it could be explained that with limited saltpetre supplies at least ordinary powders could be produced.

Modern mixtures of 75:15:10 have a substantially higher proportion of saltpetre than most of the recipes provided. Saltpetre, on the other hand, was the core ingredient which was the most complicated to purify and keep, and a mixture of purchase from abroad and local production was most likely. The making of saltpetre was complex. It then required multiple stages of filtration and reduction to produce raw saltpetre which yet needed further purification before use.[69] By the mid-fifteenth century there is ample evidence of saltpetre production, while, by the sixteenth century, it had reached an industrial scale.[70] Burgundian sources in the 1470s rarely mention charcoal in the mixture of gunpowder, but frequently refer to saltpetre and sulphur.[71] The Burgundian troops on campaign in 1475 had a recorded 1,200 handmills amongst their soldiers, as well as one windmill and four people employed as millers.[72] This seems to imply that grinding powder took place at the point of use, and that powder is likely to have been in a different physical state when troops set out.

---

[68] Smith, *Rewriting Gunpowder History*, 62. The first known suggested ratio on record is of 41:29:29, based on Roger Bacon's recipe from between 1248 and 1267 (see DeVries, 'Gunpowder and Early Gunpowder Weapons', 123).

[69] See Smith, *Reports of the HO Group*, Report 2014.

[70] See Partington, *Greek Fire and Gunpowder*, 314–23, Simon Pepper and Nicholas Adams, *Firearms and Fortifications: Military Architecture and Siege Warfare in Sixteenth-Century Siena* (Chicago: University of Chicago Press, 1986), for Tuscany, 8–17, and for England, Richard Winship Stewart, *The English Ordnance Office, 1585–1625* (Woodbridge: Boydell Press, 1996), 80–95.

[71] Smith and DeVries, *Artillery of Burgundy*, 244–48.

[72] Kay Smith (publ. under former name of Robert Douglas Smith), 'Good and Bold: A Late 15th-Century Artillery Train', *Royal Armouries Yearbook* 6 (2001), 88–97, at 103, and Kay Smith (publ. under former name of Robert Douglas Smith) and Kelly DeVries, *Rhodes Besieged* (Stroud: History Press, 2011), 341. The listing of the mills among other arms and armour devices, and not as general supplies, suggests that these mills were less likely to be used for grinding foodstuffs.

It could also be that the mills were used to grind charcoal. Charcoal was widely available and the consistency (and origin) of the charcoal was less important for making a successful powder.[73] Most powder mixtures are relatively light on charcoal. From an economic viewpoint, charcoal would be the most attainable of the three core ingredients for the fifteenth-century practitioner.

Some of the listed recipes (fols 8v and 9r) do not include saltpetre as an ingredient, but when the book later explains about making hundredweights, this calculation only adds up if saltpetre is included (at about three times the sulphur ratio). This is an example where either the author did not see the need to add explicitly something that was seemingly obvious, or where the scribe omitted to mention saltpetre at the earlier stage.

It is no accident that a number of authors who have written about the *Firework Books* were chemists or physicists.[74] This provided detailed knowledge of one aspect of the subject, but working without substantial medievalist historical skills made their work susceptible to criticism for lack of historical thoroughness.[75] As a result their translations and transcriptions increasingly deviate from the original as the text goes on, as they reflect the authors' frustrations at the above-mentioned shortfall of quantifiable, factual information in the recipes. It might be better to view the existing recipes instead as a representation of the knowledge available in the fifteenth century.

On Guns and Techniques, and How to Use Them

This category is strangely unbalanced, providing a relatively small amount of information for what must have been the majority of activities for a master gunner. A total of 30 sections are devoted to this, but half of them concern exceptional circumstances or projectiles (fire balls, flying fire, stakes, keeping fire secret, and seemingly special measures), or how to be particularly 'frightening' (fol. 7v). Comparatively few provide instructions on practical matters, e.g. loading a gun correctly and safely (fols 15v and 32r), making stones and plugs (fols 13r and 15v), the range of guns (fol. 31r), their mounting (fol. 31v), instructions on how to fire accurately (fol. 41r), and from key locations (e.g. gabions or siege towers, fol. 27v). Loading and firing are relatively straightforward processes, and it could be argued that they did not require further explanation.

---

[73] Hall, *Warfare in Renaissance*, 89.

[74] Most notably Gerhard Kramer, James Partington, Ferdinand Nibler, and Wilfried Tittmann.

[75] Tittmann and Nibler on Kramer (Tittmann, 'Ende von Berthold Schwarz', and Tittmann et al., *Salpetergewinnung*).

Gunpowder Technology in the Fifteenth Century

One of the core questions of gunpowder technology concerns the space required in the barrel for the powder to explode effectively.[76] As the first Master Gunner's Question explains, it is the 'vapour that drives the stone out of the gun', but the stone can only be driven if it is enclosed within the barrel, without space for the vapour to escape. On fol. 15v a reference to the importance of the measurement of the inside of the gun has long been interpreted as the proportions of powder, plug, and stone. This section is repeated on fol. 31v, but with different wording. The section is preceded by a very short section on the dimensions of a gun (fol. 31r) – although it is not entirely clear what is gained from this text segment which seems to provide a very different type of information.

There are very few other instructions on how to load or fire a gun under ordinary circumstances. Rather more effort is made to describe how to fire multiple shots (fol. 38r–v), or how to fire when the powder is wet (fol. 38v). All of these examples are rather short, and it could be argued that they were summarizing the daily tasks of a master gunner which would not require specific detail.

The section from fols 25v–27v is uncharacteristically long and describes how to use a gun, setting it apart in the context of the much shorter sections before and after. In some studies of *Firework Books*, this section was referred to as the 'epilogue'.[77] In language and format – with a move away from down-to-earth practical explanations towards the more general attitudes of a master gunner – it is in fact more reminiscent of the *Firework Book*'s preamble.[78] In no *Firework Book* viewed, however, does this section appear at the end, which makes it unlikely ever to have been an 'epilogue'.

The section on emptying a loaded gun (fol. 49v) is potentially helpful (if it works), but it is questionable how often such a high-risk procedure would have been applied. Nevertheless, it may well have been the last option if, for

---

[76] These are usually described as five equal parts, made up of three parts gunpowder, one part free space (to allow the ignited powder vapour to expand), and the fifth part for the wooden plug to make the powder chamber airtight, as described in Leng, *Anleitung Schiesspulver*, 41–44 and 87. The stone would be located outside the chamber. Kramer and Leibnitz provide an alternative interpretation of 'one quarter to one third of the chamber' to be occupied by the powder (Kramer and Leibnitz, *Das Feuerwerkbuch*, 23).

[77] Kramer and Leibnitz, *Das Feuerwerkbuch*, 99, or the 'Einleitung' (Jähns, *Kriegswissenschaften*, 395).

[78] This section repeats the phrase 'prince, earl, lord, knight, squire, or town' from the opening section, in the form of a listing of elements which must have had a recognition factor by a reader or audience.

one reason or another, it was not possible for the gun to be fired to empty its charge.

Fol. 32r has a noteworthy section on how to break a gun. This section is relatively rare among the *Firework Book* manuscripts, and it is not clear to what it may refer.[79] It could be that it was advice for last-resort action when retreating from a battlefield, so that a working gun would not fall into the hands of an opponent. The reverse of this section is picked up in the second part of I.34 where the text provides instructions on how to avoid the gun breaking (fol. 60v).

The aforementioned imbalance of ordinary vs. extraordinary circumstances raises questions on what was perceived to be 'widely known' and what were 'extra beneficial facts'. There are many elements which are not explained in the *Firework Book*, and one may wonder why this is so. For instance, little reference is made to the ways of loading a gun, although the illustration in the Munich Cgm. 600 manuscript implies that guns were placed upright for loading.[80] This way it would be possible to wedge the stone in thoroughly without gravity pulling it sideways. It may be that at the time of the production of the *Firework Book* this knowledge was either outdated or no longer worth mentioning, being too basic to be written down. No details are provided about the size of the gun (shorter or longer barrelled), the size of the powder chamber, or their design.[81]

I.34 also makes little reference to the substantially different ways of using gunpowder artillery as a tactical device: either in a stationary setting in a castle/town for defensive purposes, or on the road for use in battle. While early gunpowder artillery to defend towns and castles goes back to the fourteenth century (with associated records on the production of the cannon, the raw materials, the makers, and the profession), their use in open field warfare came only gradually.[82] A large logistical exercise was required to move and use them, involving many interacting factors. Aside from the weight of the cannons, it

---

[79] Similar sections could only be traced in Darmstadt Ms. 1074, fol. 37v.

[80] See Leng, *Anleitung Schiesspulver*, 86, or Schmidtchen, *Kriegswesen*, 198–99.

[81] This has long been an area for discussion. Generally, it is believed that the barrel of a gun was quite short and that the powder chamber was subdivided into five parts (based on the instructions in Munich Cgm. 600), but that still leaves much scope for interpretation. See Leng, *Anleitung Schiesspulver*, 46–47, and Schmidtchen, *Kriegswesen*, 194–97, or even Hassenstein, *Feuerwerkbuch*, 100, or Kramer and Leibnitz, *Das Feuerwerkbuch*, 23.

[82] There was a clear progression of use of gunpowder artillery in sieges, and with improvements in technology and the increased use of smaller guns, use on the battlefield became more frequent (DeVries and Smith, *Military Technology*, 140–47).

was necessary to know how to keep the powder dry and safe and how to adjust to the environment – landscape, weather, time of day, and season. Further factors included the time available in which to fire, the whereabouts of trained staff, how to avoid accidents, how to persuade 'rulers' to enlist gunpowder artillery troops, and so on. While considerable resources were required, by the mid-fifteenth century the ability to move artillery was deemed to be a necessary component of warfare, but the subject is not mentioned in I.34.[83]

On Auxiliary Incendiary Devices

This category of the *Firework Book* is the smallest (with 11 sections) – at least in Part 1 – and it includes a wide range of incendiary devices, only some of which may be fired from a gun. As they are all related to powder-making skills, they were probably tasks carried out by a master gunner. By far the largest subsection in this category concerns fire arrows (five sections on fols 30r, 41v, 48v, and 49r). The instructions include storage advice which would suggest that the I.34 illustrations (fols 87v and 88r, see Figure 10) of a mass production of fire arrows may be a reflection of actual practice.[84]

Other incendiaries topics include fire balls (fol. 7r), setting fire to a pole (fol. 40v), setting water on fire (fol. 41r), firing a 'glowing ball' (fol. 49v), and making a hardened arrow tip (fol. 50v). While these instructions seem to make sense overall, they all appear to be fairly high-risk. For instance, it is worth questioning why one would need to set a pole on fire. It could be that it was to act as a way marker, but surely this would be an extremely unlikely occurrence. Using quicklime would create a fire effect, but the risk of personal injury would be particularly high. A display or ceremonial use cannot be ruled out, but no record of such an occurrence could be traced. Firing a 'glowing ball' is a section that is not included in most *Firework Books*.[85] It is a particularly hazardous endeavour to fire two balls in one gun, with the second ball heated up to a high temperature which would mean fitting it fairly awkwardly into the gun. The first ball was to serve as a safety device to keep the heated ball away from the powder. It is only in Part 2 of I.34 that other incendiary devices, such as barrels and wheel hubs, are added as potential tools for defence and attack.

---

[83] Smith and DeVries, *Artillery of Burgundy*, 48–54.

[84] Reconstruction experiments by the HO Group have shown that the description of the production of fire arrows can be recreated. Omission of any of the suggested stages was likely to result in unsuccessful firing (see Smith, *Reports of the HO Group*, Report 2009).

[85] This section can be found in Darmstadt Ms. 1074, fol. 51r, and Dillingen Ms. XV 50, fol. 32r, but not in Freiburg Ms. 362 and others.

The section on hardening an iron arrowhead to make it into a 'house arrow' (fol. 50v) occupies a special position within the *Firework Book* tradition. It appears at the end of the majority of *Firework Books*, and all manuscripts which are not perceived to be fragmented or incomplete seem to refer to this. Comparing this section in different copies of the *Firework Book* shows a closer match in the text used, word by word, word order, and seemingly fewer mistakes made.[86] This would be likely if this section indeed was the known, formal last part of a *Firework Book*. Any scribe would pay particular attention to keeping the text to the wording known to a potential reader. The 'house arrow' section seems, however, to be at odds in content and style with the rest of the *Firework Book*. It is not clear what a house arrow might have been.

Concepts

Throughout the *Firework Book*, there are a number of concepts and deeper ideas present. The term '*kunst*' is used frequently (14 times as a noun, and twice as the adjective '*kunstlich*'); the literal translation of '*kunst*' is 'art'. Just as the English term 'art' developed in the late Middle Ages to mean 'skills in doing something, esp. as a result of knowledge or practice', 'technical skill', 'practical application', or 'trade', the same applied to the German term.[87] At times it is referred to as '*besunder kunst*' ('a special art'). The term '*Lere*' is used in the same context – it is some form of 'instruction' or 'recipe', but its literal translation would be 'teaching'.

For a twenty-first-century reader, a longstanding rivalry and distinction exists between '*ars*' and '*scientia*', which is typically translated into 'art' vs. 'knowledge'. The Latin term '*ars*' is applied to all things created, fashioned, or made by a human hand to distinguish them from all things in 'nature'. This embraces the production of everyday items such as metal, wood, and wicker-ware, to more substantial productions such as the construction of cathedrals. The distinction between 'knowledge' and 'art' was already fully developed by the thirteenth century.[88] The Latin term *scientia* referred broadly to the accumulated written knowledge and theory associated with a particular subject

---

[86] See Dresden Ms. App. 463, fol. 71v, Dillingen Ms. XV 50, fol. 32v, Darmstadt Ms. 1074, fols 54r and 54v, Göttingen 2° Cod. Ms. philos. 64, fols 146r and 146v, Heidelberg Cod. Pal. germ. 122, fols 45v and 46r, Munich Clm. 30150, fol. 149r, as well as the prints by Stainer (Stainer 1529, 36) and Egenolph (Egenolph 1529, 44).

[87] *Oxford English Dictionary Online*, definitions 1–3 (accessed 10 August 2023).

[88] One of the earliest examples in technical writings are the 'sketchbooks' of Villard de Honnecourt, produced around 1235. They combine the technological advances with function (what it is for) and design (what is achievable). See Popplow, 'Militärtechnische Bildkataloge des Spätmittelalters', 254–58.

Fig. 10. Royal Armouries, I.34, fols 87v (above) and 88r (opposite) (pictures provided by Royal Armouries).

lxxxviij

Gunpowder Technology in the Fifteenth Century

area. A proper *scientia* was required for planning and constructing cathedral vaults with appropriate buttressing. For the thirteenth-century architect Jean Mignot, this knowledge (*scientia*) also included his favoured geometric and theological schemes. Apparently his French perspectives did not coincide with Italian regional preferences of the time, and controversies arose. Theory and practice could not be separated in Mignot's mind. Similarly, Aquinas refers to theology as *scientia*.[89] For medieval scholastics, the practice of an art (*ars*) without proper knowledge (*scientia*) would accomplish 'nothing'; the two were inseparable and one without the other would be *nihil*. Thus, the practice of 'art without knowledge is nothing' ('*ars sine scientia nihil est*').[90] A fifteenth-century author, editor, copyist, or reader of a text such as the *Firework Book* is likely to have been exposed to some levels of this dichotomy, but only to a limited extent. The structure of the 12 questions, their scholastic format and tone, as well as the ability to read and write and to know the occasional Latin term, suggests some kind of grammar school education. However, it would be impossible to distinguish the different levels of education between these groups of readers or users.[91]

Building on the theme of '*scientia*', more populist modern publications view gunpowder as part of science, positioning it within the fields of early chemistry or alchemy, but often with little critical analysis.[92] Alchemy emerged in Western Europe via China and the Islamic world as a 'branch of knowledge',

[89] Geoffrey Turner, 'St Thomas Aquinas on the "Scientific" Nature of Theology', *New Blackfriars* 78 (1997), no. 921, 464–76, at 469.

[90] This quote is widely attributed to Mignot; see, for example, Otto G. von Simson, 'The Gothic Cathedral: Design and Meaning', in *Change in Medieval Society: Europe North of the Alps, 1050–1500*, ed. Sylvia L. Thrupp (Toronto: University of Toronto Press in association with the Medieval Academy, 1988), 168–87, 174. The connection between scholarly tradition and practical application can reach into all areas of technology. See, for example, Steven A. Walton and Thomas E. Boothby, 'What is Straight Cannot Fall: Medieval Architectural Statics in Theory and Practice', *History of Science*, 52:4 (2014), 347–76, for the link of scholarly tradition and architectural developments.

[91] See David Sheffler, *Schools and Schooling in Late Medieval Germany: Regensburg 1250–1500*, Education and Society in the Middle Ages and Renaissance 33 (Leiden: Brill, 2008), 17–84, about levels of education, scholarly activities, and their impact on fifteenth-century society in South-Western Germany.

[92] See, for example, Jack Kelly, *Gunpowder: A History of the Explosive that Changed the World* (London: Atlantic, 2004), 109–11, Wayne D. Cocroft, *Dangerous Energy: The Archaeology of Gunpowder and Military Explosives Manufacture* (Swindon: English Heritage, 2000), 4–5, Alfred W. Crosby, *Throwing Fire: Projectile Technology through History* (Cambridge: Cambridge University Press, 2002), 96, or Werrett, *Fireworks*, 23–41.

Analysis of the Text

initially focusing on the 'possibility of changing one metal into another' while always having some more practical application such as in medicine. It quickly developed into an intellectual discipline with its own 'specialized vocabulary, symbols and images which often render alchemical texts more or less impenetrable'.[93] Peter Maxwell-Stuart qualifies this by commenting that its 'obfuscating rhetoric' was introduced for the reason 'that alchemy was too dangerous a science to be put into the hands of the ignorant or half-trained, and so constructing a kind of jargon would effectively confine its practice to those worthy and intelligent enough to use it for proper ends'.[94] Amongst those considered 'worthy and intelligent enough' were the friars. The thirteenth-century Franciscan friar and scholar Roger Bacon, in his *Opus Majus* of 1267, was the first to mention having witnessed gunpowder explosions without mentioning gunpowder directly. It could be argued that the reference to Niger Bertholdus (fol. 20r), a 'necromancer and alchemist', who is credited with having discovered gunpowder, could be seen as a direct continuation from Roger Bacon. It could even be argued that this is why Niger Bertholdus is often assumed to have been a Franciscan.[95]

That said, the *Firework Books* and their use of chemical processes and interactions are otherwise distinctly different from the alchemical tradition. While gunpowder technology is understood to have travelled via similar geographical regions, it retained a relatively straightforward language, even if some parts of it are difficult to understand as a result of a loss of practical knowledge for a non-expert. This greater accessibility can also be seen in publications of alchemical texts being increasingly produced in vernacular languages in the early decades of the fifteenth century.[96]

---

[93] Maxwell-Stuart, *A History of Alchemy*, x.

[94] Maxwell-Stuart, *A History of Alchemy*, 73.

[95] For example, there is a statue of Bertholdus in front of Freiburg Town Hall presenting him as a Franciscan.

[96] Maxwell-Stuart, *A History of Alchemy*, 80. In the fifteenth century an increasing number of vernacular writings appeared across a wide spectrum of genres, many of them of a practical nature, from medicine, surgery, cookery, and dyeing, as well as alchemy. For discussions on vernacularization, see Pereira, 'Alchemy and the Use of Vernacular', or Carmel Ferragud, 'Vernacularization as an Intellectual and Social Bridge: The Catalan Translations of Teodorico's *Chirurgia* and of Arnau De Vilanova's *Regimen Sanitatis Salerni*, *Early Science and Medicine* 4:2 (1999), 127–48. Pereira argues that the development of 'instructive prose' ('*Lehrdichtung*') did not emerge earlier in Germany than elsewhere, but provides little evidence for this (Pereira, 'Alchemy and the Use of Vernacular', 347).

While there are clear connections with the areas of interest of alchemy, gunpowder technology seems to fall into a somewhat different category.[97] *Firework Books* focus on how matters work, and to what effect, without any apparent intention of seeking reasons why, or any explanation for their working. This might explain why such works as the *Firework Book* were written in the vernacular and not in Latin. In contrast to the vernacularization debate where Latin texts were translated into the vernacular to act as an 'intellectual and social bridge' to a wider public, the *Firework Book* seems to have originated in German without a Latin predecessor, nor was it ever translated into Latin.[98] It bypassed what was seen to be the language of learning and thus of large segments of technological writing.

In the *Firework Books* only a very small number of incidences occur where the author uses Latin terms instead of German ones. When he does use Latin he provides both the Latin and the German (with the exception of some of the special ingredients). A good example of this is the '*exemplum*' (fol. 2v), a device used in a sermon as an illustrative point, but it is unclear whether it was meant to be a scientific term or a 'term of art'. It is used in this context as a label to mark its special function within the German narrative text.[99] Otherwise, the text is very careful to use non-technical terms in all instructions. Even if Latin terms are used, they are explained and translated, meaning that '*exemplum*' is followed by a translation in German – '*ein peispil*'. The same applies in the first of two listings of '*in quartu gradu*', where the author immediately follows the Latin term with a translation into German 'which is called the fourth' (fol. 23v). In one case, the text lists '*benefencio*' (fol. 38v) which is most likely a misspelling of '*beneficio*', and a possible indicator of some knowledge of foreign language terms, but lacking the certainty of how to spell it. In another case, the author uses the Latin term to explain the origin of saltpetre when stating that saltpetre is 'called in Latin "rock salt"' (fol. 23v), without, however, providing any further explanation.

Very occasional references are made to theoretical models which were under discussion at the time. The second Master Gunner's Question relates to a 'system of qualities' or 'humouralism', established by Greek, Roman, and Islamic physicians to describe a balanced body, and widely known and used

---

[97] The fact that one *Firework Book* copy, nowadays Kassel 4º Ms. Math. 14, is attributed to Albertus Magnus instead of the more mysterious figure of Niger Bertholdus provides a good example of a possible conflation of alchemy and gunpowder technology in the fifteenth century.

[98] Ferragud, 'Vernacularization as an Intellectual and Social Bridge', 140.

[99] Nibler, *Feuerwerkbuch*, 49.

in the fifteenth century.[100] It refers to sulphur being 'hot' and saltpetre being 'cold', and the consequent need to balance 'two opposing parts which do not [normally] tolerate each other' (fol. 2v). This reference is repeated later in the *Firework Book* in a section where saltpetre is described as being 'by nature cold and dry', while sulphur is described as 'by nature hot and dry', which the author goes on to say 'easily catches fire' (fol. 23v). This is a clear reference to the humoural theories known at the time, and the understanding of the interrelation of the principles of qualities of substances.

Royal Armouries I.34 Part 2

The second part of I.34 includes a total of 14 separate sections, from making incendiary devices with barrels and wheel hubs, smoking-out devices, and fire balls, to extreme fire and other instructions. Compared to Part 1, this section moves away from firing cannons to focus on other things that catch fire, with a far greater emphasis on incendiary devices and how to prepare them. The skills and experience required, however, stay the same, and build on the elements on auxiliary incendiary devices in Part 1. There is a different emphasis in the text and in the information offered, providing individual recipes in larger segments of text without even an attempt to link the individual sections. Gunpowder and incendiary devices are used to make fire barrels, fire balls, and other devices which can be projected at the enemy. It is not, however, explained how these incendiary devices might reach the enemy.

Unusually for most *Firework Books*, Part 2 of I.34 makes numerous references to illustrations located at the end of the manuscript. In contrast to Strasbourg Ms. 2259, the sheet references in I.34 are written in the same colour ink and apparently at the same time as the other text – seemingly with little or no hesitation by the scribe or copyist as to whether they refer to an actual page.[101] However, in I.34 all references to page numbers seem to have been added after the original text in brown/black was produced. The numbers added are always in a different size from the surrounding text. The only explanation is that the numbers were added after the illustrations were made, but within a brief timeframe shortly after the production of the text. On three occasions (fols 52v, 54r, and 56r), the number added is too large for the space

---

[100] Sara M. Butler, *Forensic Medicine and Death Investigation in Medieval England* (New York: Routledge, 2014), 224–27.

[101] The relationship of the Strasbourg manuscript to I.34 is discussed in Chapter 3 under 'Content and Illustrations', where the sheet reference numbers are the same as I.34, but lack the images.

Fig. 11. Royal Armouries, I.34, fol. 89r (above) – possible depiction of mass manufacturing of wheel hub incendiaries – top right, and fol. 88v (opposite) – possible mass production of fire arrows (pictures provided by Royal Armouries).

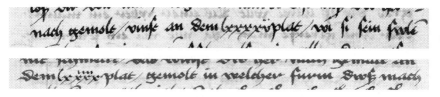

Fig. 12. Royal Armouries, I.34, fols 52v (top) and 57r (bottom) (pictures provided by Royal Armouries).

provided and touches or overwrites the existing text (see Figure 12, left). More frequently, the number is smaller than the space available (fols 53r, 54r, 55v, 57r, 57v, and 60r) (see Figure 12 right), and on one occasion (fol. 53v) the page number is missing; most likely the author forgot to add the page number, or the illustration page had not (or not yet) been added to the illustrations. This provides some indication about the production of the I.34 manuscript as a copy produced in stages, by multiple authors, copyists, or scribes, and not the product of a single author.

The detailed use of scales is another important point to highlight in I.34 Part 2. The text pays great attention to scales and their correct use, always making sure to remind the user to take items off the scales after weighing (fols 52r, 53r, 54v, 56r, 57v, 58v, and 59r – this section is only once mirrored in Part 1, on fol. 14r). There are a number of possible explanations: either the user (the author or the reader) was not very accustomed to balancing scales, or the text expresses the need to remind the reader about this. It also highlights the need for accuracy with precious and dangerous materials, at the same time with the implication that any user of the text was less likely to be a skilled artisan and trader who would have been experienced in the use of scales.

As previously indicated, along with the spread and development of gunpowder technology during the fifteenth century, the role and position of gunner became increasingly specialized. Instead of making guns himself, most of the elements were commissioned to be produced by specialist craftsmen. This is reflected in the language used by the author of I.34 Part 2, who was clearly further removed from the production stage. In contrast to Part 1, here the author more frequently refers to 'have made for yourself' (fols 53v, 54r, 55v, 57v, or 59v – a rather odd phrase in the original, indicating a special emphasis) or 'have made' (fols 52r, 52v, 53r, 54r, 54v, 56r, or 59v), implying that he neither has the time/leisure, nor the knowledge, to make specific equipment, and/or is financially affluent enough in an environment where he has sufficient tradesmen around him to commission items to be made. This relates specifically to components in iron and wood. The language makes the author appear much

Analysis of the Text

more a figure of authority who orders things to be done, rather than doing them himself.

The subsequent sections on fire arrows are very different in content and in style and are much more instructional. While they act as a stage-by-stage guide to follow in order to make fire arrows, the sections themselves get shorter as the explanations proceed, leaving some gaps in the production stages. This section builds on the instructions in I.34 Part 1, but more emphasis is placed on the practical use of fire arrows, how to produce them so that they have different properties, and how to mark them accordingly through colour. The section on colouring arrows in white, red, blue, brown, and black (fol. 59r) can be explained by subsequent use in combat so that the arrows can be distinguished, as they have different uses in a combat situation. The author refers to this by stating 'so that you can remember them' (fol. 59v). Parallels can be drawn to I.34 Part 1 where powder was mixed in different colours (fols 29v–30v). There the author fails to explain why the powder needs to be applied in different colours (or even how). Here the instructions relate to painting the outside of the fire arrow bag (made out of fustian wool). The instruction is entirely plausible and would be a sensible instruction for later use of the arrows. This could also be the case for the coloured powder mentioned in Part 1, but only if charcoal was left out of the mixture.

The section on how to harden a fire arrow with water (fol. 59v) states that in order to make good fire arrows they should be made to burn slowly or have delayed ignition (i.e. igniting only when they hit their target after flying).[102] This implies that soaking the arrow in water does benefit the result. However, if an arrow was not given sufficient time to dry it would make the arrow and its charge too wet, which in turn would mean that it would not burn and explode at all. Soaking it too little might mean an explosion in flight, or a less effective result on impact. The wetting process shows close similarities to the production of *Knollenpulver*, but omits the essential drying stage (without which *Knollenpulver* would not work).

On fol. 60r, I.34 focuses on '*olium petroleum*' – used here as a generic term for all sorts of hydrocarbon products, often used for Greek fire but also for

---

[102] Described in more detail in Blosen and Olsen, *Bengedans*, xxx. It has been suggested that the key to a successful fire arrow was to treat the powder and the arrow after mixing it, as firing the arrow without soaking it meant that it would most likely explode before hitting the intended target. While the HO Group carried out some experiments with fire arrows, more experiments in reconstructing fire arrows would be desirable. See Smith, *Reports of the HO Group*, especially the report of experiments in 2009.

other forms of burning oils.[103] This recipe is hard to follow: either the author omitted some essential stages, or he himself did not understand how to make it. This could imply that this recipe was passed on to the author from elsewhere, without a practical testing of its validity. Reassuringly, at the end of this passage, the author confirms that this would be the 'best oil' for all types of fire. This statement gives the reason for including this segment in the text, but also reassures a potential reader that they may be in possession of the recipe for the 'best oil', even if they were not yet able to follow it. This provides some explanation of the use and function of these texts. It places the likely user as someone not (yet) skilled in the various aspects of incendiary devices, but potentially not at the absolute beginner stage.

The section on cooling a gun (fol. 60v) raises a number of questions. While a gun warms up a little when firing, it cools down very quickly to a point when it would be safe to reload it. Hand guns may get hotter and be more likely to warm up, but not to such high temperatures as implied by the need for cooling.[104] It is also worth mentioning that heat on its own does not ignite powder; a spark is required. Hence guns were always swabbed after each shot to ensure that no embers remained. So why is this section included in a *Firework Book*? One theory may be that this is an indication of the background and interests of the author or the reader or the recipient of this section. Any experienced gunner must have known that the overheating of a gun would be extremely unlikely, but not so anyone with less front-line experience. It is conceivable that a medieval master gunner might well have worried that his gun might overheat, break, or fail with increased temperature, and this text section would act as reassurance. Equally, a less well-trained reader/recipient of the text (of whatever social status) might perceive that there could be a risk of overheating, and would feel reassured to find an instruction on how to prevent this.

In Part 2, ingredients are mentioned which do not occur in Part 1, such as 'saltpetre salt' (fols 52r, 54v, 56r, 57v, and 59r) and 'ground-up rotten beech wood' (fols 52r, 53r, 54r, 54v, 55r, 57r, 57v, 58v, and 59r). Similarly, others are more clearly defined in Part 2, such as the use of 'lime wood charcoal' (fols 57v,

---

[103] For a summary on the development of Greek fire, see Partington, *Greek Fire and Gunpowder*, especially chapter 1.

[104] There are sixteenth- and seventeenth-century references to a gun overheating, but it would not have been possible to reload a gun in time. It was only by the nineteenth century that repeat fire in machine guns required cooling down with water. Recent test firings of a seventeenth-century gun, led by Fred Hocker at the Vasa Museum, Stockholm, were intending to include the measurement of the temperature of the gun, but the results have not yet been published. This 'myth' of a gun overheating continues to be repeated (e.g. Andrade, *The Gunpowder Age*, 106).

58v, 59r, 59v) instead of merely 'charcoal'. The benefits of using lime charcoal had been described already in Part 1 (fol. 8v), but that information was not repeated when charcoal was mentioned in subsequent sections. This suggests two possible explanations: a) gunpowder artillery had progressed by the time of the creation of Part 2; or b) the eagerness of an individual to experiment with the potential improvement of gunpowder to make up supply shortages of ingredients or to improve effectiveness. He would not necessarily have possessed the technology to work out whether it improved or worsened the mixture, but was nevertheless keen to write his 'discoveries' down. The latter seems more likely – as indicated by the individual's unfamiliarity with basic tasks such as the very detailed instructions on how to use scales.

Features Common to Both Parts

Both Parts 1 and 2 have a number of references to fish, which is common to all other *Firework Books*. In Part 1, the references to fish are used as a measure for timekeeping: on fols 5r and 18r 'poaching fish', and on fols 22v and 37v to 'boil fish'. In Part 2, the references on fols 58v and 59r refer to the making of 'fish powder'. This suggests practical knowledge of the maker on cooking or processing fish, and it provides a clear positioning of the author of these *Firework Books* in a social stratum.

The interpretation that *Firework Books* were part of a culture of secret knowledge and only kept within closed societies has been raised on numerous occasions. There is, however, little evidence to sustain this claim. Throughout I.34, only four references mention the 'secrecy' contained in the *Firework Book*, with the associated request to keep the 'art secret so that you do not teach what is not meant for everyone' (fol. 59v). This section comes at the end of instructions on how to harden iron arrowheads, which is also the last section in Part 1 (fol. 50v). This is a small number of references in the light of the widely held assumption that secrecy surrounded gunpowder artillery. The other three sections occur in Part 1 where the secrecy refers to ways in which to keep any fire hidden (fol. 34v) for covert operations, to be ignited after numerous days (this is mirrored in a slightly different fashion on fols 57r and 58r). No further explanation is given as to why it would not be for everyone. Is it too dangerous? Is it for economic reasons?

There has been a long tradition of secret text and secret writings, most famously the pseudo-Aristotelian *Secretum Secretorum* (*Sirr al-asrar*) which emerged in the ninth century, dealing with a range of questions for rulers on

'Science of Government, on the Good Ordering of Statecraft'.[105] The *Secretum Secretorum* is not to be confused with the *Book of Secrets (Liber Secretorum)* by Muhammed ibn Zakariya al-Razi, which focuses on alchemy, providing recipes and descriptions of technical equipment and procedures. All these compilations or instructional manuals were highly influential and widely known to be a crucial part of the well-stocked library of a ruler in the High and Later Middle Ages. Within the wider field of dissemination of knowledge, there has long been a prevailing assumption of intended secrecy, of keeping the information within a controlled group, as passing this knowledge on to a broader audience would risk its misuse. William Eamon writes in detail about the various aspects of this during the fifteenth century and especially in Germany. The secrets of the *Firework Book* would fall mostly into Eamon's first definition in his 'taxonomy of secrets' as the 'social secret', 'involving the intentional suppression of information in order to protect knowledge from outsiders who might corrupt or abuse it'.[106]

I.34 Part 1 only refers to secrecy in the section on hidden fire.[107] Some of the recipes (e.g. fol. 11r) are incomplete and cannot fully be recreated. This could result either from a scribal error or from the fact that the author felt that he was not required to state what may be obvious to a contemporary reader. On the other hand, it could be that he deliberately wanted to withhold information, but that seems rather unlikely at this point. I.24 Part 2 more explicitly refers to keeping this 'art' secret so that you do not teach what is not meant

---

[105] Regula Forster, *Die Geheimnisse der Geheimnisse: die arabischen und deutschen Fassungen des pseudo-aristotelischen Sirr al-asrar / Secretum Secretorum* (Wiesbaden: Reichert, 2006), 3.

[106] William Eamon, *Science and the Secrets of Nature* (Princeton: Princeton University Press, 1994), 11. See also Pereira, 'Alchemy and the Use of Vernacular', and more recently Sylvie Neven, 'Recording and Reading Alchemy and Art-Technology in Medieval and Premodern German Recipe Collections', *Nuncius: Journal for the Material and Visual History of Early Modern Science* 31:1 (2016), 32–49. Rainer Leng dispels some of the issues of secrecy of the master gunner's knowledge which – to him – refer less to role-specific technical knowledge, but rather to military secrets related to the strength and weaknesses of one's own forces (Leng, '*getruwelich dienen*', 315–16). There has also been some speculation that there were missing or deliberately misleading components in the recipes. Some *Firework Books* make a reference to the use of quicklime, which has been argued may render some recipes unusable. More detailed research would be beneficial in this area, as the experiments carried out so far have been on a rather small scale and seem only to provide anecdotal insights. See, for example, Kramer and Leibnitz, *Das Feuerwerkbuch*, 72, Smith, *Reports of the HO Group*, especially from 2004 and 2005, and Smith, 'Gunpowder Chemistry', 151.

[107] Fols 34v and 35r.

for everyone and 'if you want to make the "courtly art" of a secret fire[*work*] that is called "secret"'.[108] However, 'secret' here refers to 'something unknown', without the intent to keep it unknown. The *Oxford English Dictionary Online* definitions seem to suggest that the intent ('the aim of keeping something a secret') became more dominant from the nineteenth century onwards.[109] Even earlier, John Wecker in his *Eighteen Books of the Secrets of Art and Nature*, published in 1660, gave rise to the concept of nature hiding its knowledge from individuals. If it really was intended to keep the knowledge in the *Firework Book* 'secret', other measures would have been put in place to ensure that it was kept unknown.[110]

In line with the reference to secrecy, and any possible appeal to a more scholarly audience of readers, and in common with the beginning of Part 1 of I.34, the Part 2 refers at various stages (in eight out of the 12 section headings) to the 'courtly art'. This term combines two complex issues: both the terms 'courtly' and its German original 'hoflich' have modern connotations of chivalry, gentlemanliness, and high status. 'Courtly' in the context of the *Firework Book* refers to items which could be expected to be known, or appreciated, at any of the courts stated in the preamble, whether that of 'any prince, earl, lord, knight, squire, or town'. This could be seen as a term of admiration, almost as an elevation of its seemingly mundane nature to something very special and noteworthy; at the same time, it indicates an aspirational and advertising aspect – capable of attracting any new reader/practitioner who, by reading this text, might have aspired to be present at court to follow these instructions. This would also explain the increased use of 'courtly' in Part 2 (eight times) in comparison with Part 1 (four times). This repeated use of 'courtly' emphasizes the target audience of the *Firework Book*.

Very few actual scribal omissions occur – where the text copied from one copy to another misses out a single letter, word, or line of text – but there are other areas where some core key ingredients (such as saltpetre in gunpowder on fols 8v and 9r, or charcoal on fol. 52r) are missing. It could be argued that the item was too obvious to be listed, but it could also provide an indication of how the text was produced. It is clear that some texts had been produced from a copy of another *Firework Book* – hence the copying of the same amounts of currency even when they were written much later. Other manuscripts may

---

[108] Fols 57r and 59v.

[109] *Oxford English Dictionary Online*, definition 1 (accessed 10 August 2023).

[110] John Wecker, *Eighteen Books of the Secrets of Art & Nature, being the Sum and Substance of Natural Philosophy* (London: Simon Miller, 1660).

have been based on knowledge recall of other manuscripts, or on dictation.[111] Signs of oral transmission include the fact that many *Firework Books* contain several of the same paragraphs but in a different order, indicating that the text was written down from memory and then dictated to a scribe. This is reinforced by the reference 'as you will hear' on fols 54r and 19v. These are stated at a common location, just after the header or at the end of a section, but in all other cases the phrase used is 'written below' (e.g. fols 5r or 9r, 60r, or 60v). It is likely that either the writer or the person dictating had the basic technical knowledge for most of the recipes. It is less likely that they knew where saltpetre came from, although they knew how to purify saltpetre and sulphur, how to put recipes together, and how to operate a gun. Furthermore, they possessed the knowledge and experience of how to make incendiary devices, and understood each individual step. The rhetorical forms of question and answer do imply that the *Firework Book* was produced to inform a pupil or a new audience, but only by conveying basic, standard information without passing on additional 'tricks of the trade' learned by a master gunner with many years of active service. That is also why the language of the text is German, and very few technical terms, whether in Latin or any other language, are used. It is most likely to have been meant as an introductory piece of information upon which someone could build a future career.

Was there a distinctive change in the fifteenth century that brought about the emergence of the *Firework Book* (alongside other writings in vernacular German, often of a technical nature)? What they do provide is an insight into the level of the knowledge of the author (or originator) of a *Firework Book*, the state of the raw materials available, and a glimpse into the role of a master gunner – for instance, the inclusion of fire arrows and incendiary devices. This knowledge seems to have been expanded in Part 2, but it is not clear whether this indicates a change of practice or simply the filling of a perceived gap in what was present in Part 1. Missing from the *Firework Books* – except in the illustrations in I.34 – are any instructions on the use of guns in battle, on strategy, or even how to mount them. They fail to explain whether a master gunner was involved (and at what level) in battle. They do, however, provide an indication of the transition towards further specialization, removing the master gunner from mundane physical tasks into the role of the person 'in charge'.

---

[111] See also Chapter 1 under '*Urtext*, Production and Transmission'.

Conclusion

The *Firework Book*, and in particular Royal Armouries manuscript I.34, provides a unique insight into fifteenth-century gunpowder technology. Among the written manuals available, it emerges at a pivotal point in the first decades of the fifteenth century. While, by the end of the fifteenth century, gunpowder technology had become omnipresent in society, the speed and format of the dissemination of the technology are not very clear. There are still many questions and enigmas arising from a lack of research findings in gunpowder technology. This book has added a valuable piece to the much bigger jigsaw.

Firework Books were produced within a short period of time by different scribes in the early part of the fifteenth century; their texts provided a comprehensive range of instructions which practitioners of gunpowder technology could follow step by step. While we cannot explain the purpose of the *Firework Book* with much certainty, this study and analysis point towards likely answers to the questions with which we began – who made the book, for what audience, who kept it, and what happened to the manuscripts after they were written.

Based on all the evidence presented we can be certain that the *Firework Book* is likely to have been written two or three generations after gunpowder technology had spread across Europe. It was felt by the author or authors to be a necessary tool to pass on to a new generation of gunners, and to showcase to any potential employers that the owner of a *Firework Book* knew about the basics of gunpowder technology, and how to handle it safely and effectively. This reinforces the theory of several types of users/readers, as summarized by Pamela Long:

> The *Feuerwerkbuch* [...] addresses a double readership – gunners and the princes and nobles who supported them. The author offers advice concerning how members of each group should comport themselves to their mutual advantage. Undoubtedly this anonymous author was himself a gunner seeking patronage. He offered a written text that could enhance an image of learning and technical competence of gunner and patron alike.[1]

---

[1] Pamela O. Long, *Openness, Secrecy, Authorship: Technical Arts and the Culture of Knowledge from Antiquity to the Renaissance* (Baltimore: Johns Hopkins University Press, 2001), 120.

Royal Armouries I.34 turns out to be a truly exceptional manuscript. It is a rare example of a copy which was seemingly not taken apart in the post-medieval period, and thus provides us with a glimpse of the use of the *Firework Book* in its originally bound format: as a compendium, and as a notebook to be added to. By examining the manuscript content and its recipes, this study locates the Firework Book within an emerging tradition of technical military treatises and manuals. My viewing of almost all of the surviving 65 *Firework Book* manuscripts reveals that few of them applied a similar comprehensive range of information, as most of them have been rebound with other texts.

I.34 is unique in that it gives us several sections of a manuscript. The presence of Part 2 particularly shows that there was continued usage and continued practice, and a development of the technology in use in the fifteenth century. I.34 is the only copy where there are textual references to the illustrations, along with the illustrations themselves – a circumstance which will almost certainly have aided the survival of this manuscript.

This study points the way to future research needed in this field. Linguistic analysis may allow for a closer localization of each of the existing *Firework Books*, and a more interdisciplinary comparison of all extant copies of the *Firework Book* may still provide more valuable insights, in comparing not just their content but also their codicological and library histories. This would be an ideal project for an international research group.

It would be beneficial to explore the corpus of material in much more detail, using in particular Royal Armouries I.34. A detailed art historical analysis of the manuscript images would be desirable in reference to clothing, tools, body language, knowledge transfer of critically important information – especially as we are dealing with ephemeral artefacts largely made of wood and cloth, which have not survived throughout the centuries. Similarly, comparative works on other aspects of documented knowledge in material culture may shed a further light.[2]

Experimental archaeology may explore whether the diverse recipes work, whether the addition of 'bonus' ingredients effected a change in the powder and its properties. The on-going work by the HO Group – and more recently the US Military Academy at West Point – have provided a good foundation to build on, and more remains to be discovered with full application and use of contemporary scientific skills and equipment. Equally, the world of economic records has barely been touched. The works of Thom Richardson on the Tower of London and Dan Spencer in a wider English context provide hints on

---

[2] Ongoing projects such as the 'Material Culture in Medieval Towns' Project at the Universität Bern show great promise to provide valuable insights in the interaction of the key brokers of material culture, and the transfer of technical knowledge.

Conclusion

records of saltpetre, sulphur, and other ingredient purchases in the fourteenth and fifteenth centuries, and more work on these and other related economic records may provide further insights, along with a thorough investigation of German archival records.

It only now starts to become more clear about who was using gunpowder technology and whether anyone in power could afford not to have it. While it remains debatable as to what extent gunpowder artillery and the knowledge of using it gave a defensive or offensive advantage, gunpowder technology was employed at large expense – following the words of warning in the *Firework Book* that any ruler worth their salt has to make sure they have 'good master gunners and gunners on whom they can depend', so as to avoid losing any potential advantage enjoyed by an enemy.[3]

All recipes for any purpose contain a large amount of tacit knowledge on how you produce an end result. It is important how you apply these recipes – whether for glass making, armoury, cooking, or of course fighting manuals. They are mostly written in vernacular languages, with the inclusion of a wide spectrum of society, including hidden people ('Have yourself made ...') who make the everyday items – so common at the time that their format and use is not described in more detail – used in the production of gunpowder.[4] Historian of Science Steven Shapin describes them as 'invisible actors' who deserve further research.[5]

What is the reason for many of the sources to emerge in this particular geographic region of what is now south-east Germany in such a high number? It may have been a reflection of the booming industrialization of Augsburg and Nuremberg and their hinterlands, connected to trans-alpine trade, as well as other key river trade routes along the rivers Rhine, Danube, and Main. Perhaps it was more a reaction to new political independence, and resulting further vulnerability with the urgency to defend against external pressures. This is similar to the reasons put forward for the economic and political precociousness of Northern Italy from the twelfth century. It is hoped that this book will open up further discussion on all these issues.

The *Firework Book* showcases knowledge available and of interest at the time. As we have seen, it contains recipes which worked and had a function (not the antiquated and non-practical knowledge as suggested by some scholars). It offers pathways to emerging questions related to the imaginative and

---

[3] Fol. 1v.

[4] Fol. 8r, and much more prominently in Part 2 on fols 52r, 54r, 55v, 57v, 58v, 59r, 59v.

[5] Steven Shapin, 'The House of Experiment in Seventeenth-Century England', *Isis* 79 (1988), 373–404, at 395.

emotive aspect of gunpowder (brighter, louder, further-firing) and the marketing aspects of gunnery and their practitioners.

Most importantly, given the nature of earlier doubts and questions, it is now clear that the *Firework Book* does reflect practice in operation at the time of its production in the early fifteenth century, but also that there remains a gap between textuality and other sources available from the time. This is both a knowledge gap on the part of the modern scholar (whether as historian or technology expert) and a gap of knowledge for gunners at the time, who were confronted by the difficulty of explaining their developing production methods in the context of a previously unfamiliar format of a text.

The question still remains as to how effective this technology was – did it really have a substantial impact in changing fortunes in battle, which justified the expense and effort to bring artillery to the battlefield, train the troops, and purchase and produce the ingredients? If it was not particularly effective, this then leads to the question of why there was such an exponential increase in use and investment in this technology, as evidenced by accounts, trade records, archaeology, or texts such as the *Firework Book*. It is hoped that this book has provided some valuable insights into the types and usages of gunpowder technology at the time and will encourage others to undertake further research in the future.

In the Introduction I referred to the concept of a Military Revolution. I have shown in this volume that the change was not quite as sudden and imminent as the term 'revolution' implies. Hence, it would be more opportune to use what Tonio Andrade described as the 'age of gunpowder' or James Belich called a 'gunpowder transition'.[6] However, there is no doubt that the *Firework Book* played an integral part in the change of gunpowder technology, and thus to warfare and society at large.

---

[6] Andrade, *The Gunpowder Age*, and James Belich, *The World the Plague Made: The Black Death and the Rise of Europe* (Princeton: Princeton University Press, 2022), 132–36.

Bibliography

List of known manuscript copies of the *Firework Book*

Austria, Vienna (Wien), Österreichische Nationalbibliothek
    Cod. 2952, 31v–80r
    Cod. 2987
    Cod. 3062, 1r–22r
    Cod 3064, 53r–70r
    Cod. 10855, 56r–69r
    Cod. 10940, 115r–148v
France, Paris, Bibliothèque nationale de France, Ms. Latin 17873, 193r–209r
France, Strasbourg, Bibliothèque nationale et universitaire, Ms. 2259, 1r–18v, 28r–29v
Germany, Augsburg
    Staats- und Stadtbibliothek, 2° Cod. 164, 1r–62v
    Staats- und Stadtbibliothek, 4° Cod. 129, 35r–99v
    Staats- und Stadtbibliothek, 4° Cod. 143, 1r–43v
    Universitätsbibliothek, III. 1.2° 44, 2r–52v
    Universitätsbibliothek, III. 1.8° 59, 2r–35r
Germany, Bad Arolsen, Fürstliche Waldecksche Hofbibliothek, IV, Ms. 83
Germany, Berlin, Staatsbibliothek zu Berlin – Preußischer Kulturbesitz
    Manuscript germanica folio 710a, 1r–26v
    Manuscript germanica folio 1117, 294r–322r
    Manuscript germanica folio 1129, 68r–82r
    Manuscript germanica quart. 621, 1r–48r
    Manuscript germanica quart. 867, 1r–41r and 48r–96r
    Manuscript germanica quart. 1018, 32r–66r
    Manuscript germanica quart. 1187, 13v–45v
    Manuscript germanica quart. 2041, 1r–29r
Germany, Darmstadt, Universitäts- und Landesbibliothek, Ms. 1074, 1r–52v
Germany, Dillingen, Studienbibliothek, Ms. XV 50, 1r–33r
Germany, Dresden, Sächsische Landesbibliothek
    Ms. App. 463, 8r–72v
    Ms. C 262, 223r–239r
Germany, Frankfurt a. M.
Universitätsbibliothek, Ms. germ. quart. 14 (Ausst. 48) 'Rüst- und Feuerwerkbuch'
Bibliothek, Institut für Stadtgeschichte, Reichssachen Nachträge, No. 741 'Anonymous, 'Büchsenmeister – fewerwercker"

Bibliography

Germany, Freiburg i. Br., Universitätsbibliothek, Ms. 362, 73r–89r

Germany, Gotha, Universitäts- und Forschungsbibliothek Erfurt-Gotha
  Cod. Chart A 756, 184r–200v
  Cod. Chart B 428, 1r–48v
  Cod. Chart B 1032 'Feuerwerk- und Büchsenmeisterbuch'

Germany, Göttingen, Niedersächsische Staats- und Landesbibliothek, 2° Cod.
  Ms. philos. 64, 94r–147v

Germany, Heidelberg, Universitätsbibliothek
  Cod. Pal. germ. 122, 1r–46r
  Cod. Pal. germ. 301, 6v–20v 'puchlein von pusschen schissen'
  Cod. Pal. germ. 502
  Cod. Pal. germ. 562
  Cod. Pal. Germ. 585
  Cod. Pal. germ. 787, 2r–26r and 34r–45r

Germany, Karlsruhe, Badische Landesbibliothek, Cod. St. Georgen 71,
  131v–[143?]

Germany, Kassel, Universitäts – Landes – und Murhardsche Bibliothek, 4°
  Ms. math. 14, 1r–46r

Germany, Leipzig, Universitätsbibliothek, Ms. 1597, 1r–88r

Germany, Memmingen, Wissenschaftliche Stadtbibliothek, 4° 2.39, 116r–121r

Germany, Munich (München)
  Bayrisches Hauptstaatsarchiv, Kurbayern, Äußeres Archiv 3904
  Bayrische Staatsbibliothek, Cgm. 356
  Bayrische Staatsbibliothek, Cgm. 399, 1r–48v
  Bayrische Staatsbibliothek, Cgm. 599, 48r–62v
  Bayrische Staatsbibliothek, Cgm. 734, 1r–59v
  Bayrische Staatsbibliothek, Cgm. 973, 91v–123v
  Bayrische Staatsbibliothek, Cgm. 4902
  Bayrische Staatsbibliothek, Cgm. 5437, 1r–8v
  Bayrische Staatsbibliothek, Clm. 30150, 94r–150r

Germany, Nuremberg (Nürnberg), Germanisches Nationalmuseum
  Ms. 719, 16r–60v
  Ms. 1480 1r–50v
  Ms. 1481a, 14r–48v

Germany, Weimar, Herzogin Anna Amalia Bibliothek, Q 342, 55r–82v

Germany, Wolfenbüttel, Herzog August Bibliothek
  Cod. Guelf. 19.28. Aug. 2°
  Cod. Guelf. 226 Extravag., 7r–32v

Italy, Rome, Città del Vaticano, Bibliotheca Apostolica Vaticana, Cod. Pal. lat.
  1889, 94r–106v

Romania, Sibiu (Hermannstadt)/Bucharest, Arhivele Statului, Ms. Varia II,
  374, 1r–36v

Switzerland, formerly sold by Antiquariat Heribert Tenschert, Kat. XXV, No. 21, now Switzerland, private owner (no further information available), 83v–94r – location could not be confirmed, so copy was not available to be viewed.

Switzerland, St. Gallen, Kantonsbibliothek, VadSlg Ms. 396, 1r–46r

UK, Leeds, Royal Armouries, MS I.34, 1r–61r

USA, Cambridge (MA), Harvard College Library – Houghton Library, Ms Type 320, 1r–37v

USA, New York, Public Library, Spencer Collection, Ms. 104, 1r–55r

Editions of *Firework Books* and related texts

Anon, 'Dye nachuolget vonn Büchen geschoß, Pulver, Fewerwerck ...' as appendix to *Flauii Vegetii Renati vier Bücher der Ritterschaft*, Augsburg: Stainer, 1529, 91r–101v – printed in Hassenstein (1941)

Anon, *Büchsenmeysterei. Von Gschoß, Büchsen, Puluer, Salpeter vnd Feuerwerk etc.* (Strassburg: Christian Egenolph, 1529) [reprinted in Frankfurt/Main 1531, 1534 and 1550], Stadt- und Universitätsbibliothek Frankfurt/Main and Bibliothèque nationale et Universitaire Strasbourg

Anon, 'Petit tractié contenant plusieurs artifices du feu ...', appendix to *Livre du canonnerie et artifice de feu* (Paris, 1561)

Anon, *Feuer Buech, durch Eurem gelertten Kriegs verstenndigen mit grossem Vleis auss villen Probiertten Kunsten* (1584)

Baetz, Manuel, *Das Feuerwerkbuch von 1420. Faksimile mit Übertragung in modernes Deutsch* (Radolfzell: Survival Press, 2001)

Eldred, William, *The Gynners glasse* (London: Printed by T. Forcet Boydel, and are to be sold at his shop in the Bulwark neere the Tower, 1646/47), *Early English Books Online*, https://go.openathens.net/redirector/leeds.ac.uk?url=https://www.proquest.com/books/gvnners-glasse-vvherein-dili-gent-practicioner-may/docview/2264183063/se-2 (accessed 10 August 2023)

Hassenstein, Wilhelm, *Das Feuerwerkbuch von 1420. 600 Jahre Deutsche Pulverwaffen und Büchsenmeisterei. Nachdruck des Erstdruckes aus dem Jahre 1529 mit Übertragung ins Hochdeutsche und Erläuterungen von Wilhelm Hassenstein* (München: Verlag der deutschen Technik, 1941)

Kramer, Gerhard, *Berthold Schwarz: Chemie und Waffentechnik im 15. Jahrhundert, Abhandlungen und Berichte des Deutschen Museums, NF 10* (München: Oldenbourg, 1995)

Meyer, Werner, 'Eine Abschrift des Feuerwerkbuchs. Die Hs. XV 50 der Studienbibliothek Dillingen an der Donau', *Liber Castellorum* (1981), pp. 288–301

Bibliography

Printed primary sources

Babington, John, and John Droeshout, *Pyrotechnica or a Discovrse of artificiall Fire-Work* (London: Thomas Harper, 1635; repr. Delhi: Facsimile Publisher, 2018)

Bacon, Francis, *Novum Organum*, ed. Joseph Devey (New York: P. F. Collier, 1902), https://oll.libertyfund.org/title/bacon-novum-organum#Bacon_0415_198 (accessed 10 August 2023)

Barnes, Carl F. (ed.), *The Portfolio of Villard de Honnecourt (Paris, Bibliothèque nationale de France, MS Fr 19093): A New Critical Edition and Colour Facsimile* (Farnham: Ashgate, 2009)

Beck, J. H., ed., *Mariano Taccola, Liber Tertius de Ingeneis ac edifitiis non usitatis* (Milano: Edizioni il Polifilo, 1969)

Ehlert, Trude, ed., *Küchenmeisterei: Edition, Übersetzung und Kommentar zweier Kochbuch-Handschriften des 15. Jahrhunderts* (Frankfurt am Main: Peter Lang, 2010)

Greco, Gina, and Christine Rose (trans), *The Good Wife's Guide:* Le Ménagier de Paris, *A Medieval Household Book* (Ithaca and London: Cornell University Press, 2009)

Knobloch, Eberhard, ed., *Mariano Taccola, De rebus militaribus (De machinis, 1449)* (Baden-Baden: Koener, 1984)

Kyeser, Conradus, et al., *Bellifortis Feuerwerkbuch*, Codices figurati-libri picturati 3 (München: Edition Lengenfelder, 1995)

Leng, Rainer, *Franz Helm und sein 'Buch von den probierten Künsten': ein handschriftlich verbreitetes Büchsenmeisterbuch in der Zeit des frühen Buchdrucks* (Wiesbaden: Reichert, 2001)

Panse, Melanie, *Hans von Gersdorff: 'Feldbuch der Wundarznei'. Produktion, Präsentation und Rezeption von Wissen*, Trierer Beiträge zu den historischen Kulturwissenschaften 7 (Wiesbaden: Reichert, 2012)

Prager, Frank D., and Ulrich Montag, eds, *Mariano Taccola, De ingeneis* (Cambridge, MA: MIT Press, 1971)

Smith, Cyril Stanley, and Martha Teach Gnudi, eds, *The Pirotechnia of Vannoccio Biringuccio* (New York: Dover, 1990)

Secondary Sources

Alexander, Jonathan J. G., et al., eds, *The Splendor of the Word: Medieval and Renaissance Illuminated Manuscripts at the New York Public Library* (New York: Harvey Miller, 2005)

Bibliography

Algazi, Gadi, *Herrengewalt und Gewalt der Herren im späten Mittelalter: Herrschaft, Gegenseitigkeit und Sprachgebrauch*, Historische Studien 17 (Frankfurt am Main: Campus, 1996)

Allenby, Michael, ed., *A Dictionary of Plant Sciences Online*, 3rd edn (Oxford: Oxford University Press, 2013) (accessed 10 August 2023)

Andrade, Tonio, *The Gunpowder Age: China, Military Innovation, and the Rise of the West in World History* (Princeton and Oxford: Princeton University Press, 2016)

Andresová, Klára, 'A Bestseller among Artillery Handbooks of the 16th Century: Printed Editions of the Late Medieval *Feuerwerkbuch*', *International Journal of Military History and Historiography* (2022), 1–27, doi: https://doi.org/10.1163/24683302-bja10041 (accessed 10 August 2023)

Arnold, Klaus, 'Bilder des Krieges – Bilder des Friedens', in *Träger und Instrumentarien des Friedens im hohen und späten Mittelalter*, ed. Johannes Fried, Vorträge und Forschungen 43 (Sigmaringen: Thorbecke, 1996)

Arnoux, Mathieu, and Pierre Monnet, eds, *Le technicien dans la cité en Europe occidentale, 1250–1650*, Collection de l'École française de Rome 325 (Rome: École française de Rome, 2004)

Backhouse, Janet, 'The Royal Library from Edward IV to Henry VII', in *The Cambridge History of the Book in Britain, Vol. III, 1400–1557*, eds Lotte Hellinga and Joseph Burnley Trapp (Cambridge: Cambridge University Press, 1999), pp. 267–81

Barter Bailey, Sarah, 'The Royal Armouries "Firework Book"', in *Gunpowder: The History of an International Technology*, ed. Brenda Buchanan (Bath: Bath University Press, 1996), pp. 57–86

Bassnett, Susan, *Translation Studies* (London: Routledge, 2002)

Baufeld, Christa, *Kleines frühneuhochdeutsches Wörterbuch: Lexik aus Dichtung und Fachliteratur des Frühneuhochdeutschen* (Tübingen: Max Niemeyer, 1996)

Baumann, Reinhard, *Söldnerwesen im 16. Jahrhundert im bayerischen und süddeutschen Beispiel. Eine gesellschaftskritische Untersuchung (Neue Schriftenreihe des Stadtarchivs München)* (München: Kommissionsbuchhandlung R. Wölfle, 1978)

Baumann, Reinhard, *Landsknechte. Ihre Geschichte und Kultur vom späten Mittelalter bis zum Dreißigjährigen Krieg* (München: C. H. Beck, 1994)

Bec, Christian, 'Une librarie florentine de la fin du xve siècle', *Bibliothèque d'humanisme et renaissance* 31 (1969), 321–32

Beck, Theodor, *Beiträge zur Geschichte des Maschinenbaus* (Berlin: Julius Springer, 1899)

Belich, James, *The World the Plague Made: The Black Death and the Rise of Europe* (Princeton: Princeton University Press, 2022)

Bell, Adrian R., Anne Curry, et al., eds, *The Soldier Experience in the Fourteenth Century* (Woodbridge: Boydell Press, 2011)

Bibliography

Bell, Adrian R., et al., eds, *The Soldier in Later Medieval England* (Oxford: Oxford University Press, 2013)

Benoit, Paul, 'Artisans ou combattants? Les canoniers dans le royaume de France à la fin du Moyen Age', *Actes de congrès de la Societé des historiens médiévistes de l'enseignement supérieur public* 18 (1987), 287–296, https://www.persee.fr/doc/shmes_1261-9078_1991_act_18_1_1499 (accessed 210 August 2023)

Benzing, Josef, 'Egenolff, Christian', *Neue Deutsche Biographie* 4 (1959), 325–26, [online version] https://www.deutsche-biographie.de/pnd122968468.html#ndbcontent (accessed 10 August 2023)

Berg, Theresia, and Udo Friedrich, 'Wissenstradierung in spätmittelalterlichen Schriften zur Kriegskunst: Der "Bellifortis" des Konrad Kyeser und das anonyme "Feuerwerkbuch"', in *Wissen für den Hof. Der spätmittelalterliche Verschriftlichungsprozess am Beispiel Heidelberg im 15. Jahrhundert*, ed. Jan-Dirk Müller (München: Wilhelm Fink, 1994), pp. 169–232

Berninger, Ernst, 'Die technischen Handschriften des 15. Jahrhunderts in der Bayerischen Staatsbibliothek München', *Bellifortis, Clm 30150* (*Patrimonia*, 137) (München: KulturStifung der Länder und Bayrische Staatsbibliothek, 2000), 61–91

Berthelot, Marcelin, 'Pour l'histoire des arts méchaniques et de l'artillerie vers la fin du moyen âge', *Annales de chimie et de physique*, ser. 6, 24 (1891), 433–521

Biggs, Douglas, et al., *Traditions and Transformations in Late Medieval England,* The Northern World 2 (Leiden: Brill, 2002)

Biggs, Douglas, et al., *Reputation and Representation in Fifteenth-Century Europe,* The Northern World 8 (Leiden: Brill, 2004)

Blosen, Hans, and Rikke Agnete Olsen, eds, *Kriegskunst und Kanonen: Das Büchsemeister- und Kriegsbuch des Johannes Bengedans* (Aarhus: Aarhus Universitetsforlag, 2006)

Bodemann, Ulrike, and Klaus Grubmüller, 'Schriftliche Anleitung zu mündlicher Kommunikation: die Schülergesprächsbüchlein des späten Mittelalters', in *Pragmatische Schriftlichkeit im Mittelalter. Erscheinungsformen und Entwicklungsstufen*, eds Hagen Keller et al., Münstersche Mittelalter-Schriften 65 (München: Wilhelm Fink, 1992), pp. 177–93

Boffey, Julia, 'Bodleian Library, MS Arch. Selden. B.24 and Definitions of the "Household Book"', in *The English Medieval Book: Studies in Memory of Jeremy Griffiths*, eds Anthony Edwards et al. (London: British Library, 2000), pp. 125–34

Boffey, Julia, and John Jay Thompson, 'Anthologies and Miscellanies: Production and the Choice of Texts', in *Book Production and Publishing in Britain, 1375–1475*, eds Jeremy Griffiths and Derek Pearsall (Cambridge: Cambridge University Press, 1989), pp. 279–315

Bibliography

Booton, Diane E., *Manuscripts, Market and the Transition to Print in Late Medieval Brittany* (Farnham: Ashgate, 2010)

Brachert, Thomas, *Nachträge und Corrigenda zum "Lexikon historischer Maltechniken. Quellen – Handwerk – Technologie – Alchemie, München 2001"* (Hildesheim: Hornemann Institut, 2010)

Brévart, Francis B., 'Between Medicine, Magic, and Religion: Wonder Drugs in German Medico-Pharmaceutical Treatises of the Thirteenth to the Sixteenth Centuries', *Speculum* 83 (2008), 1–57

Brock, Alan St Hill, *A History of Fireworks* (London: Harrap, 1949)

Brown, G. I., *The Big Bang: A History of Explosives* (Stroud: Sutton, 1998)

Brunner, Horst, 'Bilder vom Krieg in der deutschen Literatur des Mittelalters und der frühen Neuzeit', in *Strukturen der Gesellschaft im Mittelalter. Interdisziplinäre Mediävistik in Würzburg*, eds Dieter Rödel and Joachim Schneider (Wiesbaden: Reichert, 1996), pp. 101–14

Brunner, Horst, ed., *Der Krieg im Mittelalter und in der Frühen Neuzeit: Gründe, Begründungen, Bilder, Bräuche, Recht* (Wiesbaden: Reichert, 1999)

Brunner, Horst, ed., *Die Wahrnehmung und Darstellung von Kriegen im Mittelalter und in der Frühen Neuzeit*, Imagines medii aevi 6 (Wiesbaden: Reichert, 2000)

Buchanan, Brenda, ed., *Gunpowder: The History of an International Technology* (Bath: Bath University Press, 1996)

Buchanan, Brenda J., ed., *Gunpowder, Explosives and the State: A Technological History* (Aldershot: Ashgate, 2006)

Bugge, Günther, *Schieß- und Sprengstoffe und die Männer, die sie schufen* (Stuttgart: Franckh'sche Verlagshandlung, 1942)

Burgh, Patrick, *Gunpowder, Masculinity, and Warfare in German Texts, 1400–1700* (Rochester, NY: University of Rochester Press, 2019)

Butler, Sara M., *Forensic Medicine and Death Investigation in Medieval England* (New York: Routledge, 2014)

Canning, Joseph, et al., eds, *Power, Violence and Mass Death in Pre-Modern and Modern Times* (Aldershot: Ashgate, 2004)

Carr, A. D., 'War in Fourteenth-Century Europe', in *Power, Violence and Mass Death in Pre-Modern and Modern Times*, eds Joseph Canning et al. (Aldershot: Ashgate, 2004), pp. 67–89

Chase, Kenneth, *Firearms: A Global History to 1700* (Cambridge: Cambridge University Press, 2003)

Cocroft, Wayne D., *Dangerous Energy: The Archaeology of Gunpowder and Military Explosives Manufacture* (Swindon: English Heritage, 2000)

Connolly, David E., 'Ulrich Rülein von Kalbe's Bergbüchlein in the Context of Sixteenth-Century German Mining/Metallurgical Literature', in *De Re Metallica: The Uses of Metal in the Middle Ages*, eds Robert O. Bork et al. (Farnham: Ashgate, 2005), pp. 347–66

Bibliography

Contamine, Philippe, *War in the Middle Ages*, trans. M. Jones (Oxford: Blackwell, 1984)

Crosby, Alfred W., *Throwing Fire: Projectile Technology Through History* (Cambridge: Cambridge University Press, 2002)

Curry, Anne, 'Guns and Goddams: Was There a Military Revolution in Lancastrian Normandy 1415–50?', *Journal of Medieval Military History* 8 (2011), 171–88

Curry, Anne, and Elizabeth Matthew, eds, *Concepts and Patterns of Service in the Later Middle Ages*, The Fifteenth Century 1 (Woodbridge: Boydell Press, 2000)

Davies, Jonathan, *Guns and Gunpowder 1267–1603* (Guisborough: HMA Ltd, 2003)

Davies, Jonathan, *The Medieval Cannon 1326–1494* (Oxford: Osprey Publishing, 2019)

De Reuck, Anthony, 'The Nature of Saltpeter in the *Firework Book*', *Journal of the Ordnance Society* 20 (2008), 5–10

Derrida, Jacques, 'What is a "Relevant" Translation?', trans. Lawrence Venuti, *Critical Inquiry*, 27:2 (2001), 174–200

DeVries, Kelly, 'The Impact of Gunpowder Weaponry on Siege Warfare in the Hundred Years' War', in *The Medieval City under Siege*, eds Ivy A. Corfis and Michael Wolfe (Woodbridge: Boydell, 1995), pp. 227–44

DeVries, Kelly, 'Gunpowder and Early Gunpowder Weapons', in *Gunpowder: The History of an International Technology*, ed. Brenda Buchanan (Bath: Bath University Press, 1996), pp. 121–36

DeVries, Kelly, 'Gunpowder Weaponry at the Siege of Constantinople, 1453', in *War and Society in the Eastern Mediterranean, 7th–15th Centuries*, ed. Yakoov Lev, The Medieval Mediterranean 9 (Leiden: Brill, 1996), pp. 343–62

DeVries, Kelly, *Infantry Warfare in the Early 14th Century* (Woodbridge: Boydell, 1996)

DeVries, Kelly, 'The Use of Gunpowder Weaponry by and against Joan of Arc during the Hundred Years' War', *War and Society* 14:1 (1996), 1–15

DeVries, Kelly, 'The Technology of Gunpowder Weaponry in Western Europe during the Hundred Years' War', *XXII. Kongress der internationalen Kommission für Militärgeschichte* (Wien: Heeresgeschichtliches Museum, 1997), pp. 285–99

DeVries, Kelly, 'Catapults are not Atomic Bombs: Towards a Redefinition of "Effectiveness" in Premodern Military Technology', *War in History* 4 (1997), 454–70

DeVries, Kelly, 'The Forgotten Battle of Beverhoutsveld, 3 May 1382: Technological Innovation and Military Significance', in *Armies, Chivalry, and Warfare in Medieval Britain and France*, ed. Matthew Strickland (Stamford, CT: Paul Watkins, 1998), pp. 289–303

Bibliography

DeVries, Kelly, 'Gunpowder Weaponry and the Rise of the Early Modern State', *War in History* 5:2 (1998), 127–45

DeVries, Kelly, 'Review of Gerhard W. Kramer, ed., and Klaus Leibnitz, trans. *The Firework Book: Gunpowder in Medieval Germany (Das Feuerwerkbuch, c. 1440)*', *Ambix* 50:2 (2003), 237–38

DeVries, Kelly, 'Reassessment of the Gun Illustrated in the Walter de Milimete and Pseudo-Aristotle Manuscript', *Journal of the Ordnance Society* 15 (2003), 5–17

DeVries, Kelly, '"The walls come tumbling down": The Campaigns of Philip the Good and the Myth of Fortification Vulnerability to Early Gunpowder Weapons', in *The Hundred Years' War: A Wider Focus*, eds L. J. Andrew Villalon and Donald J. Kagay, History of Warfare 25 (Leiden: Brill, 2005), pp. 429–46

DeVries, Kelly, 'Facing the New Military Technology: Non-Trace Italienne Anti-Gunpowder Weaponry Defenses', in *Heirs of Archimedes: Science and Art of War through the Age of Enlightenment*, eds Brett D. Steele and Tamera Dorland (Cambridge, MA: MIT Press, 2005), pp. 37–71

DeVries, Kelly, 'Sites of Military Science and Technology', in *The Cambridge History of Science. Vol. 3: Early Modern Europe*, eds Katherine Park and Lorraine Daston (Cambridge: Cambridge University Press, 2006), pp. 306–19

DeVries, Kelly, and Robert D. Smith, 'Breech-Loading Guns with Removable Powder Chambers: A Long-Loved Military Technology', in *Gunpowder, Explosives, and the State*, ed. Brenda Buchanan (Aldershot: Ashgate, 2006), pp. 251–65

DeVries, Kelly, and Robert D. Smith, *Medieval Military Technology*, 2nd edn (Toronto: University of Toronto Press, 2012)

DeVun, Leah, *Prophecy, Alchemy, and the End of Time: John of Rupecissa in the Late Middle Ages* (New York: Columbia University Press, 2009)

Dijkmann, Jessica, *Shaping Medieval Markets: The Organisation of Commodity Markets in Holland, c. 1200–c. 1450*, Global Economic History Series 8 (Leiden: Brill, 2011)

Donkin, Robin A., *Between East and West: The Moluccas and the Traffic in Spices up to the Arrival of Europeans* (Philadelphia: American Philosophical Society, 2003)

Duchart, Heinz, ed., *Krieg und Frieden im Übergang vom Mittelalter zur Neuzeit. Theorie – Praxis – Bild* (Mainz: Philipp von Zabern, 2000)

Eamon, William, *Science and the Secrets of Nature* (Princeton: Princeton University Press, 1994)

Edson, Evelyn, *The World Map, 1300–1492: The Persistence of Tradition and Transformation* (Baltimore: Johns Hopkins University Press, 2007)

Ehlert, Trude, and Rainer Leng, 'Frühe Koch- und Pulverrezepte aus der Nürnberger Handschrift GNM 3227a (um 1389)', in *Medizin in Geschichte,*

Bibliography

Philologie und Ethnologie. Festschrift für Gundolf Keil, eds Dominik Groß and Monika Reininger (Würzburg: Königshausen & Neumann, 2003), pp. 289–313

Eis, Gerhard, *Mittelalterliche Fachliteratur* (Stuttgart: Metzler, 1962)

Elkar, Rainer S., 'Lernen durch Wandern? Einige kritische Anmerkungen zum Thema Wissenstransfer durch Migration', in *Handwerk in Europa: Vom Spätmittelalter bis zur Frühen Neuzeit*, ed. Knut Schulz, Schriften des historischen Kollegs, Kolloquien 41 (München: Oldenbourg, 1999), pp. 213–32

Ertl, Thomas, *Seide, Pfeffer und Kanonen: Globalisierung im Mittelalter* (Darmstadt: Primus, 2008)

Essenwein, August von, *Quellen zur Geschichte der Feuerwaffen*, 2 vols (Leipzig and Graz: Akademische Druck- und Verlagsanstalt, 1877; repr. 1969)

Feldhaus, Franz Maria, 'Was wissen wir von Berthold Schwarz?', *Zeitschrift für Historische Waffenkunde* 4 (1906–8), 65–69 and 113–18

Feldhaus, Franz Maria, *Die Technik der Antike und des Mittelalters* (Wildpark-Potsdam: Athenaion, 1931; repr. Hildesheim: Georg Olms Verlag, 1971)

Feldhaus, Franz Maria, *Die Machine im Leben der Völker. Ein Überblick von der Urzeit bis zur Renaissance* (Basel and Stuttgart: Birkhäuser, 1954)

Ferragud, Carmel, 'Vernacularization as an Intellectual and Social Bridge: The Catalan Translations of Teodorico's *Chirurgia* and of Arnau De Vilanova's *Regimen Sanitatis*', *Early Science and Medicine* 4:2 (1999), 127–48

Fiedler, Siegfried, *Kriegswesen und Kriegsführung im Zeitalter der Landsknechte*, Heerwesen der Neuzeit 12 (Koblenz: Bernard & Graefe, 1985)

Flachenecker, Helmut, 'Kanonen, Räderuhr und Brille: zur technischen Revolution des Spätmittelalters', in *Überall ist Mittelalter: zur Aktualität einer vergangenen Epoche*, ed. Dorothea Klein (Würzburg: Königshausen & Neumann, 2015), pp. 303–29

Foard, Glenn, and Anne Curry, *Bosworth 1485: A Battlefield Reconsidered* (Oxford: Oxbow, 2013)

Forbes, Ir. R. J., '4000 Jahre Schwefel', *CIBA Rundschau* 5/6 (1965), 2–18

Ford, Margaret Lane, 'Importation of Printed Books into England and Scotland', in *The Cambridge History of the Book in Britain, Vol. III, 1400–1557*, eds Lotte Hellinga and Joseph Burnley Trapp (Cambridge: Cambridge University Press, 1999), pp. 179–201

Forster, Regula, *Die Geheimnisse der Geheimnisse: die arabischen und deutschen Fassungen des pseudo-aristotelischen Sirr al-asrar / Secretum Secretorum* (Wiesbaden: Reichert, 2006)

Fox, Robert, ed., *Technological Change: Methods and Themes in the History of Technology*, Studies in the History of Science, Technology & Medicine 1 (Amsterdam: Harwood Academic, 1996)

Bibliography

Friedrich, Udo, 'Herrscherpflichten und Kriegskunst. Zum intendierten Gebrauch früher "Bellifortis"-Handschriften', in *Der Codex im Gebrauch: Akten des Internationalen Kolloquiums 11.–13. Juni 1992*, eds Christel Meier et al. (München: Wilhelm Fink, 1996), pp. 197–210

Gaier, Claude, *L'Industrie et le Commerce des Armes dans les Anciennes Principautés belges du XIIIme à la fin du XVme siècle* (Paris: Les Belles lettres, 1973)

Gaier, Claude, *Armes et combats dans l'univers medieval* (Brussels: De Boeck, 1995)

Galluzzi, Paolo, *Prima di Leonardo. Cultura delle machine a Siena nel Rinascimento* (Milano: Mondadori Electa, 1991)

Geibig, Alfred, 'Waffen und kriegerische Ereignisse', in *Chronik der Bischöfe von Würzburg 742–1495, Vol. VI: Die Miniaturen der Bischofschronik*, ed. Lorenz Fried (Würzburg: Ferdinand Schöningh, 1996), pp. 217–85

Geibig, Alfred, 'Pyrotechnic Devices from Coburg Castle', in *Royal Armouries Yearbook*, Vol. 6, ed. P. J. Turner (Leeds: Trustees of the Armouries, 2001), pp. 88–97

Geibig, Alfred, *Die Macht des Feuers – Might and Fire* (Coburg: Kunstsammlung der Veste Coburg, 2012)

Gelfand, Toby, 'The History of the Medical Profession', in *Companion Encyclopaedia of the History of Medicine*, eds William F. Bynum and Roy Porter (London and New York: Routledge, 1993), pp. 119–50

Gerardy, Theodor, *Datieren mit Hilfe von Wasserzeichen, beispielhaft dargestellt an der Gesamtproduktion der Schaumburgischen Papiermühle Arensberg von 1604–1650* Schaumburger Studies 4 (Bückeberg: n. pub., 1964)

Gerardy, Theodor, 'Die Beschreibung des in Manuskripten und Drucken vorkommenden Papiers', *Codicologia* 5 (1980), 37–51

Gessler, Eduard A., 'Die Entwicklung des Geschützwesens in der Schweiz von seinen Anfängen bis zum Ende der Burgunderkriege', *Mitteilungen der Antiquarischen Gesellschaft Zürich* 28 (1918), 183–460

Gille, Bertrand, 'Études sur les manuscrits d'ingénieurs du XVe siècle', *Techniques et civilisations* 5 (1956), 77–86

Gille, Bertrand, *The Renaissance Engineer* (London: Lund Humphries, 1966)

Gillespie, Vincent, and Anne Hudson, eds, *Probable Truth: Editing Medieval Texts from Britain in the Twenty-First Century*, Texts and Transitions 5 (Turnhout: Brepols, 2013)

Ginsburger, M., 'Les Juifs et l'art militaire au Moyen-Âge', *Revue des Études Juives* 88 (1929), 156–66

Goetz, Dorothea, *Die Anfänge der Artillerie* (Ostberlin: Militärverlag der DDR, 1985)

Götze, Alfred, *Frühneuhochdeutsches Glossar*, 7th edn (Berlin: de Gruyter, 1967)

Graf zu Waldburg Wolfegg, Christoph, *Venus and Mars: World of the Medieval Housebook* (London: Prestel, 1998)

Graf zu Waldburg Wolfegg, Christoph, 'Der Münchner "Bellifortis" und sein Autor', *Patrimonia* 137 (2000), 21–60

Grieve, Maud, *A Modern Herbal: The Medicinal, Culinary, Cosmetic and Economic Properties, Cultivation and Folk-lore of Herbs, Grasses, Fungi, Shrubs, & Trees with All Their Modern Scientific Uses*, Vol. 1 (New York: Dover, 1971)

Grimm, Jacob and Wilhelm, *Deutsches Wörterbuch von Jacob und Wilhelm Grimm Online*, 16 vols (Leipzig: Hirzel, 1854–1961; Online 1998–2003), http://woerterbuchnetz.de/cgi-bin/WBNetz/wbgui_py?sigle=DWB (accessed 10 August 2023)

Grummit, David, 'The Defence of Calais and the Development of Gunpowder Weaponry in England in the Late Fifteenth Century', *War in History* 7:3 (2000), 253–72

Guilmartin, John F., 'Ballistics in the Black Powder Era', in *British Naval Armaments*, ed. Robert D. Smith (London: Royal Armouries Conference Proceedings, 1989), pp. 73–98

Habermann, Mechthild, *Deutsche Fachtexte der frühen Neuzeit: Naturkundlich-medizinische Wissensvermittlung im Spannungsfeld von Latein und Volkssprache*, Studia linguistica Germanica 61 (Berlin: de Gruyter, 2002)

Hagemann, Karen, ed., *Landsknechte, Soldatenfrauen und Nationalkrieger. Militär, Krieg und Geschlechterordnung im historischen Wandel*, Geschichte und Geschlechter 26 (Frankfurt am Main: Campus, 1999)

Hagenmeyer, Christa, 'Kriegswissenschaftliche Texte des ausgehenden 15. Jahrhunderts', *Leuvensche Bijdragen* 57 (1967), 182–95

Hale, John Rigby, *Artists and Warfare in the Renaissance* (New Haven and London: Yale University Press, 1990)

Hall, Bert S., *The So-Called "Manuscript of the Hussite Wars' Engineer" and its Technological Milieu: A Study and Edition of the* Codex Latinus Monacensis 197, Part 1 (PhD dissertation, University of California Los Angeles, 1971 – Ann Arbor: University Microfilms, 1972)

Hall, Bert S., "'Der Meister sol auch kennen schreiben und lesen': Writings about Technology ca. 1400–ca. 1600 A.D. and their Cultural Implications', in *Early Technologies*, ed. Denise Schmandt-Besserat (Los Angeles: Undena Publications, 1979), pp. 47–58

Hall, Bert S., *The Technological illustrations of the So-Called "Anonymous of the Hussite Wars": Codex* Latinus Monacensis 197, Part 1 (Wiesbaden: Reichert, 1979)

Hall, Bert S., 'The Corning of Gunpowder and the Development of Firearms in the Renaissance', in Buchanan, *Gunpowder: The History of an International Technology* (1996), pp. 87–120

Hall, Bert S., 'The Didactic and the Elegant: Some Thoughts on Scientific and Technological Illustrations in the Middle Ages and Renaissance', in *Picturing Knowledge: Historical and Philosophical Problems concerning the Use of Art in Science*, ed. Brian Baigrie (Toronto: University of Toronto Press, 1996), pp. 3–39

Hall, Bert S., *Weapons and Warfare in Renaissance Europe: Gunpowder, Technology, and Tactics* (Baltimore: Johns Hopkins University Press, 1997)

Hall, Bert S., 'Foreword', in *Gunpowder, Explosives, and the State*, ed. Brenda Buchanan (Aldershot: Ashgate, 2006), pp. xxii–xxiii

Hammer, Paul E. J., *Warfare in Early Modern Europe, 1450–1660* (Aldershot: Ashgate, 2007)

Hanna, Ralph, *Editing Medieval Texts: An Introduction, Using Exemplary Materials Derived from Richard Rollo, 'Super Canticum' 4* (Liverpool: Liverpool University Press, 2015)

Hartig, Otto, *Die Gründung der Münchner Hofbibliothek durch Albrecht V. und Jakob Fugger* (München: Königlich Bayerische Akademie der Wissenschaften, 1917)

Harvey, John, *The Mediaeval Architect* (New York: St. Martin Press, 1972)

Harvey, Paul Dean Adshea, ed., *The Hereford World Map: Medieval World Maps and their Context* (London: British Library, 2006)

Hawthorne, John G., and Cyril Stanley Smith, ed., *Theophilus. On Divers Arts* (New York: Dover, 1979)

Hellinga, Lotte, and Joseph Burnley Trapp, ed., *The Cambridge History of the Book in Britain, Vol. III, 1400–1557* (Cambridge: Cambridge University Press, 1999)

Hilaire-Perez, Liliane, and Catherine Verna, 'Dissemination of Technical Knowledge in the Middle Ages and the Early Modern Era: New Approaches and Methodological Issues', *Technology and Culture* 47:3 (July 2006), 536–65

Hime, Henry W. L., *Gunpowder and Ammunition: Their Origin and Progress* (Waltham Abbey: Royal Gunpowder Mills, 1904)

Hime, Henry W. L., *The Origins of Artillery* (London: Longmans, 1915)

Huuri, Kalervo, *Zur Geschichte des mittelalterlichen Geschützwesens aus orientalischen Quellen* (Helsinki: Finnische Literaturgesellschaft, 1941)

Jähns, Max, *Atlas zur Geschichte des Kriegswesens von der Urzeit bis zum Ende des 16. Jahrhunderts* (Berlin: Lith. Institut v. Wilh. Greve, 1878)

Jähns, Max, *Handbuch einer Geschichte des Kriegswesens von der Urzeit bis zur Renaissance*, 2 vols (Leipzig: F. E. Grunow, 1878–80)

Jähns, Max, *Geschichte der Kriegswissenschaften vornehmlich in Deutschland*, 3 vols (München and Leipzig: R. Oldenbourg, 1889–91), http://archive.org/details/geschichtederkroojhgoog (accessed 10 August 2023)

Jullien, Ev,a and Michel Pauly, *Craftsmen and Guilds in the Medieval and Early Modern Periods* (Stuttgart: Franz Steiner, 2016)

Kalning, Pamela, 'Funktionalisierung von Geschichtsschreibung in Kriegslehren des späten Mittelalters', in *Krieg und Frieden in der historischen*

Gedächtniskultur, ed. Johannes Burkhardt (München: E. Vögel, 2000), pp. 31–43

Karg-Gasterstädt, Elisabeth, and Theodor Frings, *Althochdeutsches Wörterbuch* (Berlin: Akademie, 1952), http://awb.saw-leipzig.de/cgi/WBNetz/wbgui_py?sigle=AWB (accessed 10 August 2023)

Karpienski, Marc-André, 'Gunpowder and Cannons: Gunnery in the Late Middle Ages', in *The Means to Kill: Essays on the Interdependence of War and Technology from Ancient Rome to the Age of Drones*, ed. Gerrit Dworok and Frank Jacob (Jefferson, NC: McFarland, 2001), pp. 57–70

Kaye, Joel, *A History of Balance, 1250–1375: The Emergence of a New Model of Equilibrium and its Impact on Thought* (Cambridge: Cambridge University Press, 2014)

Keen, Maurice (ed.), *Medieval Warfare: A History* (Oxford: Oxford University Press, 1999)

Kelly, Jack, *Gunpowder: A History of the Explosive that Changed the World* (London: Atlantic, 2004)

Ker, Neil R., *Medieval Libraries of Great Britain* (London: Royal Historical Society, 1987)

King, Andy, 'Gunners, Aides and Archers: The Personnel of the English Ordnance Companies in Normandy in the Fifteenth Century', *Journal of Medieval Military History* 9 (2011), 65–75

Kirchner, Joachim, *Germanistische Handschriftenpraxis* (München: Beck, 1950)

Klemm, Friedrich, *Die Geschichte des technischen Schrifttums. Form und Funktion des gedruckten technischen Buchs vom ausgehenden 15. bis zum beginnenden 19. Jahrhundert* (München: Diss. Masch, 1948)

Köhler, Gustav, *Die Entwicklung des Kriegswesens und der Kriegsführung in der Ritterzeit von der Mitte des 11. Jahrhunderts bis zu den Hussitenkriegen*, 3 vols (Breslau: Koebner, 1886–89)

Kortüm, Hans-Henning, ed., *Krieg im Mittelalter* (Berlin: Akademie, 2001)

Kramer, Gerhard W., 'Das Feuerwerkbuch, eine unausgeschöpfte chemie- und sprengstoffgeschichtliche Quelle', *Nobel-Hefte* 49:3/4 (1983), 89–99

Kramer, Gerhard W., *Berthold Schwarz: Chemie und Waffentechnik im 15. Jahrhundert*. Abhandlungen und Berichte der Deutschen Museum, N.F. 10 (München: Oldenbourg, 1995)

Kramer, Gerhard W., '*Das Feuerwerkbuch*: Its Importance in the Early History of Black Powder', in Buchanan, *Gunpowder: The History of an International Technology* (1996), pp. 45–56

Kramer, Gerhard W., and Klaus Leibnitz, *Das Feuerwerkbuch: German, circa 1400: Translation of MS 362 dated 1432 in the Library of the University of Freiburg*, Journal of the Arms & Armour Society 17.1 (London: The Arms & Armour Society, 2001)

Bibliography

Kümper, Hiram, *Regimen von der Wehrverfassung. Ein Kriegsmemorandum in der Gießener Handschrift 996, zugleich ein Beitrag zur städtischen Militärgeschichte des 15. Jahrhunderts*, Berichte und Arbeiten aus der Universitätsbibliothek und dem Universitätsarchiv Gießen 55 (Gießen: Universitätsbibliothek Gießen, 2005)

Lawn, Brian, *The Salernitan Questions: An Introduction to the History of Medieval and Renaissance Problem Literature* (Oxford: Clarendon Press, 1963)

Lazar, Thomaž, *Poznosrednjeveško topništvo na Slovenskem. Raziskave dveh zgodnjih topov iz Pokrajinskega muzeja Ptuj-Ormož / Late-Medieval Artillery in Slovenia. A Study of Two Early Artillery Pieces from the Regional Museum Ptuj-Ormož* (Ljubljana: Narodni muzej Slovenije, 2015)

Lefèvre, Wolfgang, ed., *Picturing Machines, 1400–1700* (Cambridge, MA: MIT Press, 2004)

Lehmann, Paul, *Eine Geschichte der alten Fuggerbibliotheken* (Tübingen: Kommission für Bayerische Landesgeschichte/Schwäbische Forschungsgemeinschaft, 1956)

Leicester, Henry Marshall, *The Historical Background of Chemistry* (New York: Wiley, 1956)

Leng, Rainer, *"getruwelich dienen mit Buchsenwerk"*. Ein neuer Beruf im späten Mittelalter: Die Büchsenmeister', in *Strukturen der Gesellschaft im Mittelalter. Interdisziplinäre Mediävistik in Würzburg*, ed. Dieter Rödel and Joachim Schneider (Wiesbaden: Reichert, 1996), pp. 302–21

Leng, Rainer, 'Gründe für berufliches Töten. Büchsenmeister und Kriegshauptleute zwischen Berufsethos und Gewissensnot', in *Der Krieg im Mittelalter und in der Frühen Neuzeit: Gründe, Begründungen, Bilder, Bräuche, Recht*, ed. Horst Brunner, Imagines medii aevi 3 (Wiesbaden: Reichert, 1999), pp. 307–48

Leng, Rainer, *Anleitung Schiesspulver zu bereiten, Büchsen zu laden und zu beschiessen: eine kriegstechnische Bilderhandschrift im cgm 600 der Bayerischen Staatsbibliothek München*, Imagines medii aevi 5 (Wiesbaden: Reichert, 2000)

Leng, Rainer, *Ars belli: deutsche taktische und kriegstechnische Bilderhandschriften und Traktate im 15. und 16. Jahrhundert*, 2 vols (Wiesbaden: Reichert, 2002)

Leng, Rainer, 'Deutsche kriegstechnische und taktische Bilderhandschrifen und Traktate. Festvortrag anläßlich der Verleihung des Werner-Hahlweg-Preises 2002 in Halle', *Zeitschrift für Heereskunde* 67:3 (2003), 50–55

Leng, Rainer, 'Feuerwerk zu Ernst und Schimpf. Die spielerische Anwendung der Pyrotechnik im Lustfeuerwerk', in *Homo faber ludens: Geschichten zu Wechselbeziehungen von Technik und Spiel*, ed. Stefan Poser and Karin Zachmann (Frankfurt am Main: Peter Lang, 2003), pp. 85–111

Leng, Rainer, 'Social Character, Pictorial Style, and the Grammar of Technical Illustration in Craftsmen's Manuscripts in the Late Middle Ages', in *Picturing Machines 1400–1700* ed. Wolfgang Lefèvre (Cambridge, MA: MIT Press, 2004)

Leng, Rainer, 'Zum Verhältnis von Kunst und Krieg in den illustrierten Kriegslehren des 15. und 16. Jahrhunderts', in *'Mars und die Musen': Das Wechselspiel von Militär, Krieg und Kunst in der Frühen Neuzeit*, ed. Jutta Nowosadtko and Matthias Rogge (Münster: Lit Verlag, 2008), pp. 33–58

Leng, Rainer, 'Feuerwerks- und Kriegsbücher', in *Katalog der deutschsprachigen illustrierten Handschriften des Mittelalters*, vol. 4/2, eds Norbert H. Ott et al. (München: C. H. Beck. 2009), pp. 145–512, http://www.manuscripta-mediaevalia.de/?xdbdtdn:%22hsk%200622a%22&dmode=doc#|3 (accessed 10 August 2023)

Lindgren, Uta, 'Technische Enzyklopädien des Spätmittelalters – Was ist daran technisch?', Bellifortis, Clm 30150, *Patrimonia* 137 (München: KulturStiftung der Länder und Bayrische Staatsbibliothek, 2000), pp. 9–20

Lohrmann, Dietrich, 'Das Maschinenbuch des Konrad Gruter für Erich VII., König von Dänemark (1424)', *Deutsches Archiv für Erforschung des Mittelalters* 63:1 (2007), 71–92

Long, Pamela O., 'Power, Patronage, and the Authorship of Ars: From Mechanical Know-How to Mechanical Knowledge in the Last Scribal Age', *Isis* 88:1 (1997), 1–41

Long, Pamela O., *Openness, Secrecy, Authorship: Technical Arts and the Culture of Knowledge from Antiquity to the Renaissance* (Baltimore: Johns Hopkins University Press, 2001)

Long, Pamela O., *Artisan/Practitioner and the Rise of the New Sciences, 1400–1600* (Corvallis: Oregon State University Press, 2011)

Lynn, John A., ed., *Tools of War: Instruments, Ideas, and Institutions of Warfare, 1445–1871* (Urbana: University of Illinois Press, 1990)

Lynn, John A., ed., *Feeding Mars: Logistics in Western Warfare from the Middle Ages to the Present* (Oxford: Westview Press, 1993)

Lynn, John A., *Battle: A History of Combat and Culture* (Cambridge: Cambridge University Press, 2004)

Lynn, John A., *Women, Armies, and Warfare in Early Modern Europe* (Cambridge: Cambridge University Press, 2008)

McCleery, Iona, 'Both "Illness and Temptation of the Enemy": Melancholy, the Medieval Patient and the Writings of King Duarte of Portugal (r. 1433–38)', *Journal of Medieval Iberian Studies* 1:2 (2009), 163–78

McKitterick, David, *Print, Manuscript and the Search for Order, 1450–1830* (Cambridge: Cambridge University Press, 2003)

Mallett, Michael, 'The Transformation of War, 1494–1530', in *Italy and the European Powers: The Impact of War, 1500–1530*, ed. Christine Shaw, History of Warfare 38 (Leiden: Brill, 2006), pp. 3–22

Bibliography

Marzell, Heinrich, *Frühneuhochdeutsches Wörterbuch der Deutschen Pflanzennamen* (Leipzig: Hirzel, 1943)

Maxwell-Stuart, P. G., *The Chemical Choir: A History of Alchemy* (London: Continuum, 2008)

Menhardt, Hermann, *Das älteste Handschriftenverzeichnis der Wiener Hofbibliothek von Hugo Blotius 1576* (Wien: Rudolf M. Rohrer, 1957)

Merten, Bettina, Ulrich Reinisch, and Michael Korey, eds, *Festungsbau: Geometrie – Technologie – Sublimierung* (Berlin: Lukas, 2012)

Miller, Peter, *History and Its Objects: Antiquarianism and Material Culture since 1500* (Ithaca and London: Cornell University Press, 2017)

Moffett, Randall, 'Military Equipment in the Town of Southampton during the Fourteenth and Fifteenth Centuries', *Journal of Medieval Military History* 9 (2011), 167–99

Molino, Paula, *L'impero di carta: Hugo Blotius, Hofbibliothekar nella Vienna di fine Cinquecento* (unpublished PhD thesis, European University Institute, Fiesole, 2011)

Moss, Ann, *Printed Commonplace Books and the Structuring of Renaissance Thought* (Oxford: Clarendon Press, 1996)

Multhauf, Robert Philipp, *The Origins of Chemistry* (London: Oldbourne, 1966)

Neddermeyer, Uwe, *Von der Handschrift zum gedruckten Buch*, 2 vols (Wiesbaden: Harrassowitz, 1998)

Needham, Joseph, *Military Technology: The Gunpowder Epic*, Part 7 of *Science and Civilisation in China*, Vol. 5, *Chemistry and Chemical Technology* (Cambridge: Cambridge University Press, 1986)

Needham, Joseph, *Military Technology: Missiles and Sieges*, Part 6 of *Science and Civilisation in China*, Vol. 5, *Chemistry and Chemical Technology* (Cambridge: Cambridge University Press, 1994)

Neven, Sylvie, 'Recording and Reading Alchemy and Art-Technology in Medieval and Premodern German Recipe Collections', *Nuncius: Journal for the Material and Visual History of Early Modern Science* 31:1 (2016), 32–49

Nibler, Ferdinand, 'Das Feuerwerkbuch: Eine verspätete Buchbesprechung etwa 600 Jahre nach dem Erscheinen des Feuerwerkbuches', *Zeitschrift für Heereskunde* 67:2 (2003), 147–54

Nibler, Ferdinand, *Feuerwerkbuch: Anonym, 15. Jahrhundert; Synoptische Darstellung zweier Texte mit Neuhochdeutscher Übertragung* (online publication, 2005), https://www.ruhr-uni-bochum.de/technikhist/tittmann/5%20 Feuerwerkbuch.pdf (accessed 10 August 2023)

Nicolai, Ferdinand Friedrich von, *Nachrichen von alten und neuen Kriegs-Büchern, welche den Feld- und Festungs-Krieg entweder abhandeln oder erläutern nebst einer kurzen Beurteilung derselben* (Stuttgart: n. pub., 1765)

Bibliography

Oman, Charles W. C., *The Art of War in the Middle Ages, A.D. 378–1515* (Ithaca: Cornell, 1953/60)

Ott, Norbert H., 'Steiner, Heinrich', *Neue Deutsche Biographie* 25, 183 [online version] (2013), https://www.deutsche-biographie.de/pnd119838451.html#ndbcontent (accessed 10 August 2023)

Päsler, Ralf G., 'Sachliteratur (Artillerie-, Fecht-, und Ringbücher)', in *Handbuch Höfe und Residenzen im spätmittelalterlichen Reich, vol. 15.III: Hof und Schrift*, eds Werner Paravicini et al. (Ostfildern: Thorbecke, 2005), pp. 573–84

Pászthory, Emmerich, 'Salpetergewinnung und Salpeterwirtschaft vom Mittelalter bis in die Neuzeit', *Chemie in unserer Zeit* 29:1 (1995), 8–20

Parker, David, 'The Importance of the Commonplace Book: London, 1450–1550', *Manuscripta* 40 (1996), 29–48

Parker, Geoffrey, *The Military Revolution: Military Innovation and the Rise of the West, 1500–1800* (Cambridge: Cambridge University Press, 1988; rev. edn 2002)

Partington, James R., *A History of Greek Fire and Gunpowder*, intro. Bert S. Hall (Baltimore: Johns Hopkins University Press, 1960; repr. 1999)

Partington, James R., *A History of Chemistry*, 4 vols (London: Macmillan, 1961–70)

Pepper, Simon, and Nicholas Adams, *Firearms and Fortifications: Military Architecture and Siege Warfare in Sixteenth-Century Siena* (Chicago: University of Chicago Press, 1986)

Pereira, Michela, 'Alchemy and the Use of Vernacular Languages in the Late Middle Ages', *Speculum* 74:2 (1999), 336–56

Pfeiffer, Franz, ed., *Konrad von Megenberg: Das buch der natur* (Stuttgart: K. Aue, 1861), https://archive.org/details/dasbuchdernaturoopfeigoog/page/n548 (accessed 10 August 2023)

Plimpton, George, *Fireworks: A History and Celebration* (New York: Doubleday, 1984)

Pope, Dudley, *Guns* (Feltham: Spring Books, 1969)

Popplow, Marcus, 'Militärtechnische Bildkataloge des Spätmittelalters', in *Krieg im Mittelalter*, ed. Hans-Henning Kortüm (Berlin: Akademie, 2001), pp. 251–68

Prestwich, Michael, *Armies and Warfare in the Middle Ages: The English Experience* (New Haven: Yale University Press, 1996)

Prinzler, Heinz W., *Pyrobolia: Vom griechischen Feuer, Schießpulver und Salpeter* (Leipzig: VEB Deutscher Verlag für Grundstoffindustrie, 1981)

Quarg, Götz, 'Der Bellifortis von Konrad Kyeser aus Eichstätt 1405', *Technikgeschichte* 32 (1965), 293–324

Rae, John, and Rudi Volti, *The Engineer in History*, Worchester Polytechnic Institute Studies in Science, Technology and Culture 14 (New York: Peter Lang, 1999)

Bibliography

Rathgen, Bernard, *Pulver und Salpeter: Schießpulver Kunstsalpeter Pulvermühlen im frühen Mittelalter* (München: Barbara-Verlag, 1926)

Rathgen, Bernard, *Das Geschütz im Mittelalter* (Berlin: VDI-Verlag, 1928)

Rathgen, Bernard, 'Schiesspulver, Kunstsalpeter, Pulvermühlen im frühen Mittelalter', *Zeitschrift für Naturwissenschaften* 81:3/4 (1941), 64–100

Rathgen, Bernard, and Karl Heinrich Schäfer, 'Feuer- und Fernwaffen beim päpstlichen Heere im 14. Jahrhundert', *Zeitschrift für historische Waffen- und Kostümkunde* 7 (1917), 1–15

Reichmann, Oscar, et al., eds, *Frühneuhochdeutsches Wörterbuch* (Berlin: de Gruyter, 1976), https://fwb-online.de/ (accessed 10 August 2023)

Restall, Matthew, *Seven Myths of the Spanish Conquest* (Oxford: Oxford University Press, 2004)

Rial Costas, Benito, *Print Culture and Peripheries in Early Modern Europe*, Library of the Written World 24, The Handpress World 18 (Leiden: Brill, 2013)

Richardson, Thom, *The Tower Armoury in the Fourteenth Century* (Leeds: Royal Armouries, 2016

Rieckenberg, Hans Jürgen, 'Berthold, der Erfinder des Schießpulvers. Eine Studie zu seiner Lebensgeschichte', *Archiv für Kulturgeschichte* 36 (1956), 316–22

Ritchie, Tessy S., Kathleen E. Riegner, et al., 'Evolution of Medieval Gunpowder: Thermodynamics and Combustion Analysis', *ACS Omega* 6:35 (2021), 22848–22856 https://pubs.acs.org/doi/10.1021/acsomega.1c03380 (accessed 10 August 2023)

Robertson, Haileigh Elouise, *'Imitable Thunder': The Role of Gunpowder in Seventeenth-Century Experimental Science* (unpublished PhD dissertation, University of York, 2015)

Roelcke, Thorsten, 'Die Periodisierung der deutschen Sprachgeschichte', in Sprachgeschichte 2.1, eds Werner Besch et al., 2nd edn (Berlin and New York: de Gruyter, 1998), pp. 798–815

Rogers, Clifford J., ed., *The Military Revolution Debate: Readings on the Military Transformation of Early Modern Europe* (Oxford: Westview Press, 1995)

Rogers, Clifford J., 'The Medieval Legacy', in *Early Modern Military History, 1450–1815*, ed. Geoff Mortimer (Basingstoke: Palgrave Macmillan, 2004), pp. 6–24

Rogers, Clifford J., 'Gunpowder Artillery in Europe, 1326–1500: Innovation and Impact', in *Technology, Violence, and War: Essays in Honor of Dr. John F. Guilmartin, Jr.*, eds Robert S. Ehlers, Jr., Sarah K. Douglas, and Daniel P. M. Curzon, History of Warfare 125 (Leiden: Brill, 2019), pp. 39–71

Rogers, Clifford J., 'Four Misunderstood Gunpowder Recipes of the Fourteenth Century', *Journal of Medieval Military History* 18 (2020), 173–82

Romocki, S. J. von, *Geschichte der Explosivstoffe* (Hannover: Gebrüder Gänecke, 1895; repr. Hildesheim: Gerstenberg, 1976)

Schmeller, Johann Andreas, ed., *Bayerisches Wörterbuch*, Vols 1 and 2 (München: Oldenbourg 1872–1877; repr. 2008), http://publikationen.badw.de/de/022964277.pdf and http://publikationen.badw.de/de/022964287.pdf (both accessed 10 August 2023)

Schmidtchen, Volker, *Bombarden, Befestigungen, Büchsenmeister: Von den ersten Mauerbrechern des Spätmittelalters zur Belagerungsartillerie der Renaissance – eine Studie zur Entwicklung der Militärtechnik* (Düsseldorf: Droste, 1977)

Schmidtchen, Volker, *Festung, Garnison, Bevölkerung: Historische Aspekte der Festungsforschung*, Schriftenreihe Festungsforschung 2 (Wesel: Deutsche Gesellschaft für Festungsforschung, 1982)

Schmidtchen, Volker, *Kriegswesen in späten Mittelalter: Technik, Taktik, Theorie* (Weinheim: VCH, 1990)

Schmidtchen, Volker, 'Mittelalterliche Kriegstechnik zwischen Tradition und Innovation', in *Europäische Technik im Mittelalter. 800 bis 1400. Tradition und Innovation. Ein Handbuch*, ed. Uta Lindgren (Berlin: Gebr. Mann, 1996), pp. 305–16

Schmidtchen, Volker, 'Ius in Bello und militärischer Alltag – Rechtliche Regelungen in Kriegsordnungen des 14. bis 16. Jahrhunderts', in *Der Krieg im Mittelalter und in der Frühen Neuzeit: Gründe, Begründungen, Bilder, Bräuche, Recht*, ed. Horst Brunner, Imagines medii aevi 3 (Wiesbaden: Reichert, 1999), pp. 25–56

Schneider, Karl, 'Zusammenstellung und Inhalts-Angabe der artilleristischen Schriften und Werke in der Bibliothek Seiner Exzellenz des Herrn Feldzeugmeisters Ritter v. Hauslab', *Mittheilungen über Gegenstände der Artillerie-und Kriegs-Wissenschaften. Hg. vom K. K. Artillerie-Committé* (Wien: Braumüller, 1868), pp. 123–211

Schulz, Knut, 'Büchsenmeister des Spätmittelalters: Migration und Ausbreitung des neuen Wissens', in *Craftsmen and Guilds in the Medieval and Early Modern Periods*, eds Eva Jullien and Michel Pauly (Stuttgart: Franz Steiner, 2016), pp. 221–42

Seel, Fritz, 'Sulphur in History: The Role of Sulphur in "Black Powder"', in *Sulphur: Its Significance for Chemistry, for the Geo-, Bio- and Cosmosphere and Technology*, eds Achim Müller and Bernt Krebs (Amsterdam: Elsevier, 1984)

Shapin, Steven, 'The House of Experiment in Seventeenth-Century England', *Isis* 79 (1988), 373–404

Sheffler, David, *Schools and Schooling in Late Medieval Germany: Regensburg 1250–1500*, Education and Society in the Middle Ages and Renaissance 33 (Leiden: Brill, 2008)

Bibliography

Sherwood, Foster Hallberg, *Studies in Medieval Uses of Vegetius' "Epitoma Rei Militaris"* (unpublished PhD dissertation, University of California Los Angeles, 1980)

Shrader, Charles R., 'A Handlist of Extant Manuscripts Containing the *De Re Militari* of Flavius Vegetius Renatus', *Speculum* 33 (1979), 280–305

Singer, Charles, ed., *A History of Technology*, 2 vols, Vol. 2 (Oxford: Clarendon Press, 1954–84)

Smith, Geoff, 'The Pre-History of Gunpowder' (online publication, 2012), https://independent.academia.edu/GeoffSmith17 (accessed 10 August 2023)

Smith, Geoff, 'Medieval Gunpowder Chemistry: A Commentary on the Firework Book', *Journal of the International Committee for the History of Technology* 21 (2015), 147–66

Smith, Geoff, 'Saltpetre: The Soul of Gunpowder', *Journal of the Ordnance Society* 27 (2020), 5–24

Smith, Geoff, 'Sulphur: The Trigger of Gunpowder', *Journal of the Ordnance Society* 28 (2021), 115–19

Smith, Kay (publ. under former name of Robert Douglas Smith), 'Artillery and the Hundred Years War: Myth and Interpretation', in *Arms, Armies and Fortifications in the Hundred Years War*, eds Anne Curry and Michael Hughes (Woodbridge: Boydell, 1994), pp. 151–60

Smith, Kay (publ. under former name of Robert Douglas Smith), 'Good and Bold: A Late 15th-Century Artillery Train', *Royal Armouries Yearbook* 6 (2001), 88–97

Smith, Kay (partially publ. under former name of Robert Douglas Smith), *Reports of the HO Group Medieval Gunpowder Research* (2002–2020) https://ahc.leeds.ac.uk/downloads/download/35/fields_of_conflict or https://www.middelalderakademiet.dk/krudt-og-kanoner (both accessed 10 August 2023)

Smith, Kay (publ. under former name of Robert Douglas Smith), 'All manner of peeces: Artillery in the Late Medieval Period', *Royal Armouries Yearbook* 7 (2002), 130–38

Smith, Kay (pub. under former name of Robert Douglas Smith) and Kelly DeVries, *The Artillery of the Dukes of Burgundy, 1363–1477* (Woodbridge: Boydell, 2005)

Smith, Kay (pub. under former name of Robert Douglas Smith), *Rewriting the History of Gunpowder* (Nykøbing Falster: Middelaldercentret, 2010)

Smith, Kay (publ. under former name of Robert Douglas Smith) and Ruth Rhynas Brown, *Bombards: Mons Meg and her Sisters* (London: Royal Armouries, 1989)

Smith, Kay (pub. under former name of Robert Douglas Smith) and Kelly DeVries, *Rhodes Besieged* (Stroud: History Press, 2011)

Smith, Trevor Russell, 'The Earliest Middle English Recipes for Gunpowder', *Journal of Medieval Military History* 18 (2020), 183–92

Spencer, Dan, 'The Provision of Artillery for the 1428 Expedition to France', *Journal of Medieval Military History* 13 (2015), 179–92

Spencer, Dan, '"The Scourge of the Stones": English Gunpowder Artillery at the Siege of Harfleur', *Journal of Medieval History* 43:1 (2017), 59–73

Spencer, Dan, *Royal and Urban Gunpowder Weapons in Late Medieval England* (Woodbridge: Boydell Press, 2019)

Spufford, Peter, *Handbook of Medieval Exchange* (London: Royal Historical Society, 1986)

St John Hope, William, 'The Last Testament and Inventory of John de Vere, 13th Earl of Oxford', *Archaeologia* 66 (1914–15), 310–48

Stammler, Wolfgang, et al., eds, *Die deutsche Literatur des Mittelalters: Verfasserlexikon* (Berlin: de Gruyter, 1933–55)

Stewart, Richard Winship, *The English Ordnance Office, 1585–1625* (Woodbridge: Boydell Press, 1996)

Stone, Peter G., and Philippe G. Planel, *The Constructed Past* (London: Routledge, 2003)

Stratford, Jenny, 'The Early Royal Collection and the Royal Library to 1461', in *The Cambridge History of the Book in Britain, Vol. III, 1400–1557*, eds Lotte Hellinga and Joseph Burnley Trapp (Cambridge: Cambridge University Press, 1999), pp. 255–66

Striedl, Hans, *Der Humanist Johann Albrecht Widmanstetter 1506–57 als klassischer Philologe* (Wiesbaden: Harrassowitz, 1953)

Stuart, Malcolm, ed., *The Encyclopedia of Herbs and Herbalism* (London: Orbis Books, 1979)

Stummvoll, Josef, 'Die Druckschriftenbestände der Österreichischen Nationalbibliothek und die Abschreibung des alphabetischen Kataloges 1501 bis 1929', in *Buch und Welt: Festschrift für Gustav Hofmann zum 65. Geburtstag*, eds Hans Striedl and Johannes Wieder (Wiesbaden: Harrassowitz, 1965), pp. 105–16

Sutton, Anne F., *Richard III's Books* (Stroud: Sutton, 1997)

Tallett, Frank, and D. J. B. Trim, eds, *European Warfare: 1350–1750* (Cambridge: Cambridge University Press, 2010)

Tether, Leah, *Publishing the Grail in Medieval and Renaissance France* (Cambridge: D. S. Brewer, 2017)

Tittmann, Wilfried, 'Der Mythos vom "Schwarzen Berthold"', *Waffen- und Kostümkunde* 25 (1983), 17–30

Tittmann, Wilfried, 'Die importierte Innovation. China, Europa und die Entwicklung der Feuerwaffen', in *Europäische Technik im Mittelalter. 800 bis 1400. Tradition und Innovation. Ein Handbuch*, ed. Uta Lindgren (Berlin: Gebr. Mann, 1996), pp. 317–36

Bibliography

Tittmann, Wilfried, '"Büchsenwerk" – die Kunst aus Büchsen zu schießen. Mit einer Entgegnung auf Klaus Leibnitz', *Waffen- und Kostümkunde* 42 (2000), 141–82

Tittmann, Wilfried, 'Das unaufhaltsame Ende von Berthold Schwarz. Anmerkungen zu Gerhard W. Kramer: 'Das Pyr Autómaton – die selbstentzündlichen Feuer des Mittelalters' (online publication, 2002), http://www.ruhr-uni-bochum.de/technikhist/tittmann/2%20Ende.pdf (accessed 10 August 2023)

Tittmann, Wilfried, et al., 'Salpeter und Salpetergewinnung im Übergang vom Mittelalter zur Neuzeit' (online publication, 2017), http://www.ruhr-uni-bochum.de/technikhist/tittmann/4%20Salpeter.pdf (accessed 10 August 2023)

Tout, Thomas Frederick, 'Firearms in England in the Fourteenth Century', *English Historical Review* 26 (1911), 666–702

Trapp, Joseph Burnley, 'Literacy, Books and Readers', in *The Cambridge History of the Book in Britain, Vol. III, 1400–1557*, eds Lotte Hellinga and Joseph Burnley Trapp (Cambridge: Cambridge University Press, 1999), pp. 31–43

Trenkler, Ernst, 'Die Frühzeit der Hofbibliothek (1368–1519)', in *Geschichte der Österreichischen Nationalbibliothek. Erster Teil. Die Hofbibliothek (1368–1922)*, ed. Josef Stummvoll (Wien: Georg Prachner, 1968), pp. 1–58

Turner, Geoffrey, 'St Thomas Aquinas on the "Scientific" Nature of Theology', *New Blackfriars* 78:921 (1997), 464–76

Vale, Malcolm, *The Princely Court: Medieval Courts in North-West Europe, 1270–1380* (Oxford: Oxford University Press, 2001)

Vaupel, Elisabeth, 'Schießpulver und Pyrotechnik', in *Europäische Technik im Mittelalter. 800 bis 1400. Tradition und Innovation. Ein Handbuch*, ed. Uta Lindgren (Berlin: Gebr. Mann, 1996), pp. 301–4

Von Simson, Otto G., 'The Gothic Cathedral: Design and Meaning', in *Change in Medieval Society: Europe North of the Alps, 1050–1500*, ed. Sylvia L. Thrupp (Toronto: University of Toronto Press in association with the Medieval Academy, 1988), pp. 168–87

Wachinger, Burghart, et al., *Die deutsche Literatur des Mittelalters: Verfasserlexikon*, 2nd edn (Berlin: de Gruyter, 1977–2008)

Walton, Steven A., 'The Art of Gunnery in Tudor England' (unpublished PhD dissertation, University of Toronto, 1999)

Walton, Steven A., 'Proto-Scientific Revolution or Cookbook Science? Early Gunnery Manuals in the Craft Treatise Tradition', *Proceedings of Craft Treatises and Handbooks: The Dissemination of Technical Knowledge in The Middle Ages, a conf. held in Cordoba, 6–8 October 2005* (Cordoba: Faculty of Arts, 2005)

Walton, Steven A., 'Mathematical Instruments and the Creation of the Scientific Military Gentleman', in *Instrumental in War: Science, Research, and*

Instruments between Knowledge and the World, ed. Steven A. Walton, History of Warfare 28 (Leiden: Brill, 2005), pp. 17–46

Walton, Steven A., 'Perception of the Performance of Cannon Shot before 1700', *Journal of the Ordnance Society* 20 (2008), 69–80

Walton, Steven A., and Thomas E. Boothby, 'What is Straight Cannot Fall: Medieval Architectural Statics in Theory and Practice', *History of Science* 52:4 (2014), 347–76

Wecker, John, *Eighteen Books of the Secrets of Art & Nature, being the Sum and Substance of Natural Philosophy* (London: Simon Miller, 1660)

Weiss Adamson, Melitta, 'Vom Arzneibuch zum Kochbuch, vom Kochbuch zum Arzneibuch: Eine diätetische Reise von der arabischen Welt und Byzanz über Italien ins spätmittelalterliche Bayern', in *Der Koch ist der bessere Arzt: Zum Verhältnis von Diätetik und Kulinarik im Mittelalter und der Frühen Neuzeit*, eds Andrea Hofmeister-Winter et al. (Frankfurt am Main: Peter Lang, 2014), pp. 39–62

Weiss Adamson, Melitta, '"mich dunckht ez sein knöllell": Von den Mühen eines bayrischen Übersetzers mittelalterlicher Fachliteratur', in *Fachtexte des Spätmittelalters und der Frühen Neuzeit: Tradition und Perspektiven der Fachprosa- und Fachsprachenforschung*, ed. Lenka Vanková (Berlin: de Gruyter, 2014), pp. 143–54

Welch, Evelyn, *Shopping in the Renaissance: Consumer Cultures in Italy 1400–1600* (New Haven: Yale University Press, 2005)

Werrett, Simon, *Fireworks: Pyrotechnic Arts and Sciences in European History* (Cambridge: Cambridge University Press, 2010)

White, Lynn, Jr, *Medieval Technology and Social Change* (London: Oxford University Press, 1962)

White, Lynn, Jr, 'Kyeser's Bellifortis: The First Technological Treatise of the Fifteenth Century', *Technology and Culture* 10 (1969), 436–41

Williams, A. R., 'The Production of Saltpetre in the Middle Ages', *Ambix* 22 (1975), 125–33

Williard, Thomas, 'Astrology, Alchemy and other Occult Sciences', in *Handbook of Medieval Culture*, ed. Albrecht Classen (Berlin: de Gruyter, 2015), pp. 102–19

Witthöft, Harald, 'Maß und Regio – Herrschaft, Wirtschaft und Kultur. Von aequalitas, Einheitlichkeit und langer Dauer', *Jahrbuch für Regionalgeschichte und Landeskunde* 24 (2006), 49–75

Woolgar, Chris M., 'Medieval Colour and Food', *Journal of Medieval History* 44 (2018), 1–20

Wunderle, Elisabeth, *Die mittelalterlichen Handschriften der Studienbibliothek Dillingen* (Wiesbaden: Harrassowitz, 2006)

Würdinger, Josef, *Kriegsgeschichte von Bayern, Franken, Pfalz und Schwaben: Band II von 1347 bis 1506* (München: Literarisch-Artistische Anstalt der Cotta'schen Buchhandlung, 1868)

Index

Page references in *italics* refer to illustrations.

Agricola, Georgius, *De Re Metallica* 29
Albrecht III, duke of Austria 51
Albrecht IV, duke of Austria 51
Albrecht V, duke of Bavaria 50, 53
alchemy/alchemists 17, 25, 43, 48n.45,
 120–1, 154–5, 332–4, 342
Alexander the Great 228–9
alum 128–31, 134–7, 146–7, 166–7, 298–9
Aquinas, Thomas 332
Aristotle 228–9
arrows 188–9, 341
 fire 28, 65–6, 88–9, 166–7, 186–9,
  220–7, 240–1, 246–9, 263n.14, 280–1,
  288–95, 321, 328, *336*, *337*, 339, 344
 gun, fired from 212–13
 'house arrow' 66, 252–7, 329
ars as concept 329, 332
Arsenal Book (*Zeughausbuch*) 52
arsenicum (*album*) 106–9, 122–3, 158–9,
 206–9, 220–1, 318, 320n.58
atrimentum/atramentum 122–3, 132–5,
 318
audience and reception
 for *Bellifortis* 24–5, 33
 for *Büchsenmeister Book* 25–8, 33
 for *Firework Book* 9, 17, 25–6, 33–4,
  35, 42–3, 60, 78, 306, 332, 340, 343–4,
  345
Augsburg 40, 46n.38, 50–1, 347
authorship 15–17, 35, 40, 54, 60, 68, 78

Bacon, Francis 1
Bacon, Roger 333
balls 37, 102–3, 114–15, 246–7, 262–3,
 266–71, 274–9, 309, 311, 319, 323
 fire (glowing) 64, 66, 88–91, 110–13,
  166–7, 176–7, 182–3, 220–1, 248–51,
  276–7, 280–1, 312, 325, 328, 335

Bellifortis 4
 audience 24–5, 33
 authorship 25
 Firework Book, compared to 24–6
 language 25
 manuscripts 22–4
 as source text 27
Bengedans, Johannes, *War Book*
 (*Kriegsbuch*) 27–9
Bianca Mary Sforza, wife of Maximilian
 I 51
bindings 16, 34, 42, 53–5, 57, 60, 78, 346
book trade 44, 48–50
Bosworth, battle of 311
brandy 106–11, 152–3, 160–1, 166–7,
 188–9, 226–7, 288–9, 302–3, 317–18,
 322
Brunschwig, Hieronymus 29
Büchsenmeister Book 11
 audience 25–8
 authorship 27–8
 Firework Book, compared to 23, 25–6,
  28, 304, 308
 manuscripts 22–3

camphor 106–7, 120–3, 158–9, 168–9,
 184–5, 206–9, 276–9, 288–9, 313,
 317–18, 320n.58
cannons *see* guns/cannons
cats *see* siege towers/cats/gabions
charcoal 10, 52, 64–5, 68, 106–9, 118–23,
 126–7, 132–5, 138–9, 152–65, 176–7,
 182–9, 196–7, 200–3, 210–11, 226–35,
 238–45, 252–3, 264–5, 270–3, 282–7,
 290–5, 298–301, 313–14, 316–17, 320–1,
 323–5, 339–41, 343
concepts, analysis of 329–35
Copernicus, Nicolaus 29

Index

'courtly art' of firework   170–1, 202–3, 258–71, 274–89, 296–303, 343

dating of *Firework Book*   12, 15–16, 23, 59, 304–5
De Regimine Principum (*On the Government of Rulers*)   4
dialects *see* language/dialects
dialogue, didactic form of   6, 9, 18, 309, 344; *see also* gunners, master, Master Gunner's Questions
Duarte, king of Portugal   48
Dürer, Albrecht   30

Eck, Benedict, abbot of Mondsee   53
editions, previous/early printed versions   5–6, 10, 12–13, 43–4
Edward IV, king of England   49

fish, cooking as timekeeping   102–3, 148–9, 162–3, 210–11, 341
Formschneider, Johann, master gunner or gun maker   27
Frederick III (of Austria), Holy Roman Emperor   16, 51
Fuchs, Leonard   29
Fugger, Georg   50
Fugger, Johann Jakob   50, 53
Fugger, Ulrich   50–1

gabions *see* siege towers/cats/gabions
Galicia, stone of   104–5
genre of *Firework Book*   3–4, 10–22, 28, 41
Great Book (of John Paston)   45
Greek fire   66, 229n.248, 339
gunners, master   2, 17, 20, 26–8, 33, 40, 42, 310
core skills   43, 55, 86–9, 196–9, 304–7, 316, 321, 323
in illustrations   69, 70, 71, 72, 73, 74, 75, 261n.7, 283n.58, 330, 331
literacy   43, 196–7, 306, 332
Master Gunner's Questions   9, 10, 29–30, 63, 90–103, 304, 306–9, 322, 326, 332, 334

moral qualities   65, 194–9, 306–7
status   5, 35–40, 54, 338–40, 344
The Gvnners Glasse   308
gunpowder   1–5, 9–10, 26, 30, 33, 34–5, 37, 43, 47, 63–8, 91–5, 150–1, 304, 309, 314, 345–9
analysis of text on   319–25
coloured   184–7, 321, 339
common/ordinary   156–61, 218–19, 240–3, 320
corning   23, 101n.51, 321–2
fire powder, strong   230–3
good/better/strong   106–7, 118–29, 136–41, 218–19, 242–5, 307, 320, 322–4, 348
for guns or fire arrows   240–1
historiography of   2–3
Knollenpulver (lumped powder)   23n.54, 66, 100–3, 141n.136, 200–1, 244–7, 307, 309, 319, 321–2, 339
loading guns *see under* guns/cannon
long-range   106–9
loud   188–9, 320, 322–3
miraculous   182–5, 320
origins   1, 13
paulum currasine   192–3
safety   196–9
separation of   160–5
spoiled, recovery of   108–11, 160–1, 164–5, 208–11, 316–17, 319, 321
tinder powder   154–5, 192–5, 198–201
water in   216–17
See also individual ingredients
guns/cannons   306, 335
analysis of text on   325–8
breaking of   92–5, 192–3, 327
cooling   300–3, 340
dimensions   190–1
emptying   248–9, 326–7
loading and firing   90–5, 100–1, 114–15, 140–3, 192–3, 212–25, 325, 327–8, 344; *See also* plugs
placement of   190–1
safety   192–5, 198–9, 224–5, 325
terminology   309–12

374

Index

hardening 66, 114–15, 246–7, 252–7, 290–5, 328–9, 339, 341
Hassenstein, Wilhelm 5, 12–15
Hauslab, Franz Ritter von 78
hedgehogs 66, 214–15
Heidelberg 50–1
Helm, Franz, *Buch von den probierten Künsten* 29, 52
Henry VII, king of England 49
historiography (overview) 9–10, 13–22
Honnecourt, Villard de 22
Household Book 45
humouralism 334–5

illustrations
  of *Bellifortis* 33, 69
  of *Büchsenmeister Book* 26, 28, 33, 69
  of *Firework Book* 7, 20–1, 26–7, 33, 35, 43, 54–7, 68–9, 70, 71, 72, 73, 74, 75, 76, 77, 78, 305, 327–8, 330, 331, 335, 336, 337, 338, 338, 344, 346
  of *Medieval Housebook* 30
incendiary devices, auxiliary 69, 76, 77, 335, 344
  analysis of text on 328–9
  large-scale 66, 258–71, 274–81, 306, 328, 336, 337
  See also arrows, fire; balls, fire (glowing)
Ingenieurkunst- und Wunderbuch ('Book of the Art of Engineering and Miracles') 27
ingredients and recipes, analysis of 314–19
Innsbrucker Zeughausbuch ('Innsbruck Arsenal Book') 52

Jähns, Max 18–19, 307–8, 311
jaspanicum see verdigris
John de Vere, earl of Oxford 49

Kramer, Gerhard 6, 17–18, 31–2, 304–5
kunst as concept *see ars* as concept
Kyeser, Konrad 25, 27

language/dialects 6, 10, 16–18, 21, 25, 39, 43, 63, 67–8, 305, 334, 344, 346

Leeds, Royal Armouries, MS I.34 *see* manuscript of *Firework Book*, Leeds, Royal Armouries, MS I.34
Leibnitz, Klaus 17–18
Leng, Rainer 13–15, 26, 32, 39
Leopold II, Holy Roman Emperor 53
libraries 46–55
London, Tower of 2, 37, 47, 346
lye 102–3, 116–19, 144–7, 198–9, 238–9, 296–7

manuscript of *Firework Book*, Leeds, Royal Armouries, MS I.34 5–7
  analysis of text 304–44
  catalogue entry 56–7
  codicology 9, 56–60, 335, 338
  content 63–9
  date 56–7, 305–6
  edition/transcription of 5, 9, 80–2, 84–302 (even pages), 309
  as exemplar 9, 345–6
  illustrations 7, 54–5, 56–7, 68–9, 70, 71, 72, 73, 74, 75, 76, 77, 78, 305, 330, 331, 335, 336, 337, 338, 338, 344, 346
  initials 63, 81, 81
  language 63, 67–8, 80, 82
  ownership 78
  palaeography 60, 61, 62, 63, 67, 335, 338
  preamble 63, 305–6, 323, 326
  scribal errors 67, 80, 310–11, 317, 321, 342–3
  translation of 5, 9, 81–2, 85–303 (odd pages)
  watermarks 58, 58–60
manuscripts of *Firework Book* 33–4, 50
  comparison of 7–9, 346
  list of all manuscripts 349–51
  Berlin, Staatsbibliothek zu Berlin – Preußischer Kulturbesitz, Manuscript germanica folio 710a 307n.8
  Berlin, Staatsbibliothek zu Berlin – Preußischer Kulturbesitz, Manuscript germanica quart. 1187 307n.8

375

Index

Bucharest, Arhivele Statului, Ms.
Varia II 165n.166
Darmstadt, Universitäts- und
Landesbibliothek, Ms.
1074 165n.166, 209n.218, 310,
327n.79, 328n.85, 329n.86
Dillingen Ms. XV 50 8n.20, 15–16,
46, 87n.6, 171nn.170–1, 201n.204,
207n.210, 207n.212, 207nn.214–15,
209n.218, 213n.229, 219n.236,
229n.248, 310, 313n.35, 314n.36,
317n.45, 328n.85, 329n.86
Dresden, Sächsische
Landesbibliothek, Ms. App.
463 103nn.52–3, 165n.166, 201n.204,
215n.231, 313n.35, 314n.36, 317n.45,
329n.86
Freiburg i. Br., Universitätsbibliothek,
Ms. 362 5, 6n.16, 8n.20, 15, 17–18,
31–2, 46, 91n.17, 103nn.52–3, 117n.88,
135nn.27–8, 135n.30, 141n.135,
143n.140, 147n.144, 159n.162,
165n.166, 171nn.170–1, 181n.184,
183n.185, 193n.197, 201n.202,
201n.204, 207n.210, 207nn.212–15,
211n.221, 213n.229, 215n.231, 215n.233,
219n.236, 241n.265, 245n.273,
251n.283, 311, 313n.35, 314n.36, 317n.45,
328n.85
Göttingen, Niedersächsische Staats-
und Landesbibliothek, 20 Cod.
Ms. philos. 64 179n.178, 183n.185,
247n.276, 251n.281, 251n.283, 255n.285,
255n.287, 329n.86
Heidelberg, Universitätsbibliothek,
Cod. Pal. germ. 122 141n.135,
171n.171, 183n.185, 185n.190,
201nn.203–4, 247n.276, 251n.281,
251n.283, 255n.287, 313n.35, 314n.36,
317n.45, 321n.60, 329n.86
Heidelberg, Universitätsbibliothek,
Cod. Pal. germ. 502 26n.71, 42n.26,
46, 51, 103n.52, 201n.204
Heidelberg, Universitätsbibliothek,
Cod. Pal. germ. 562 42n.26,
231n.251, 310

Heidelberg, Universitätsbibliothek,
Cod. Pal. germ. 585 103n.52
Heidelberg, Universitätsbibliothek,
Cod. Pal. germ. 787 31n.94, 46n.38,
165n.166
Kassel, Universitäts – Landes – und
Murhardsche Bibliothek, 40, Ms.
math. 14 64n.13, 229n.249, 231n.251,
334n.97
Leeds, Royal Armouries, MS I.34
see manuscript of Firework Book,
Leeds, Royal Armouries, MS I.34
Leipzig, Universitätsbibliothek, Ms.
1597 41n.22
Munich, Bayrische Staatsbibliothek,
Cgm. 356 23n.52
Munich, Bayrische Staatsbibliothek,
Cgm. 399 26n.71, 41n.22
Munich, Bayrische Staatsbibliothek,
Cgm. 4902 31n.94, 165n.166,
251n.283
Munich, Bayrische Staatsbibliothek,
Clm. 30150 8n.20, 109n.68,
229n.248, 329n.86
New York, Public Library, Spencer
Collection, Ms. 104 42n.27, 60,
171n.171
Nuremberg, Germanisches
Nationalmuseum, Ms. 1481a 46n.38
St. Gallen, Kantonsbibliothek, VadSlg
Ms. 396 135n.128
Strasbourg, Bibliothèque nationale et
universitaire, Ms. 2259 42n.27, 67,
165n.166, 193n.197, 335
Vienna, Österreichische
Nationalbibliothek, Cod. 2952 32,
52–3
Vienna, Österreichische
Nationalbibliothek, Cod.
3064 26n.71
Weimar, Herzogin Anna Amalia
Bibliothek, Q 342 8n.20, 87n.6
Mary of Burgundy, wife of Maximilian
I 51
Maximilian I, Holy Roman
Emperor 51–2

376

Index

Medieval Housebook (*Das mittelalterliche Hausbuch*) 30, 45
Memmingen, Abraham von 16
mercury 116–17, 120–3, 152–3, 158–9, 166–7, 188–9, 192–3, 276–9, 313n.34, 317–18, 320
'Military Revolution' 4, 348
Mönch, Philipp, *Kriegsbuch* 30
Mondsee 52–3
Mosbach, Johann von 46, 51
Muhammed ibn Zakariya al-Razi, *Liber Secretorum* ('*Book of Secrets*') 342
Munich 32, 50, 53

Nibler, Ferdinand 6–8, 17, 310
Niger Bertholdus *see* Schwarz, Berthold (Niger Bertholdus)

oleum benedictum 188–9, 216–17, 222–3
oleum compomitum distillatum 208–9
olium petroleum see petroleum/*olium petroleum*
opperment/orpiment 122–3, 318
oral transmission 5, 31, 33, 269n.30, 317, 344
ownership of *Firework Book* 15–16, 34, 35–6, 39, 43–52, 54–5, 60, 78, 345

Paston, John 45
petroleum/*olium petroleum* 67, 206–7, 259n.3, 260–1, 278–81, 296–301, 339–40
Philip the Upright, Elector Palatine of the Rhine 30
plugs 30, 64, 66, 94–7, 100–1, 112–15, 132–3, 140–3, 174–5, 178–9, 188–93, 212–17, 220–1, 224–5, 248–9, 266–9, 307, 309–10, 325–6
preamble 31, *61*, 63, 305–7, 323, 326
production stages 31–4, 78, 304–5, 338, 348
provenance *see* libraries; ownership of *Firework Book*
purpose of *Firework Book see* uses and purpose of *Firework Book*

quicklime 116–17, 146–7, 184–5, 226–9, 328, 342n.106

reception *see* audience and reception
resin 112–13, 172–3, 176–7, 180–1, 200–1, 216–17, 224–7, 230–1, 259n.3, 260–1, 264–5, 268–75, 278–81, 286–7, 292–3, 298–301
Richard III, king of England 47
Rülein, Ulrich 29

salammoniac 104–11, 118–23, 158–9, 168–9, 184–5, 208–9, 216–17, 220–1, 317–18, 320n.58
  purification of 65, 170–1, 313
salniter 166–7, 184–5, 188–9, 210–11, 222–3, 230–1, 317
salpratica/salpertica 65, 166–9, 208–9, 316, 318
salt 64, 114–15, 128–31, 134–5, 142–7, 150–1, 166–7, 214–15, 232–5, 258–9, 272–3, 278–9, 286–7, 292–3, 315–16, 334, 340
saltpetre 10, 52, 63–6, 68, 92–3, 102–3, 108–15, 118–23, 156–69, 174–7, 182–7, 196–205, 216–17, 220–1, 226–7, 240–45, 258–61, 264–5, 268–79, 286–7, 290–5, 300–1, 304, 307, 312–18, 320–1, 323–5, 334–5, 340, 343–4, 347
  purification of 28, 64, 66, 104–7, 116–17, 124–39, 142–51, 160–1, 166–7, 210–13, 232–41, 313–17, 324, 344
scales 122–3, 136–9, 158–9, 226–7, 258–9, 264–5, 272–3, 276–9, 286–7, 290–3, 313, 338, 341
Schedel, Hartmut 53
Schmidtchen, Volker, categorization of medieval military publications 20–1, 31, 33, 311
Schwarz, Berthold (Niger Bertholdus) 13, 43, 64, 154–7, 333
scientia as concept 329, 332
scribes/script 17–18, 33, 40, 43, 60, 69, 329, 345
  scribal errors 32, 53, 55, 67, 80, 310–11, 317, 321, 342–3
secret firework 280–9, 341–3
Secretum Secretorum ('*The Secret Book of Secrets*') 341–2

377

siege towers/cats/gabions 66, 174–7, 196–7, 224–5, 325

sieges 65–6, 172–83, 258–63, 327; *See also* siege towers/cats/gabions

smoking out devices 272–5, 335

stones, fire 224–5

structure of *Firework Book* 304–9, 317

sublimata mercurius/sublimate mercury 122–3, 158–9, 220–1, 318

sulphur 10, 52, 64–5, 68, 92–3, 106–13, 116–23, 138–9, 150–3, 156–67, 174–9, 182–9, 196–7, 200–1, 210–11, 216–17, 220–31, 240–9, 260–1, 264–5, 270–3, 276–9, 286–7, 290–9, 307, 314, 316–7, 320, 323–5, 335, 344, 347

 candles 200–5, 222–3

 oil of 65–6, 204–7, 226–7, 317

terminology 9, 304, 309–14

Theophilus, *De diversis artibus* 308–9

tinder (powder and resin) 65–6, 154–5, 192–5, 198–201, 216–17, 224–5, 248–53

title of *Firework Book* 12, 52

urine 116–17, 150–1, 210–11, 219n.237, 254–5, 315, 317

urtext 31–2

uses and purpose of *Firework Book*

 purpose 4–5, 26, 30–4, 39–40, 42, 345–7

 use, manuscript evidence of 40–3, 54, 305–6, 346

Valterius, Robert, *De Re Militari* 54

Venice 130–1, 204–5

verdigris/*jaspanicum* 104–5, 118–19, 122–3, 146–7, 162–3

Vienna 50–2

Vigevano, Guido da, *Texaurus regis Francie acquisitionis terre sancte* 22

vinegar 124–9, 144–51, 162–3, 198–9, 206–7, 211, 244–5, 252–3, 294–5

Völki, Jodocus, priest 15–16

wax 100–1, 200–1, 216–17, 230–3, 276–7

wedges 30, 98–101, 114–15, 190–3, 216–17, 307, 308n.9

wicks 200–3, 260–1

Widmanstetter, Johann Albrecht 53

wine/wine barrels 90–1, 104–5, 108–11, 115n.87, 116–17, 143n.140, 144–51, 158–9, 166–71, 192–3, 198–9, 202–3, 208–11, 244–5

Previously Published

The Medieval Tournament as Spectacle:
Tourneys, Jousts and *Pas d'Armes*, 1100–1600
edited by Alan V. Murray and Karen Watts

The Funeral Achievements of Henry V at Westminster Abbey:
The Arms and Armour of Death
edited by Anne Curry and Susan Jenkins